D0454451

Regis St. Louis

Rio de Janeiro

The Top Five

1 Lapa
Dance to the samba beat in the streets of cinematic old Rio (p136)

2 Carnaval
Revel at the world's largest, wildest street party (p23)

3 Pão de Açúcar
Marvel at the view from Rio's most iconic peak (p76)

4 Ipanema Beach
Laze on one of Brazil's most beautiful beaches (p61)

5 Cristo Redentor
Be captivated by the landscape beneath the redeemer (p79)

Contents

Introducing Rio de Janeiro   5

City Life   7

Carnaval   23

Arts   31

History   45

Sights   55

Walking & Cycling Tours   95

Eating   103

Entertainment   127

Activities   149

Shopping   157

Sleeping   173

Excursions   189

Directory   203

Language   219

Index   227

Maps   235

Published by Lonely Planet Publications Pty Ltd
ABN 36 005 607 983

Australia Head Office, Locked Bag 1, Footscray,
Victoria 3011, ☎ 03 8379 8000, fax 03 8379 8111,
talk2us@lonelyplanet.com.au

USA 150 Linden St, Oakland, CA 94607,
☎ 510 893 8555, toll free 800 275 8555,
fax 510 893 8572, info@lonelyplanet.com

UK 72–82 Rosebery Ave, Clerkenwell, London,
EC1R 4RW, ☎ 020 7841 9000, fax 020 7841 9001,
go@lonelyplanet.co.uk

The Authors

Regis St. Louis

A longtime admirer of the *cidade maravilhosa*, Regis can't seem to get enough of marvelous Rio de Janeiro. The city's vibrant music scene, its colorful *botecos* (neighborhood bars) and samba clubs, and the alluring energy of the Cariocas are just a few of the reasons why he's returned so often. Regis speaks both Portuguese and Spanish, and he has written many articles on Rio and the tropics. He was also the coordinating author of Lonely Planet's *Brazil* guide and covered both Rio and Brazil's southern states for LP's recent *South America on a Shoestring*. He lives in New York City.

CONTRIBUTING AUTHORS

PAULA GOBBI
Argentinean-born Paula has been reporting on Rio de Janeiro since the early 1980s. In 1999 Paula won an NFCP Golden Reel Award for her story on the legacy of slavery. For this book she wrote about racial identity (p12), recycling efforts (p21) and the favelas (p58).

THOMAS KOHNSTAMM
Thomas moved to Rio in 2000, intending to work as a translator and English-language teacher. When the job didn't go as planned, he traded in his dictionaries for a surf board

and Havaianas. Thomas wrote about surfing in Rio (p155).

DAN LITTAUER
Originally from Israel, Dan settled in Rio after he fell in love with Brazil. He is the director of G Brazil, a travel agency and tour operator for lesbian and gay travelers to South America. Dan contributed the boxed text on Gay Rio (p144).

CASSANDRA LOOMIS
Cassandra is a New York–based fashion designer. She wrote about a company in Rio that is making a positive contribution to the Amazon (p171).

CARMEN MICHAEL
Carmen is an Australian writer living and working in Rio. She contributed boxed texts on *gafieiras* (p33), *malandros* (p53) and *samba* (p140).

TOM PHILLIPS
British journalist Tom lived and worked in Rio and Belo Horizonte for two years. Tom wrote pieces on Gilberto Gil (p36) and *bailes* (p146).

MARCOS SILVIANO DO PRADO
Born and raised in Ipanema, Marcos used 40 years of Carnaval experience to develop the Carnaval Party Planner (p25). He operates a travel agency in Rio.

PHOTOGRAPHERS

Ricardo Gomes & John Maier Jr
For both Ricardo Gomes and John Maier Jr, there is no better city to live in than Rio de Janeiro. Both Ricardo and John work with photographs and video; they also have a production company, which covers news and feature stories from Latin America. Their work has appeared in the *New York Times*, *Time* and *Spiegel*, and on the BBC, HBO and Discovery.

Introducing Rio de Janeiro

Be warned: Rio's seductive powers can leave you with a serious case of *saudade* (indescribable longing) when you leave. Planted between lush, forest-covered mountains and breathtaking beaches, the *cidade maravilhosa* (marvelous city) has many charms at her disposal.

You've probably heard a thing or two about joie de vivre. Sure, the French invented the term (just as they invented the bikini), but it's the Cariocas (Rio dwellers) who've made it their own. How else to explain the life-lusting zeal with which the city's inhabitants celebrate their days? While large-scale festivities like Carnaval and Reveillon (New Year's Eve) pack the calendar year, there are plenty of other occasions for revelry – a Saturday at Ipanema beach, a *festa* (party) atop magnificent Pão de Açúcar, a soccer match at Maracanã, an impromptu gathering on the sidewalks of Lapa, Santa Teresa, Copacabana or any other corner of the city.

Wherever you find yourself in the city, you'll be faced with that incredibly seductive sound – samba – which permeates so many facets of Carioca life. Any day of the week is the right time to follow the beat to the dance halls, bars, and open-air cafés proliferating in Rio. Whether it's the heart-pounding rhythms of the *batucada* (percussion jams) or the lyrical ballads of *samba-canção* (melody-driven samba), the music is meant to move you, and if it doesn't, then you'd better check your pulse.

Of course, a city like Rio has much more than just samba, and the nightclubs, lounges and myriad drinking spots host an amazing range of sounds – from hip-hop, funk and jazz to old-school bossa nova, house, trip-hop and some Brazilian styles you may not have heard of, like *forró* (traditional, fast-paced music from the northeast), electro-samba or *maracatu* (percussion-heavy rhythms from Bahia). Music is the meeting ground for some of Brazil's most creative artists, and not surprisingly nets an audience diverse as the city itself. This is another of Rio's disarming traits: its rich melting pot of cultures. Cariocas they all may call themselves, but the city's enticing variety of cuisines speaks volumes about its long history of immigration. The culinary delights from Bahia, Minas Gerais and even the Amazon vie for attention among classic recipes from Southern France, Northern Italy, Bavaria, Tokyo, Lebanon and beyond.

LOWDOWN

Population 6.2 million; Greater Rio 11.8 million
Time zone GMT minus 3 hours
Three-star room around US$110
Coffee US$1
Metro ticket US$1.30
Suco (juice) from a juice bar US$1.40
Essential accessory Havaianas (rubber sandals)
No-no It's considered rude to greet a woman with a handshake; instead, kiss her on both cheeks (go left then right)

Perhaps the only thing matching Rio's wide cultural mix is the diversity of its landscape. One phrase you'll still hear bandied about is *Deus é Brasileiro* (God is Brazilian), usually in reference to the seemingly unfair distribution of gorgeous mountains, white-sand beaches, verdant rainforests and deep blue sea with which Rio has been blessed. Yet far from being a static backdrop, Rio's topography is the place for action. Whether it's surfing the breaks off Prainha, hiking through Tijuca's rainforests, sailing across the Baía de Guanabara or rock climbing up the face of Pão de Açúcar, there are dozens of ways to experience the beauty – though some would say you can experience plenty of beauty on Ipanema's Posto 9 without leaving your beach towel.

In truth, the Rio experience is so many varied things: it's taking an early-morning stroll along some of the world's most beautiful beaches, dancing your heart out in a Lapa nightclub or breathing in the scent of fresh passionfruit while wandering through the produce markets. It's people-watching in Leblon, drinking in the atmosphere of a faded colonial past in Centro or joining the mad circus at Maracanã.

Getting back to that *saudade* we mentioned earlier…Rio has turned heads for centuries, inspiring a string of admirers dating back to the city's earliest colonial days. (This despite a long history of social problems dogging the city from its founding up to the present.) The waves of immigrants who never looked back were preceded by the Portuguese king himself, who just couldn't tear himself away from his newly adopted city. 'No, I think I'll rule from here now,' he must have replied when his cohorts asked him to return home. It was another six years before his advisers coaxed him back to Portugal. Just keep that in mind when you're scheduling your return flight.

ESSENTIAL RIO

- Watching the sunset while sipping caipirinhas (cane-liquor cocktail) or *agua de coco* (coconut water) on **Ipanema beach** (p61).
- Discovering the hidden secrets of charming **Santa Teresa** (p87).
- Joining the weekend party on the samba-filled streets of **Lapa** (p88).
- Watching the mad spectacle of a *futebol* (soccer) match at **Maracanã** (p150).
- Enjoying the music, the drinks and the warm night air at the **Lagoa kiosks** (p131).

REGIS' TOP RIO DAY

I rise early and join Cariocas for a jog along the beach from Leblon to Copacabana. After a quick dip in the ocean, I head to Ipanema for a refreshing *açaí* (juice made from an Amazonian berry) at **Polis Sucos** (p112). While it's still fairly early, I make my way to Centro to browse for used records and antiques before catching the *bonde* (tram) up to Santa Teresa. I meet up with a few friends, grab lunch at **Espirito Santa** (p125), then spend a few hours exploring the old streets. In the late afternoon, I head back to Ipanema, in time for sunset and *agua de coco* (coconut water) on Arpoador. In the evening, I'll have dinner at **Miss Tanaka** (p114) in Jardim Botânico, followed by drinks at neighboring **Da Graça** (p132). Later, I'll check out the samba scene in Lapa, settling in at either **Carioca da Gema** (p139) or **Democráticus** (p141).

City Life

Rio Today   8

City Calendar   9
  January & February 10
  March & April 10
  May & June 10
  July & August 10
  September & October 10
  November & December 11

Culture   12
  Identity 12
  Lifestyle 13
  Food 14
  Fashion 16
  Sport 16
  Media 17
  Language 18

Economy & Costs   19

Government & Politics   19

Environment   20
  The Land 20
  Green Rio 21
  Urban Planning & Development 22

City Life

RIO TODAY

This city of beautiful scenery, wild parties and astounding musical history is certainly no stranger to the world's gaze. Long before 20th-century Hollywood illuminati ordained Rio as the jet-setters' destination *par excellence,* Rio was reveling in the attention of *arrivistes* from near and far (kings, naturalists and Frenchmen included; see p49). Today, the city continues to wend its way into the world's headlines – though not always for the reasons Rio would like. In discovering the unfolding daily dramas, you'll more often come across phrases like *cidade partida* (divided city) than *cidade maravilhosa* (marvelous city).

While it's true that the city can be classified along the lines of haves and have-nots, Rio has always united in more ways than it separated. The beaches in Rio, for instance, have always been free and democratic, and today on Ipanema beach, it's possible to stumble across soccer-playing kids from the favelas (shanty towns), cell phone–toting models, a *novela* (soap opera) actor, a few pensioners, hippies, yuppies and assorted tourists – all in the span of a few volleyball courts. Other areas of town are just as much a melting pot – from Lapa's taverns to the joy-filled soccer arenas, and the sidewalk eateries sprinkled about the Zona Sul (southern zone of the city of Rio).

Carnaval is perhaps the biggest manifestation of social democracy run wild: one and all mix it up in the dance parties, *bloco* (street party) marches and jam sessions happening around town. The parade itself is something of a gift from the favelas, where the *escolas de samba* (samba schools) basically created Carnaval as we know it today. Cariocas joke that if it were up to the Portuguese, they'd still be throwing flour on one another to the backdrop of polka music. (The joke refers to a Portuguese custom – the *entrudo* – in which pranksters threw water, flour, face powder and more at each other during Carnaval.)

Aside from staging one of the world's biggest parties, the favelas are the setting for some of the city's biggest musical experiments as young hip-hop artists create some of Brazil's more socially daring songs. Yet for most, the favelas are a place of struggle and poverty. For years, the official policy was simply to ignore them and hope that they would go away, or better yet, make them go away with bulldozers and wrecking crews. Today, however, the favelas have gained the attention of both the local and national governments, with serious lip service – if nothing more – paid to the notion of improving the lives of favela dwellers.

The Favela-Bairro project, for instance, remains a hot topic. The brainchild of Rio mayor Cesar Maia (p20), this urbanization scheme helped him get in the running for world's top mayor in 2005. Whether or not Rio can successfully integrate the favelas with the rest of the city will be a major issue in the years to come.

Outside the favelas, the city has smaller but equally urgent issues with which to contend. Beautifying the city in time for the 2007 Pan American (Pan Am) Games is at the top of people's minds – and where to fit all those extra people? Despite the city's fairly full coffers, the majority of its hotels desperately need a makeover, and some of

HOT CONVERSATION TOPICS

- Corruption – What's the latest political scandal and which officials are lining their pockets this week?
- Real estate – *How* much did that Leblon penthouse go for? And, will my friends still visit me if I move to Niterói?
- Sex – Which Brazilian actress is doing nude spreads in the glossies this week?
- Soccer – Who's the hot new player for Flamengo, and can you believe the results of the '06 World Cup?
- Parties – Did you make it to that wild funk *festa* (party) in the favela last week?
- Dating – Which Carioca playboy was spotted on Ipanema stealing kisses behind his fiancée's back?
- Crime – Which gang burned an outer-suburbs bus this week – and what was the response of Rio's draconian police force?

Ferries are good for viewing the city from the bay – board and disembark at Niterói (p205)

its colonial churches and palaces in the downtown area are crying out for attention. Not all areas of town, however, have been equally neglected. The rebirth of Lapa (derelict less than 10 years ago) and Santa Teresa (formerly the exclusive domain of artists and nearby favela residents) are symbols of Rio breaking away from its hard days.

Even the posh neighborhoods of Ipanema and Leblon are looking better than ever. Those who fled to Barra da Tijuca in the 1990s have begun to grow weary of traffic-clogged highways, long commutes and the distance separating them from Rio's unceasing energy. Residents have begun moving back into the city, and rediscovering its allure – which is one reason why housing prices continue to skyrocket all over town.

Meanwhile, the city's ever-replenishing sources of scandals and successes mean there's never a dull news day – from the latest violence shaking the favelas to surprising advances in civil rights. You'll see Cariocas gathered around the newsstands, reading the headlines on the posted newspapers, and shaking their heads – sometimes in laughter, sometimes in disgust. At the end of the day, the city continues on (not marching exactly, more dancing, along the lines of a graceful samba). Just watch the sunset from Praia do Arpoador – a favorite of fishermen as well as the up, the down, the down-and-out and everyone in between – and as the sun sinks slowly behind Dois Irmãos, bathing Ipanema beach in golden rays, you might think Rio is an enchanted city. And as many Cariocas would say, how could you believe otherwise?

CITY CALENDAR

Rio's Carnaval is the world's biggest party, but that's not the end of celebrating. Reveillon (New Year's Eve) is another citywide celebration, when Cariocas and visitors pack Copacabana beach. This is when the summer heat waves arrive, with daytime temperatures around 35°C (95°F), and often reaching 40°C (104°F). The high humidity adds even more punch to the heat. Yet this is also the rainiest time of year (see Climate, p209).

Other *festas* (parties) occur throughout the year. Those looking to escape the crowds (and the heat) might consider the mild but pleasant winter months (May to September) that feature blue skies and temperatures in

TOP FIVE QUIRKY EVENTS

- At the **Lighting of the Lagoa Christmas Tree**, catch live shows celebrating the onset of Christmas that take place against the backdrop of the glowing tree, which glows brighter each year.
- Gaze out over the city lights from atop Sugar Loaf, as lauded Brazilian bands keep the party going at **Noites Cariocas**.
- Find hundreds of ways at **Carnaval** to rack up some sins before Lent arrives.
- Put on your whites, think positive thoughts and cast your petitions out to sea on **Festa de Iemanjá**, the feast day of the well-known *orixá* (deity).
- Get in touch with your inner fisherman during **Festa da São Pedro do Mar**, an annual boat procession that ends near Urca.

the mid-20s. Aside from July, which is a school-holiday month throughout Brazil, this is the least busy time to visit the city. For the dates of Rio's many public holidays, see p211.

JANUARY & FEBRUARY

CARMEN MIRANDA ANNIVERSARY

☎ 2551 2597; Museu Carmen Miranda, facing Av Rui Barbosa 560, Flamengo

On February 9, the birthday of the Brazilian entertainer Carmen Miranda is celebrated with special exhibitions and a mini film festival that features the movies she starred in. If you're a fan, it's a kitschy good time.

CARNAVAL

In February or March, the city puts on its famous no-holds-barred party. For information on how to spend a few nights without sleep, see p24.

DIA DE SÃO SEBASTIÃO

On January 20, the patron saint of Rio is commemorated with a procession that carries the image of São Sebastião from Igreja (church) de São Sebastião dos Capuchinos in Tijuca (Rua Haddock Lobo 266) to the Catedral Metropolitana (p89), where the image is blessed in a Mass celebrated by the Archbishop of Rio de Janeiro.

MARCH & APRIL

DIA DA FUNDAÇÃO DA CIDADE

On March 1, the city commemorates its founding in 1565 by Estácio de Sá with a Mass in the church of its patron saint, Igreja de São Sebastião dos Capuchinos.

DIA DO ÍNDIO

☎ 2286 8899; www.museudoindio.org.br; Rua das Palmeiras 55; admission US$2 🕑 9:30am-5:30pm Tue-Fri, 1-5pm Sat & Sun;

April 4 is recognized in Brazil as Indians' day. Although this holiday is largely overlooked (much like the indigenous themselves), the Museu do Índio (p75) has special celebrations throughout the week. Exhibitions, dance and film presentations are staged daily.

SEXTA-FEIRA DA PAIXÃO

In March or April (depending when Easter falls), Good Friday is celebrated throughout

the city. The most important ceremony re-enacts the Stations of the Cross under the Arcos da Lapa (p88), with more than 100 actors.

MAY & JUNE

FESTAS JUNINAS

Spanning the month of June, the feast days of various saints mark some of the most important folkloric festivals in Brazil. In Rio, celebrations are held in various public squares, with lots of food stands, music, fireworks and an occasional bonfire or two. The big feast days are June 13 (Dia de Santo Antônio), June 24 (São João) and June 29 (São Pedro).

RIO MARATHON

www.maratonadorio.com.br

Set along the coast, with the ocean always at your side, this marathon course must be one of the most beautiful in the world. Rio hosts its annual 42km run in mid-to-late June, when the weather is mild and the skies are clear and blue. Entrance is around US$60.

JULY & AUGUST

FESTA DA SÃO PEDRO DO MAR

On July 3, the fishing fraternity pays homage to its patron saint in a maritime procession. Their decorated boats leave from the fishing community of Caju and sail to the statue of São Pedro in Urca.

FESTA DE NS DA GLÓRIA DO OUTEIRO

On August 15, a solemn Mass is held at the historic church overlooking Glória and the bay. From a church ablaze with decorated lights, a procession travels out into the streets of Glória to mark the Feast of the Assumption. This festa includes music and colorful stalls set up in the Praça NS da Glória. Festivities start at 8am and continue all day.

SEPTEMBER & OCTOBER

DIA DE INDEPENDÊNCIA DO BRASIL

On September 7, Independence Day is celebrated with a large military parade down Av Presidente Vargas. It starts at 8am at Candelária and goes down just past Praça XI.

FESTA DA PENHA

One of the largest religious and popular festivals in the city takes place every Sunday in October and the first Sunday in November. The lively celebrations commence in the northern suburb of Penha at Igreja NS da Penha de França, Largo da Penha 19.

PANORAMA RIO DE DANÇA

www.panoramafestival.net

One of Brazil's biggest dance festivals takes place in late October through early November and, at various locations around the city, features the work of around 200 different contemporary dance groups. The one-week festival features plenty of experimental troupes – from both Brazil and abroad – as well as traditional performers who don't get much attention.

RIO DE JANEIRO INTERNATIONAL FILM FESTIVAL

www.festivaldorio.com.br

This film festival is one of the biggest in Latin America. More than 200 films from all over the world are shown at some 35 theaters in Rio. Often the festival holds open-air screenings at Copacabana beach. It runs from the last week of September through the first week of October.

RIO JAZZ FESTIVAL

Although dates for this October music Jazz Festival vary, it's an opportunity for Rio's beautiful people to come together for three nights of great music. Local, national and international acts present a wide variety of music, playing jazz and its many relatives – samba-jazz, bossa nova, samba, and *Música Popular Brasileira* (MPB).

SAMBA SCHOOL REHEARSALS

In September (though some begin as early as July or August), samba schools host open rehearsals once a week (usually on Friday or Saturday night). In spite of the name, these are less a dress rehearsal than just an excuse to dance (to samba, of course), celebrate and pass on the good vibe before the big show come Carnaval time. Anyone can come, and it's a mixed crowd of Cariocas and tourists, though it gets more and more crowded the closer it is to Carnaval. For more information on attending the open rehearsals, see p141.

TIM FESTIVAL

Tim, the übersuccessful cell-phone service provider, throws a huge music festival in October (currently the third weekend, though dates can vary). Expect Brazil's top names in pop, jazz and MPB in an eclectic line up of performers at one of Rio's big venues – most recently at the Museum of Modern Art. Tickets often sell out well before the three-day-long event, so keep an eye on *Veja* magazine, which announces details in advance.

NOVEMBER & DECEMBER

NOITES CARIOCAS

http://oinoitescariocas.oi.com.br in Portuguese; Pão de Açúcar

Atop one of Brazil's most beguiling viewpoints, the city of Rio forms the backdrop to one of its best music fests during this annual summertime event. Beginning in November and running through February, all-night-long rock and MPB concerts are held on weekend nights, attracting a well-dressed Zona Sul crowd. See also Party on the Mountain (p135).

SKOL RIO

Over several weekends in November, one choice spot in the city (most recently Lapa) becomes the stage for live DJs and samba bands, as the prominent beer manufacturer, Skol, makes a killing – needless to say, the product would be consumed in abundance here even without the name recognition.

FESTA DE IEMANJÁ

Dwarfed by secular New Year's Eve celebrations, this Candomblé (a religion originating from Africa) festival on December 31 celebrates the feast day of Iemanjá, the goddess of the sea. Celebrants dress in white and place their petitions on small boats, sending them out to sea. If their petitions return, their prayers will not be answered. Along with the petitions, celebrants send candles, perfumes and talcum powder to appease the blue-cloaked *orixá* (spirits or deities). Until recently, devotees gathered in Copacabana, Ipanema and Leblon, but owing to the popularity of Reveillon, and its chaotic spillover, they are seeking more tranquil spots – Barra da Tijuca and Recreio dos Bandeirantes – to make their offerings.

LIGHTING OF THE LAGOA CHRISTMAS TREE

From the end of November to the first week of January, the Christmas tree glows brightly on the **Lagoa de Rodrigo de Freitas** (p64). To celebrate its lighting, the city often throws big concerts in Parque Brigadeiro Faria Lima, usually on the first Saturday in December. Big Brazilian names like Milton Nascimento have performed in the past.

REVEILLON

Rio's biggest holiday after its spectacular and rowdy Carnaval takes place on the famed Copacabana beach, where some two million people pack the sands to welcome the new year. A spectacular fireworks display lights up the night sky as top bands perform in the area. The hardiest of revelers keep things going all night long, then watch the sun rise the next morning.

CULTURE

Despite the often-simplistic media portrayals, Rio is a complicated place, with an incredibly diverse population mixing together on the streets of the city.

IDENTITY

Cariocas come from a long line of immigrants, which is reflected in the many faces on today's packed sidewalks. There you'll see Rio's cultural ancestry made flesh in the mix of Africans, Europeans and Indians who have intermarried freely since colonial times.

More recent immigrants to Rio are likely to come not from abroad but from within Brazil. On a walk through Centro at rush hour, you'll likely pass *caboclos,* descendents of the Indians, who come from Amazonia; *gaúchos* from Rio Grande do Sul, who speak a Spanish-inflected Portuguese and can't quite shake the reputation for being rough-edged cowboys; Baianos, descendents of the first Africans in Brazil, who are stereotyped as being extroverted and celebratory; Paulistanos, who inhabit Rio's rival city, São Paolo; Mineiros, who come from the colonial towns of Minas Gerais, and speak rather slowly; and Sertanejos, denizens of the drought-stricken *sertão* (interior).

A COLOR-BLIND SOCIETY Paula Gobbi

Traditionally defined as a color-blind society, Brazil has woken to a revolution of racial identity. The University of Rio de Janeiro, the largest in the state of Rio de Janeiro, has taken the lead in trying to compensate for a historical racial inequality, adopting affirmative-action quotas for 'black' students in 2003. This was the first time in Brazil that race had been used as a criterion for college admission. Forty percent of the admission slots were reserved for black and mulatto (mixed black and white ancestry) students.

The pilot project triggered 300 court cases, most of which questioned the standard that allowed applicants to self-define their color for admission purposes. Many questioned whether, in Brazil, where interracial marriages are common, resulting in an endless spectrum of skin colors, you could determine who was 'black' for affirmative-action purposes?

Perhaps in no other country in the world is the racial mix so diverse, yet the ideal of racial democracy is tarnished by the glaring inequalities that are a clear divide between rich and poor. More than 62% of Afro-Brazilian descendents live in poverty. Afro-Brazilians die younger than whites, earn less and have a greater risk of going to prison. Prior to the quota system only 2% of university students were black.

Some four million slaves were brought to Brazil over the centuries, six times as many as in the US, and it was the last country in the world to formally abolish slavery, doing so in 1888. Brazil has the largest population of Africans of any country outside Africa.

Following the example of the University of Rio de Janeiro, other universities embraced affirmative action. The University of Brasília adopted the quota system in the second semester of 2004, raising another storm. The University set up a commission to determine the racial identity of candidates by analyzing their photographs. The aim was to eliminate potential 'racial cheaters' by setting supposedly objective parameters based on anatomical traits. The application of this criterion led to widespread scientific and political dispute.

Controversial as it is, Brazil's recent embrace of affirmative action seems to be gaining momentum. So far, none of the court cases have been successful, and the University of Rio de Janeiro has refined its quota system. The challenge now lies in supporting those students to graduate and narrowing the gap of the discriminatory divide.

Out of this thick cultural and ethnic brew, a Carioca emerges – one who's been stereotyped as being spontaneous and friendly (detractors would add materialistic and self-absorbed). Stereotypes aside, Rio's citizens do have a fondness for their hometown, and vestiges of past ancestry are often jettisoned in favor of the all-encompassing ethos of the Carioca. There are very few separate ethnically defined neighborhoods, for instance, as the melting-pot ideal has been taken quite literally here. You're as likely to see those of Syrian, African and Italian descent mingling in the *botecos* (neighborhood bars) of Leblon as you are to see similarly mixed groups hanging out in Centro or Botafogo or any other neighborhood.

Although some unfortunate hints of racism persist, one of the biggest obstacles to tackling it is the denial that racism even exists. Since there are no organized hate groups here and nothing like the hate crimes seen in other countries, some Brazilians contend that all is equal. The facts show otherwise. Afro-Brazilians make up the bulk of low-paid workers, and are far more likely to live in favelas than in middle-class neighborhoods. A black political representative or even a high-ranking black employee is a rarity – clear examples of the lack of opportunities for blacks in Brazil. There are, however, some glimmers of hope that things may be changing (albeit at a glacial pace). See A Color-Blind Society, opposite.

The far more obvious way that things divide is by class, with income creating a city of haves and have-nots. Brazil has one of the world's greatest divides between rich and poor, and in few cities is the disparity more apparent than in Rio. At one end are the million-odd Cariocas living in favelas, often struggling just to get enough to eat, and at the other end are the überwealthy living in gated communities, with a maid, a driver and various other servants to attend to their needs. Often the dividing line is little more than a highway.

LIFESTYLE

Constructing a portrait of the typical Carioca is a complicated task, given the wide mix of social, cultural and economic factors at play. One way of getting a glimpse of the inner machinations of Carioca lifestyles is through the lens of neighborhood hierarchies.

The city's most well-to-do flock to apartments in the Zona Sul, though even there you'll find a wide range of lifestyles. The typical Ipanema resident, for instance, is young and well off, with an eye on the latest fashions, a cell phone permanently glued to the ear, a car in the garage and either a lucrative job in Centro or a sizable trust fund courtesy of the parents. The beach is the main stomping ground, as are the cafés and restaurants. This typical Ipanema resident, by the way, might be male or female, straight or gay. Weekends are spent away – at the beach house in Angra dos Reis or on a getaway to Búzios.

In neighboring Leblon, you'll find a similar mix, though a greater percentage of affluent older residents, and families (Praia de Leblon is a regular family affair at weekends). Those who can't afford the prices here often look in Gávea or, better yet, Jardim Botânico. All of these aforementioned residents will probably have a car (as does anyone who lives out in Barra da Tijuca), a decent-paying job and live in a secure building (which comes standard with a doorman who has a seemingly omniscient grasp of residents' lives upstairs).

Less expensive, but still desirable, is Botafogo, with its myriad *botecos,* and excellent access to the metro (many residents here do without cars). Meanwhile, Copacabana, once the star of Rio, is now a neighborhood of residents with the highest median age in the country (those smitten with the *cidade maravilhosa* in the '50s who came to stay haven't left, while younger generations have gradually moved further out). Despite their age, these older Cariocas haven't lost their adoration for the beach, evidenced in their volleyball games and power walks along the shore.

While nearly everyone in Rio has some concern about the crime problems, those with families tend to take extra precautions, opting for high-security buildings – the latest trend is even hiring bodyguards for teens as they go out at night. Well-to-do families are also very likely to send their children to private schools (usually Catholic), and off to the US or Britain to learn English during a year abroad, either during high school or college. Having domestic staff such as maids (and possibly cooks and chauffeurs) is fairly common in upper-middle-class families.

Away from the Zona Sul, you'll find working-class neighborhoods like Vila Isabel. Here the families work to earn enough to put food on the table and pay the rent; the children tend to live at home until they are married – if only because sharing an apartment with friends is a luxury not all can afford. Couples here tend to marry younger.

At the bottom of the socioeconomic ladder are the *favelados* (favela dwellers), who, despite film and media portrayals, are not all indigent street children or bloodthirsty drug lords. Many working families live in favelas, often undergoing long commutes (sometimes to domestic-help jobs in the Zona Sul) for very little money. The *favelas* may be old and traditional (like Mangueira, where you'll see old women out in their best clothes after Sunday church service) or new and disconnected from city services.

FOOD

Despite Rio de Janeiro's chefs experiencing near-total obscurity outside of Brazil's borders, culinary delights of every taste and texture abound in the *cidade maravilhosa;* visitors – and even locals – are often stunned by the enticing array of restaurants scattered throughout the city.

The vast number of immigrants ensures that every type of cuisine is well represented. Stroll about Centro and you will discover Lebanese, Spanish, German, French and Italian cuisines, all laboriously prepared according to tradition. Although the Japanese population of São Paulo dwarfs that of Rio's, the abundant coastline and steady stream of immigrants (many from São Paulo's Japanese enclave, as a matter of fact) ensure that you'll never be far from mouthwatering plates of sushi and sashimi.

A flair for the new is no small part of Rio's dining scene. In the city that brought the world the *fio dental* (dental-floss bikini), the culinary arts are no less flashy. You are likely to encounter daring – and not always successful – food combinations in Rio blending old with new (or new with newer).

Those who prefer tradition to the flash should explore the time-tested favorites of Brazil's many regional dishes. Diners can sample rich, shrimp-filled *moqueca* (seafood stew cooked in coconut milk) from Bahia or tender *carne seca* (jerked or preserved meat) covered in *farofa* (manioc flour), a staple in Minas Gerais. Daring palates can venture north into Amazonia, enjoying savory *tacacá* (manioc paste, leaves of the Brazilian vegetable *jambu*, and dried shrimp) or creamy *cupuaçu* (Amazonian fruit) ice cream. Cowboys and the *gaúcho* south bring the city its *churrascarias,* Brazil's famous all-you-can-eat barbecue restaurants where crisply dressed waiters bring piping-hot spits of fresh roasted meats to your table.

COCKTAILS FOR CARIOCAS

Perhaps owing to those long, steamy summers, Cariocas are big supporters of that most universal of institutions – the neighborhood watering hole. Here local patrons can quench their thirst with some of Rio's most delectable drinks, the most famous of which, both in Rio and abroad, is the caipirinha (cane-liquor cocktail).

The ingredients are simple – *cachaça* (cane liquor), lime, sugar and crushed ice – but a well-made caipirinha is a work of art. The key component here is the high-proof (40% or so) cane spirit, which is also known as *pinga* or *aguardente*, and is produced and consumed throughout the country. The production of *cachaça* is as old as slavery in Brazil, with the first distilleries growing up with the sugar plantations – first to satisfy local consumption and then to export to Africa in exchange for slaves.

Other ways to experience *cachaça* are to mix with fresh fruit juices to make *batidas* (often served as frothy, half-frozen cocktails) or, if it's a particularly fine label (the best *cachaças* generally come from Minas Gerais), to drink it straight. Those who've had their fill of cane spirits might prefer the *caipirosca* or *caipivodcas*, which have vodka replacing the *cachaça*.

Despite the widespread love affair with the caipirinha, draft beer or *chope* (shoh-pee) is also extremely popular in the city. This pale blond pilsner is lighter than and far superior to canned or bottled beer, and it's served ice cold in most bars, which is perhaps one reason why Cariocas are the largest consumers of *chope* in the country.

For tips on where to find the best drinks and bars in Rio de Janeiro see The Best in Town, p129, and Best Neighborhood Bars, p132.

FEIJOADA

As distinctively Carioca as Pão de Açúcar (p76) or Cristo Redentor (p79), the *feijoada completa* is a dish that constitutes an entire meal, which often begins with a caipirinha aperitif.

A properly prepared *feijoada* is made up of black beans slowly cooked with a great variety of meat – including dried tongue and pork offcuts – seasoned with salt, garlic, onion and oil. The stew is accompanied by white rice and finely shredded kale, then tossed with croutons, fried *farofa* (manioc flour) and pieces of orange.

Feijoada has its origins in Portuguese cooking, which uses a large variety of meats and vegetables; fried *farofa* (inherited from the Indians) and kale are also Portuguese favorites. The African influence comes with the spice and the tradition of using pork offcuts, which were the only part of the pig given to slaves.

Traditionally, Cariocas eat *feijoada* for lunch on Saturday. (It's rarely served on other days.) Among the top places to sample the signature dish are Petronius (p112), Galeto do Leblon (p110) and Casa da Feijoada (one of the few places in Rio that serves *feijoada* daily, p108). Vegetarians can sample tasty meat-free versions of *feijoada* at Vegetariano Social Club (p113) or Fontes (p110).

If you find yourself craving the dish after you return home, try your hand at making it.

Recipe

Ingredients

6 cups dried black beans
½kg smoked ham hocks
½kg Brazilian *lingüiça* (Brazilian sausage; substitute chorizo or sweet sausage)
½kg Brazilian *carne seca* or lean Canadian (loin-cut) bacon
1kg smoked pork ribs
The intrepid can add one each of a pork ear, foot, tail and tongue

2 bay leaves
3 garlic cloves, minced
1 large onion, chopped
3 tablespoons olive oil
4 strips smoked bacon
salt and black pepper
orange slices to garnish
rice, *farofa*, kale or collard greens to serve
hot sauce (optional) to serve

Preparation

After soaking beans overnight, bring them to a boil in 3L of water and then keep them on low to medium heat for several hours, stirring occasionally. Meanwhile, cut up the ham hocks, *lingüiça* and *carne seca* into 3cm or 4cm chunks, separate the pork ribs by twos and place them all in a separate pan full of water and bring to a boil. After the first boil, empty out the water and add the mixture, along with the bay leaves and salt and pepper, to the beans. As the pot simmers, in a separate pan sauté the garlic and onion in olive oil, adding in the smoked bacon. Take two ladles of beans from the pot, mash them and add to the frying pan. Stir around, cook for a few more minutes, then add frying-pan contents to the pot; this will thicken the mixture. Simmer for another two to three hours, until the beans are tender and the stock has a creamy consistency. Remove bay leaves and serve over rice with *farofa* and kale or collard greens. Garnish with fresh orange slices. Add hot sauce if desired, and be sure to enjoy with a cold caipirinha.

Brazil's verdant natural setting produces no shortage of delicacies. Its 4000km-long coastline ensures an abundance of fresh fish, just as its tropical forests produce savory fruits of every shape and size. In the mornings, Cariocas stop by their neighborhood juice bars for a shot of fresh-squeezed vitamins. The best juice bars offer dozens of varieties, featuring flavors from all over the country. Many don't translate – since some of these fruits don't exist elsewhere – so you'll have to try for yourself.

The setting is as much a part of the culinary experience as the food itself. (Some critics say Leblon is *only* about ambience.) Rio has 100-year-old *botecos* (which are sometimes staffed by fussy waiters who don't seem much younger), bordello-esque cafés full of models and their admirers, no-nonsense lunch bars designed for powering through a meal, and long-standing, character-filled eateries that are open late into the night – or morning, rather – perfect for those who only eat filet mignon and pineapple sandwiches at 4am.

Those who'd like to get into the cuisine scene should check out *Eat Smart in Brazil* by Joan and David Peterson. It includes an overview of Brazil's culinary heritage and regional cuisines as well as recipes and a detailed glossary. See the array of eateries beginning p106 for an idea of Rio's culinary diversity.

FASHION CONSCIENCE

Coopa Roca (www.coopa-roca.org.br) is one favela organization that is garnering attention in some surprising places – top London fashion shows included. This craftwork and sewing collective began in Rocinha in the early 1980s under the guidance of sociologist Maria Teresa Leal. The idea began during Leal's repeat trips to the favela with her housekeeper, a Rocinha resident. During her stays, Leal encountered many women who were talented seamstresses but who had no opportunity to earn money for their skills. Wanting to give something to the community, Leal set up Coopa Roca, and the organization was off and running. Initially a small group of women joined the co-op, each working from home to produce quilts, pillows and craft items made of recycled fabrics and other materials.

The work grew more complex over the years, with more women joining the ranks, and soon the co-op began creating truly eye-catching pieces, using delicate techniques such as *fuxico* (embroidering with pieces of fabric).

The fashion world came calling in the early 1990s, with commissions from Brazilian designers Osklen and Carlos Miele, as well as the ubiquitous department store C&A. More recently, Coopa Roca has begun creating colorful crochet bags for British designer Paul Smith, and window displays for Ann Taylor, as well as assorted pieces for vanguard designers in France and Holland.

Today the co-op employs more than 150 women, most of whom would have little opportunity to earn money otherwise. All of the women continue to work from home and share the production and administrative responsibilities. Despite their growing success, the headquarters of Coopa Roca remains in the favela, where it will continue to be a source of inspiration for both those within the community and abroad.

FASHION

Rio's fashion has a lot to do with the tropical climate and the belief in the body beautiful: Cariocas have them both, and they're not afraid to show them off.

Top European labels must now jockey for attention beside rising homegrown luminaries. The city's biggest fashion event is the annual Fashion Rio, a week during which some three dozen or so Brazilian designers – the majority based in Rio – launch their upcoming spring and summer collections. What began in 2002 is now a huge event with top models such as Gisele Bündchen showcasing the work of Lenny, Salinas, Walter Rodrigues, Blue Man, Complexo B and others slowly emerging onto the world stage.

In addition to the many boutiques in Ipanema and Leblon, a good opportunity to peruse the talents of upcoming designers is at the Babilônia Feira Hype market (see Markets for the Masses, p168), held throughout the year.

Although the French invented the bikini in 1946, it's Brazilian designers – and the models promoting them – who reinvent it every season. *Fio dental* ('dental floss' bikinis) emerged in the '80s, and is still an icon on beaches here. Exposed *bundas* (bottoms), at least for the women, are generally the style. Whether you're six or 60, fat or skinny, the rule on the beach is to wear as little as possible, while still covering up the essentials (topless bathing is not allowed in Rio, by the way) – this applies to men, to some extent. Maybe 15% of men wear Bermudas, while the vast majority stick to *sungas* (hip-hugging skimpy briefs).

Off the beach, women show up the men quite a bit. For most men, a night out means putting on a clean T-shirt and jeans. They are, according to one disgruntled Carioca woman, seriously fashion challenged. This is perhaps a bit unfair, as men are beginning to catch on; a growing number of boutiques in Ipanema, Leblon and the *shoppings* (shopping malls) are dedicated to pushing men in the right direction.

Regardless of gender, Havaianas are the quintessential item you'll find in every Carioca's wardrobe. The nifty rubber sandals are also one of Brazil's leading exports, with well over two billion pairs created since the inception of the company in 1962. Aside from sandals, a tan is the most common fashion accessory, and it's rare to find a Carioca who doesn't have at least some color to their skin, if not an outright deep, dark glow.

SPORT

Cariocas have a fairly one-track mind when it comes to sport. There's soccer, and then there's, well, what else? Auto racing, as a matter of fact. Brazilian drivers have won more Formula One world championships than any other nationality, a fact that probably won't surprise anyone who rents a car for the weekend. The greatest racer was three-time world champion Ayrton Senna, who was almost canonized after his death.

Tennis is growing in popularity, after Gustavo 'Guga' Kuerten helped put Brazil on the map. Volleyball, basketball – even professional bull riding – have their Brazilian advocates, if not its stars. All of this means that kids growing up in Brazil can now watch something on the TV besides soccer. Which isn't to say that any of them have an interest in anything besides soccer.

Most people acknowledge that Brazilians play the world's most creative and thrilling style of soccer, and Brazil is the only country to have won five World Cups (1958, 1962, 1970, 1994 and 2002).

Futebol (soccer) games are an intense spectacle – as much because of the crazed fans as the teams out on the field. The rivalries are particularly intense when two of Rio's club teams play each other. The major teams are Botafogo (black-and-white-striped jerseys), Flamengo (red jerseys with black hoops), Fluminense (red, green and white stripes) and Vasco da Gama (white with a black sash). Nearly every Carioca supports a team to which they are undyingly devoted. Professional club competitions are held year-round and the games can be played on any day of the week (though Saturday, Sunday and Wednesday are favorites). An excellent book on understanding Brazil's great sport, and its relationship to culture, religion and politics, is *Futebol: The Brazilian Way of Life* by Alex Bellos. For results, schedules and league tables visit www.netgol.com. For more information on watching and playing sport in Rio, turn to p150.

MEDIA

Like in many other cities in the world, news outlets are concentrated in the hands of the few. The Organizações (O) Globo empire, which was founded by patriarch Roberto Marinho in Rio in the 1920s, today has the world's fourth-largest TV network (behind NBC, CBS and ABC in the US). O Globo also includes Brazil's major radio network (Radio Globo), the country's second-biggest publishing house (Editora Globo) and of course the leading Rio newspaper *(O Globo)*. Currently, *O Globo* receives half of the total amount spent annually in Brazil on advertising.

Major dailies in Rio include the sometimes sensationalist *O Dia* as well as the nationwide *Jornal do Brasil,* a more moderate publication (not unlike *O Globo* in its political slant).

The variety of magazines on newsstands is astounding. Aside from Portuguese translations of popular magazines like *Cosmopolitan,* there are hundreds of glossies, covering everything from science, history and literature to sailing, dogs and astrology. Brazil's most popular

There's more than one way to play soccer!

THE NATIONAL ADDICTION

Although soccer is certainly near the top of the list of Brazil's national obsessions, *novelas*, or soap operas, are more watched than anything else on TV. Aired nightly between 6pm and 9pm, these one-hour soaps feature some of Brazil's top actors and certainly Brazilian TV's racier subject matter – unlike American soaps, *novelas* aren't afraid to show some nudity and bloodshed. The plots tend to deal with historical themes, in settings ranging from 17th-century Salvador to a 19th-century coffee plantation or an estate in 1930s Minas Gerais. Period costume is just part of the fun. Also unlike American variants, Brazilian soaps run for a finite period – usually six to nine months – with wild finales often featuring over-the-top gun battles or improbable marriages. Incidentally, directors aren't afraid to kill off a few characters along the way; this only adds to the excitement – particularly when audiences give unfavorable reviews of the death, and the screenwriter is compelled to resurrect the deceased character.

Novelas at times even play a political role. There was outcry when a former hooker called Fernanda was killed by a *bala perdida* (stray bullet) in the chic Rio neighborhood of Leblon. Yet it was actually just part of the storyline in *Mulheres Apaixonadas* (Women in Love). The bloodthirsty twist was part of a drive by media giant *O Globo* to promote a disarmament bill (voted down in 2005). Confusingly, the producers of the *novela* went on to film a real-life antigun demo in Copacabana and incorporate it into the program, blurring even further the distinction between *novelas* and reality.

Despite the widespread popularity of *novelas*, there are a few critics. Their most common gripe is the role to which blacks are relegated in the soaps. The maid, butler and chauffeur are invariably black, while the majority of leading characters have the fairest of skin. Defenders say this is merely a reflection of reality, particularly when filming period pieces. Regardless, things may be beginning to change as a few *novelas* are introducing meatier roles for their once-typecast actors.

magazines are *Veja*, a glossy mag full of journalism lite (not unlike *Time* magazine), and the more sophisticated *Isto É*, with more in-depth articles.

Although Internet usage is growing, there are still few conduits of alternative news sources in Brazil. Globo Online tends to dominate this field as well. For further details of newspapers and magazines available in Rio, see p213.

LANGUAGE

Portuguese is the eighth most commonly spoken language in the world, with around 200 million speakers worldwide. The majority of them – 186 million at last count – hail from Brazil, the only Portuguese-speaking country in South America. Brazilian Portuguese differs from European Portuguese, owing in part to New World influences: Portuguese colonists first arrived in the 16th century, and as they came into contact with the Tupi tribes living along the Atlantic coast, they adopted the Tupi language to such an extent that Tupi, along with Portuguese, became the lingua franca of the colony. The Jesuits had a great deal to do with this, since they translated prayers and songs into Tupi, and in so doing recorded and promoted the language. The situation lasted only as long as the priests. Tupi was banned when the crown expelled the Jesuits in 1759, and Portuguese remained the country's official language.

Tupi wasn't the only language to have an influence on the development of Brazilian

OI, CARA! (HEY, GUY/GAL)

A few phrases and gestures can go a long way in Brazil. And learning a language – or getting your point across – is all about making an effort, of which Brazilians will be most appreciative. *Díria* (slang) is a big part of the Carioca dialect. Here are a few words and phrases to help you along.

babaca (bah-*bah*-kah) – jerk
bunda (*boon*-duh) – bottom
eu gosto de você (*ey*-ooh go-shtoo zhih vo-*say*) – I like you
falou (fah-*low*) – agreed/you're welcome
fique à vontade (*fee*-kuh vahn-*tah*-jee) – make yourself at home
fio dental (*fee*-ooh den-*towh*) – dental floss, aka bikini
gata/gato (*gah*-tah/gah-too) – good-looking woman/man
nossa! (*noh*-sah) – gosh/shit/you don't say
ótimo (*ah*-tche-moo) – cool
sunga (*soohn*-guh) – tiny Speedo-type swim shorts favored by Carioca men
'ta legal (*ta* lee-*gowh*) – that's cool
tudo bem? (*too*-doo behm) – everything good?
valeu (vah-*lay*-ooh) – thanks
vamu nessa (vah-moo-*neh*-suh) – let's go

Portuguese. In the 19th century, the Bantu and Yoruba languages arrived in Brazil, brought by African slaves. At the same time, European Portuguese went through linguistic changes as it came in contact with French (Napoleon Bonaparte, who invaded Portugal, played his part in the semantic evolution), while Brazilian Portuguese retained some of its earlier features. Today, the differences between the two variations are about as pronounced as those between American English and British English.

Although Portuguese shares many lexical similarities with its romance-language cousin Spanish, the two are quite different. Spanish speakers will be able to read many things in Portuguese, but will have great difficulty understanding Brazilians. Fortunately, Brazilians are quite patient, and they appreciate any effort to speak their language. Incidentally, English is still not commonly taught in Brazil, except in the more exclusive private schools. See the Language chapter, p220, for a more detailed look at Portuguese.

ECONOMY & COSTS

As well as being the most popular tourist destination in Brazil, Rio is a thriving shipping, banking, cultural, publishing and pharmaceutical center. Within 500km of the city are more than 30% of Brazil's population, 60% of its industries and 40% of its agricultural production. Its port trades more than 30 million metric tons of goods each year. More than 80% of Brazil's visitors pass through the city's airports. Most of Brazil's main film and record companies are based in the city, as are O Globo and Manchete – the country's largest and most influential TV networks.

As far as visitors are considered, Brazil is less expensive than European or North American cities, and costs here are about half those found in Paris or New York. That said, Rio will seem expensive if you come with unrealistic expectations. As a budget guideline, if you're traveling with another person, and split the cost of a decent hotel room (US$90 and up), eat in restaurants and have a few drinks in bars every night, US$90 to US$120 per person would be a rough estimate for what you'll spend per day.

Brazil is not the cheapest destination for solo travelers. The cost of a single room in a hotel is not much less than for a double, and when you eat, you'll find most dishes in restaurants are priced for two people. Those who aren't averse to staying in one of the city's many hostels can cut their costs considerably.

HOW MUCH?
Liter of gas US$1.20
Liter of bottled water US$0.90
Glass of chope (draft beer) US$2
Souvenir T-shirt US$12
Agua de coco (coconut water) on the beach US$1
Metro ticket US$1
Pair of Havaianas US$6
Admission to samba club US$4–9
Dinner for two at Yorubá US$60
Cable-car ride to top of Pão de Açúcar US$16

If you have more money to spend, the quality of your vacation increases substantially. For US$150 per person, a couple can get a good hotel room in Copacabana or Ipanema on or near the beach, eat at excellent restaurants, and still have money left over for shopping.

Keep in mind that during the December-to-February holiday season, lodging costs generally increase by 25% to 30% (and sometimes more in places like Buzios and other popular resorts near Rio). You'll pay a premium if you come during Carnaval or Reveillon, with accommodation prices doubling or even tripling.

GOVERNMENT & POLITICS

Rio de Janeiro is the capital of the eponymous state (Brazil has 26 states), which manages its affairs in the Palácio Tiradentes (p85) under the guidance of the state assembly. The head of Rio state is the governor, who is elected in four-year terms. On a city level, Rio is headed by a mayor, also elected for four-year terms, and a *câmara municipal* (municipal council), which meets at Praça Floriano (p86).

RIO'S MIGHTY CESAR

Although Rio has had its share of controversial figures, Cesar Maia is certainly one of the more eccentric mayors the city has known in recent years. Currently in his third term (which began in 2004), Maia has undertaken some ambitious projects for Rio. He is best known for championing the Favela-Bairro project, having gained millions for favela development since unveiling the plan back in 1994. This has earned him much praise in certain favelas (though some favela dwellers feel left out of the equation). He has also spoken out about the hypocrisy of the rich, who benefit from favela cheap labor the favelas provide, but want the poor to disappear from sight.

Yet despite his seemingly soft-hearted concern for the poor, Maia has said other things that reveal there's more to his politics than liberal rhetoric. In regards to the growing homeless population, he has suggested spraying toxic chemicals on the roads to discourage people from sleeping on the sidewalks. He has also said that police should be given more authority to shoot to kill – and that 'elimination' of drug lords is the best way to curtail drug trafficking.

The more one learns about Maia, the more his contradictions emerge. He was born not far from Maracanã to middle-class parents, and became active in politics when he joined the Communist party in college. In time this saw him exiled to Chile. When he returned he eventually began working for the left-of-center PDT (Democratic Labor Party), but ended up jumping the fence to the conservative PFL (Liberal Front Party) when the Labor Party refused to endorse him in 2000.

Cesar Maia's legacy still remains uncertain. While Favela-Bairro has many advocates, it has its equal share of detractors who say funds are being mismanaged. His bid to bring the Olympics to Rio in 2012 failed, although the city did secure the Pan American Games in 2007. How the city manages the games will certainly reflect on the mayor, who has presidential ambitions. Whether he can reign in the feeling of lawlessness in Rio will undoubtedly play a big part in his success or failure.

Political parties proliferate in Brazil, and at present there are over two dozen parties, the majority having formed in the last 10 years.

The current head of Rio state is Rosinha Garotinho, elected in 2003. She owes her election to her husband, who was previous governor of the state and stepped down following his two successive terms (the constitutional limit in Brazil). Although Mrs Garotinho is governor, critics think her husband still wields the real power in the state, which was hard to refute when she handed the reigns over to him during a particularly violent favela uprising early on in her term. Mr Garotinho, though, has presidential ambitions, and has made no secret of his plans to run against the current Brazilian president, Luiz Inácio Lula da Silva, in 2006.

Speaking of the Garotinhos, nepotism is just one of the ailments afflicting the administration in Rio (and Brazil in general). Corruption is the greater ill, with one government scandal after another forming the better part of the media's news week. This has led to much disillusionment on the part of many Brazilians, who have long given up on the idea of honest political leadership.

Law and order is probably an even hotter topic when it comes to governmental woes. Periodically, the violence in the favelas erupts, and so far the response has either been effete or extremely draconian. In the past, the state has even asked the federal government to send army troops into the city to secure the areas around the favelas. In 2005, the police adopted a new tactic, performing assassination-style hits on several drug lords in the favelas.

'Favela' remains the buzzword of Rio. How to resolve the problems affecting over 25% of the population (favela residents) remains the biggest talking point – not only in Rio but in Brazil as a whole. One major step toward addressing these grievances is the multimillion-*reais* Favela-Bairro project, which aims to bring city services such as electricity, running water, schools and medical clinics to the favelas – though it too has its critics.

ENVIRONMENT

THE LAND

Rio – with its spectacular scenery – is more than blessed by nature. Its location between the mountains and the sea, bathed by the sun, has entranced visitors for many centuries. Darwin called it 'more magnificent than anything any European has ever seen in his country of origin.'

It all started millions of years ago, when the movement of the earth pushed rock crystal and granite, already disturbed by faults and fractures, into the sea. Low-lying areas were flooded and the high granite peaks became islands.

The plains and swamps on which the city is built were slowly created through centuries of erosion from the peaks and the gradual accumulation of river and ocean sediment.

The mountains, their granite peaks worn by intense erosion and their slopes covered with Atlantic rainforest, form three ranges: the Rural da Pedra Branca massif, the Rural Marapicu-Gericinó massif and the Tijuca-Carioca massif.

The Tijuca-Carioca massif can be seen from almost everywhere in Rio and is responsible for the coastline, which alternates between bare granite escarpments and Atlantic beaches. Its most famous peaks are Pão de Açúcar (Sugarloaf; p76), Morro do Leme, Ponta do Arpoador, Morro Dona Marta, Corcovado and Dois Irmãos at the end of Praia de Leblon.

The sea has also played its part. The stretch of coast between Dois Irmãos and Arpoador was once a large spit, and Lagoa Rodrigo de Freitas (p64) was a bay. Between Arpoador and Morro do Leme the sea created the beautiful curved beach of Copacabana. Praia Vermelha, the smallest of Rio's Atlantic beaches, is the only one with yellow sand instead of white. Inside Baía de Guanabara, river sediment and reclamation projects formed the present bay rim.

GREEN RIO

Rio still has a long way to go toward protecting its natural beauty, and there are serious environmental problems affecting the city.

Although nowhere near as bad as burgeoning São Paulo to the south, the air quality in Rio is poor, a result of both the heavy volume of traffic throughout the metropolitan area and industrial emissions in neighboring regions. The mountains that surround the city enclose the air pollution, aggravating the problem. (One effect of this air pollution is abnormally high rates of asthma among children.)

Despite initial efforts to clean up the Baía de Guanabara following the Earth Summit (the UN Conference on Environment and Development) in 1992, an oil spill in 2000 brought further ecological damage to the bay, and no concerted efforts have been made to clean it up since then. It is foolish to swim at bay beaches. Ocean beaches are also polluted, although

RECYCLING FRENZY *Paula Gobbi*

During the rainy season, the piles of garbage in the favelas come down the hills with such force that they destroy whatever is in their path. With no sewage in most favelas, waste and nature are a lethal mix. Much of the garbage is made up of cans and plastic bottles. But now an increasingly popular recycling scheme has the Complexo do Mare, a group of 12 favelas in Rio de Janeiro, cashing in on this waste.

It is a common sight to see people walking around the favelas with huge bags of bottles and cans, which can be exchanged for discounts on electricity bills. Recyclers are of both genders and all ages but the scheme is particularly popular with housewives – with lower electricity bills there is more money for food.

The competition for cans and bottles has become so intense that it has spread to the trendiest beaches in town. Don't be surprised to find that, after quenching your thirst on the beach, you have a shadow tailing you. The chances are, that shadow is out for the can and it won't be long before you are asked for it. Downtown Rio is another hunting ground for the 'collectors' who search in the rubbish for what has become precious waste indeed.

With such a collective effort it is no wonder that Brazil has become a world champion in aluminum-can recycling, with almost 95% of cans recycled in 2004. The price for 1kg of cans is about US$1.40. In Rio de Janeiro there are close to 10,000 people working in the can-collecting business, and those numbers can double during Carnaval or a hot summer day. It's estimated that each collector can gather about 5kg of cans per day, making US$7 from the waste. In a country where the minimum salary is US$135 per month, making an extra US$204 is a great deal.

Recycling has become so topical that in 2006 municipal law required all schools in Rio, private and public, to include information about recycling in their school curriculum. Students will learn at an early age the importance of keeping the environment clean and how to do so. With this army of new recruits, at least this kind of litter will be history in the streets of Rio.

less so than the bay. Ipanema is cleaner than Copacabana, and as you get further from the city, the cleaner the waters will be. Refuse from storm drains and the open sewers still prevalent in the city add to the pollution after heavy rains (some 30% of households still lack access to sewer connections).

Another disturbing problem in the city is the continued destruction of Mata Atlântica (Atlantic rainforest) that remains on some of the hillsides around the city, as favelas continue to spread. Until recently, very few citizens took much interest in environmental cleanups. New projects, however, are beginning to reflect a growing concern over the degradation of Rio's natural beauty. Beach cleanup groups, spearheaded by nongovernmental organizations (NGOs) such as Aqualung, have begun appearing on the shores of Rio, and other groups have even set their sights on cleaning up the polluted Baía de Guanabara.

Other modest advances in environmental consciousness in some parts of the city include the clean-up of Lagoa Rodrigo de Freitas. The elegant egret has even returned to its shores.

Although Rio is nothing like it was when tropical rainforest covered its landscape, there is still a variety of wildlife in the city. In Campo de Santana, *agoutis* (hamster-like native rodents), peacocks, white-faced tree ducks, geese, egrets and curassows abound.

The park near Leme (p66) has many plants and birds native to the Atlantic rainforest, such as saddle and bishop tanagers, thrushes and the East Brazilian house wren, which has a distinctive trill. The nearby Parque Nacional da Tijuca (p93) contains many more rainforest species.

The Jardim Botânico (p64) has a huge variety of native and imported plant species, including the Vítoria Régia water lilies from the Amazon and impressive rows of royal palms, whose seeds originally came from France. It has over 8000 plant species, including 600 varieties of orchid. Watch for the brightly plumed hummingbirds, known in Brazil as *beija-flores* (literally, flower-kissers).

Micos (capuchin monkeys) and macaws can be seen in surprising places in the city, including Pista Cláudio Coutinho (p77) in Urca and Parque Lage (p64) on the south side of Corcovado.

URBAN PLANNING & DEVELOPMENT

Rio suffers from the same urban sprawl affecting most other cities. Today Rio occupies around 1200 sq km, with 4800 people packed into each square kilometer, which makes it one of the world's 25 most populous cities.

Favelas contribute to much of this urban density. The number of people living in them grows at an annual rate (7.5%) three times that of overall population growth (2.5%). In the last decade, the city has begun addressing the needs of Rio's 500 favelas, where an estimated 1.8 million Cariocas live.

Several hundred million *reais* have been poured into Mayor Maia's Favela-Bairro project so far, with as much as a billion *reais* earmarked for the project's lifespan. Maia claims that the project has already benefited 500,000 people.

The biggest challenge facing the city at the time of writing was the development planned to take place to accommodate the 2007 Pan Am Games, when 80,000 people are expected to descend upon the city. Much of the building activity is focused on Barra da Tijuca.

In other contexts, 'urban planning' amounts to very little planning at all. The city continues to expand north and west, taxing the environment with unbridled growth.

Carnaval ■

History 25

Sights & Activities 26
  Carnaval Balls 26
  Samba-School Parades 27
  Samba City, Samba Land 30
  Samba-School Rehearsals 30
  Dates 30

Carnaval

One of the world's largest parties, Carnaval – in all its colorful, hedonistic bacchanalia – is virtually synonymous with Rio. Although Carnaval is ostensibly just five days of revelry (Friday to Tuesday preceding Ash Wednesday), Cariocas begin the partying months in advance. The parade through the Sambódromo, featuring elaborate floats flanked by thousands of pounding drummers and twirling dancers, is the culmination of the festivities – though the real action, Cariocas profess, is at the wild parties about town.

Adding to the welcome mayhem are visitors, who can join Cariocas in the revelry, heading to nightclubs and bars that throw special costumed events. There are free live concerts happening all over the city (like those in Largo do Machado, Arcos da Lapa and Praça General Osório), while those seeking a bit of decadence can head to the various balls about town. Whatever you do, prepare yourself for sleepless nights, an ample dose of caipirinhas and samba, and mingling with the joyful crowds spilling out of the city.

Joining the *bandas* (street parties, also called *blocos*) is one of the best ways to celebrate à la Carioca. These *bandas* consist of a procession of drummers and vocalists followed by anyone who wants to dance through the streets of Rio. Some *bandas* require costumes (drag, Amazonian attire etc), while others simply expect people to show up and add to the good cheer.

Although the city is blazing with energy during Carnaval, don't expect the party to come to you. To get more information on events during Carnaval, check *Veja* magazine's *Veja Rio* insert (sold on Sundays at newsstands) or visit **Riotur** (Map pp238–9; www.rio.rj.gov.br/riotur; 9th fl, Rua Assembléia 10; Ⓜ Carioca). This is the organization in charge of Carnaval, by the way. See Sights & Activities, p26, to get some ideas on how to celebrate the return of King Momo, the lord of the Carnaval. For those unacquainted with Momo, he's the modern embodiment of Momos, the Greek god of trickery, and when the chosen Momo is announced, Cariocas expect a portly, jolly ruler who can dance a mean samba. The revelry officially begins when the mayor hands King Momo the keys to the city on the Friday before Carnaval.

For a complete rundown on the latest Carnaval info, visit the excellent website www.rio-carnival.net.

All smiles for Carnaval in Ipanema

CARNAVAL PARTY PLANNER *Marcos Silviano do Prado*

Rio starts revving up for Carnaval long before the colorful parades take place, but the partying reaches boiling point from Friday to Tuesday before Ash Wednesday. To make the most of your time, check out the long-standing *festas* (parties) listed below. You can dance through the streets in a *banda* (street party), party like a rock star at one of many dance clubs (p143) scattered throughout town, or find your groove at one of the samba-school rehearsals (highly recommended) listed on p141. Those looking for free, open-air, neighborhood-wide celebrations shouldn't miss Rio Folia in Lapa or the Cinelândia Ball in Centro. For up-to-date listings of what's on, visit www.ipanema.com.

Saturday Two Weeks Before Carnaval

- Banda de Ipanema (p26) at 4pm
- Rehearsals at samba schools (p30)

Weekend Before Carnaval

- Banda Simpatia é Quase Amor (p26), Saturday at 4pm
- Monobloco, Praia de Leblon, Sunday at 4pm
- Rehearsals at samba schools

Carnaval Friday

- Carnaval King Momo is crowned by the mayor at 1pm
- Shows start at Terreirão do Samba (Samba Land; p30) and Rio Folia (in front of the Lapa Arches in Lapa) from 8pm
- Cinelândia Ball (p26) from 9pm
- Red and Black Ball at the Scala (p26) from 11pm
- Gay ball at **Le Boy** (Map pp244–5; ☎ 2513 4993; www.leboy.com.br in Portuguese; Rua Raul Pompéia 102, Copacabana)
- Dance party at **Cine Ideal** (☎ 2252 7766; www.idealparty.com.br in Portuguese; Rua da Carioca 62, Centro)

Carnaval Saturday

- Cordão do Bola Preta (p26) from 9:30am
- Banda de Ipanema at 4pm
- Deluxe costume competition at Glória (p186) from 7pm
- Parade of Group A samba schools at the Sambódromo (p27) from 7pm
- Street band competition (Av Rio Branco, Centro, admission free) from 8pm
- Shows start at Terreirão do Samba and Río Folia from 8pm
- Copacabana Palace Luxury Ball (costumes or black tie mandatory; p26) from 11pm

- Carnaval balls at Scala (p26), Help (p26) and other venues from 11pm
- Gay balls at Le Boy and **Incontrus** (☎ 2549 6498; Praça Serzedelo Correia 15, Copacabana)
- X-Demente Party at Fundição Progresso (p89)
- Parties at 00 (p143) and other dance clubs

Carnaval Sunday

- Shows start at Terreirão do Samba and Rio Folia from 8pm
- Samba parade at the Sambódromo from 9pm to 6am
- Carnaval balls at Scala and Help from 11pm
- Gay balls at Le Boy and Elite (p142)
- Rave party at theme park Terra Encantada (p94)
- Parties at 00 and other dance clubs

Carnaval Monday

- Shows start at Terreirão do Samba and Rio Folia from 8pm
- Samba parade at the Sambódromo from 9pm to 6am
- Carnaval balls at Scala, Help and others from 11pm
- Gay balls at Le Boy and Elite
- Parties at 00 and other dance clubs

Carnaval Tuesday

- Banda de Ipanema at 4pm
- Shows start at Terreirão do Samba and Rio Folia from 8pm
- Parade of Group B samba schools at the Sambódromo from 9pm
- Scala Gay Costume Ball from 11pm
- Carnaval balls from 11pm at Help and other venues
- Gay balls at Le Boy and **Garden Hall** (☎ 2430 8400; Shopping Barra Garden, Av das Américas 3255, Barra da Tijuca)
- X-Demente Party at Fundição Progresso
- Parties at 00 and other dance clubs

HISTORY

Carnaval, like Mardi Gras, originated from various pagan spring festivals. During the Middle Ages, these tended to be wild parties, until tamed in Europe by both the Reformation and the Counter-Reformation. But not even the heavy hand of the Inquisition could squelch Carnaval in the Portuguese colony, where it came to acquire Indian costumes and African rhythms.

Some speculate that the word *carnaval* derives from the Latin *carne vale*, 'goodbye meat.' The reasoning goes something like this: for the 40 days of Lent, the nominally Catholic

Brazilians give up liver and steak fillets, in addition to luxuries such as alcohol and pastries. To compensate for the deprivation ahead, they rack up sins in advance with wild parties in honor of King Momo.

SIGHTS & ACTIVITIES

There are dozens of ways to take part in Carnaval, from participating in a *banda*, to attending one of the society balls, to watching the phantasmagoric parade live and up close at the Sambódromo. If you smile at the thought of putting on a costume and dancing before thousands (millions if you include the TV audience), now's your chance – just pick out a samba school and join up (opposite).

CARNAVAL BALLS

Carnaval balls are surreal and erotic events. The most famous one is held at the Copacabana Palace (p180). It's a formal affair, so you'll need a tux; there you'll have the opportunity to celebrate with Rio's glitterati as well as international stars. Tickets cost upwards of US$500. Popular but less pricey balls are held at the Glória (p186) and Río Scenarium (p142).

BANDAS: CARNAVAL ON THE STREETS

Attending a *banda* is one of the best ways to celebrate Carnaval and to join in, all you have to do is show up. Note that some *bandas* require that you to march in one of the *banda's* colors. Often you can buy shirts on the spot (around US$8) or you can just show up in the right colors. Dozens of *bandas* party through the streets before Carnaval. For complete listings, check **Riotur** (Map pp238–9; www.rio.rj.gov.br/riotur; 9th fl, Rua Assembléia 10; Ⓜ Carioca).

Banda Carmen Miranda (Praça General Osório, Ipanema; ☯ 4pm Carnaval Sun) A hilarious good time, Banda Miranda features lots of men decked out like the proverbial Brazilian bombshell. A lively mix of straights and gays parades through Ipanema's streets.

Banda de Ipanema (Praça General Osório, Ipanema; ☯ 4pm 2nd Sat before Carnaval & Carnaval Sat) This longstanding *banda* attracts a wild crowd, complete with drag queens and others in costume. Don't miss it.

Banda de Sá Ferreira (cnr Av Atlântica & Rua Sá Ferreira, Copacabana; ☯ 4pm Carnaval Sat & Sun) This popular Copacabana *banda* marches along the ocean from Posto 1 to Posto 6.

Banda Simpatia é Quase Amor (Praça General Osório, Ipanema; ☯ 3pm 2nd Sat before Carnaval & Carnaval Sun) A big *bloco* with 10,000 participants and a 50-piece percussion band.

Barbas (cnr Ruas Assis Bueno & Arnoldo Quintela, Botafogo; ☯ 3pm Carnaval Sat) One of the oldest *bandas* of the Zona Sul parades through the streets with a 60-piece percussion band. A water truck follows along to spray the crowd of some 2500, all decked out in red and white.

Bloco das Carmelitas (cnr Rua Dias de Barros & Ladeira de Santa Teresa, Santa Teresa; ☯ 6pm Carnaval Fri) Crazy mixed crowd (some dressed as Carmelite nuns) parades through Santa Teresa's streets.

Bloco de Bip Bip (Rua Almirante Gonçalves 50, Copacabana; ☯ Carnaval Sat & 9:30pm Carnaval Tue) Has perhaps the best music of any *banda*, owing to the professional musicians who sometimes play in the procession. Leaves from the old samba haunt Bip Bip (p137).

Bloco de Segunda (Cobal Humaitá, Rua Voluntários de Pátria 446, Botafogo; ☯ 6pm Carnaval Mon) Excellent percussion band joins 2000 or so revelers. T-shirt is obligatory; buy at Cobal Humaitá (p167) beforehand.

Cordão do Bola Preta (cnr Ruas 13 de Maio & Evaristo da Veiga, Centro; ☯ 10am Carnaval Sat) The oldest *banda* still in action features lots of straight men dressed as women, and a chaotic march that often leads the group to stop at bars along the way. Costumes are always welcome, especially those with black-and-white spots.

Dois Pra Lá, Dois Pra Cá (Carlinho de Jesus Dance School, Rua da Passagem 145, Botafogo; ☯ 2pm Carnaval Sat) This fairly long march begins at the dance school and ends at the Copacabana Palace hotel. Bring along your swimsuit for a dip in the ocean afterward.

Other balls, which are decidedly less upper class, are held at **Scala** (Map pp246–7; Av Afránio de Melo Francoin 296, Leblon), at **Canecão** (Map pp242–3; ☎ 2105 2000; www .canecao.com.br in Portuguese; Av Venceslau Brás 215, Botafogo) and at **Help** (☎ 2522 1296; Av Atlântica 3432, Copacabana). The most extravagant gay balls are found at **Le Boy** (☎ 2513 4993; www.leboy.com.br; Rua Raul Pompéia 102, Copacabana). The most popular ball is held in Praça Floriano (p86) in Cinelândia, attracting 60,000 revelers. Every night of the Carnaval period (from 9pm on Friday to Tuesday), bands take to the stage in front of the câmara municipal (town hall) in the Praça Floriano. This ball is free.

Tickets go on sale about two weeks beforehand, and the balls are held nightly during Carnaval and the preceding week. The *Veja Rio* insert in *Veja* magazine has details.

SAMBA-SCHOOL PARADES

The main Carnaval parade takes place in the Sambódromo, and it's nothing short of spectacular. Before an exuberant crowd of some 30,000, each of the 14 best samba schools has its hour and 20 minutes to dazzle the audience.

The parades begin in moderate mayhem and work themselves up.

Each school enters the Sambódromo with amped energy levels, and dancers take things up a notch as they dance through the stadium. Announcers introduce the school, the group's theme colors and the number of *alas* (literally, wings – subgroups within a school, each

Plenty of glitter – and plumage – for the Carnaval parade at Sambódromo

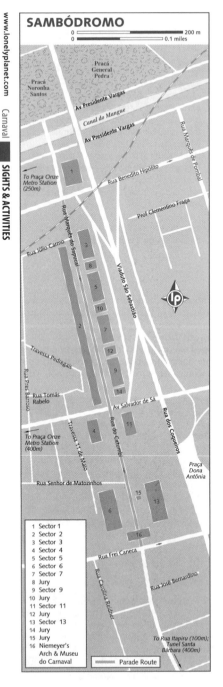

SAMBÓDROMO

1	Sector 1
2	Sector 2
3	Sector 3
4	Sector 4
5	Sector 5
6	Sector 6
7	Sector 7
8	Jury
9	Sector 9
10	Jury
11	Sector 11
12	Jury
13	Sector 13
14	Jury
15	Jury
16	Niemeyer's Arch & Museu do Carnaval

playing a different role). Far away the lone voice of the *puxador* (interpreter) starts the samba. Thousands more voices join him, and then the drummers kick in, 200 to 400 per school. The pounding drums drive the parade. Sambas, including the themes for each group, have flooded the airwaves for weeks Next come the main wings of the school, the big allegorical floats, the children's wing, the drummers, the celebrities and the bell-shaped *baianas* (women dressed as Bahian aunts) twirling in elegant hoopskirts. The *baianas* honor the history of the parade itself, which was brought to Rio from Salvador da Bahia in 1877.

Costumes are fabulously lavish: 1.5m feathered headdresses, long, flowing capes that sparkle with sequins, and rhinestone-studded G-strings.

The whole procession is also an elaborate competition. A handpicked set of judges chooses the best school on the basis of many components, including percussion, the *samba do enredo* (theme song), harmony between percussion, song and dance, choreo-graphy, costumes, story line, floats and decorations. The dance championship is hotly contested, with the winner becoming not just the pride of Rio but all of Brazil.

The Sambódromo parades start with the *mirins* (young samba-school members) on the night of Carnaval Friday, and continue on through Saturday night when the Group A samba schools strut their stuff. Sunday and Monday are the big nights, when the Grupo Especial – the 14 best samba schools in Rio – parade: seven of them on Sunday night and into the morning, and seven more on Monday night. The following Saturday, the eight top schools strut their stuff again in the Parade of Champions. Each event starts at 9pm and runs until 6am.

Tickets

Getting tickets at legitimate prices can be tough. Many tickets are sold well in advance of the event. Check with **Riotur** (Map pp238–9; www.rio.rj.gov.br/riotur; 9th fl, Rua Assembléia 10; M Carioca) about where you can get them, as the official outlet can vary from year to year. People line up for hours, and travel agents and scalpers snap up the best seats. Riotur reserves seats in private boxes for tourists for US$200, but you should be able to pick up regular tickets for much less from a travel agent or from the **Maracanã football stadium box office** (Map pp236–7; ☎ 2568 9962) for around US$40. Try to get seats in the center, as this is the liveliest section and has the best views.

By Carnaval weekend, most tickets will have sold out, but there are lots of scalpers. If you buy a ticket from a scalper (no need to worry about looking for them – they'll find you!), make sure you get both the plastic ticket with the magnetic strip and the ticket showing the seat number. The tickets for different days are color coded, so double-check the date as well.

If you haven't purchased a ticket but still want to go, during Carnaval you can show up at the Sambódromo at around midnight, three or four hours into the show. This is when you can get grandstand tickets for about US$10 from scalpers outside the gate. Make sure you check which sector your ticket is for. Most ticket sellers will try to pawn off their worst seats.

And if you can't make it during Carnaval proper, there's always the cheaper (but less exciting) Parade of Champions the following Saturday.

Getting to the Sambódromo

Don't take a bus to or from the **Sambódromo** (Map p28; Rua Marquês do Sapucaí, near Praça Onze metro station). It's much safer to take a taxi or the metro, which runs round the clock during Carnaval until 11pm Tuesday. This is also a great opportunity to check out the paraders commuting in costume.

Make sure you indicate to your taxi driver which side of the stadium you're on. If you take the metro, the stop at which you get off depends on the location of your seats. For sectors 2, 4 and 6, exit at Praça Onze. Once outside the station, turn to the right, take another right and then walk straight ahead (on Rua Júlio Carmo) to Sector 2. For sectors 4 and 6, turn right at Rua Carmo Neto and proceed to Av Salvador de Sá. You'll soon see the Sambódromo and hear the roar of the crowd. Look for signs showing the entrance to the sectors. If you are going to sectors on the other side (1, 3, 5, 7, 9, 11 and 13) exit at the metro stop Central. You'll then walk about 700m along Av Presidente Vargas until you see the Sambódromo.

THE INSIDERS GUIDE TO SAMBÓDROMO

Alas – literally the 'wings.' These are groups of samba-school members responsible for a specific part of the central *samba do enredo* (theme song). Special *alas* include the *baianas*, women dressed as Bahian 'aunts' in full skirts and turbans. The *abre ala* of each school is the opening wing or float.

Bateria – the drum section is the driving beat behind the school's samba and is the 'soul' of the school.

Carnavalescos – the artistic directors of each school, responsible for the overall layout and design of the school's theme.

Carros alegóricos – the dazzling floats, usually decorated with near-naked women. The floats are pushed along by the school's maintenance crew.

Desfile – the parade. The most important samba schools *desfilar* (parade) on the Sunday and Monday night of Carnaval. Each school's *desfile* is judged on its samba, drum section, master of ceremonies and flag bearer, floats, leading commission, costumes, dance coordination and overall harmony.

Destaques – the richest and most elaborate costumes. The heaviest ones usually get a spot on one of the floats.

Diretores de harmonia – the school organizers, who usually wear white or the school colors; they run around yelling and 'pumping up' the wings, making sure there aren't any gaps in the parade.

Enredo – the central theme of each school. The *samba do enredo* is the samba that goes with it.

Passistas – a school's best samba dancers. They roam the parade in groups or alone, stopping to show their fancy footwork along the way. The women are usually scantily dressed and the men usually hold tambourines.

Puxador – the interpreter of the theme song. He (a *puxador* is invariably male) works as a guiding voice, leading the school's singers at rehearsals and in the parade.

SAMBA CITY, SAMBA LAND

One of the biggest new developments in Rio is **Cidade do Samba** (Samba City; Rua Rivadávia Correa 60, Gamboa), which opened in early 2006. Constructed near the port, the 'city' is actually made up of 14 large buildings (one for each school) among which the assembly of all Carnaval floats will take place. At time of research, they were just opening the area for viewing (admission free), with shows, exhibitions and other events planned in the future. Check with **Riotur** (Map pp238–9; www.rio.rj.gov.br/riotur; 9th fl, Rua Assembléia 10; ⓜ Carioca) for the latest details.

An even more important staging ground is the **Terreirão do Samba** (Samba Land), an open-air courtyard next to the Sambódromo's sector 1, where bands play to big crowds throughout Carnaval (beginning the weekend before).

CARNAVAL DATES

The following are the Carnaval dates in coming years:

2007 February 16–20	**2009** February 20–24
2008 February 1–5	**2010** February 12–16

SAMBA-SCHOOL REHEARSALS

Around August or September, rehearsals start at the *escolas de samba* (samba schools or clubs). Some schools begin as early as July. Rehearsals usually take place in the favelas and are open to visitors. They're fun to watch, but go with a Carioca for safety. Mangueira and Salgueiro are among the easiest schools to get to. See p141 for a complete listing of samba schools.

Arts ■

Music   33
  Samba 33
  Bossa Nova 35
  Tropicália 35
  MPB & the Modern Sound 35

Cinema   37

Literature   39

Architecture   40

Visual Arts   42

Theater & Dance   43

Arts

Although Brazil's *governo federal* (federal government) is no longer headquartered in Rio, the *cidade maravilhosa* (marvelous city) is still far and away the country's cultural capital. The arts are flourishing in Rio, with both the traditional and the avant-garde vying for space on the stages, screens and gallery walls throughout the city. Visitors need only look around or peruse the weekly arts listings to discover the breadth of today's offerings.

Rio's fascinating museums are good destinations to seek when the rain – or the heat – arrives. There you can discover Brazil's indigenous cultures, come face-to-face with Brazilian modern art or stroll through the chambers from which kings and demagogues once ruled.

The city that gave birth to samba and bossa nova has become one of the world's music capitals, with an ever-growing crop of new talent lending the city its tremendous creative energy. While the samba has undergone a rebirth in Rio – particularly in the cinematic streets of old Lapa – a plethora of other musical styles continues to evolve in the *botecos* (neighborhood bars), nightclubs and open-air settings around town. Throughout the week, in some of the most seductive settings, one can hear *Música Popular Brasileira* (MPB), samba, hip-hop (called 'black music'), reggae, funk, jazz, electronic music, regional styles like *choro* (romantic, intimate samba) and *forró* (traditional, fast-paced music from the northeast), as well as the many fusions among these styles, such as samba-jazz, samba-funk, electro-samba and bossa-jazz.

Music is only one part – admittedly a big one – of the city's booming arts scene. In the fine arts, Rio's galleries and museums continue to host some of Brazil's best exhibitions, with Museu de Arte Moderna (MAM; p89) and Centro Cultural Banco do Brasil (p83) leading the way. Film is also well supported in Rio with dozens of theaters hosting everything from arthouse cinema to foreign classics, and with more and more Brazilian films appearing alongside Hollywood ones. There are also plenty of places at which to get a taste of classical music, theater and dance. Whatever your passion, annual festivals are the best places to see what's hot and new in Brazil. Check the City Calendar (p9) for special events happening during your stay. Those with good Portuguese can immerse themselves in the literary world, catching local poets at spoken-word events and big names such as José Saramago and Paulo Coelho on tours through town.

No matter the genre, Rio's enchanting tropical climate plays a part in some of the city's performances. Throughout the year, open-air concerts (on Copacabana beach,

THE IPOD 25: SOUNDS FROM BRAZIL

One of the world's great music cultures, Brazil has an astounding array of talented musicians, playing in a range of addictive styles. A list of our favorite songs could easily fill this chapter, but we've limited our (highly subjective) pick to 25 songs from 25 different artists.

- 'Aquarela do Brasil' – Ary Barroso
- 'Viagem' – Baden Powell
- 'Samba da Bênção' – Bebel Gilberto
- 'Soy Loco Por Ti, America' – Caetano Veloso
- 'Apesar de Você' – Chico Buarque
- 'Flor de Lis' – Djavan
- 'O Mar' – Dorival Caymmi
- 'Alô, Alô Marciano' – Elis Regina
- 'ABC da Vida' – Elza Soares
- 'Namorinho de Portão' – Gal Costa
- 'Quilombo, o El Dorado Negro' – Gilberto Gil
- 'Muito à Vontade' – João Donato e Seu Trio
- 'Desafinado' – João Gilberto
- 'Ponta de Lança Africana' – Jorge Benjor
- 'Asa Branca' – Luiz Gonzaga
- 'Alibi' – Maria Bethânia
- 'Recado' – Maria Rita
- 'Chuva no Brejo' – Marisa Monte
- 'Travessia' – Milton Nascimento
- 'Último Desejo' – Noel Rosa
- 'Panis et Circenses' – Os Mutantes
- 'Garota de Ipanema' – Tom Jobim
- 'Velha Infância' – Tribalistas
- 'Felicidade' – Vinícius de Moraes
- 'Minha Tribo Sou Eu' – Zeca Baleiro

Marina da Glória and even Pão de Açúcar), art exhibitions and film screenings make ample use of Rio's green space, and visitors are never far from an open-air music setting – whether it be at the kiosks of Lagoa (p131), Lapa's weekend street parties or the casual sidewalk settings of the many *botecos* around town.

For the latest information about what's on, be sure to browse local listings in *Veja Rio* or the weekend sections of *Jornal do Brasil* and *O Globo*.

MUSIC

Few cities in the world can compete with Rio's enormous musical heritage. Music here is a deeply ingrained part of life, a form of both celebration and escape, and is heard everywhere on the streets, taking forms that run the gamut from cutting-edge pieces created in the studio to old classics, reinvented anew on stages and in neighborhood sidewalk cafés.

Indeed, innovation is perhaps the greatest feature of Brazilian music. Ever in search of the new, Rio boasts a long line of songwriters who have made tremendous contributions not only to Brazilian music but to musical traditions across the globe. Today the wave continues unabated with renowned musicians – along with scores of unknowns – weaving together the city's complex and deeply enriching harmonies.

SAMBA

The birth of Brazilian music essentially began with the birth of samba, first heard in the early 20th century in a Rio neighborhood near present-day Praça Onze. Here, immigrants from northeastern Brazil (mostly from Bahia) formed a tightly knit community in which traditional African customs thrived – music, dance and the Candomblé religion. Local homes provided the setting for impromptu performances and the exchange of ideas among Rio's first great instrumentalists. Such an atmosphere nurtured the likes of Pixinguinha, one of samba's founding fathers, as well as Donga, one of the composers of 'Pelo Telefone,'

THE DANCE HALLS OF OLD Carmen Michael

If you're interested in Brazilian music and dance, shine up your dancing shoes and head for some of Rio's old-school-style dance halls, known as *gafieiras*. Originally established in the 1920s as dance halls for Rio's urban working class, *gafieiras* nowadays attract an eclectic combination of musicians, dancers, *malandros* (con men) and, of course, the radical chic from Zona Sul. Modern and sleek they are not. Typically held in the ballrooms of old colonial buildings in Lapa, the locations are magnificently old world. Bow-tied waiters serve ice-cold *cerveja* (beer) under low yellow lights and, while the setup initially looks formal, give it a few rounds and it will dissolve into a typically raucous Brazilian evening.

Before *gafieiras* were established, Rio's different communities were polarized by their places of social interaction, whether it was opera and tango for the Europeans or street *choro* (romantic, intimate samba) for the Africans. Responding to a social need and in tandem with the politics of the time, *gafieiras* quickly became places where musicians and audiences of black and white Brazilians alike could mix and create new sounds. Through the *gafieiras*, the street-improvised *choro* formations became big-band songs and a new Brazilian sound was born. The best and oldest dance halls are Democráticus (p141), attracting a young yet fashionably bohemian crowd on Wednesday, and Estudantina (p142) on Praça Tiradentes, which operates from Friday to Sunday.

The standard of dancing is outstanding in Brazil, so expect to see couples who would be considered professional in Europe or the US dancing unnoticed across the polished floors. While just about anything goes in Rio, it's an opportunity for the Cariocas to dress up a little, so you will see quite a few dresses and smart shoes. Don't be intimidated by the other dancers. Unlike in Buenos Aires, where the tango is for experts only, Brazilians are pretty relaxed about newcomers dancing. For those traveling solo, *gafieiras* are fantastic places to meet some intriguing locals and learn a few steps. Dance around the edge of the dance floor with the rest of the dancers to get a closer look at how the dance works – if you are a woman, you won't wait long before someone asks you to dance. Alternatively, you can take a lesson and perhaps meet some fellow beginners to dance with. Estudantina has an in-house dance instructor with whom you can arrange lessons; otherwise, head for one of the nearby dance schools, such as **Nucleo de Dança** (☎ 2221 1011; Rua da Carioca 14, Centro), or check the listings in Activities (p156).

Rio rhythm at bar Bip Bip (p137)

the first recorded samba song (in 1917) and an enormous success at the then-fledgling Carnaval.

Samba continued to evolve in the homes and *botequims* (bars with table service) around Rio. The 1930s are known as the golden age of samba. By this point, samba's popularity had spread beyond the working-class neighborhoods of Central Rio, and the music evolved at the same time, into diverse, less percussive styles of samba. Sophisticated lyricists like Dorival Caymmi, Ary Barroso and Noel Rosa popularized *samba-canção* (melody-driven samba). Songs in this style featured sentimental lyrics and an emphasis on melody (rather than rhythm), foreshadowing the later advent of cool bossa nova. One of the big radio stars of the 1930s was Carmen Miranda, who would become one of the first ambassadors of Brazilian music.

The 1930s were also the golden age of samba songwriting for the Carnaval. *Escolas de samba* (samba schools), which first emerged in 1928, soon became a vehicle for samba songwriting and by the 1930s, samba and Carnaval would be forever linked. Today's theme songs still borrow from that golden epoch.

Great *sambistas* (samba singers) continued to emerge in Brazil over the next few decades, although other emerging musical styles diluted their popularity. Artists like Cartola, Nelson Cavaquinho and Clementina de Jesus made substantial contributions to both samba and styles of music that followed from samba.

Traditional samba went through a rebirth a little over a decade ago with the opening of old-style *gafieiras* (dance halls) in Lapa. (See the Dance Halls of Old, p33.) Today, Rio is once again awash with great *sambistas*. Classic sambistas like Alcione and Beth Carvalho still perform, while rising stars like Teresa Christina and Grupo Semente are intimately linked to Lapa's rebirth. You can see Teresa Christina and other talented musicians live at Carioca da Gema, Democráticus and other settings in Lapa (p139).

BOSSA NOVA

In the 1950s came bossa nova (literally, new wave), sparking a new era of Brazilian music. Bossa nova's founders – songwriter and composer Antonio Carlos (Tom) Jobim and guitarist João Gilberto, in association with the lyricist-poet Vinícius de Moraes – slowed down and altered the basic samba rhythm to create a more intimate, harmonic style. This new wave initiated a new style of playing instruments and of singing.

Bossa nova's seductive melodies were very much linked to Rio's Zona Sul, where most bossa musicians lived. Songs like Jobim's 'Corcovado' and Roberto Meneschal's 'Rio' evoked an almost nostalgic portrait of the city with their quiet lyricism. Bossa was also associated with the new class of university-educated Brazilians, and its lyrics reflected the optimistic mood of the middle class in the 1950s.

By the 1960s, bossa nova had become a huge international success. The genre's initial development was greatly influenced by American jazz and blues, and over time, the bossa nova style came to influence those music styles as well. Bossa nova classics were adopted, adapted and recorded by such musical luminaries as Frank Sinatra, Ella Fitzgerald and Stan Getz, among others.

In addition to the founding members, other great Brazilian bossa nova musicians include Marcos Valle, Luiz Bonfá and Baden Powell, whose talented 20-something son Marcel Powell carries on the musical tradition (catch him live in Rio). Bands from the 1960s like Sergio Mendes & Brasil '66 were also quite influenced by bossa nova, as were other artists who fled the repressive years of military-dictatorship rule to live and play abroad.

For the full story, check out Ruy Castro's *Bossa Nova: The Story of the Brazilian Music that Seduced the World*.

TROPICÁLIA

One of Brazil's great artistic movements, emerging in the late 1960s, was *tropicália*, a direct response to the repressive military dictatorship that seized power in 1964 (and remained in power until 1984). Bahian singers Caetano Veloso and Gilberto Gil led the movement, making waves with songs of protest against the national regime. (Gil, ironically, is today's Minister of Culture – see Gil, p36.) In addition to penning defiant lyrics, *tropicalistas* introduced the public to electric instruments, fragmentary melodies and wildly divergent musical styles. In fact, the *tropicalistas'* hero was poet Oswald de Andrade, whose 1928 *Manifesto Antropofágico* (Cannibalistic Manifesto), supported the idea that anything under the sun could be devoured and re-created in one's music. Hence, the movement fused elements of American rock and roll, blues, jazz and British psychedelic styles into bossa nova and samba rhythms. Important figures linked to *tropicália* include Gal Costa, Jorge Benjor, Maria Bethânia, Os Mutantes and Tom Zé. Although *tropicália* wasn't initially embraced by the public, who objected to the electric and rock elements (in fact, Veloso was booed off the stage on several occasions), by the 1970s its radical ideas had been absorbed and accepted, and lyrics of protest were ubiquitous in songwriting of the time.

The world is still coming to grips with the complex musical legacy of the *tropicalistas*. A 2006 exposition at London's Barbican Centre was dedicated to the movement, and included the music of AfroReggae, one of Rio's leading funk groups, whose songs have elements of *tropicália*. Those who want a deeper understanding of the movement and its aftermath should read Caetano Veloso's erudite book *Tropical Truth*.

MPB & THE MODERN SOUND

Música Popular Brasileira (MPB) is a catchphrase to describe all popular Brazilian music after bossa nova. It includes *tropicália*, *pagode* (relaxed and rhythmic form of samba), and Brazilian pop and rock. All Brazilian music has roots in samba; even in Brazilian rock, heavy metal, disco or pop, the samba sound is often present.

MPB first emerged in the 1970s along with talented musicians like Edu Lobo, Milton Nascimento, Elis Regina, Djavan and dozens of others, many of whom wrote protest songs not unlike the *tropicalistas*. Chico Buarque is one of the first big names from this epoch, and is easily one of Brazil's greatest songwriters. His music career began in 1968 and spanned a time during which many of his songs were banned by the military dictatorship – in fact his music became a symbol of protest during that era. Today the enormously successful Carioca artist continues to write new albums, though lately he has turned his hand to novel writing (See Words without Song, p40).

Jorge Benjor is another singer whose career, which began in the 1960s, has survived up to the present day. Highly addictive rhythms are omnipresent in Benjor's songs, as he incorporates African beats and elements of funk, samba and blues in his eclectic repertoire. The celebratory album *África Brasil,* along with his debut album *Samba Esquema Novo,* is among his best.

More recent MPB stars include Bebel Gilberto, the sweet-voiced daughter of João Gilberto, who blends bossa nova with modern beats. Perhaps the true heiress of bossa, however, is the Rio-born artist Marisa Monte, who's popular both at home and abroad for her fine songwriting and sensuous voice. Mixing samba, *forró,* pop and rock, Marisa has been part of a number of successful collaborations in the music world, most recently with Arnaldo Antunes and Carlinhos Brown to create the hit album *Tribalistas* (2003). Two other notable young singers who hail from a bossa line include Fernanda Porto and Cibelle.

Speaking of family lines, one artist not to be overlooked is Maria Rita, the incredibly talented singer and songwriter whose voice is remarkably similar to that of her late mother, Elis Regina – one of Brazil's greatest singers. Rita's 2005 album *Segundo* followed on from the success of her debut album two years earlier, and showed that she's on her way to carving a name for herself.

Carlinhos Brown is another popular artist (and workaholic) who continues to make immeasurable contributions to Brazilian music, particularly in the realm of Afro-Brazilian rhythms. Born in Bahia, Brown has influences that range from merengue (lively, joyful music originating in the Domincan Republic) to Candomblé music to James Brown, the US

GIL *Tom Phillips*

An active participant in both the World Economic Forum and the World Social Forum, Gilberto Gil is not exactly your cookie-cutter politico. Perhaps only in Brazil would you expect to find a pop star in government. Forget Silvio Berlusconi's crooning, or Tony Blair's attempts at Christian rock – Gilberto Gil has been one of Brazil's best-loved musicians since the 1960s.

Gil was always an *engajado* (activist) – during the 1960s he spent two years exiled in London after offending the dictatorship with his surreal, provocative lyrics. It's just that these days he's engaged in a different way, occupying an office in Brazil's Planalto, where he is the Minister of Culture in President Lula's cabinet.

A household name for decades, 'Gil' hails from the northeastern state of Bahia. Born in 1942, he was raised in a middle-class family near Salvador. His career as a troubadour began in 1965, when he moved south to São Paulo with another Bahian musician, Caetano Veloso. Between them they were responsible for *tropicália,* an influential though short-lived cultural movement that blended traditional Brazilian music with the electric guitars and psychedelia of the Beatles. Years later Veloso even recorded a Tupiniquim (an indigenous group in the northeast) tribute to the Liverpudlian rockers – called *Sugar Cane Fields Forever.*

Over the decades Gil has notched up hit after hit – morphing from quick-footed *sambista* (samba dancer) to Stevie Wonderesque balladeer to dreadlocked reggae icon. His latest album, *Kaya N'Gan Daya,* was a tribute to his idol Bob Marley. In 2003 he even took to the stage in New York with the UN secretary general: Kofi Annan on bongos, Gil on guitar.

In between world tours, book launches and his ministerial duties, the slender 60-something-year-old even finds time for the beach. Keep your eyes peeled – it's not uncommon to find Gil sunning himself at Ipanema's Posto 9.

Here is some essential listening:

- *Gilberto Gil,* Gilberto Gil
- *MTV Unplugged,* Gilberto Gil
- *Quanta,* Gilberto Gil
- *Refazenda,* Gilberto Gil
- *Tropicália 2,* Gilberto Gil and Caetano Veloso
- *Tropicália, ou Panis et Circencis,* Gilberto Gil, Caetano Veloso, Gal Costa and Os Mutantes

funk artist from whom Carlinhos took his stage name. In addition to creating the popular percussion ensemble Timbalada, he has a number of excellent albums of his own (notably *Alfagamabetizado*).

The list of emerging talents gets longer each day, but Brazilian hip-hop is reaching its stride with talented musicians like Marcelo D2 (formerly of Planet Hemp) dazzling audiences with albums like *A Procura da Batida Perfeita* (2005). Seu Jorge, who starred in the film *Cidade de Deus,* has also earned accolades for the release of *Cru* (2005), an inventive hip-hop album with politically charged beats.

In other genres, indie-rock favorites Los Hermanos are among the best bands competing for airtime. Check out their excellent album *Ventura.* Another of our indie favorites is *Monokini Mondo Topless* (2004), an album that blends pop with electro grooves – think vaguely Stereolab in the tropics.

There's no doubt that more great artists will have emerged by the time you read this. Your best bet: upon arrival get yourself to a record store in Rio (try Modern Sound, p165, or Plano B, p171) and find out who's the hottest pop star of the moment. It's unlikely the store clerk will answer Madonna, or any non-Brazilian artist for that matter. For a more detailed history of Brazilian music, check out the book *The Brazilian Sound* by Chris McGowan and Ricardo Pessanha.

CINEMA

Brazil's film industry has been booming in recent years, with a number of great feature films and documentaries emerging from the country. One of the most recent hits is the 2005 *Dois Filhos do Francisco* (The Two Sons of Francisco), a film based on the true story of two brothers – Zeze and Luciano di Camargo – who overcame their humble origins to become successful country musicians. Despite some unfortunate melodrama, the film has plenty of merit, including a curious soundtrack created under the direction of Caetano Veloso.

Although made by two Americans, *Favela Rising* (2005) is so quintessentially 'Rio' that it deserves mention. A fine counterpoint to *Cidade de Deus* (more on that later), this documentary shows a different side of the favela through the eyes of Anderson Sá, founder of the very talented *Grupo Cultural Afro Reggae* (Afro-Reggae Group) and massive symbol of hope for many poor children growing up in the favela. In the film, Sá, who turned his life around after involvement in gangs, starts a music school for youths and makes an enormous contribution to a number of lives as the Afro-Reggae movement spreads to other favelas.

Another worthwhile film, made in 2005, is the documentary *Vinícius,* a paean to the great poet and songwriter Vinícius de Moraes, directed by his ex-son-in-law Miguel Faria Jr. The film features archival footage of old interviews as well as performances of Vinícius' music as played by some of Brazil's best artists.

For a trip back to 1930s Lapa, check out Karim Aïnouz's compelling *Madame Satã* (2002). Rio's gritty red-light district of that time (which hasn't changed much in the last 75 years) is the setting for the true story of Madame Satã (aka João Francisco dos Santos), the troubled but good-hearted *malandro* (con artist), transvestite, singer and *capoeira* master, who became a symbol of Lapa's midcentury bohemianism.

One of Brazil's top directors, Fernando Meirelles earned his credibility with *Cidade de Deus* (City of God), the 2002 film based on a true story by Paolo Lins. The film, which showed brutality and hope coexisting in a Rio favela, earned four Oscar nominations, including one for best director. More importantly, it brought much attention to the plight of the urban poor in Brazil. After his success with *Cidade de Deus,* Meirelles went Hollywood with *The Constant Gardener* (2004), an intriguing conspiracy film shot in Africa.

Eu, Tu, Eles (Me, You, Them), Andrucha Waddington's social comedy about a northeasterner with three husbands, was also well received when it was released in 2000. It has beautiful cinematography and a score by Gilberto Gil (see Gil, opposite) that contributed to the recent wave of popularity of that funky northeastern music, *forró.*

Walter Salles is one of Brazil's best-known directors, whose Oscar award–winning *Central do Brasil* (Central Station, 1998) should be in every serious Brazilophile's film library. The central character is an elderly woman who works in the main train station in Rio writing

STARRING RIO...

Rio has featured prominently in a number of Hollywood films, from the earliest Fred Astaire–Ginger Rogers collaboration, *Flying Down to Rio* (1933) to the Hitchcock classic *Notorious* (1946), with James Bond (in *Moonraker;* 1979), Michael Caine (*Blame it on Rio,* 1984) and others making their appearance in the city.

Our favorite film starring Rio, however, is not a feature film but a documentary. *Rio de Jano* (2003) shows Rio in all its complexity from the point of view of French cartoonist Jano, who illustrates the city in richly detailed, color drawings. His portrait of Cariocas is a skillful one – the characters here come neither from the favela nor from well-heeled suburbs. Instead they work, go to funk shows, bask on the beach, drink at open-air bars and work blue-collar jobs. Director Anna Azevedo did a marvelous job bringing Jano's works to life, giving both an insider and an outsider perspective of Rio.

letters for illiterates with families far away. A chance encounter with a young homeless boy leads her to accompany him into the real, unglamorized Brazil on a search for his father. Salles' latest foray into film was his big-budget biopic *Diarios de Motocicleta* (The Motorcycle Diaries, 2004), detailing the historic journey of Che Guevara and Alberto Granada across South America.

As with many filmmakers, some of Salles' best works came much earlier. In fact, his first feature film *Terra Estrangeiro* (Foreign Land), shot in 1995, holds an important place in the renaissance of Brazilian cinema. The film won seven international prizes and was shown at over two dozen film festivals. It was named best film of the year in Brazil in 1996, where it screened for over six months. Salles is also a great documentary filmmaker; *Socorro Nobre* (Life Somewhere Else, 1995), *Krajcberg, O Poeta dos Vestígios* (Krajcberg, the Poet of the Remains, 1987) and others of his films have won awards at many international festivals.

Bruno Barreto's *O Que É Isso Companheiro* (released as *Four Days in September* in the US, 1998) was based on the 1969 kidnapping of the US ambassador to Brazil by leftist guerrillas. It was nominated for an Oscar in 1998.

Another milestone in Brazilian cinema is the visceral film *Pixote* (1981), directed by the acclaimed Hector Babenco. This film shows life through the eyes of a street kid in Rio, who gets swept along on a journey from innocent waif to murderer by the currents of the underworld. The film was a damning indictment of Brazilian society, made all the more poignant when the actor who played Pixote was killed by police during a bungled robbery six years after the making of the film.

Another important film is *Bye Bye Brasil* (1980) by Carlos Diegues. The first major film produced after the end of the dictatorship, it chronicles the adventures of a theater troupe as they tour the entire country, charting the profound changes in Brazilian society in the second half of the 20th century. Diegues went on to direct *Orfeu* (1999), a lackluster remake of the Camus classic.

Prior to the military dictatorship (1964–85), which stymied much creative expression in the country, Brazil was in the grip of Cinema Novo. This 1960s movement focused on Brazil's bleak social problems, and was influenced by Italian neorealism. One of the great films made during this epoch was the 1962 *O Pagador de Promessas* (The Payer of Vows), a poetic story about a man who keeps his promise to carry a cross after the healing of his donkey. It won the Palme D'Or at the Cannes film festival. Another great pioneer of Cinema Novo is the director Glauber Rocha. In *Deus e o Diabo na Terra do Sol* (Black God, White Devil, 1963), Rocha touched on many of the elements in northeastern Brazil of struggle, fanaticism and poverty. It's one of the great films of the period.

Another important film of the 20th century was made a few years before Rocha's excellent film. *Orfeu Negro* (Black Orpheus), Marcel Camus' 1959 film, opened the world's ears to bossa nova by way of the Jobim and Bonfá soundtrack. Music aside, the film did a clever job recasting Ovid's original Orpheus-Eurydice myth in the setting of Rio's Carnaval (a fertile ground for mythmaking). Making an arguably larger impact yet on Brazilian cinema was the Nelson Pereira dos Santos film *Rio 40 Graus* (1955). This classic of Cinema Novo followed a number of characters and plots that intertwine at an electric pace. Because of its unglamorized portrait of the poor, it was banned on release and wasn't shown in theaters until a year later.

Brazilian cinema began in Rio; appropriately, the city itself starred in the first film made in the country – a slow pan of Baía de Guanabara, made in 1898.

LITERATURE

Since the mid-1990s Brazilians have been buying books in record numbers, and good Brazilian novels are increasingly being translated into English. Best-selling author Paulo Coelho, a Carioca, has written 15 books, and his work has been translated into 56 languages. He's Latin America's second-most-read novelist (after Gabriel García Márquez). Coelho continues to churn out books, with his most recent efforts, *The Zahir* (2005) and *Eleven Minutes* (2003), returning to the theme of spiritual journeys. He explored different material in *Veronika Decides to Die,* which tackles the story of a writer committed to a psychiatric hospital after a suicide attempt, and *The Fifth Mountain,* a fictionalized tale about the prophet Elijah. Still, his most popular works are the simple spiritual fables, like *The Alchemist* and *The Pilgrimage,* with which he sprang to fame in the mid-1990s.

A far-different worldview is presented in works from the detective genre, with popular novels finally available in English. Often called the Raymond Chandler of Brazil, Luis Alfredo Garcia-Roza writes hard-boiled page-turners, often set in his Copacabana neighborhood. To explore the noir side of Rio check out his novels *Southwesterly Wind* (2004) and *Window in Copacabana* (2005). Patrícia Melo is another Brazilian crime novelist (and playwright), who's received praise from both readers and academics for her smart, psychologically complex thrillers. Among her best works are *The Killer* (1998) and *Inferno* (2002).

More widely respected in literary circles is the great Brazilian writer Jorge Amado, who died in August 2001. Born near Ilhéus in 1912, and a longtime resident of Salvador, Amado wrote colorful romances of Bahia's people and places, with touches of magical realism. His early work was strongly influenced by communism. His later books were lighter in subject, but more picturesque and intimate in style. The two-most-acclaimed are *Gabriela, Clove and Cinnamon,* which is set in Ilhéus, and *Dona Flor and Her Two Husbands,* which is set in Salvador. The latter relates the tale of a young woman who must decide between two lovers – the first being the man she marries after her first husband drops dead at Carnaval, the second being her deceased husband who returns to her as a ghost. The ensuing ménage

So much to choose from at Toca do Vinicius (p163 & 164) bookstores, Ipanema

à trois is delightfully portrayed. Amado's other works include *Tent of Miracles,* which explores race relations in Brazil, and *Pen, Sword and Camisole,* which exposes the petty political maneuverings in the realms of academic and military politics. *The Violent Land* is an early Amado classic – something of a dark frontier story. *Shepherds of the Night,* three short stories about a group of Bahian characters, provides another excellent and witty portrait of Bahia.

In the 19th century, José de Alencar became one of Brazil's most famous writers. Many of his works are set in Rio, including *Cinco Minutos* and *Senhora,* both published in 1875. Another from that era, Joaquim Manoel de Macedo was a great chronicler of the customs of his time. In addition to such romances as *A Moreninha,* he also wrote *Um Passeio Pela Cidade do Rio de Janeiro,* published in 1863, and *Memórias da Rua do Ouvidor,* published in 1878.

Joaquim Maria Machado de Assis, another Carioca, is widely regarded as Brazil's greatest writer. The son of a freed slave, Assis worked as a typesetter and journalist in late-19th-century Rio. A tremendous stylist with a great command of humor and irony, Assis had a sharp understanding of human relations, which he used to great effect in his brilliantly cynical works. He used Rio as the background for most of the works he produced in the late 19th century, such as *The Posthumous Memoirs of Bras Cubas* and *Quincas Borba.*

Mario de Andrade is another great Brazilian writer. He led the country's artistic renaissance in the 1920s, and became one of the leading figures in the modernist movement in Brazil. In works such as *Macunaíma* he pioneered the used of vernacular language in national literature. He stressed the importance of Brazilian writers drawing from their own rich heritage. His work showed elements of surrealism and was later seen as a precursor to magical realism.

WORDS WITHOUT SONG

When compiling a list of the best Brazilian singer-songwriters, the name Chico Buarque invariably rises toward the top. Not one to rest on his achievements, Buarque in recent years has reinvented himself as an author, writing three novels – all currently available in English. Usually when musicians try their hand at fiction writing, the results are lukewarm at best, but Buarque seems to have jumped the fence successfully in his latest effort, *Budapest* (his first book was less of an achievement). He admits he's no pro. 'I'm an amateur,' he told a reporter. Modesty aside, his imaginative story is an engaging portrait of both Budapest and Rio, and makes for some gripping reading.

ARCHITECTURE

Formerly the capital of Brazil for many years, Rio has been the architectural setting for the beautiful, the functional and the avant-garde. Today one can see the sweeping range of styles that span the 17th to the 20th centuries in archetypal buildings that often jockey for attention right alongside one another.

Vestiges of the colonial period live on in downtown Rio. Some of the most impressive works are the 17th century churches built by the Jesuits. The best examples from this, the baroque period, are the Convento de Santo Antônio (p84) and the Monasteiro de São Bento (p84). The incredibly ornate interiors, which appear almost to drip with liquid gold, show little of the restraint that would later typify Brazilian architecture.

The artist mission (a group of artists and architects chosen to bring new life to the city) that arrived from France in the early 19th century introduced a whole new design aesthetic to the budding Brazilian empire. Neoclassicism became the official

---

CITY SYMBOLS: TOP FIVE ARCHITECTURAL ICONS

- Copacabana Palace (p180) – The neoclassical gem that came to represent a glitzy new era.
- Arcos da Lapa (p88) – Often used as a symbol of Lapa's bohemian rebirth.
- Maracanã football stadium (p150) – Brazil's temple to football and once the world's largest stadium.
- Cristo Redentor (p79) – The subject of many songs and stories, Christ the Redeemer still looms large over Rio's mythic and real-life landscape.
- Teatro Municipal (p86) – The flower of the Belle Epoque and also the costliest opera house constructed outside of Europe.

Spread your wings and view the architectural features of rooftops in Centro

style and was formally taught in the newly founded Imperial Academy. The works built during this period were grandiose and monumental, dominated by classical features such as elongated columns and wide domes. Among the many fine examples of this period are the Instituto Nacional de Belas Artes (p64), the Teatro Municipal (p86) and the Casa França-Brasil (p82) – considered the most important from this period. There are a few curious features of the Casa: its alignment to the cardinal points, the large cross-shaped space inside, and its monumental dome.

The end of the 19th century saw the continuation of this trend of returning to earlier forms and featured works like the Real Gabinete Português de Leitura (p85). Completed in 1887, the Royal Reading Room shows inspiration from the much earlier manueline period (early 1500s), with a Gothic facade and the highlighting of its metallic structure.

Across the 20th century, Rio became the setting for a wide array of architectural styles – including neoclassical, eclectic, art-deco and modernist works. During the same period, Rio also restored some of its colonial gems (others fell to the wrecking ball), becoming one of Latin America's most beautiful cities.

This, of course, didn't happen by chance. In the early-20th century, as capital of Brazil, Rio was viewed as a symbol of the glory of the modern republic and the president lavished beautiful neoclassical buildings upon the urban streetscape. The early 1900s was also the period when one of Rio's most ambitious mayors, Pereira Passos, was in office. These twin factors had an enormous influence in shaping the face of Brazil's best-known city.

Mayor Passos (1902–06) envisioned Rio as the Paris of South America, and ordered his engineers to lay down grand boulevards and create manicured parks, as some of Rio's most elegant buildings rose overhead. One of the most beautiful buildings constructed during this period was the Palaçio Monroe (1906), a recreation of a work built for the 1904 St Louis World's Fair. The elegant neoclassical Monroe Palace sat on the Praça Floriano and housed the Câmara dos Deputados (House of Representatives). Unfortunately, like many other of Rio's beautiful buildings, it was destroyed in 1976 in the gross 'reurbanization' craze sweeping through the city.

The fruits of this period were displayed at the International Exposition held in Rio in 1922. This was not only the showcase for neocolonial architecture and urban design; it also

TOP FIVE GREEN SPACES

- Floresta da Tijuca (p93) – Rio's crown jewel of green spaces, with rainforests teeming with plant and animal life.
- Sítio Burle Marx (p94) – Out of the way, but worth the trip, with thousands of plant species on an old, lushly landscaped estate.
- Parque do Flamengo (p78) – Best on Sundays when through-streets close to traffic and joggers, cyclists and Rollerbladers claim the myriad pathways through the seaside park.
- Jardim Botânico (p64) – Stately royal gardens best suited to leisurely strolls.
- Parque do Catete (p81) – Small but elegant, complete with swan-filled pond and garden-side bistro.

introduced Brazil's most modern city to the rest of the world. Another big event of the 1920s was the completion of the Copacabana Palace hotel (p180), the first luxury hotel in South America. Its construction would lead to the rapid development of the beach regions.

Rio's 1930s buildings show the currents of modern European architecture, which greatly impacted upon the city's design. Rio's modernism was born along with the rise of President Vargas, who wanted to leave his mark on federal Rio through the construction of public ministries, official chambers and the residences of government power. The Ministry of Health & Education, the apotheosis of the modernist movement in Brazil, is one of the city's most significant public buildings, as it's one of the few works designed by French architect Le Corbusier in conjunction with several young Brazilian architects. (Another work of Le Corbusier–influenced design is the Aeroporto Santos Dumont, completed in 1937.)

The 1930s were also the era of the art-deco movement, which was characterized by highly worked artistic details and an abundance of ornamentation. Good specimens include the central train station and the statue of Cristo Redentor (p79) on Corcovado.

One of the young Brazilians who assisted on Le Corbusier's project would turn out to be a monumental name in architectural history: Oscar Niemeyer. Working in the firm of Lúcio Costa at the time of his initial collaboration with Le Corbusier, Niemeyer – along with Costa – championed the European avant-garde style in Brazil, making a permanent impact on the next 50 years of Brazilian design. Costa and Niemeyer collaborated on many works, designing some of the most important buildings in Brazil.

In Rio, Niemeyer and Costa broke with the neoclassical style and developed the functional style, with its extensive use of steel and glass, and lack of ornamentation. The Museu de Arte Moderna (inaugurated in 1958, p89) and the Catedral Metropolitana (begun in 1964, p89) are good examples of this style. One of the most fascinating modern buildings close to Rio is the Niemeyer-designed Museu do Arte Contemporânea (MAC; p91) in Niterói. Its fluid form and delicate curves are reminiscent of a flower in bloom (though many simply call it spaceshiplike). It showcases its natural setting and offers stunning views of Rio.

Niemeyer, whose work has often been described as harmonious, graceful and elegant, has continued to design innovative buildings for over half a century. He collaborated with Le Corbusier on the design of the UN completed in 1953. Now nearing 100, Niemeyer shows no sign of slowing down, and he still maintains an office in Copacabana. At last count, in 2006, he was working on a series of buildings in Niterói – called Niemeyer Way – as well as a monument in Havana dedicated to Cuba. (Niemeyer, incidentally, was forced into exile in 1964 for his association with the Communist party, and he still maintains ties today.)

Other big building projects on the horizon include Christian de Portzamparc's plans to build the enormous concert hall Cidade de Música (Music City), currently scheduled for construction in 2007. And by the time you read this, the much-vaunted design of Phillip Starck's Rio Universe hotel (p178) should be turning heads on Ipanema beach – not an easy feat given the competition.

VISUAL ARTS

Although currently little known outside of Brazil, Rio's artists are slowly carving a name for themselves in the contemporary art world. At the forefront of the art movement are avant-gardists like Ducha, who utilizes the city's unique topography to create some of his boldest works. His best-known work is his 2001 *Projeto Cristo Redentor,* in which he turned the Christ statue blood red by covering the white spotlights with red gelatin film. This of course required breaking the law, which earned him a fair bit of notoriety.

Another Rio-based artist doing daring work is Jarbas Lopes. His politically and socially incisive work often takes aim at the corruption inherent in many spheres of Brazilian government. Lopes' *O Debate* (The Debate) series was created by manipulating posters, found on the street, of political candidates. Taking the posters of two opposing candidates, he'd weave them together, then place them back on the street, offering his views on the lack of choice in the elections.

Although he's not from Rio, the photographer Sebastião Salgado is Brazil's best-known contemporary artist outside the country. Noted for his masterful use of light, the black-and-white photographer has earned international acclaim for his stunningly beautiful and highly evocative photos of migrant workers and others on the fringes of society.

Going back a few years, the Carioca artist Hélio Oiticica (1937–80) was one of the most significant figures of the avant-garde of the '60s and '70s. He's best known for interactive works, like his controversial *Cosmococa,* an installation that invited viewers to lie on sand covered with plastic sheeting, while watching a projection in which lines of cocaine were arranged across a photo of Marilyn Monroe. Despite his short life, his impact on Brazilian art was profound. Today, there's even a cultural center named after him (p83).

Rio-born artist Cildo Meireles (b 1948) also made a sizable contribution to the contemporary art movement. Creating at the height of the military dictatorship, Meireles focused on the social environment, using silk screens and installations to question the legitimacy of the regime. In the US he garnered much attention for his designing and printing of fake banknotes that featured an image of Uncle Sam on one side and Fort Knox on the other, which he reintroduced into circulation.

Anna Bella Geiger (b 1933) is another important artist active since the 1960s. Following the warm reception of her early photographic work, she expanded her range, becoming one of Brazil's pioneers in video art. Her most recent work was her 2004 exhibition at Paço Imperial, entitled *Obras em Arquipélago,* a sublime composition uniting the language and design of cartography with the geography of the human body.

Getting his start a few decades earlier was the experimental artist Abraham Palatnik, one of the first Brazilians to explore the use of technology in art. He delighted critics with his masterful mixing of light and movement, which he fused in 'cinechromatic machines' – projections of colored light forms onto clear surfaces, innovative work for the 1950s. His last solo exhibition was held in Rio in 1986.

Throughout Brazil's recent history, the influence of European and other foreign art on Brazilian work was significant. In the 19th and 20th centuries, Brazilian artists followed international trends such as neoclassicism, romanticism, impressionism and modernism. The best-known Brazilian painter internationally is Cândido Portinari (1903–62). Early in his career he made the decision to paint only Brazil and its people. Strongly influenced by the Mexican muralists, such as Diego Rivera, he fused native, expressionist influences with a sophisticated, socially conscious style.

Rio's earliest painters were quite taken with the landscape – a tradition that continues today. The 19th-century French artists Jean-Baptiste Debret and Nicolas Taunay, who came via the French artistic mission, set the tone for the development of art over the next 100 years (some critics say they stifled Brazilian art by keeping it rooted in old-fashioned traditions). Regardless, Debret's and Taunay's works in watercolor are some of the first visual records of life in the colony. The neoclassical strand was continued in later works like Victor Meirelles' *A Primeira Missa* (the First Mass, 1861), which depicts the first Mass celebrated in the new colony, with Pedro Álvarez Cabral (Portuguese discoverer of Brazil) and his men in attendance.

THEATER & DANCE

One of the big names in Brazilian theater today is the avant-garde director Gerald Thomas. Born in Rio, Thomas now lives in New York, but continues to have some of his biggest successes on Rio's stages. His work, which he calls Dry Opera, features the almost cinematic use of blackouts and atmospheric lighting, along with prerecorded music and marionette-like acting. For some, it amounts to a complete reinvention of theater. The political comedy *Um Circo de Rins e Fígados* (A Circus of Kidneys and Livers) remains one of his long-running successes (already seen by over 80,000 people in both Brazil and Argentina). His drama isn't strictly limited to his plays: in 2003, following his production of *Tristan und Isolde,* several belli-gerent audience members shouted at the director, and he mooned them from onstage. This even led to criminal proceedings, though his name was eventually cleared.

Rio's lively theater scene began long before the term 'indecent exposure' was in circulation. In fact, the first theater troupes were founded just after Brazil's independence in 1822, and playwrights soon developed a national style. The poet and writer Gonçalves Dias (1823–64) was among the first Brazilians to write plays. Only a handful of Dias' work survives, and the romantic figure (who later died in a shipwreck) is better known for his poetry. His lyric 'Canção do Exílio' (Song of Exile) is his dedication to Brazil's natural beauty.

During the early days of the Republic, other great theater works were produced. Well-known writers, such as José de Alencar, Machado de Assis and Artur Azevedo, wrote plays in addition to literary works, expanding the national repertoire of Brazil's proliferating theaters.

In the 1940s, Nelson Rodrigues (1912–80), who's often characterized as the Eugene O'Neill of Brazil, was instrumental in transforming theater. His socially conscious plays revealed the moral hypocrisy of upper-class Brazilian families. The 1950s saw a flourishing of the theater arts as playwrights like Gianfranco Guarnieri, Jorge Andrade and Ariano Suassuna created more experimental works, creating a dynamic theater scene in Rio and São Paolo.

History

The Recent Past   46

From the Beginning   47
  The Portuguese Arrival 47
  Of Noble Savages & Savage Nobles 47
  Africans in Brazil 47
  Rio's Early Days 48
  The Dom Comes to Town 49
  The Belle Époque 50
  The 20th Century 52

History

The city known for its breathtaking beauty and startling contrasts has never had much trouble capturing the world's attention. Today's Rio continues to grab headlines around the globe. Despite a foiled attempt to bring the 2012 Olympics to Rio, controversial mayor Cesar Maia still basked in the limelight as Rio prepared to host the 2007 Pan Am Games. A flurry of building projects accompanied the preparation, from the modernization of Maracanã football stadium to the building of new hotels and high-tech stadiums in the Barra da Tijuca area, all in expectation of the 80,000 visitors Rio hopes to attract. At last count, Cesar was enumerating his successes in preparation for a bid at the 2008 presidential elections.

In the city, other major projects continue apace, with the long-term Favela-Bairro project entering its third phase. Hundreds of millions of *reais* have been spent on this major development scheme to integrate the favelas (shanty towns) with the rest of the city, providing long-neglected communities with access to decent sanitation, health clinics, schools and public transportation. In 2006 evidence of the success of Favela-Bairro was anecdotal at best, with mixed reports from beneficiaries and the city yet to publish a meaningful report on its progress. Meanwhile, urban renewal and gentrification continues (albeit at a slow pace) in Centro, Santa Teresa and Lapa, and parts of the Zona Sul.

THE RECENT PAST

The favela, once a foreign word to English speakers, has become one of the hottest topics in Rio in the last 10 years. Policy towards these extremely poor communities was…well, until the 1990s, there wasn't much official policy aside from simply destroying the communities and hoping they would go away. Now that Rio has over a million residents living in these towns, the local government has begun to actually address their existence, thus instigating the above-mentioned Favela-Bairro project. One of the reasons that local and national politicians can no longer ignore the favela is the spread of pop culture. The favelas have always been the focus of Carnaval, but today they have also become the focus of Brazilian films (*Cidade de Deus* among others helped focus the world's attention) and music – many top performers have emerged from the favelas – and in Rio, the favelas are the settings for the wildest parties.

Since the 1990s the city has been investing in cleaning up its downtown, renovating some of its early-19th-century gems and doing its best to attract new investment to the area. The metro has gone through several phases of expansion, opening its most recent Copacabana station in 2004, and the work continues (Ipanema stations are in the distance).

Rio has also attempted to curtail its high crime rates, beefing up the numbers of police officers on the beach, in Santa Teresa and in other tourist areas. Unfortunately, the police still have a bad reputation when it comes to excessive use of force, and *bolas perdidas* (stray bullets) remain a constant danger when the cops arrive.

Eco 92, the UN Conference on Environment and Development, was the first of several conferences and hardly anyone remembers what happened before the Kyoto Protocol of 1997. But for Rio the conference was a boon to the then neglected city, and the federal government poured in almost US$1 billion to improve Rio's infrastructure. Eco 92 also laid the foundation for more environmental sensitivity. And although things have been off to a slow start, the Green movement is slowly finding its footing in Rio, with more awareness of the ecological problems the city is creating.

TIMELINE	8000 BC	AD 1502
	Ancestors of Tupinambá living along Baía de Guanabara	Portuguese ships sail into Baía de Guanabara after an eight-month voyage

FROM THE BEGINNING

THE PORTUGUESE ARRIVAL

In the 15th century the small country of Portugal, ever infatuated with the sea, began its large-scale explorations that would eventually take the Portuguese to the coast of Brazil in 1500. A little over a year later, Gonçalo Coelho sailed from Portugal and entered a huge bay in January 1502. It was his chief pilot, Amerigo Vespucci, however, who would give the name. Mistaking the bay for a river (or possibly making no mistake at all since the old Portuguese 'rio' is another word for bay), he dubbed it Rio de Janeiro (River of January).

Although the Portuguese were the first European *arrivistes*, the French would become the first non-natives to settle along the great bay. Like the Portuguese, the French had been harvesting dyewood along the Brazilian coast, but unlike the Portuguese they hadn't attempted any permanent settlements in this region until Rio de Janeiro. Regardless, the Portuguese were far from being the first to set foot on the tropical shoreline, as the land had already been inhabited for at least 10,000 years.

OF NOBLE SAVAGES & SAVAGE NOBLES

Some believe that the Guanabara Indians, the Tupinambá, inspired works such as Sir Thomas Moore's *Utopia* (1516) and would later inspire Rousseau's Enlightenment-era idea of the 'noble savage'. This all started from the letters credited to Amerigo Vespucci on his first voyage to Rio in 1502. The idea common at the time was that there existed on earth an Eden, and that it lay undiscovered. Vespucci claimed to have found that Eden, from his cursory observations of the Tupi. They were described as innocent savages, carefree and well-groomed, with the unusual custom of taking daily baths in the sea. The fact that native women were freely offered to the strange foreigners probably added to the enthusiasm with which they spoke about the region upon their return.

In fact, the honeymoon didn't last long. The conquerors soon came to see the forest-dwelling Indians as raw manpower for the Portuguese empire, and enslaved them and set them to work on plantations. The Indians, too, turned out to be different than the Europeans imagined. The Tupinambá were warlike and ate their enemies – through ritualistic cannibalism they would receive the power and strength of the consumed opponent. They also didn't take to the work as the Portuguese had expected, and were dying off in large numbers from introduced diseases. By the 17th century the Tupinambá had been completely eradicated. To fulfill their growing labor demands, the Portuguese would soon turn to Africa.

AFRICANS IN BRAZIL

The Portuguese began bringing blacks stolen from Africa into the new colony shortly after Brazil's founding. Most blacks were brought from Guinea, Angola and the Congo and would constitute some four million souls brought to Brazil over its 3½ centuries of human trafficking. The port of Rio had the largest number of slaves entering the colony – as many as two million in all. At open-air slave markets these new immigrants were sold as local help or shipped to the interior, initially to work on the thriving sugar plantations, and later – when gold was discovered in Minas Gerais in 1704 – to work back-breaking jobs in the mines.

Although slavery was rotten anywhere in the New World, most historians agree that the Africans in Rio had it better than their rural brethren. Those that came to Rio worked in domestic roles as maids and butlers and out on the streets as dock workers, furniture movers, delivery boys, boatmen, cobblers, fishermen and carpenters. The worst job was transporting the barrels of human excrement produced in town and emptying them into the sea.

1567	1763
Portuguese set up the first settlement on Morro do Castelo	Rio's population swells to 50,000 and the capital of Brazil moves from Salvador to Rio

As Rio's population grew, so too did the number of slaves imported to meet the labor needs of the expanding coffee plantations in the Paraíba Valley. By the early 19th century African slaves made up two-thirds of Rio's population.

Lots of illicit liaisons occurred between master and slave and children born into mixed backgrounds were largely accepted into the social sphere and raised as free citizens. This contributed considerably to creating Brazil's melting pot. While escape attempts were fewer in Rio than in the more brutal climate of the northeast, there were attempts. Those seeking freedom often set their sights on *quilombos*, communities of runaway slaves. Some were quite developed – as was the case with Palmares, which had a population of 20,000 and survived through much of the 17th century before it was wiped out by Federal troops.

Rio's nearest *quilombo* in the 19th century was in Leblon – then quite distant from the city. Unlike other *quilombos*, it was headed by a white, progressive businessman who was in favor of slave abolition. Luggage manufacturer Jose de Seixas Magalhães kept farmland in Leblon, which was staffed entirely by runaway slaves, whom he hid and protected in his Leblon mansion.

This was during Brazil's incipient abolition movement, and the farm operated under the eyes of the government, with Magalhães enjoying the special patronage of Princesa Isabel. Abroad, the country was receiving pressure to outlaw slavery, and trafficking in human cargo was outlawed in 1830. This move, however, did nothing to improve the lives of slaves in Brazil, who would have to wait another two generations to gain their freedom. Despite the ban, shipment of human cargo continued well into the 1850s, with half a million slaves smuggled into Brazil between 1830 and 1850. The British (out of economic self-interest) finally suppressed Brazil's trafficking with naval squadrons.

Pressure from home and abroad reached a boiling point toward the end of the 19th century and slavery was finally abolished from the steps of Royal Palace overlooking Praça Quinze de Novembro (p85) in 1888. Brazil was the last country in the New World to end slavery.

RIO'S EARLY DAYS

In order to get the colony up and running, the Portuguese built a fortified town on Morro do Castelo in 1567 to maximize protection from European invasion by sea and Indian attack by land. They named their town São Sebastião do Rio de Janeiro, in honor of King Sebastião of Portugal. Cobbled together by the 500 founding Cariocas, early Rio was a poorly planned town with irregular streets in the medieval Portuguese style. It remained a small settlement through the mid-17th century, surviving on the export of brazilwood and sugarcane. In Rio's first census (in 1600), the population comprised 3000 Indians, 750 Portuguese and 100 blacks.

With its excellent harbor and good lands for sugarcane, Rio became Brazil's third most important settlement (after Salvador da Bahia and Recife-Olinda) in the 17th century.

The gold rush in Minas Gerais had a profound effect on Rio and caused major demographic shifts on three continents. The rare metal was first discovered by *bandeirantes* (explorers and hired slave hunters) in the 1690s, and as word spread gold seekers arrived in droves. Over the next half-century an estimated 500,000 Portuguese arrived in Brazil and many thousands of African slaves were imported. Rio served as the natural port of entry for this flow of people and commerce to and from the Minas Gerais goldfields.

In the 18th century Rio morphed into a rough-and-tumble place attracting a swarthy brand of European immigrant. Most of the settlement was built near the water (where today stands Praça Quinze de Novembro), beside rows of warehouses, with noisy taverns sprinkled along the main streets. Rio was a rough city full of smugglers and thieves, tramps and assassins, and slaves on the run. Smuggling was rampant, with ships robbed and the sailors murdered, with bribes given over to the cops. Gold flowing through the city created the constant menace of pirates. Adding a note of temperance to the place were the religious orders that came in small bands and built Rio's first churches.

1807	1822
Napoleon invades Portugal and the Portuguese prince regent (later known as Dom João VI) flees for Brazil	Dom Pedro I declares independence from Portugal and crowns himself emperor

THE FRENCH CONNECTION

Cariocas and the French share much more than just a few romance-language cognates. In fact, Franco-Brazilian history goes back five centuries. Within two years of the Portuguese landing, French sailors (pirates, mostly) began appearing in the bay. In contrast to the more aggressive methods of the Portuguese, the French developed a strong friendship with the Tupinambá, and by 1710 there were bilingual people on both sides. The French also brought back brazilwood, parrots and tobacco, but they were also the first to bring back a living Tupi, and paraded him before Franco King Henri II at a decadent 'Brazilian Festival'.

France was also the first in the region to set up a colony in what they called Antarctic France. They settled an island in the bay and present-day Flamengo beach, and called their 'town' Henriville. Unfortunately, the colony didn't last as the Portuguese battled for control over the region, eventually driving the French off the land in 1565.

The French returned a few times in the early 18th century to try to get a piece of Brazil but, ironically, it wasn't until Dom João's arrival from Portugal that French culture truly thrived in Brazil. The king, who adored French culture (but was still an archenemy of Napoleon), invited to Brazil a French mission – a talented assortment of architects, painters, sculptor and other artists. They made substantial contributions to the young country, creating among other things the Imperial Academy of Fine Arts, Brazil's first school for the education of architects. This was headed by the architect Grandjean de Montigny, who ushered in Rio's neoclassical architectural period (see p40).

Early in the 19th century, Rio captured the public imagination in Paris at an exhibition of Felix-Émile Taunay's colorful panoramas. Rio was billed as the new Arcadia, a city whose emphasis was on natural beauty. This fired the imagination of some Parisians, and hot on the heels of the artistic mission came other elements of high culture – French dressmakers, florists, perfumers and wine sellers – who set up shop on Rua do Ouvidor, which quickly became the French quarter of the city.

Some of Rio's most important buildings that rose over the next century were decidedly French in flavor. The Opera house, for instance, was modeled on the Paris Opera House, and Rio's grand avenue (today Av Rio Branco) was laid down in an attempt to recreate the Champs Elysées in the tropics. In the 20th century French architects such as Le Corbusier were extremely influential on urban design.

On the political front, the French influence was again significant. In fact, the most commonly seen slogan in Brazil – Order and Progress (visible on any Brazilian flag) – comes from French philosopher Auguste de Comte (1797–1857), whose elevation of reason and scientific knowledge over traditional religious beliefs was extremely influential on the young Brazilian Republic.

Today, the tropical mystique continues to entrance Parisians. The 'Year of Brazil in France' was celebrated in 2005 with hundreds of exhibitions, parties and events, celebrating Brazilian music, film, art and dance, held throughout France. Paris nightclubs have also tapped into Rio's allure with places like Favela Chic serving up caipirinhas (cane liquor cocktails) as DJs spin hip-hop straight out of the baile-funk, while samba parties by the Seine are becoming a regular summertime event. Meanwhile, French visitors continue to flock to the *cidade maravilhosa* (marvelous city). Only the US and Germany send more travelers to Rio.

Rio for its part continues to hold French culture in high esteem. Top culinary honors consistently go to French restaurants and French chefs (Le Pré Catalan, and Le Saint Honoré often battling for top billing). And French filmmaking, French art and French fashion are usually regarded in Rio as the pinnacles of achievement. The perfect day in Rio for a Zona Sul *garota* (young woman) would probably entail a quick shop at Louis Vuitton or the French boutique **Clube Chocolate** (p171), catching the latest French film at **Casa França-Brasil** (p147), followed by dinner at **Olympe** (p114).

THE DOM COMES TO TOWN

In 1807 Napoleon's army marched on Lisbon. Two days before the French invasion, 40 ships carrying the Portuguese prince regent (later known as Dom João VI) and his entire court of 15,000 set sail for Brazil under the protection of British warships. After the initial landing in Bahia (where their unkempt state was met with bemusement), the royal family moved down to Rio, where they settled.

This had momentous consequences for the city as the king, missing the high culture of Europe, lavished his attention on Rio, envisioning a splendid European-style city for

1888	1889
Slavery abolished	Brazilian Republic declared

his new hometown. European artisans flooded the city. The British, rewarded for helping the king safely reach Brazil, gained access to Brazil's ports, and many Anglo traders and merchants set up shop in the town center. Anti-Napoleon French also arrived, as did other Europeans, creating an international air unknown until then. When the German Prince and noted naturalist Alexander Philip Maximilian arrived in Brazil in 1815 he commented on the many nationalities and mixtures of people he encountered.

Dom João VI fell in love with Rio. A great admirer of nature, he founded the botanical gardens and introduced sea bathing to the inhabitants of Rio. He had a special pier built at Caju, with a small tub at the end, in which he would immerse himself fully clothed as the waves rocked gently against it. (His wife Carlota Joaquina bathed in the nude.) This was long before Copacabana was opened to the rest of the city, remaining a virgin expanse of white sand framed by rainforest covered mountains, reachable only by an arduous journey.

With the court came an influx of money and talent that helped build some of the city's lasting monuments, such as the palace at the Quinta da Boa Vista. Within a year of his arrival, Dom João VI also created the School of Medicine, the Bank of Brazil, the Law Courts, the Naval Academy and the Royal Printing Works.

Dom João VI was expected to return to Portugal after Napoleon's Waterloo in 1815, but instead stayed in Brazil. The following year his mother, mad queen Dona Maria I, died, and Dom João VI became king. He refused demands to return to Portugal to rule, and he declared Rio the capital of the United Kingdom of Portugal, Brazil and the Algarves. Brazil became the only New World colony to ever have a European monarch ruling on its soil.

Five years later Dom João VI finally relented to political pressure and returned to Portugal, leaving his 23-year-old son Pedro in Brazil as prince regent. In Portugal the king was confronted with the newly formed Côrtes, a legislative assembly attempting to reign in the powers of the monarchy. The Côrtes had many directives, one of which was restoring Brazil to its previous status as subservient colony. Word was sent to Dom Pedro that his authority was greatly diminished. According to legend, when Pedro received the directive in 1822, he pulled out his sword and yelled 'Independência ou morte!' ('Independence or death!'), putting himself at the country's head as Emperor Dom Pedro I.

Portugal was too weak to fight its favorite son, not to mention the British, who had the most to gain from Brazilian independence and would have come to the aid of the Brazilians. Without spilling blood, Brazil had attained its independence and Dom Pedro I became the head of the Brazilian 'empire' (despite Pedro's claims to the contrary, Brazil was a regular monarchy, not an empire since it had no overseas colonies).

Dom Pedro I ruled for only nine years. From all accounts, he was a bumbling incompetent who scandalized even the permissive Brazilians by siring numerous illegitimate children. He also strongly resisted any attempts to weaken his power by constitutional means. Following street demonstrations in Rio in 1831, he surprised everyone by abdicating, leaving the power in the hands of his five-year-old, Brazilian-born son.

Until Dom Pedro II reached adolescence, Brazil suffered through a turbulent period of unrest, which finally ended in 1840 when Dom Pedro II, at the age of 14, took the throne. Despite his youth he proved to be a stabilizing element for the country, and ushered in a long period of peace and relative prosperity. The period of industrialization began with the introduction of the steamship and the telegraph, and the king encouraged mass immigration from Europe. His shortcomings during his half-century of rule were a bloody war with Paraguay (1865–70) and his slowness at abolishing slavery. He was well-liked by his subjects, but they finally had enough of a monarchy and he was pushed from power in 1889.

THE BELLE ÉPOQUE

Rio experienced boom days in the latter half of the 19th century. The spreading wealth of coffee plantations in Rio state (and in São Paulo) revitalized Brazil's economy, just as the city was going through substantial growth and modernization. Regular passenger ships

1917	1928
The world's first samba, 'Pelo Telefone', is released; a whole new genre of music is born	The first escola de samba, Deixa Falar, is created; Carnaval is the buzz of Rio

Pedestrians crossing Av Rio Branco, Centro

began sailing to London (1845) and Paris (1851), and the local ferry service to Niterói began in 1862. A telegraph system and gas streetlights were installed in 1854. By 1860 Rio had more than 250,000 inhabitants, making it the largest city in South America.

For the wealthy the goal of creating a modern European capital grew ever closer, as the city embraced all things European – with particular influence from the customs, fashion and even cuisine of Paris. The poor, however, had a miserable lot. In the 1870s to 1880s, as the rich moved to new urban areas by the bay or in the hills, Rio's marginalized lived in tenement houses in the old center of town. There conditions were grim: streets were poorly lit and poorly ventilated, with a stench filling the narrow alleyways.

Rio's flood of immigrants added diversity to the city. On the streets, you could hear a symphony of languages – African, Portuguese, English, French – mixing with the sounds of the *bonde* (tram), of carts drawn by mules, as the cadence of various dances – maxixes, lundus, polkas and waltzes – interpreted by anonymous performers.

The city went through dramatic changes in the first decade of 1900, owing in large part to the work of mayor Pereira Passos. He continued the work of 'Europeanization' by widening Rio's streets and creating grand boulevards such as Av Central and Mem de Sá. The biggest of these boulevards required the destruction of 600 buildings to make way for Av Central (later renamed Rio Branco), which became the Champs Élysées of Rio, an elegant boulevard full of sidewalk cafés and promenading Cariocas.

Passos also connected Botafogo to Copacabana by building the tunnel, paving the way for the development of the southern beaches. Despite his grand vision for Rio, his vision for the poor was one of wide-scale removal from the city center – a short-sighted policy that would dog Rio (and Brazilian) government for the next 80 years. In truth, the *cortiços* – poor collective lodgings – were breeding grounds for deadly outbreaks of small pox, yellow fever and typhus. Sighting the widespread health and sanitation problems, the city destroyed thousands of shacks (with no homes, the poor fled to the hills, later creating some of the earliest favelas). The city also exterminated rats and mosquitoes and created a modern sewage system.

By the time Passos' term ended in 1906, Rio was the Belle Époque capital par excellence of Latin America. Its only possible rival in beauty was Buenos Aires. One visitor who

1950	1960
Pelé plays his last match at Maracanã; 200,000 fans come to watch	The capital of Brazil transfers from Rio to Brasília

commented on Rio's transformation was former US President Teddy Roosevelt. In 1913, during his tour through town, he noted that since Brazil became a republic in 1889, Rio de Janeiro had gone 'from a picturesque pest-hole into a singularly beautiful, healthy, clean and efficient modern great city.'

THE 20TH CENTURY

At the end of the 19th century, the city's population exploded because of European immigration and internal migration (mostly ex-slaves from the declining coffee and sugar regions). By 1900 Rio boasted more than 800,000 inhabitants, a quarter of them foreign-born (by contrast, São Paulo's population was only 300,000).

Following Passos' radical changes, the early 1920s to the late 1950s were one of Rio's golden ages. With the inauguration of the grand luxury resort hotels (the Glória in 1922 and the Copacabana Palace in 1924), Rio became a romantic, exotic destination for Hollywood celebrities and international high society, with Copacabana its headquarters. In some ways Rio's quasi-mythic status as a tropical arcadia spans its entire history, but in the 1940s and '50s its reputation as the urban Eden of Latin America was vouchsafed as the world was introduced to Carmen Miranda, an icon for Rio.

This was also a time when radical changes were happening in the world of music (see below), and when Rio was first beginning to celebrate its 'Brazilianness', or its mixed heritage and multicolored population. Sociologist Gilberto Freyre's influential book *Masters and Slaves* (1933) turned things upside down as Brazilians, long conditioned to think of their mixed-race past with shame, began to think differently about their heritage – as an asset that set them apart from other nations of the world.

The 1930s was the era of President Vargas, who had a vision for Brazil, and wanted desperately to improve the level of education among all Brazilians and to increase the country's industrial output. As industry flourished, so too did the arts. The city was buzzing with energy as the downtown became the center of bohemianism.

The world's fascination with Rio was severely curtailed during the rise of the military dictatorship of the 1960s. The era of repression began with press censorship, silencing of political opponents (sometimes by torture and violence) and an exodus of political defectors

---

MOTHER OF SAMBA

In 20th century Rio, one of the most momentous events was transpiring not inside the presidential palace but in the working-class neighborhood of Praça Onze near downtown. In 1915 this was considered 'Africa in miniature' for the influx of immigrants from Bahia, who had been flocking to the region since the end of slavery in 1888. There Afro-Brazilian culture – music, dance and religion (Candomblé) – thrived in the homes of old Bahian matriarchs, called *tias* (aunts). At the center of this thriving community was Tia Ciata, something of a self-made woman who rented out costumes for the Carnaval balls, worked as a healer (she was even consulted by president Wenceslau Brás, who had a leg wound she allegedly healed), and hosted large parties on Candomblé saints' days – all while looking after her 15 children. Within time, Ciata's house became the meeting point for the city's journalists, bohemians, Bahian expats and musicians. Today's now-legendary names – Pixinguinha, Donga, Heitor dos Prazeres and others – met regularly to play music and experiment with new forms, never imagining that their result – samba – would become one of the world's great musical forms. Coincidentally, this was also around the time that African-Americans in New Orleans were paying the music that would later be called jazz.

After the earliest musical creations, the performers gathering at Tia Ciata's went on to make records, and samba's popularity spread like wildfire across the city. They came first through the working class and, after initial resistance, on into the houses of the wealthy. Samba continued to evolve throughout the next few decades as it was adopted for Carnaval, yet the songs developed in those early years would live on (many are still played), and laid the foundation for which so much of Brazilian music is based on today.

1964	1985
President Goulart overthrown by a military coup and the era of heightened repression begins	Civilian rule returns to Brazil under José Sarney

RIO'S MALANDROS Carmen Michael

In the suffocating heat of a summer afternoon sometime in the 1930s, João Francisco dos Santos walked into the shabby, corrupt Lapa police station with vengeance on his mind. Wearing a silk shirt stretched across his taut frame and a gold ring engraved with St George, the formidable *capoeirista* (*capoeira* – Brazilian martial arts – practitioner) attacked five policemen who had previously assaulted his transvestite friends... At least, that's the story they tell in the more notorious drinking dens of Lapa. Born to slaves in the impoverished northeast of Brazil, swapped at age eight for a horse, and later emerging as the flamboyant transvestite cabaret performer, João Francisco dos Santos (or Madam Satã as he was later called) became the first of a new breed of social misfits known in Rio as *malandros* (con men).

In the tumultuous era of the 1930s, Lapa emerged as a seedy bohemian enclave of gambling houses, cabaret and brothels. In this setting, *malandros* consorted with a cast of exotic dancers, transvestites, penniless musicians and angst-ridden poets. Their exploits were told by the likes of Noel Rosa, Nelson Gonçalves and other musicians who sang of Meia Noite, Camisa Preta, Miguel Zinho and other legendary *malandros*. Originally portrayed as complicated Robin Hood types, the *malandro* today is more likely to be described as a sly con artist.

'First samba, then make love and then sleep,' wrote Chico Buarque, summing up the idle *malandro* philosophy of life in one of his many odes to Malandragem. For the poor and discriminated, *malandros* also became a symbol of rebellion. Carefully dodging the title of thief or gigolo, *malandros* used charm, persuasion and manipulation to fund their flamboyant lifestyle, and they often played the part in eye-catching white patent shoes, and silk shirts and scarves.

Rio's con artists have been largely relegated to the pages of history, though there are some who say a new breed of *malandro* has emerged, playfully targeting those who possess money and naïveté in equal quantities. When Brazilians talk about *malandros* today, mostly they mean that unnaturally good-looking *capoeirista*, *sambista* (samba dancer) or surfer who offers to 'show you around' and who will spend your money so fast it will make your head spin. And then, as all good *malandros* should do, he will disappear into the night to the local *botequim* (bar with table service), ensuring his exploits are well known in the barfly history books. As they say in Rio: as long as *otários* (the gullible) exist, there will always be *malandros*.

abroad (including musicians, writers and artists). There were numerous protests during that period (notably in 1968 when some 100,000 marched upon the Palácio Tiradentes). And even Rio's politicians opposed the military regime, which responded by withholding vital federal funding for certain social programs.

Despite the repression, the '60s and '70s witnessed profound changes in the city, with the opening of tunnels and the building of viaducts, parks and landfills. (Perversely, this time of autocratic rule was also marked by a booming economy.) In the realm of public transportation, modernization was on the way. In the 1970s builders connected Rio with Niterói with the construction of the bay-spanning bridge, while beneath the city, the first metro cars began to run. This outmoded *bonde* has nearly disappeared: Rio's last streetcar line (p87) runs from Centro to Santa Teresa, and still conjures up those nostalgic prewar days.

Meanwhile, the Zona Sul saw skyscrapers rising over the beaches of Copacabana and Leblon, with the wealthy moving further away from neglected downtown Rio. The moving of Brazil's capital to Brasília in 1960 seemed to spell the end for Centro, which became a ghost town after hours and retained none of the energy of its past. By the 1970s, its plazas and parks were dangerous places, surrounded by aging office towers.

The heart of old Rio remained a bleak place until around 1985, when Brazil held its first direct presidential election in 20 years. With the slow return to civilian rule, Cariocas turned their attention to sadly abandoned parts of the city, like downtown. Over the next decade citizens, particularly local shop owners, launched a downtown revitalization campaign, sometimes collecting money by going door-to-door.

By 1995 it was clear that the drive was a success. Whole blocks in downtown received much-needed facelifts. Handsomely restored buildings attracted new investment, with new shops and cultural centers opening their doors alongside book publishers and art galleries. And nightlife returned to Lapa.

1992	1994
Rio hosts Eco 92, the UN Conference on Environment and Development	The Favela-Bairro project is unveiled; Brazil wins its fourth World Cup

Unfortunately, the latter half of the 20th century was also an era of explosive growth in the favelas, as immigrants poured in from poverty-stricken areas of the northeast and the interior, swelling the number of urban poor in the city. The *'cidade maravilhosa'* (marvelous city) began to lose its gloss as crime and violence increased, and in the 1990s it became known as the *cidade partida* (divided city), a term that reflected the widening chasm between the affluent neighborhoods of the Zona Sul and the shanty towns spreading across the region's hillsides.

Today crime and its root, poverty, are the single biggest issues affecting Rio. Whether the city can improve the lot of the poor will undoubtedly play a major role in defining Rio's image in the coming years.

2002	2007
After four unsuccessful attempts, Lula is elected president; Brazil wins its fifth World Cup	Rio hosts the Pan American Games

Itineraries 56
Organized Tours 58

Ipanema & Leblon 61

Gávea, Jardim Botânico & Lagoa 63
Gávea 63
Jardim Botânico 64
Lagoa 64

Copacabana & Leme 65

Botafogo & Urca 66
Botafogo 75
Urca 76

Flamengo, Laranjeiras & Cosme Velho 77
Flamengo 78
Laranjeiras 79
Cosme Velho 79

Catete & Glória 80
Catete 80
Glória 81

Centro & Cinelândia 81
Centro 82
Cinelândia 86

Santa Teresa & Lapa 86
Santa Teresa 87
Lapa 88

Greater Rio 89
São Cristóvão 90
Baía de Guanabara & Niterói 91

Barra da Tijuca & West of Rio 92

Sights

Sights

Rio's star attractions are its white-sand beaches and the heady culture that has grown up beside them, but the *cidade maravilhosa* (marvelous city) has much more up her sleeve than just steamy days out on the sands and samba-filled nights. In fact, with a history dating back more than five centuries, the once mighty 'capital of the Brazilian empire' (as one Portuguese king crowned Rio) has scores of atmospheric old streets, magnificent churches and cathedrals, and plazas teeming with activity in the colonial part of town. Urban wanderers have much to discover, from the bohemian lanes of old Santa Teresa to the idyllic charm of Urca, with countless secrets just waiting to be unearthed.

Those who'd rather revel in the city's natural beauty, can do so from breathtaking heights atop Pão de Açúcar (Sugarloaf) or beneath the open arms of Cristo Redentor (Christ the Redeemer). There are also splendid imperial gardens, tranquil islands out in the bay and wild markets, alive with the sights and sounds (and tastes) of northeastern Brazil.

ITINERARIES
One Day
In 24 hours in Rio, you can take in a lot – though you'll probably wish you had many more days at your disposal. Start the morning with a quick juice – go for *açaí* (juice made from an Amazonian berry) and a *misto quente* (hot ham-and-cheese sandwich) at a local juice bar on your way to Ipanema beach (p61). Once you reach the sands, you can join the action – *futebol* (soccer), surfing, volleyball, *frescobol* (beach game with two paddles and a ball),

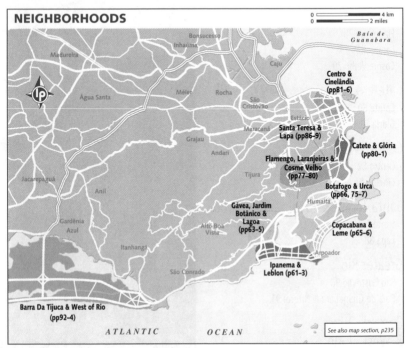

wave frolicking – or just take in the lovely scenery. After you've gotten a bit of color, order an *agua de coco* (coconut water) and make your way to **Lagoa** (p64). Take a stroll along the lake, go for a jog or even hire a bike. Afterward, reward yourself with a meal at **Arab Da Lagoa** (p114) or one of the other lakeside kiosks. As the afternoon wanes, grab a taxi to Urca and take the cable car to **Pão de Açúcar** (p76), where you can watch a spectacular sunset over the *cidade maravilhosa*. For dinner, fresh seafood and more great views await at **Azul Marinho** (p107). Finish the night with samba and caipirinhas (cane liquor cocktails) at **Carioca da Gema** (p139) or one of the many other samba clubs in Lapa.

Three Days

Following your first action-packed day in Rio, catch the *bonde* (tram) up to **Santa Teresa** (p87) for a stroll through picturesque streets lined with old mansions and colorful restaurants and bars. Have lunch at the Amazonian restaurant **Espírito Santa** (p125). While it's still light, head up to Corcovado, where you can admire the craftsmanship of the **Redeemer** (p79) and the splendid city beneath him. That evening, catch some live music in Copacabana either at **Severyna** (p139), **Clan Café** (p138) or **Bip Bip** (p137). On your third day, it's time for a bit of Mata Atlântica (coastal rainforest), which you can experience in all its tropical splendor at **Parque Nacional da Tijuca** (p93). After a walk past waterfalls and lush scenery, go back to the Zona Sul for a bite and *chope* (draft beer) at one of Leblon's classic *botecos* (small neighborhood bars, such as **Jobi**, p131). Walk it off on **Praia de Leblon** (p61), going all the way to Arpoador for a (hopefully) perfect sunset over the beach.

One Week

By the fourth day, it's time to return to the beach – this time to **Copacabana** (p65) for a jog or cycle alongside of it. Refuel on *agua de coco* or something more substantial at one of Av Atlântica's many eateries. After lunch take the metro up to Centro for a walk through history. In addition to checking out the baroque cathedrals, the teeming pedestrian streets and the faded palaces, be sure to stop in the **Centro Cultural Banco do Brasil** (p83) to see what exhibitions are on. As Cariocas call it a day (around 5pm or 6pm), head to the **Arco do Teles** (p135) for outdoor drinking and revelry amid charming old lanes. From there, catch a cab to Leblon for a drink at stylish **Bar d'Hotel** (p130) or **Melt** (p147).

By the fifth day, you may need a respite from Rio's intensity. The untouched beauty of **Ilha Grande** (p195), two hours west of Rio, offers a mix of lush forests and breathtaking beaches. Further east lies **Paraty** (p192), whose charming colonial streets make for fine evening strolls after a day exploring the region's natural wonders – beaches, forests, islands. Spend two days in these locations, then return for a final day in Rio.

On your last day in town, join the madness at **Maracanã football stadium** (p150), or for a more low-key day, visit the boutiques of Ipanema, check out the state of contemporary art at **Museu de Arte Moderna** (MAM, p89), or have a cruise along the bay (p58). At night, make your way to Botafogo for a Bahian feast at **Yorubá** (p119), after which you'll be primed for more live music at **Democráticus** (p141), **Praia Vermelha** (p138) or **Vinícius piano bar** (p139). To end the week with a bang, check out the club scene at **Baronneti** (p146) or **00** (zero zero, p143), only calling it a night as the sun rises over Ipanema beach.

Ride a bonde (tram) through the streets of Santa Teresa

FAVELAS: THE OTHER SIDE OF RIO *Paula Gobbi*

What do we know about the favelas? That the *cidade maravilhosa* has over 700; that more than 1 million people live in these notoriously violent, drug ridden slums, where poverty prevails, and public power is nonexistent. Many steer away, yet the glow and fascination for 'world of favelas' drives thousands of tourists each year to satisfy their curiosity on the close-knit hillside communities and capture with their lenses the passageways clustered with vestiges of urban poverty. Films have grasped insights into this mysterious world, from the romanticized 1959 classic *Orfeu Negro* (Black Orpheus) to the recent unsettling *Cidade de Deus* (City of God).

Over a century ago the first favela in Rio, the Morro da Providencia, was founded by excombatants of the Guerra dos Canudos (Canudos War). The 10,000 soldiers came to Rio in 1897, the federal capital at the time, to collect their promised payoff with homes. They settled on the hillside waiting. Since then, Rio's housing problem has only multiplied and favelas sprawled out embracing the city.

Bob Nadkarni, English filmmaker and painter, fell in love with the enchanting world of the shanty towns and moved to Tavares Bastos favela 25 years ago. Conquering the art of the best caipirinhas in town, he enjoys sharing his revealing stories of crime and police corruption in a favela overlooking the stunning Baía de Guanabara. At 'The Maze' art gallery attached to his home, he provides painting classes to the local community. Bob argues that Rio's favelas compare to London's 19th-century slums.

Favelas exhale cultural vitality. Rocinha is next to Rio's wealthiest neighborhood and famed as the largest favela in Latin America. This bustling community of over 150,000 has its own cable TV network with 32 channels and 30,000 subscribers, three community radio stations and two newspapers. And it's also home of the Casa da Cultural (Culture Home), founded in 2003 by Gilberto Gil, Minister of Culture, singer and neighbor. Drawing on the favela's rich artistic tradition, it promotes music, theater and painting. The house (on Estrada da Gávea number one) was declared a historic landmark.

The favela next door, Vidigal, perched on a hillside overlooking Ipanema beach, is the base of the group 'Nos do Morro' (Us from the Favela). This theater group won fame after some of its young actors appeared in the award-winning *Cidade de Deus*. Ten of its members performed in the *Two Gentlemen of Verona* for the Royal Shakespeare Company in August 2006.

The cultural group AfroReggae is an expression of favela life – experiences, frustrations and police violence. What started in 1993 in the favela of Vigario Geral as a newspaper called *Afro Reggae News*, five years later had a radio station, production company and a contract for a CD, *Nova Cara*, with Universal Studios.

The favelas brew rich musical expression – *forró* (traditional fast-paced music from the northeast), funk, hip-hop, *pagode* (relaxed, rhythmic form of samba, first popularized in the 1970s), rap, gospel, rock. And they are the home of the most famous samba schools who work all year round to enchant the world with its glittering parade.

ORGANIZED TOURS

Bay Cruises

With its magnificent coastline and pristine islands nearby, Rio makes a lovely backdrop for a cruise. Tours depart from the Marina de Glória (Map pp238–9), and you can purchase tickets in advance from 8am to 4pm Monday to Friday.

MACUCO RIO Map pp238-9

☎ 2205 0390; www.macucorio.com.br in Portuguese; Marina da Glória, Glória; boat tours US$35-45 ☺ 10am & 2pm

Macuco offers two daily tours in a high-velocity speed boat which can carry 28 people. The first trip heads south to the pristine Cagarras Archipelago all the way to Redondo Island, where you can spot migratory birds and perhaps dolphins, turtles and even whales at certain times

of the year. The other route heads to the north passing beside the Museu do Arte Contemporânea (MAC) and historic sites along the bay. Both tours last just under two hours, with a choice of morning or afternoon cruises.

MARLIN YACHT TOURS Map pp238-9

☎ 2225 7434; www.marlinyacht.com.br; Marina da Glória, Glória; cruise 2/4½hr US$20/30; ☺ 10am & 3pm

Marlin offers two daily tours aboard their large 30-person schooners. The morning cruise departs for Cagarras at 10am, passing by Niterói beaches along the way. You'll stop for a 30-minute swim along a particularly lovely beach, and return at 2:30pm. The other route, identical to that offered by Saveiros, travels along the bay departing at 3pm and returning at 5pm. Marlin also offers fishing tours (p152).

SAVEIROS TOURS Map pp238-9

☎ 2225 6064; www.saveiros.com.br; Marina da Glória, Glória; cruise US$14; ⏱ 9:30-11:30am

Saveiros leads daily two-hour cruises out over Baía de Guanabara in large schooners. The route follows the coastline of Rio and Niterói with excellent views of Pão de Açúcar, the MAC, Ilha Fiscal and the old fort of Urca. You'll sail under the Niterói bridge.

City Tours

GRAY LINE TOURS Map pp246-7

☎ 2512 9919; www.grayline.com.br; Av Niemeyer 121, Leblon

The Rio-based branch of the international chain offers a range of sightseeing tours. They cover the usual tourist destinations – with four-hour trips to Corcovado, historic Centro and Baía de Guanabara, all of which cost around US$30. It also has day trips to Buzios (US$28) and Petropólis (US$22). Look for its brochures on the reception desks of most hotels or check its website for more details. Some readers have complained of spending more time on the bus (while it picks up passengers from other hotels) than on the actual tour itself.

LUIZ AMARAL TOURS

☎ 2259 5532; www.travelrio.com

Luiz strives to lead small groups (maximum of four people) that make participants feel llike they're on an outing among friends. A friendly, well-traveled Carioca with a good command of English, Luiz can put together a tour to do whatever you want. His more popular excursions include a trip up Pão de Açúcar combined with an exploration of historical Centro and Santa Teresa (US$45 per person for groups of two), an exploration of beaches south of Barra (US$45 per person for groups of four), and nightlife tours in Rio (US$35 per person for two or more).

PRIVATE TOURS

☎ 2232 9710; www.privatetours.com.br

Recommended for his tailor-made tours, Pedro Novak has been leading excursions around the city and further afield since 1992. One of his unique offerings is his sunset tour, where you watch the sun set over Rio and the bay from atop the 270m-high Niterói city park. The trip also includes a visit to the old Santa Cruz fortress (constructed in 1567), followed by dinner.

www.lonelyplanet.com

SHOULD I STAY OR SHOULD I GO?

Favela tours are now among the most popular day tours you can book in the city, but many visitors wonder if it's little more than voyeurism taking a trip into the Rocinha 'slums'. In fact, there can be some positive things that come out of the experience. Local residents, who feel marginalized by their own government, are often flattered that foreigners take such an interest in them. Projects focused on the arts are growing in the favelas; and one of the best ways to support the community directly is to purchase locally made paintings and handicrafts.

Choosing a guide is also essential. Try to get the lowdown before you sign up. Does he or she give time or money to the community? If so, how much and where does it go? Does the guide live in the favela? While the majority of agencies operating in Rocinha are simply opportunists, there are a few who are bringing more than just tourists to the neighborhood. Ask around, as for those who are interested in seeing Rocinha from the inside – as a volunteer – there are numerous ways to get involved.

Favela Tours

MARCELO ARMSTRONG

☎ 3322 2727, 9989 0074; www.favelatour.com.br; per person US$30

Marcelo is the pioneer of favela tourism, and takes small groups on half-day tours to the favelas of Rocinha and Vila Canoas near São Conrado. The itinerary includes an explanation of the architecture and social infrastructure of the favela – particularly in relation to greater Rio de Janeiro. The trip also includes a walk through the streets, and a stop at both a community center and a handicraft center where visitors can purchase colorful artwork made by locals. A portion of Marcelo's profits goes toward social causes in the favela. To avoid paying a commission, call him direct (don't book through hotels or other middle men).

Helicopter Tours

HELISIGHT

☎ 2511 2141 weekdays, 2542 7895 weekends; www.helisight.com.br; from US$75-240 per person

In business since 1991, Helisight offers eight different tours, lasting from six to 60 minutes. From one of its four helipads, helicopters travel around Cristo Redentor, from where you can glimpse the statue's

Sights

ORGANIZED TOURS

excellent craftsmanship. Helisight also has flights over the Parque Nacional da Tijuca and above the mountains and beaches woven into Rio's lush landscape. Helipad locations are in Parque Nacional da Tijuca facing Corcovado; on Morro da Urca, the first cable-car stop up Pão de Açúcar; on the edge of Lagoa; and Pier Mauá downtown at the docks. Sample prices per person are US$75 for a six-minute flight and US$240 for a 30-minute one (three-person minimum).

Hiking Tours
RIO ADVENTURES
☎ 2705 5747; www.rioadventures.com; hiking/climbing/rafting tours from US$25/65/80
Offering a range of outdoor activities, Rio Adventures leads hikes through Tijuca National Park, including short treks up Pico Tijuca and Pedro Bonito. They also offer sightseeing tours, rock climbs (Pão de Açúcar, Corcovado and Pico da Tijuca), rafting excursions (to Paraibuna River, 175km northwest of Rio) and even parachuting and paragliding trips. They employ experienced guides, who speak Portuguese, English and Spanish among other languages.

TANGARÁ ECOLOGICAL HIKES
☎ 2252 8202, 9656 1460; www.tangarapasseios.com.br
Run by two Brazilians who love the outdoors, Tangara offers an enormous variety of excursions, from kayaking excursions off Praia Vermelha to climbs up Pedra da Gávea, while hang gliders soar nearby. They also have two-day trips: exploring Ilha Grande, rafting excursions in Mont Serrat and climbing treks up Pedra do Baú. They rate hikes according to level of difficulty (easy, moderate and hard), and their outings remain popular with young Brazilians. Guides speak English, Spanish and Portuguese.

TRILHARTE ECOTURISMO Map pp242-3
☎ 2556 3848; www.trilharte.com.br in Portuguese; Suite 01, Rua Almirante Tamandaré 77, Flamengo; from US$17-75
Although the guides don't speak English, this ecologically minded organization offers exceptional excursions, catering to adventurers 'with a passion for photography.' It offers hiking, rappelling, rafting and horse-back riding trips, which range in price from US$17 to US$75. It also hosts photographic safaris, where participants study under a professional photographer on a day- or weekend-long excursion. Past trips have ranged from the aesthetic (Holy Week in Ouro Preto) to the far out (nudes in nature). For a list of scheduled excursions, visit its website (click on 'sugestões de passeios'). Most activities are held at weekends.

Jeep Tours
JEEP TOUR
☎ 2108 5800; www.jeeptour.com.br
Travel to the lush Parque Nacional da Tijuca in a large, convertible jeep. Four-hour tours, which cost around US$40 per person, consist of a stop at the Vista Chinesa, then on to the forest for an easy hike, and a stop for a swim beneath a waterfall, before making the return journey. On the way back, you'll stop at Pepino beach, the landing strip for hang gliders from nearby Pedra Bonita. Other excursions offered by Jeep Tour include trips to Angra dos Reis (where forest meets sea) and a coffee *fazenda* (plantation). The price of all tours includes pick up and drop off at your hotel.

Motorcycle Tours
ROUGH TRIP
☎ 2572 9991; www.roughtrip.com.br
Head off-road on a 200cc motorcycle on one of Rough Trip's tours of Rio's beaches, forests and mountains. Guides are provided, as are helmets and gloves. In addition to its Rio tour, Rough Trip also offers excursions to Buzios or will custom-design a tour to your liking.

Tram Tours
BONDE HISTORICO
☎ 2240 5709, 2524 2508; per person US$6; ☽ 10am Sat
Run by the Museu do Bonde (Tram Museum), guided tours of the Santa Teresa neighborhood illuminate historic points along the journey from downtown to Silvestre and back, with a stop at the Museu do Bonde. Trams depart every Saturday at 10am, from the tram station on Rua Profesor Lélio Gama in Centro.

Walking Tours

CULTURAL RIO
☎ 3322 4872, 9911 3829; www.culturalrio.com.br;
from US$50

Run by art historian Professor Carlos
Roquette, who speaks English and French
as well as Portuguese, Cultural Rio offers
visitors an in-depth look at social and historical aspects of Rio de Janeiro. Roquette
has a wealth of Carioca knowledge (and
a quirky sense of humor), and he feels as
comfortable discussing Jobim and the
bossa nova scene as he does the sexual
indiscretions of the early Portuguese rulers.
Itineraries include a night at the Teatro Municipal, colonial Rio, baroque Rio, imperial
Rio and a walking tour of Centro. In business for over 20 years, Professor Roquette
charges US$50 for a four-hour tour and
US$10 for each additional hour.

FABIO SOMBRA
☎ 2275 8605; www.fasombra.cjb.net

A multilingual artist still active as an arte
naïf painter, Fabio leads tours highlighting
historical and cultural Centro and Santa Teresa. His most popular tour covers the ruins
of the old port and historical sites around
Praça 15 de Novembro, the monastery of
São Bento and the Catedral Metropolitana,
passing through Lapa and ending in Santa
Teresa. Fabio also enjoys having visitors to
his studio at Rua Dr Xavier Sigaud 205 (10
minutes' walk from Pão de Açúcar in Urca),
where he gives a colorful slide show called
'Rio Fold Experience.' Call in advance to get
directions before you drop by.

IPANEMA & LEBLON
Eating p106; Shopping p158; Sleeping p174

Truly some of the world's more enchanting places, Ipanema and Leblon are blessed
with a magnificent beach and open-air
cafés, bars and restaurants hidden along the
tree-lined streets just back from the beach.
This is Rio's premier zip code and favored
stomping ground for wealthy Cariocas,
young and old, gay and straight.

Ipanema acquired international fame in
the early '60s as the home of the bossa nova
character 'Girl from Ipanema.' It became the
hangout of artists, intellectuals and wealthy
liberals, who frequented the sidewalk cafés
and bars. After the 1964 military coup and
the resulting crackdown on liberals, many
of these bohemians were forced into exile.
During the '70s, Leblon became the nightlife
center of Rio. The restaurants and bars of
Baixo Leblon, on Av Ataúlfo de Paiva between Ruas Aristídes Espínola and General
Artigas, were the meeting point for a new
generation of artists and musicians. While
Lapa is where the live music is at, Leblon
still has its allure – you'll find both old-time
favorites and alluring newcomers here.

Orientation

Situated in the Zona Sul, Ipanema and Leblon face the same stretch of beach and are
separated by the Jardim de Alah, a canal
and adjacent park. A few blocks to the
north lies Lagoa Rodriga de Freitas, while
the rocky outcropping of Ponta do Arpoador (a surfer favorite) forms the eastern
boundary. To the west looms the Morro
(mountain) Dois Irmãos, nicely framing
the already lovely stretch of sand.

IPANEMA & LEBLON BEACH Map pp246-7
Av Delfim Moreira & Av Vieira Souto

Although the beaches of Ipanema and Leblon are one long beach, the *postos* (posts)
along them subdivide the beach into areas
as diverse as the city itself. Posto 9, right
off Rua Vinícius de Moraes, is Garota de
Ipanema, which is where Rio's most lithe
and tanned bodies tend to migrate. The
area is also known as the Cemetério dos
Elefantes because of the old leftists, hippies
and artists who hang out there. In front of
Rua Farme de Amoedo the beach is known
as Bolsa de Valores or Crystal Palace (this is
the gay section), while Posto 8 further up is
mostly the domain of favela kids. Arpoador,
between Ipanema and Copacabana, is Rio's
most popular surf spot. Leblon attracts

TRANSPORT

Bus Botafogo (503); Corcovado train station (583,
584); Urca (511 and 512); São Conrado (591, 592);
Praça Quinze de Novembro (415); Novo Rio bus
station (128 and 172); Centro (Rio Branco, 132);
Copacabana (503, 569 and 570).

Metrô-Ônibus (metro buses) connect Siqueira
Campos station with Ipanema and Leblon (see p206
for more information).

a broad mix of single Cariocas, as well as families from the neighborhood.

Whatever spot you choose, you'll enjoy cleaner sands and sea than those in Copacabana. Keep in mind that if you go on Saturday or Sunday, the sands get fearfully crowded. Go early to stake out a spot.

Incidentally, the word *ipanema* is Indian for 'bad, dangerous waters' – not so far off given the strong undertow and often oversized waves crashing on the shore. Be careful, and swim only where the locals do.

MIRANTE DO LEBLON Map pp246-7
Av Niemeyer
A few fishermen, casting out to sea, mingle with couples admiring the view at this overlook at the western end of Leblon beach. The luxury Sheraton Hotel looms to the west, with the not so luxurious favela of Vidigal nearby.

MUSEU AMSTERDAM SAUER
Map pp246-7
☎ 2512 1132; www.amsterdamsauer.com; Rua Garcia D'Ávila 105; admission free; ⏰ 9:30am-2:30pm Mon-Fri, 10am-2pm Sat
Next door to Museu H Stern, the Amsterdam Sauer Museum also houses an impressive collection of precious stones – over 3000 items in all. Visitors can also take a peek at the two life-sized replicas of mines.

MUSEU H STERN Map pp246-7
☎ 2259 7442; hstern@hstern.com.br; Rua Garcia D'Ávila 113; admission free; ⏰ 8:30am-6pm Mon-Fri, 8:30am-noon Sat
The headquarters of the famous jeweler H Stern incorporates a museum displaying a

permanent exhibition of fine jewelry, some rare mineral specimens and a large collection of tourmalines. There is a 12-minute tour, which displays the process of turning the rough stones into flawlessly cut jewels as the gems pass through the hands of craftsmen, cutters, goldsmiths and setters. With a coupon, you can get a free cab ride to and from the shop and anywhere in the Zona Sul. Call them at ☎ 2274 6171 and they'll pick you up from your hotel.

PARQUE GAROTA DE IPANEMA
Map pp246-7
Off Rua Francisco Otaviano near Rua Bulhões Carvalho; ⏰ 7am-7pm
This small park next to the Arpoador rock features a tiny playground and a small concrete area popular with skaters, as well as a lookout with a good view of Ipanema beach. On weekends in summer, concerts are sometimes held here.

TOCA DO VINÍCIUS Map pp246-7
☎ 2247 5227; www.tocadovinicius.com.br; Rua Vinícius de Moraes 129; ⏰ 9am-9pm Mon-Fri, 10am-5pm Sun
A quintessential stop off for bossa nova fans, Toca do Vinícius is a **music store** (p163) named in honor of the famous Brazilian

Enjoying a stroll along Ipanema Beach (p61)

musician, Vinícius de Moraes. The 1st floor has a good selection of bossa, while upstairs a tiny museum displays original manuscripts and photos of the great songwriter and poet. Live bossa nova concerts are held in the small space several nights a week.

GÁVEA, JARDIM BOTÂNICO & LAGOA

Eating p113; Shopping p164

Beginning just north of Ipanema and Leblon, these well-heeled neighborhoods front the Lagoa Rodrigo de Freitas, a picturesque saltwater lagoon ringed with a walking and biking trail and dotted with lakeside kiosks serving up cuisine al fresco and live music on warm nights. The other big draw here is the royal garden (Jardim Botânico) that gave the neighborhood its name. Here you'll find stately palms, rare orchids and a rich variety of flowering plants. Aside from its natural attractions, these neighborhoods have some excellent restaurants, lively nightlife, a planetarium and one of the Zona Sul's best cultural centers.

Orientation

Located behind Ipanema, Lagoa Rodrigo de Freitas forms the centerpiece to these three charming neighborhoods. The lake itself, with a path looping around it, is a fine place for strolling. At night, kiosks on the western and eastern sides of Lagoa draw diners from all over the city. Two small islands in the lake, Ilha Piraqué and Ilha dos Caiçaras, are private country clubs.

The district of Lagoa itself, with high-rise condominiums fronting the lake, extends along the northern shores. The tropical acreage of the Jardim Botânico lies to the west of the lake, and its residents live just

north of there. South of the gardens lies Praça Santos Dumont, a small plaza at the intersection of three busy streets that forms the backdrop to Gávea's most active bar scene. Across busy Rua Jardim Botânico lies the country club Jóquei Clube (p150).

Traffic around the lake can be a headache. Av Epitácio Pessoa, the wide boulevard on the eastern side of the lake, leads to the Túnel Rebouças, which connects Lagoa to downtown or the Linha Vermelha, the northern highway out of town. The major thoroughfare on the western edge of the lake, Rua Jardim Botânico, continues north around the lake turning into Rua Humaitá once it crosses Av Epitácio Pessoa. This is a handy shortcut to get to Botafogo or Leme.

Av Padre Leonel Franca divides Gávea from Leblon to the south, turns into the Lagoa–Barra Hwy as it goes west, passing through São Conrado before Barra.

GÁVEA

INSTITUTO MOREIRA SALLES

Map pp236-7

☎ 3284 7400; www.ims.com.br in Portuguese; Rua Marquês de Sao Vicente 476; admission free; ☿ 1-8pm Tue-Sun

This beautiful cultural center is next to the Parque da Cidade and contains an archive of more than 80,000 photographs, many portraying old streets of Rio as well as the urban development of other Brazilian cities over the last two centuries. It also hosts impressive exhibitions, often showcasing the works of some of Brazil's best photographers and artists. Check its website for details of what's on when you're in town.

The gardens, complete with artificial lake and flowing river, were designed by Brazilian landscape architect Burle Marx. There's also a craft shop and a quaint café that serves lunch or afternoon tea.

MUSEU HISTÓRICO DA CIDADE

Map pp236-7

☎ 2512 2353; www.rio.rj.gov.br/cultura in Portuguese; Estrada de Santa Marinha 505; admission US$2; ☿ 10am-4pm Tue-Sun

The 19th-century mansion located on the lovely grounds of the Parque da Cidade now houses the City History Museum. In addition to its permanent collection, which portrays Rio from its founding in 1565 to the mid-20th century, the museum has exhibitions of furniture, porcelain, photographs and paintings by well-known artists. The park itself is free, open from 7am to 6pm.

PLANETÁRIO Map pp246-7
☎ 2274 0096; www.rio.rj.gov.br/planetario in Portuguese; Rua Padre Leonel Franca 240; museum admission free, domes US$2; ☻ museum 10am-5pm Tue-Sun

Gávea's stellar attraction, the Planetário (Planetarium) features a museum, a *praça dos telescópios* (telescopes' square) and a couple of state-of-the-art operating domes, each capable of projecting over 6000 stars onto its walls (40-minute sessions in the domes are at 4pm, 5:30pm and 7pm Saturday, Sunday and holidays; admission US$2). Visitors can take advantage of free guided observations through the far-seeing telescopes on Monday, Wednesday and Thursday from 6:30pm to 8:30pm. The hyper-modern Museu do Universo (Universe Museum) houses sundials, a Foucault's Pendulum and permanent exhibitions, and good temporary ones – the recent Mars exhibit garnered much attention. Periodically, the planetarium hosts live *chorinho* (romantic, intimate samba) concerts on weekends. Check the website or the newspaper for information.

JARDIM BOTÂNICO

JARDIM BOTÂNICO Map pp246-7
☎ 2294 9349; www.jbrj.gov.br in Portuguese; Rua Jardim Botânico 920; admission US$2; ☻ 8am-5pm

This exotic 1.41-sq-km garden, with over 5000 varieties of plants, was designed by order of the Prince Regent Dom João in 1808. It's quiet and serene on weekdays and blossoms with families and music on

weekends. The row of palms (planted when the garden first opened), the Amazonas section and the lake containing the huge Vitória Régia water lilies are some of the highlights. A pleasant outdoor café overlooks the gardens. Take insect repellent.

PARQUE LAGE Map pp246-7
☎ 2538 1091; www.eavparquelage.org.br in Portuguese; Rua Jardim Botânico 414; ☻ 7am-6pm

This is a beautiful park at the base of Parque Nacional da Tijuca, about a kilometer from Jardim Botânico. It has English-style gardens, little lakes and a mansion that now houses the Instituto Nacional de Belas Artes, which often hosts art exhibitions and occasional performances. The park is a tranquil place – a favorite of families with small children. Native Atlantic rain forest surrounds Parque Lage. This is the starting point for challenging hikes up Corcovado (not recommended to go alone).

LAGOA

FUNDIÇÃO EVA KLABIN RAPAPORT
Map pp246-7
☎ 2523 3471; Av Epitácio Pessoa 2480; ☻ 1-5pm Wed-Sun

An old mansion full of antiques, the former residence of Eva Klabin Rapaport houses the works of art she collected for 60 years. Reflecting Eva's diverse interests, the collection has 1100 pieces from ancient Egypt, Greece and China. Paintings, sculptures, silver, furniture and carpets are also on display.

LAGOA RODRIGO DE FREITAS
Map pp246-7

One of the city's most picturesque spots, Lagoa has 7.2km of cycling/walking path around the lake. Bikes are available for hire (p204) near Parque Brigadeiro Faria Lima. It may sound cheesy, but hiring a paddle boat is another way to enjoy the lake, especially when the Christmas tree is lit up across the water. Boat rental is available on the lake's east side in Parque do Cantagalo, December through early January. For those who prefer caipirinhas to plastic swan boats, the kiosks in Parque dos Patins offer lakeside dining al fresco, often accompanied by live *forró* (traditional, fast-paced music from the northeast).

PARQUE DA CATACUMBA Map pp246-7

Av Epitácio Pessoa; ☾ 8am-7pm

Inaugurated in 1979, Catacumba is the site of Brazil's first outdoor sculptural garden. The site of a former favela (which was demolished to create the park), Catacumba sits atop Morro dos Cabritos, which rises from the Lagoa Rodrigo de Freitas. It's a choice place to escape the heat while strolling through some fascinating works by artists such as Roberto Moriconi and Bruno Giorgi. Superb views await those willing to climb to the top of the hill (385m). During summer, Catacumba hosts free Sunday afternoon concerts featuring top performers in its outdoor amphitheater. Check *O Globo*'s weekend listings for details.

COPACABANA & LEME

Eating p115; Shopping p164; Sleeping p179

Framed by mountains and deep blue sea, Rio's most beautiful beach is a long, curving shoreline stretching 4.5km from end to end. Packing the beach are sun-worshippers of every age and background – from favela kids to aging socialites, with tourists, families and hipsters all thrown into the mix. While no longer the pre-eminent symbol of Rio (Ipanema has long since earned that distinction), Copacabana is still a fascinating place, with many gems hidden beneath its theatrical façade. Old-school *botecos* (small open-air bars), eclectic restaurants and nightclubs, myriad shops and of course the handsome beach still cast a spell on many visitors.

Today, the neighborhood is a mix of chaos and beauty – of gorgeous beach fronted by luxury hotels, with the favelas ever present along the perimeters. Copacabana is also the heart of Rio's red-light district. After dark, prostitutes trawl the restaurants along Av Atlântica while overstimulated foreigners stumble toward the strip clubs around Av Princesa Isabel.

TRANSPORT

Bus Ipanema and Leblon (503, 569 and 570), Gávea (462 and 433). Centro (buses marked 'Praça XV,' 'Castelo,' and 'Praça Mauá')

Metro Siqueira Campos and Cardeal Arcoverde

The name Copacabana comes from a small Bolivian village on Lake Titicaca. Historians believe a statue of the Virgin Mary (Our Lady of Copacabana) was brought to Rio and consecrated inside a small chapel near Arpoador. Copacabana remained a small fishing village until Túnel Velho opened in 1891, connecting it with the rest of the city.

The construction of the neoclassical Copacabana Palace Hotel in 1923 heralded a new era for Copacabana – and Rio – as South America's glitziest destination for the Hollywood jetsetter. Copacabana remained Rio's untarnished gem until the 1970s, when the area began to fall into decline.

Orientation

Bordered by mountains on three sides and ocean to the east, congested Copacabana contains only three parallel streets traversing its entire length. Av Atlântica runs along the ocean. The one-way Av Nossa Senhora (NS) de Copacabana is two blocks inland, and runs east. One block further inland, Rua Barata Ribeiro is also one-way, running west (toward Ipanema and Leblon). The names of all these streets change when they reach Ipanema. As in Ipanema, part of the beachside street (Av Atlântica in this case) closes on Sundays and holidays (until 6pm), giving freer reign to the joggers, cyclists and Rollerbladers normally jostling for space on the sidewalks. Av Princesa Isabel, which serves as the boundary between Copacabana and Leme, is the principal thoroughfare to Botafogo, Centro and points north.

COPACABANA & LEME BEACH
Map pp244-5

A magnificent confluence of land and sea, the long, scalloped beach of Copacabana and Leme runs for 4.5km, with a flurry of activity always stretching along its length: over-amped footballers singing their team's anthem, Cariocas and tourists lining up for caipirinhas at kiosks, favela kids showing off their football skills, beach vendors shouting out their wares among the beached and tanned bodies.

As in Ipanema, each group stakes out their stretch of sand. Leme is a mix of older residents and favela kids, while the area between the Copacabana Palace Hotel and Rua Fernando Mendes is the gay and transvestite section, known as the Stock or Stock Market – easily recognized by the rainbow

COPACABANA & LEME TOP FIVE

- Following the beat of Brazilian music at the live jam sessions of **Bip Bip** (p137).
- Drinking poolside at the **Copacabana Palace** (p134).
- Taking a sunrise stroll along the **beach** (p65).
- Browsing for records and catching evening jazz at **Modern Sound** (p165).
- Enjoying a decadent meal **Le Pré Catalan** (p117).

flag. Young football and *futevôlei* (soccer volleyball) players hold court near Rua Santa Clara. Posts five and six are a mix of favela kids and Carioca retirees, while the beach next to the Forte de Copacabana is the fishermen's community beach. In the morning, you can buy the fresh catch of the day.

The beach is lit at night and police are in the area, but it's still not wise to walk there after dark – stay on the hotel side of Av Atlântica if you take a stroll. Av NS de Copacabana is also dangerous – watch out at weekends, when the shops are closed and there are few locals around.

MORRO DO LEME Map pp244-5

☎ 2275 7696; admission US$1; ☽ 9am-noon Sat & Sun, reservations required

East of Av Princesa Isabel, Morro do Leme contains an environmental protection area. The 11 hectares of Atlantic rain forest are home to numerous species of birds, such as the saddle and bishop tanagers, thrushes and the East Brazilian house wren. An hour-long tour is available by booking ahead.

MUSEU HISTÓRICO DO EXÉRCITO E FORTE DE COPACABANA Map pp244-5

☎ 2521 1032; Av Atlântica & Rua Francisco Otaviano; admission US$2; ☽ 10am-4pm Tue-Sun

Built in 1914 on the promontory of the old Our Lady of Copacabana chapel, the fort of Copacabana was one of Rio's premier defenses against attack. You can still see its original features, including walls up to 12m thick, defended by Krupp cannons. The several floors of exhibits tracing the early days of the Portuguese colony to the mid-19th-century aren't the most tastefully done, but the view alone is worth a visit. Be sure to stop in the recently opened **Confeitaria Colombo** (p116).

BOTAFOGO & URCA

Eating p118; Shopping p166; Sleeping p184

One of Rio's most traditional neighborhoods, Botafogo may lack the sensuality of Ipanema, but it has an energy all its own, with its old colonial buildings now set with charming bars and restaurants. For discovering Rio beneath the stereotypes, Botafogo is an excellent place to wander.

Neighboring Urca with its peaceful, tree-lined streets seems a world away from the noisy bustle of Copacabana. Here, you'll find an eclectic mix of building styles and manicured gardens along its streets, with local residents strolling among them. Along the seawall, which forms the northwestern perimeter of Pão de Açúcar, fishermen cast for dinner as couples lounge beneath palm trees, taking in views of Baía de Guanabara and Cristo Redentor. Tiny Praia Vermelha in the south has one Rio's finest beach views. A lovely walking trail begins there.

Although it was the site of one of the first Portuguese garrisons in the region, almost 300 years elapsed before Urca developed into a residential neighborhood. Today it is one of the safest and – in spite of the Pão de Açúcar cable car in its midst – least discovered by foreign visitors.

Botafogo, on the other hand, was developed early on. It's named after the Portuguese settler João Pereira de Souza Botafogo, and reached its peak in the late 1800s when the Portuguese Court arrived in Brazil. Carlota Joaquina, the wife of Dom João VI's had a country villa. With royalty established in the area, arriving aristocrats built many mansions, some of which still stand as schools, theaters and cultural centers.

TRANSPORT

Botafogo

Bus Leblon (503). Numerous lines pass along Praia de Botafogo heading north and south (including 569, 570, 571 and 572).

Metro Botafogo.

Urca

Bus Centro (107), Leblon, Ipanema and Copacabana (511 and 512).

(Continued on page 75)

1 *Row-boats with Pão de Açúcar (Sugarloaf, p76) in background* **2** *Even at night Ipanema beach (p61) has loads of atmosphere* **3** *Fishermen at Arpoador rock, Ipanema (p62)* **4** *Join the* gata *and* gato *on Ipanema beach (p61)*

1 *(previous page) The statue of Cristo Redentor (p79) stands at the top of Corcovado mountain, overlooking Rio de Janeiro*

1 *Characteristic 'wavy tile' pavement, Copacabana beach (p65)* **2** *Taking a walk on Copacabana beach at sunrise (p65)* **3** *Catch a wave or two at Arpoador, Ipanema (p61)* **4** *Samba performers on Copacabana beach (p65)*

1 *Museu do Arte Contemporânea (MAC), Niterói (p91)* 2 *Santa Teresa bonde (p87)* 3 *Bright lights of Rio taken from Corcovado (p79)* 4 *The facade of Rio's ultramodern Catedral Metropolitana (p89)*

1 Colorful streamers flutter above this narrow shopping street in an old part of the Centro district (p81)
2 Inside Igreja de Nossa Senhora de Candelária, Centro (p84)
3 Stepping out at Escadaria Selarón, Santa Teresa (p89)
4 Petrobras building, Centro (p97)

1 *Fresh fruit from the Hortifruti market (p111)* 2 *A traditional music performance of Asa Branca (a classic by Brazilian Luiz Gonzaga), in the Sambódromo (p24)* 3 *Meal at Centro's Cais do Oriente (p123)* 4 *Dining at Nam Thai, Leblon (p112)*

1 *Hang gliding (p153) over Sao Conrado with a bird's-eye view of Ipanema* **2** *Rock-climbing Pão de Açúcar (Sugarloaf, p76)* **3** *Bicycle riding is a popular activity (p152)* **4** *Skateboarder in midjump off ramp*

1 Revelers at Brazil's famous annual Carnaval (p23) 2 Dancing in the streets at Carnaval (p26) 3 Who needs an excuse to dress up when it's party time (p26)? 4 She's sure to attract the judges' attention at the Sambódromo (p27)

(Continued from page 66)

In the 19th century, development was spurred by the construction of a tram that ran to the botanical garden (Jardim Botânico), linking the bay with the lake (Lagoa). This artery still plays a vital role in Rio's traffic flow, though Botafogo's main streets are now extremely congested.

Orientation

Botafogo lies just north of Copacabana and borders the Baía de Guanabara to the east. A small beach faces the bay, but unlike in Dona Carlota Joaquina's time, the water here is now too polluted for swimming. To the north lies the Flamengo district, while heading west along Rua Humaitá leads to Lagoa. Rua Voluntários da Pátria, which runs the length of Botafogo, is one of the main thoroughfares in the region. The region's eastern boundary is Av Lauro Sodré, the chaotic artery that feeds into Copacabana. Along this stretch are some of Botafogo's more mammoth attractions: Canecão (p143), the large concert hall; Rio Sul Shopping (p166), an enormous shopping mall; and Rio-Off Price Shopping (p166), a discount mall.

To the east of Av Laura Sodré runs Av Pasteur. This is the only road into Urca. It continues past the Praça Euzebio Oliveira to the Pão de Açúcar cable car, which is a stone's throw from Praia Vermelha. Northeast from there is the pleasant neighborhood, of only a handful of quiet streets – all built on landfill. The neighborhood's most prominent features are visible from the other side of the city. Morro da Urca and Pão de Açúcar loom majestically overhead, while Morro de Cara de Cão (Face of the Dog Mountain) lies hidden behind them

---

BOTAFOGO & URCA TOP FIVE

- Ascending **Pão de Açúcar** (p76).
- Taking in the live samba beats to the backdrop of crashing waves at **Praia Vermelha** (p77).
- Looking for monkeys along **Pista Cláudio Coutinho** (p77).
- Dining on Bahian cuisine at **Yorubá** (p119).
- Wandering through the entrancing neighborhood of **Urca** (p101).

(to the northeast). At the tip of this hill lies Fortaleza de São João, site of one of Rio's first settlements.

BOTAFOGO
MUSEU CASA DE RUI BARBOSA
Map pp242-3

☎ 2537 0036; www.casaruibarbosa.gov.br in Portuguese; Rua São Clemente 134; admission US$0.50; ❧ 9:30am-5pm Tue-Fri, 2-5pm Sat & Sun

The former mansion (completely restored in 2003) of famous Brazilian journalist and diplomat Rui Barbosa is now a museum housing his library and personal belongings, along with an impressive archive of manuscripts and first editions of other Brazilian authors, such as Machado de Assis and José de Alençar. Barbosa played a major role in shaping the country's socio-economic development in the early 20th century.

MUSEU DO ÍNDIO Map pp242-3
☎ 2286 8899; www.museudoindio.org.br; Rua das Palmeiras 55; admission US$2; ❧ 9:30am-5:30pm Tue-Fri, 1-5pm Sat & Sun

Featuring multimedia exhibitions on Brazil's northern tribes, the small Museu do Índio provides an excellent introduction to the economic, religious and social life of Brazil's indigenous people. Next to native food and medicinal plants, the four life-size dwellings in the courtyard were actually built by four different tribes. As a branch of Funai (the National Indian Foundation), the museum contains an excellent archive of more than 14,000 objects, 50,000 photographs and 200 sound recordings. Its indigenous ethnography library containing 16,000 volumes by local and foreign authors is open to the public during the week.

MUSEU VILLA-LOBOS Map pp242-3
☎ 2266 3845; Rua Sorocaba 200; admission free; ❧ 10am-5:30pm Mon-Fri

Housed in a century-old building, the modest museum is dedicated to the memory of Brazil's greatest classical composer – and founder of the Brazilian Academy of Music – Heitor Villa-Lobos. In addition to scores, musical instruments – including the piano on which he composed – and personal items, the museum contains an extensive sound archive. The gardens were designed by landscape architect Burle Marx.

Sights

Small Botafogo beach faces Baía de Guanabara

PASMADO OVERLOOK Map pp242-3
Rua Bartolomeu Portela

Sweeping views of Enseada de Botafogo (Botafogo Inlet), Pão de Açúcar and Corcovado await visitors who make the journey up Pasmado. It's best reached in early morning or late afternoon, when the light is at its best for capturing the postcard panorama. Visitors will also be able to see details of a favela from above. The overlook is best reached by taxi via Rua General Severiano.

URCA
MUSEU DE CIÊNCIA DA TERRA
Map pp242-3

☎ 2546 0200; Av Pasteur 404; admission free;
⊙ 10am-4pm Tue-Sun

With curved staircases and statues looming out front, this majestic building went through a number of incarnations before it finally ended up housing the Earth Science Museum. The museum appeals mostly to children, who still marvel at some of the life-sized dinosaurs on display. The four-room exhibit gives a quick overview of the natural history of Brazil since the Big Bang. Other rooms showcase the museum's extensive collection of minerals, rocks and meteorites – 5000 pieces in all.

PÃO DE AÇÚCAR Map pp242-3

☎ 2546 8400; Praça General Tibúrcio; admission US$10; ⊙ 8am-10pm

One of Rio's dazzling icons, Pão de Açúcar (Sugarloaf) offers a vision of Rio at its most disarming. Following a steep ascent up the mountain, you'll be rewarded with superb views of Rio's gorgeous shoreline, and the city planted among the green peaks. For prime views of the *cidade maravilhosa*, go around sunset on a clear day.

Everyone must go to Pão de Açúcar, but if you can, avoid it from about 10am to 11am and 2pm to 3pm, which is when most tourist buses arrive. Avoid cloudy days as well.

To reach the summit, 396m above Rio and the Baía de Guanabara, you take two cable cars. The first ascends 220m to Morro da Urca. From here, you can see Baía de Guanabara and along the winding coastline. On the ocean side of the mountain is Praia Vermelha, in a small, calm bay. Morro da Urca has a restaurant, souvenir shops, a playground, outdoor theater and a **helipad** (p59).

The second cable car goes up to Pão de Açúcar. At the top, the city unfolds beneath you, with Corcovado mountain and Cristo Redentor off to the west, and the long curve of Copacabana beach to the south. If the breathtaking heights unsteady you, a drink stand is on hand to serve caipirinhas or cups of Skol (beer). The two-stage cable cars depart every 30 minutes.

Those who'd rather take the long way to the summit should sign up with one of the granite-hugging climbing tours offered by various outfits in Rio (p151).

PISTA CLÁUDIO COUTINHO Map pp242-3
☽ 6am-sunset
Everyone loves this paved 2km trail winding along the southern contour of Morro do Urca. It's a lush treed area, with the waves crashing on the rocks below. Look out for families of *micos* – small, coastal-dwelling capuchin monkeys with gray fur, striped tails and tiny faces. About 300m along the path, there's a small unmarked trail leading off the path to Morro da Urca. From there you can go up to Pão de Açúcar by cable car, saving a few *reais*. Pão de Açúcar can also be climbed – but it's not recommended without climbing gear.

PRAIA DA URCA Map pp242-3
This tiny beach is popular with neighborhood kids who gather here for pickup football games when school is not in session (and sometimes when it is). A small restaurant, Garota da Urca (p119), lies near the beach.

PRAIA VERMELHA Map pp242-3
Beneath Morro da Urca, narrow Praia Vermelha has superb views of the rocky coastline from the shore. Its coarse sand gives the beach the name *vermelha* (red). Because the beach is protected by the headland, the water is usually calm.

FLAMENGO, LARANJEIRAS & COSME VELHO
Eating p120; Shopping p166; Sleeping p185
Graced with one of Rio's most recognizable landmarks (Christ the Redeemer), this trio of neighborhoods has much history hidden in its old streets. Some believe Flamengo in fact was the site of the first Portuguese house built in Rio. It was certainly its finest residential district in the 19th century, though it lost its luster when the tunnel to Copacabana was completed in 1904, and the upper classes migrated to the southern

shores. Today this region contains both remnants from the colonial past and symbols of its future – notably among the corridors of the sleek new cultural center that recently opened here. Its other gems are the Palácio de Laranjeiras and the beach-fronting Parque do Flamengo, one of the world's largest urban parks. Flamengo itself has old-school charm in its juice bars, *botecos* and no-nonsense restaurants, set along shady streets.

Bordering Flamengo to the west, Laranjeiras is among the most tightly interwoven communities of the Zona Sul. The connected backyards, small businesses and chatter among neighbors on the streets bring a small-town feel to the district.

Cosme Velho lies west of Laranjeiras and is one of the city's most visited neighborhoods – if only for the statue of Cristo Redentor soaring above its streets. The district also contains a museum of arte naïf and the charming Largo do Boticário, a preserved plaza that gives onlookers a glimpse of 19th-century Rio. Cosme Velho and Laranjeiras both have their share of nightlife options; their jazz cafés and discreet dance clubs cater to Cariocas tired of the Zona Sul scene.

Orientation
The small neighborhood of Flamengo lies north of Botafogo overlooking the bay. Its eastern boundary is formed by several wide roads – Praia do Flamengo and Av Infante Dom Henrique – leading north and south.

Sights

FLAMENGO, LARANJEIRAS & COSME VELHO

TRANSPORT

Flamengo
Bus Leblon, Ipanema and Copacabana (571 and 572), which travel north along Rua Sen Vergueiro and south along Rua Marques de Abrantes.
Metro Flamengo, Largo do Machado.

Laranjeiras
Bus From Ipanema, 456 (Praça General Osório) travels through Copacabana and along Rua das Laranjeiras; from Largo do Machado take 406A.

Cosme Velho
Bus Centro, Glória or Flamengo (180); Copacabana, Ipanema or Leblon (583 and 584).

FLAMENGO, LARANJEIRAS & COSME VELHO TOP FIVE

- Admiring the magnificent view from beneath **Cristo Redentor** (opposite).
- Finding the perfect beat at **Casa Rosa** (p140).
- Browsing the eye-catching exhibits at **Centro Cultural Telemar** (right).
- Feasting on *churrasco* (roasted meat) to panoramic views at **Porcão Rio's** (p120).
- Catching live bands at easy-going **Severyna** (p139).

The verdant Parque do Flamengo begins just across these roads and contains a restaurant, museum, sports fields and many paths winding along the manicured landscape as it parallels the Praia do Flamengo. Southward-running Rua Marquês de Abrantes is Flamengo's main street and site of its most prominent restaurant scene. Inland, the Praça São Salvador is one of Flamengo's small, charming parks worth a stroll for those interested in taking in the neighborhood. A few blocks north of this park is the bigger Parque Guinle (opposite) containing the Palácio de Laranjeiras (opposite), seat of the state government. Between the two parks is Rua das Laranjeiras, a thoroughfare that runs west, eventually becoming Rua Cosme Velho as it leads into the neighborhood of the same name. Off this main road you'll reach the cog railway station of Corcovado, the Museu Internacional de Arte Naïf do Brasil (p80) beyond it, and the Largo do Boticário a few blocks further west.

North of Laranjeiras is the picturesque neighborhood of Santa Teresa, though access to its tortuous roads is difficult from here owing to Morro So Judas Tadeu separating the two neighborhoods.

FLAMENGO
ARTE-SESC CULTURAL CENTER
Map pp242-3

☎ 3138 1343; Rua Marquês de Abrantes 99; admission free; ◷ noon-6pm Tue & Wed, noon-8pm Thu-Sat, 11am-5pm Sun

This small cultural center is housed in an early-20th-century mansion built by Czech entrepreneur Frederico Figner. His record company is better known than he is – Odeon records being one of the top labels

in the country. The small gallery features good exhibits, often highlighting Rio's development in the early 20th century. Downstairs is the excellent **Senac Bistrô** (p121).

CENTRO CULTURAL TELEMAR
Map pp242-3

☎ 3131 6060; www.centroculturaltelemar.com.br in Portuguese; Rua Dois de Dezembro 63; admission free; ◷ 11am-8pm Tue-Sun

One of Rio's most visually exciting new additions is this modern arts center on the edge of Flamengo. With 2000 sq meters of exhibition space spread across six floors, the center features temporary multimedia installations that run the gamut between architecture and urban design to photojournalism to pop art, to eye-catching video art. There's also a permanent exhibition on the history of telecommunications in Brazil. The top floor houses an auditorium where visitors can attend concerts (admission US$5) and plays, watch documentaries and even more experimental video art. There's quite a buzz about this new space.

MUSEU CARMEN MIRANDA
Map pp242-3

☎ 2551 2597; facing Av Rui Barbosa 560; admission US$0.50; ◷ 10am-5pm Tue-Fri, noon-5pm Sat & Sun

Carmen Miranda was once the highest-paid entertainer in the USA. She's the only Brazilian to leave her prints in Hollywood's Walk of Fame. Although she's largely forgotten there, the talented Brazilian singer still has her fans in Rio, and has become a cult icon among the gay community. For those interested in getting to know one of Brazil's stars of the '40s, the small museum dedicated to her is an excellent starting point. It has photographs and music of that era and the starlet's iconographic costumes and jewelry.

PARQUE DO FLAMENGO
Map pp242-3 & Map pp238-9

Officially called Parque Brigadeiro Eduardo Gomes, Parque do Flamengo was the result of a landfill project that leveled the São Antônio hill in 1965, and now spreads all the way from downtown Rio through Glória, Catete and Flamengo, and on around to Botafogo. The 1.2 million sq meters of land reclaimed from the sea now stages every manner of Carioca outdoor activity. Cyclists and Rollerbladers glide along the myriad paths, while the many football fields and sports courts are framed against the sea. On Sundays and holidays, the avenues through the park are closed (from 7am to 6pm).

Designed by famous Brazilian landscaper Burle Marx (who also landscaped Brasília), the park features some 170,000 trees of 300 different species. In addition there are three museums in the park: the **Museu de Arte Moderna** (p89), the **Monumento Nacional dos Mortos da II Guerra Mundial** (p89) and the **Museu Carmen Miranda** (opposite).

LARANJEIRAS

MARACATU BRASIL Map pp242-3

☎ 2557 4754; www.maracatubrasil.com.br; 2nd fl, Rua Ipiranga 49; ☷ 10am-6pm Mon-Sat

One of Rio's best places to study percussion, Maracatu Brasil is very active in music events throughout the city. Instructors here offer courses in a number of different drumming styles: *zabumba, pandeiro,* symphonic percussion and others. You can arrange private lessons (US$30 per hour) or sign up for group classes if you plan to stick around a while (US$20 to US$60 a month). On the 1st floor of the lime-green building, Maracatu sells instruments (p167).

PARQUE GUINLE & THE PALÁCIO DE LARANJEIRAS Map pp242-3

☎ 2299 5233; Rua Paulo Cesar de Andrade 407; ☷ palace guided visits 1pm, 2pm & 3pm Mon & Fri

Designed by French landscaper Gochet, the park has a European air, and has a small lake, lanes and lawns. Overlooking the park is the resplendent Palácio da Laranjeiras, built between 1909 and 1914 by architect Silva Telles. Today it is the official residence in Rio of the state governor, and contains the same artwork, furniture and ornamental objects from when the palace was built. You can tour parts of the palace by guided appointments (by advance notice only).

COSME VELHO

CRISTO REDENTOR Map pp236-7

☎ 2558 1329; www.corcovado.org.br; Rua Cosme Velho 513 (cog station); admission US$10; ☷ 8:30am-6:30pm

One of Rio's most identifiable landmarks, the magnificent 38m-high Cristo Redentor

(Christ the Redeemer) looms large atop Corcovado. From here, the statue – all 1145 tons of him – has stunning views over Rio (which explains the contented expression on his face). Corcovado, which means 'hunchback,' rises straight up from the city to a height of 710m, and at night, the brightly lit statue is visible from nearly every part of the city.

When you reach the top, you'll notice the Redeemer's gaze directed at **Pão de Açúcar** (p76), with his left arm pointing toward the Zona Norte, and Maracanã football stadium crowding the foreground. You can also see the international airport on Ilha do Governador just beyond and the Serra dos Órgãos mountain range in the far distance. Beneath Christ's right arm is the Lagoa Rodrigo de Freitas, Hipódromo de Gávea, Jardim Botânico, and over to Ipanema and Leblon.

Corcovado lies within the **Parque Nacional da Tijuca** (p93). You can get here by car or by taxi, but the best way is to go up in the cog train (departures every 30 minutes). For the best view, sit on the right-hand side going up. You can also drive to the top. Taxi drivers typically charge around US$20 for return trips with waiting time.

Be sure to choose a clear day to visit.

LARGO DO BOTICÁRIO Map pp242-3
Rua Cosme Velho 822
The brightly painted houses on this pictur-esque square date from the early 19th cen-tury. Largo do Boticário was named in honor of the Portuguese gentleman – Joaquim Luiz da Silva Souto – who once ran a *boticário* (apothecary), utilized by the royal family. The sound of a brook coming from the nearby forest adds to the square's charm. Occasional art and cultural events are hosted here.

MUSEU INTERNACIONAL DE ARTE NAÏF DO BRASIL Map pp242-3
☎ 2205 8612; www.museunaif.com.br; Rua Cosme Velho 561; admission US$2.50; ☺ 10am-6pm Tue-Fri, noon-6pm Sat & Sun
Vivid color and a playful perspective are two of the characteristics of arte naïf paintings, and many of the artists of this style came from outside the academy. Also known as primitivist, arte naïf paintings in this per-manent collection are extensive: over 8000 pieces, executed by artists from 130 coun-tries, dating from the 15th century to the present. This makes it the largest museum of its kind in the world. Visitors receive a 20% discount by showing a ticket stub to the Corcovado cog train – one block away.

CATETE & GLÓRIA
Eating p121; Sleeping p186
An aura of faded splendor pervades the neighborhoods of Catete and Glória. Like Flamengo, these twin districts flourished in the mid-19th century – their location at the outskirts of the city made them among the most desirable places to live. Many noble-men and merchants built stately homes in this district, including the Barão de Novo Friburgo, who built the stately Palácio do Catete. By the end of the century, though, the aristocracy had moved further out as the inner city expanded – a trend that in some ways continues today.

The Palácio do Catete, which once served as the republic's seat of power, remains the jewel of the neighborhood, and its attached gardens are a peaceful refuge from the often chaotic streets outside. Another place of his-toric interest lies a few blocks north. Atop a small hill overlooking the bay, the baroque Igreja de Nossa Senhora da Glória de Out-eiro dates from the 18th century and was

a favorite of Dom Pedro II and the royal family.

Aside from these vestiges of the past, most of the area is now an area of small-scale commerce. A handful of working-class restaurants, unkempt juice bars and a movie theater lie scattered among clothing shops and hardware stores.

Today, many former magnificent man-sions have become hotels – most in serious need of a renovation. With many budget options among these crumbling buildings, Glória and Catete attract shoestring travel-ers who don't mind the workaday bustle of the district.

Orientation
Catete and Glória lie just west of Baía de Guanabara. Glória is the northernmost neighborhood of the two. Rua do Catete, which runs north, is the main thoroughfare, and it connects the area with Flamengo to the south and Lapa to the north. Busy Praia do Flamengo separates the neighborhood from Parque do Flamengo, and there are a number of pedestrian overpasses to reach the park.

CATETE
MUSEU DA REPÚBLICA Map pp242-3
☎ 2558 6350; www.museudarepublica.org.br; Rua do Catete 153; admission US$2; ☺ noon-5pm Tue, Thu & Fri, 2-5pm Wed, Sat & Sun
The Museu da República, located in the Palá-cio do Catete, has been wonderfully restored. Built between 1858 and 1866 and easily distinguished by the bronze condors on the eaves, the palace was home to the president of Brazil from 1896 until 1954, when Presi-dent Getúlio Vargas committed suicide here.

He had made powerful enemies in the armed forces and the political right wing, and was attacked in the press as a commu-nist for his attempts to raise the minimum wage and increase taxes on the middle and

TRANSPORT
Bus To Rua da Glória: Leblon (571); Copacabana (572); Largo do Machado (569) goes to Leblon via Jóquei, while 570 also goes there via Copacabana.
Metro Largo do Machado, Catete, Glória.

upper classes. Tensions reached a critical level when one of Vargas' bodyguards fired shots at a journalist. Although the journalist was unharmed, an air force officer guarding him was killed, giving the armed forces the pretext they needed to demand the resignation of Vargas. In response, Vargas committed suicide, and his emotional suicide note read, 'I choose this means to be with you [the Brazilian people] always…I gave you my life; now I offer my death.' The bedroom in which the suicide occurred is eerily preserved on the 3rd floor.

The museum has a good collection of art and artifacts from the Republican period, and also houses a good lunch restaurant, art-house cinema and bookstore.

MUSEU DE FOLCLÓRICO EDSON CARNEIRO Map pp242-3
☎ 2205 0090; Rua do Catete 181; admission US$1; ⏱ 11am-6pm Tue-Fri; 3-6pm Sat & Sun
Created in 1968, the museum is an excellent introduction to Brazilian folk art, particularly from the northeast. Its permanent collection comprises 1400 pieces, and includes Candomblé costumes, ceramic figurines and religious costumes used in festivals. The museum also features a folklore library and a small shop, selling handicrafts, books and folk music. The museum lies next door to the Palácio do Catete.

PARQUE DO CATETE Map pp242-3
☎ 2205 0090; Rua do Catete 181; admission US$1; ⏱ 11am-6pm Tue-Fri, 3-6pm Sat & Sun
The small landscaped park on the grounds of the Palácio do Catete provides a quiet refuge from the city. Its pond and shade-covered walks are popular with neighborhood strollers and children. Special performances in the park include concerts and plays. The Bistrô Jardins (p121), overlooking the park, makes a fine spot for afternoon tea.

GLÓRIA

IGREJA DE NOSSA SENHORA DA GLÓRIA DO OUTEIRO Map pp238-9
☎ 2557 4600; www.outeirodagloria.org.br; Praça Nossa Senhora da Glória 135; ⏱ 9am-5pm Tue-Fri, 9am-noon Sat & Sun; guided visits 1st Sun of month
This tiny church atop Ladeira da Glória commands lovely views out over Parque do Flamengo and the bay. Considered one

of the finest examples of religious colonial architecture in Brazil, the church dates from 1739 and became the favorite of the royal family upon their arrival in 1808. Some of the more fascinating features of the church are its octagonal design, its single tower (through which visitors enter), the elaborately carved altar (attributed to the Brazilian sculptor Mestre Valentim) and its elegant, 18th-century tiles.

CENTRO & CINELÂNDIA
Eating p122; Shopping p167; Sleeping p187

Rio's bustling commercial district, Centro is the city's business and finance hub. By day, the wide avenues and narrow lanes adjoining them fill with lawyers and bankers, temps and delivery boys, all making their way through the crowded, noisy streets. Although hypermodern on one hand, among Centro's numerous high-rise office buildings are remnants of its once-magnificent past. Looming baroque churches, wide plazas and cobblestone streets lined with colorful colonial buildings lie scattered throughout the district.

Many pedestrian-only areas crisscross Centro. The most famous of these is known as Saara, a giant street bazaar crammed with discount stores. In the last century, Saara attracted an influx of immigrants from the Middle East, and if you're in search of authentic Lebanese cuisine, this is the place to dine.

Restaurants suit every taste and budget, from greasy diners to elegant French bistros. After lunch, Cariocas browse the bookstores, music shops, galleries and curio shops. By workday's end (5pm or 6pm), the pubs and streetside cafés buzz with life as Cariocas unwind over draughts or cocktails.

As well as its culinary attractions, Centro has a number of museums, historic churches and attractive cultural centers featuring changing exhibitions. Visitors to

Sights

CENTRO & CINELÂNDIA

TRANSPORT

Bus From the Zona Sul look for the following destinations printed in the window: 'Rio Branco,' 'Praça XV,' 'Praça Tiradentes,' 'Castelo' and 'Praça Mauá.'

Metro Cinelândia, Carioca, Uruguaiana, Presidente Vargas.

the area will also find essential services: the main airline offices are here, as are foreign consulates, Brazilian government agencies, money-exchange houses, banks and travel agencies.

At the southern edge of the business district, Cinelândia's shops, bars, restaurants and movie theaters are popular day and night. The bars and restaurants get crowded at lunch and after work, when street musicians sometimes wander the area. There's a greater mix of Cariocas here than in any other section of the city. Several gay and mixed bars stay open until late.

Orientation

Av Rio Branco is the wide, chaotic boulevard that connects Centro to the Zona Sul. In addition to banks and travel agents, the street harbors several museums, theaters and cultural centers, most near Praça Floriano at the southern end of Centro. Many blocks north of there, Av Presidente Vargas intersects Av Rio Branco at Av Praça Pio X, which fronts the impressive Igreja Nossa Senhora de Candelária – one of the city's more ornate churches. The metro travels beneath both Av Rio Branco (to the Zona Sul) and Av Presidente Vargas (to the Sambódromo and points west) as it travels in and out of Centro. Most buses leave for the Zona Sul along Av Rio Branco.

The Saara bazaar lies west of Rio Branco along Rua da Alfândega, Rua Senhor dos Passos, Rua de Buenos Aires and Av Passos. Other pedestrian streets lie west of Av Rio Branco. Cobbled Travessa do Comércio, becomes a lively scene weekday evenings. South of there is Praça Quinze de Novembro, which lies just east of the breezy Praça Mercado Municipal, the departure point for

ferries to Niterói and Paquetá. Just south of there is the Santos Dumont area, at Centro's eastern edge.

Cinelândia is a small area bounded by Praça Floriano at its eastern edge, Rua Evaristo da Veiga to the north Rua Republica de Paraguai to the west and the Passeio Público to the south. Its narrow pedestrian streets are lined with cheap restaurants and bars spilling onto the sidewalk.

CENTRO

BIBLIOTECA NACIONAL Map pp238-9

☎ 2262 8255; Av Rio Branco 219; admission free; ⓨ 9am-8pm Mon-Fri, 9am-3pm Sat, free guided tours 11am, 1pm & 4pm Mon-Fri

Inaugurated in 1910, the national library is the largest in Latin America, with more than 8 million volumes. It was designed by Francisco Marcelino de Souza Aguiar. On the ground floor, the periodical section is to the left, and general works are to the right. On the 2nd floor are many rare books and manuscripts, including two copies of the precious Mainz Psalter Bible, printed in 1492. Owing to their fragility, most of these rare books can be viewed only on microfilm.

CAMPO DE SANTANA Map pp238-9

Campo de Santana is a pleasant park that, on 7 September 1822, was the scene of the proclamation of Brazil's independence from Portugal by Emperor Dom Pedro I of Portugal. The landscaped park with an artificial lake and swans is a fine place for a respite from the chaotic streets, and you're liable to see a few agoutis (a hamster-like rodent native to Brazil) running wild here.

CASA FRANÇA-BRASIL Map pp238-9

☎ 2253 5366; www.casafrancabrasil.rj.gov.br in Portuguese; Rua Visconde de Itaboraí 78; admission free; ⓨ noon-8pm Tue-Sun

In a neoclassical building dating from 1820, the Casa França-Brasil opened in 1990 for the purpose of advancing cultural relations between France and Brazil. The main hall features changing exhibitions often dealing with political and cultural facets of Carioca society. The building is considered the most important Classical Revival structure in Brazil, and once served as a customs house.

CENTRO & CINELÂNDIA TOP FIVE

- Taking in an exhibition at **Centro Cultural Banco do Brasil** (opposite).
- Catching the happy hour ritual of drinks on **Travessa do Comércio** (p86).
- Enjoying a decadent meal inside the converted mansion **Cais do Oriente** (p123).
- Attending a concert at the lavish **Teatro Municipal** (p129).
- Wandering the busy pedestrian streets around **Saara bazaar** (p81).

Biblioteca Nacional – the largest library in Latin America (opposite)

CENTRO CULTURAL BANCO DO BRASIL Map pp238-9

☎ 3808 2000; www.cultura-e.com.br in Portuguese; Rua Primeiro de Março 66; admission free, exhibitions US$2-4; ✆ noon-8pm Tue-Sun

Reopened in 1989, the Centro Cultural do Banco do Brasil (CCBB) is housed in a beautifully restored 1906 building. It's one of Brazil's best cultural centers, with more than 120,000 visitors per month. Facilities include a cinema, two theaters and a permanent display of the evolution of currency in Brazil. CCBB hosts excellent exhibitions that are among the city's best. A recent display of African art garnered international attention.

There's always something going on at the Centro Cultural Banco do Brasil – from exhibitions, lunchtime and evening concerts, to film screenings – so look at *O Globo*'s entertainment listings before you go. Don't miss this place, even if you only pass through the lobby on a walking tour.

CENTRO CULTURAL CARIOCA

Map pp238-9

☎ 2242 9642; www.centroculturalcarioca.com.br in Portuguese; Rua do Teatro 37; ✆ noon-8pm Tue-Sun

This restored theater on Praça Tiradentes is once again a major contributor to the arts in downtown Rio. Its exposed brick walls and large wood-framed windows form the backdrop to superb musical groups – often samba – performing throughout the week (p140), and also has dance recitals, book releases and ongoing exhibitions. They also teach dance classes here (p156).

CENTRO CULTURAL JUSTIÇA FEDERAL Map pp238-9

☎ 2510 8846; Av Rio Branco 241; admission free; ✆ noon-7pm Tue-Sun

The stately building overlooking the Praça Floriano served as the headquarters of the Supreme Court (Supremo Tribunal Federal) from 1909 to 1960. Following its recent restoration, it's become the Federal Justice Cultural Center, featuring exhibitions focused above all on photography and Brazilian art, though some fascinating exhibits from abroad sometimes make their way here. The store on the 1st floor has a tiny selection of books and handicrafts.

CENTRO DE ARTE HÉLIO OITICICA

Map pp238-9

☎ 2242 1012; Rua Luis de Camões 68; admission free; ✆ 11am-7pm Tue-Fri, 11am-5pm Sat & Sun

This avant garde museum is set in a 19th-century neoclassical building that originally housed the Conservatory of Music and Dramatic Arts. Today, the center displays permanent works by the artist, theoretician and poet Helio Oiticica, as well as bold contemporary art exhibitions, well-tuned to Oiticica's forward-leaning aesthetics. In addition to six exhibition galleries, there's a bistro and a book shop on the first floor.

IGREJA DE NOSSA SENHORA DE CANDELÁRIA Map pp238-9

☎ 2233 2324; Praça Pio X; admission free;
🕑 8am-4pm Mon-Fri, 8am-1pm Sat, 9am-1pm Sun

The construction of the original church (dating from the late 16th century) on the present site was credited to a ship's captain who had nearly been shipwrecked at sea. Upon his safe return he vowed to build a church to NS de Candelária. A later design led to its present-day grandeur. Built between 1775 and 1894, NS de Candelária was the largest and wealthiest church of imperial Brazil. The interior is a spectacular combination of baroque and Renaissance styles. The ceiling above the nave reveals the origin of the church. The cupola, fabricated entirely from limestone shipped from Lisbon, is one of its most striking features. Mass is said at 9am, 10am and 11am on Sunday. But be sure to watch out for traffic as you cross to the church.

IGREJA SÃO FRANCISCO DA PENITÊNCIA & CONVENTO DE SANTO ANTÔNIO Map pp238-9

☎ 2262 0197; Largo da Carioca 5; admission free;
🕑 convent 9am-noon & 1-4pm Tue-Fri, guided visits only to church

Overlooking the Largo da Carioca is the baroque Igreja São Francisco da Penitência, dating from 1726. Recently restored to its former glory, the church's sacristy, which dates from 1745, has blue Portuguese tiles and an elaborately carved altar made out of jacaranda wood. It also has a roof panel by José Oliveira Rosa depicting St Francis receiving the stigmata. The church's statue of Santo Antônio is an object of great devotion to many Cariocas in search of a husband or wife.

A garden on the church grounds leads to the catacombs, used until 1850. Visits must be arranged in advance.

Next door, the Convento de Santo Antônio was built between 1608 and 1615. It contains the chapel of Nossa Senhora das Dores da Imaculada

Conceição. Fabiano de Cristo, a miracle-working priest who died in 1947, is entombed here.

MONASTEIRO DE SÃO BENTO

Map pp238-9

☎ 2291 7122; Rua Dom Gerardo 68; admission free; 🕑 8-11am & 2:30-6pm

This is one of the finest colonial gems in Brazil. Built between 1617 and 1641 on Morro de São Bento, the monastery has a fine view over the city. The simple façade hides a baroque interior richly decorated in gold. Among its historic treasures are wood carvings designed by Frei Domingos da Conceição (and made by Alexandre Machado) and paintings by José de Oliveira Rosa. On Sunday, the High Mass at 10am includes a choir of Benedictine monks singing Gregorian chants.

Mass is also said at 7:15am Monday to Saturday, and at 8am, 10am and 6pm on Sunday. To reach the monastery from Rua Dom Gerardo, go to No 40 and take the elevator to the 5th floor.

MUSEU HISTÓRICO E DIPLOMÁTICO

Map pp238-9

☎ 2253 7961; Av Marechal Floriano 196; 🕑 tours 2pm, 3pm, 4pm Mon, Wed & Fri

Housed in the neoclassical Palácio Itamaraty, the Museum of History and Diplomacy served as the private presidential home from 1889 until 1897. The museum has an impressive collection of art, antiques and maps. Visits are by guided 45-minute tours. Call ahead to ensure you get an English- or French-speaking guide. The museum is just a short walk west from Presidente Vargas metro station.

MUSEU HISTÓRICO NACIONAL

Map pp238-9

☎ 2550 9224; www.museuhistoriconacional.com .br; off Av General Justo near Praça Marechal Âncora; admission US$1.50; 🕑 10am-5:30pm Tue-Fri, 2-6pm Sat & Sun

Housed in the colonial arsenal, which dates from 1764, the large national history museum contains over 250,000 historic relics relating to the history of Brazil from its founding to its early days as a republic. Its extensive collection includes a full-sized model of a colonial pharmacy and the writing quill that Princesa Isabel used to sign the document abolishing slavery in Brazil.

MUSEU NACIONAL DE BELAS ARTES

Map pp238-9

☎ 2240 0068; Av Rio Branco 199; admission US$1.50; ☺ 10am-6pm Tue-Fri, 2-6pm Sat & Sun

Rio's fine arts museum houses more than 800 original paintings and sculptures ranging from the 17th to the 20th century. One of its most important galleries is the **Galeria de Arte Brasileira**, with 20th-century classics such as Cândido Portinari's *Café*. Other galleries display Brazilian folk art, African art and furniture, as well as contemporary exhibits. Guided tours are available in English (call ahead).

MUSEU NAVAL E OCEANOGRÁFICO

Map pp238-9

☎ 2533 7626; Rua Dom Manuel 15, Praça Quinze de Novembro; admission free; ☺ noon-4:30pm

Chronicling the history of the Brazilian navy from the 16th century to the present, the museum also has exhibitions of model warships, maps and navigational instruments.

Naval enthusiasts should also visit the nearby **Espaço Cultural da Marinha** (ECM; Map pp238–9; admission free; ☺ noon-5pm Tue-Sun), on the waterfront near the eastern end of Av Presidente Vargas. It contains the *Riachuelo* submarine, the *Bauru* (a WWII torpedo boat) and the royal family's large rowboat. The boat tour to **Ilha Fiscal** (p91) leaves from the docks here.

PAÇO IMPERIAL Map pp238-9

☎ 2533 4407; Praça Quinze de Novembro; admission free; ☺ noon-6:30pm Tue-Sun

The former imperial palace was originally built in 1743 as a governor's residence. Later it became the home of Dom João and his family when the Portuguese throne transferred the royal seat of power to the colony. In 1888, Princesa Isabel proclaimed the Freedom from Slavery Act from the palace's steps. The building was neglected for many years but has been restored and is used for exhibitions and concerts; its cinema frequently screens foreign and art-house films.

PALÁCIO TIRADENTES Map pp238-9

☎ 2588 1411; Rua Primeiro de Março; admission free; ☺ 10am-5pm Mon-Sat, noon-5pm Sun

In the looming building overlooking the bay, the stately Tiradentes Palace today houses the seat of the legislative assembly. Visitors can wander through exhibits on the 1st and 2nd floor that relate – through photographs and documents – some of the historic events that took place in the nearby chambers between 1926 and the present. One of its darkest hours was when the National Assembly was shut down in 1937 under the Vargas dictatorship – it later served as his Department of Press and Propaganda. Most information is in Portuguese, though you can listen to a rundown of history at the interactive machine in the foyer. The statue in front, incidentally, is not a likeness of Russian mystic Rasputin, but rather that of martyr Tiradentes, who led the drive toward Brazilian independence in the 18th century.

PASSEIO PÚBLICO Map pp238-9

Rua do Passeio; admission free; ☺ 9am-5pm

The oldest park in Rio, the Passeio Público was built in 1783 by Mestre Valentim, a famous Brazilian sculptor, who designed it after Lisbon's botanical gardens. In 1860 the park was remodeled by French landscaper Glaziou. The park features some large trees, a pond with islands and an interesting crocodile-shaped fountain. The entrance gate was built by Valentim. Before the Parque do Flamengo landfill, the sea came right up to the edge of the park.

PRAÇA QUINZE DE NOVEMBRO

Map pp238-9

Near Rua Primeiro de Março

The first residents on this historic site were Carmelite fathers who built a convent here in 1590. It later came under the property of the Portuguese crown and became Largo do Paço, which surrounded the royal palace (Paço Imperial). The square was later renamed Praça Quinze de Novembro after Brazil declared itself a republic on November 15, 1822. A number of historic events took place here: the coronation of Brazil's two Emperors (Pedro I and Pedro II), the abolition of slavery and the overthrow (deposition) of Emperor Dom Pedro II in 1889.

REAL GABINETE PORTUGUÊS DE LEITURA Map pp238-9

☎ 2221 3138; Rua Luís de Camões 30; admission free; ☺ 9am-6pm

Built in the Portuguese manueline style in 1837, the gorgeous Portuguese Reading Room houses over 350,000 works, many dating from the 16th, 17th and 18th centuries. It also has a small collection of paintings, sculptures and ancient coins.

TEATRO MUNICIPAL Map pp238-9
☎ 2299 1716, booking 2262 3501; Rua Manuel de Carvalho; guided tour US$2 ☉ 9am-5pm Mon-Fri

Built in 1905 in the style of the Paris Opera, the magnificent Municipal Theater is the home of Rio's opera, orchestra and ballet. Its lavish interior contains many beautiful details – including the stage curtain painted by Italian artist Eliseu Visconti, which contains portraits of 75 major figures from the arts: Carlos Gomes, Wagner and Rembrandt among others. Bilingual guided tours are a worthwhile investment (call ☎ 2544 2900 to book one). If you get a chance, come to a performance here (p129).

TRAVESSA DO COMÉRCIO Map pp238-9
Near Praça Quinze de Novembro

Beautiful two-story colonial townhouses line this narrow cobblestone street leading off Praça Quinze de Novembro. The archway (Arco de Teles), leading into the area was once part of an old viaduct running between two buildings. Today, the street contains half a dozen restaurants and drinking spots that open onto the streets. It's a favorite spot for Cariocas after work.

CINELÂNDIA

PRAÇA FLORIANO Map pp238-9
Av Rio Branco

The heart of modern Rio, the Praça Floriano comes to life at lunchtime and after work when the outdoor cafés are filled with beer drinkers, samba musicians and political debate. The square is also Rio's political marketplace. There are daily speechmaking, literature sales and street theater. Most city marches and rallies culminate here on the steps of the old Câmara Municipal (Town Hall) in the northwestern corner of the plaza.

SANTA TERESA & LAPA
Eating p124; Shopping p170; Sleeping p188

Set on a hill overlooking the city, Santa Teresa, with its cobbled streets and aging mansions, retains the charm of days long past. Originally named after the Carmelite convent founded here in 1750, Santa Teresa

was the uppermost residential neighborhood in the 19th century, when Rio's upper class lived here and rode the *bonde* (tram) to work in Centro. Many beautiful colonial homes stretch skyward, their lush gardens hidden behind gabled fences. Like other areas near Centro, the neighborhood fell into neglect in the early 20th century as the wealthy moved further south. During the 1960s and '70s many artists and bohemians moved into Santa Teresa's mansions, initiating a revitalization process that still continues. Today, Santa Teresa is experiencing a tremendous renaissance, and the neighborhood has become synonymous with Rio's vibrant art and music scene. Throughout the year, impromptu festivals and street parties fill the air, ranging from *maracatu* drumming along Rua Joaquim Murtinho to live jazz at the Parque Ruinas to the annual Portas Abertas event (taking place in July at the time of writing), where dozens of artists open their studios and cover the streets with living installations.

The neighborhood's ongoing restoration has led to an influx of restaurants, bars and cultural centers, and some have even compared Santa Teresa to Paris' Montmartre. Yet this unpolished gem is unlikely to ever completely lose its edginess, if only for the omnipresent favelas spreading down the hillsides. Be cautious when walking around Santa Teresa.

The streets of Lapa lie down the hill from Santa Teresa and south of Cinelândia. Formerly a residential neighborhood of the wealthy, Lapa's best days came and went before the 20th century, and its mansions are now sadly neglected. Although Lapa still recalls decades of dereliction in the minds of

TRANSPORT

Santa Teresa
Bus Centro (206A, 206B and 214), all of which travel along Av Almirante Barroso and Rua do Lavradio.
Bonde Paula Matos, Dois Irmãos.

Lapa
Bus Leblon bus (571) travels between Largo da Lapa and Leblon via Jóquei; 572 travels between the same points, going via Copacabana.
Metro Cinelândia.

many Cariocas, the district has recently experienced a cultural revival, and its old buildings are slowly being restored. Lapa is the center of a vibrant bohemian scene in Rio, and the setting for many Brazilian novels.

At night, Lapa is the setting for one of Rio's most vibrant street parties as revelers from all over the city mingle among its samba clubs and music-filled bars. At weekends it gets fearfully crowded here as thousands gather for the chaotic street scene. In spite of some restoration, this neighborhood, like Santa Teresa, still maintains its edgy side. Take care when strolling around the neighborhood.

Lapa's landmark aqueduct, Arcos da Lapa (Lapa Arches), is one of the neighborhood's most prominent features. Narrow tracks course over the 64m-high structure, carrying the famous *bonde* to and from Santa Teresa.

Orientation

Santa Teresa lies atop a hill overlooking Centro and the Zona Norte. The *bonde,* which rattles through the district, begins at the station on Rua Professor Lélio Gama off Rua Senador Dantas, then travels over the Arcos da Lapa and up into Santa Teresa.

Lapa is north of Santa Teresa and south of Cinelândia. (The boundary between Lapa and Cinelândia is marked by the modern Catedral Metropolitana and the Arcos da Lapa.) Rua do Lavradio, to the west of the cathedral, is one of Lapa's most charming streets with its antique shops and bars. South of the arches is Rua Joaquim Silva, site of Rio's burgeoning samba street scene on weekends. Its crumbling buildings also contain clubs and music halls. Parallel to this street is the much larger Rua da Lapa, which runs south to Glória and toward the Zona Sul. The tram leads up to Santa Teresa, as do the windy streets throughout Lapa.

SANTA TERESA

BONDE Map p241

☎ 2240 5709; station at Rua Lélio Gama 65; fare US$0.65; ⌚ departures every 30min

The *bonde* that travels up to Santa Teresa from Centro is the last of the historic streetcars that once crisscrossed the city. Its romantic clatter through the cobbled streets has made it the archetype for bohe-

mian Santa Teresa. The two routes currently open have been in operation since the 19th century. Both travel high atop the narrow **Arcos da Lapa** (p88) and along curving Rua Joaquim Murtinho before reaching **Largo do Guimarães** (p88). From there, one line (Paula Matos) takes a northwestern route, terminating at **Largo das Neves** (p88). The longer route (Dois Irmãos) continues from Largo do Guimarães uphill and southward before terminating near the water reservoir at Dois Irmãos (Two Brothers – named after the twin stone pyramids used to collect water from the Carioca River).

Although a policeman often accompanies the tram, the favelas down the hillsides still make this a high-crime area. Go by all means, but don't bring any valuables. Local kids jumping on and off the train lend a festive air to the journey. An unspoken tradition states that those who ride on the running board ride for free.

Tram tours (p60) depart every Saturday, highlighting historic points in the neighborhood.

CASA DE BENJAMIN CONSTANT

Map p241

☎ 2509 1248; Rua Monte Alegre 255; admission free; ⌚ guided tours 1-5pm, gardens 8am-6pm

This country estate served as the residence for one of Brazil's most influential politicians in the founding of the young Republic. Benjamin Constant (1837–91) was an engineer, military officer and professor before taking an active role in the Provisional Government. He is also remembered for founding a school for blind children. Painstakingly preserved, his house provides a window into his life and times. The lush gardens surrounding his estate provide a fine view over Centro and the western side of Santa Teresa.

SANTA TERESA & LAPA TOP FIVE

- Riding the **bonde** (left) up to Santa Teresa.
- Dancing to samba at **Democráticus** (p141).
- Dining on delectable Amazonian dishes at **Espirito Santa** (p125).
- Drinking in the Saturday night bar scene at **Largo das Neves** (p88).
- Browsing for antiques along **Rua do Lavradio** (p161).

RIO'S TOP FIVE FOR CHILDREN

- Slipping and sliding along waterfalls at the gigantic **Rio Water Planet** (p94).
- Stargazing at the **Planetário** (p64).
- Meeting some of Brazil's native creatures at the **Jardim Zoológico** (p90).
- Admiring the city skyline at sunset during a **cruise** (p58) along the bay.
- Renting **bikes** (p204) at Lagoa, followed by lunch at one of the **lakeside kiosks** (p63).

CENTRO CULTURAL LAURINDA SANTOS LOBO Map p241

☎ 2224 3331; Rua Monte Alegre 306; admission free; ⌚ 8am-5pm

The large mansion built in 1907 once served as a salon for artists from Brazil and abroad as socialite Laurinda Santos Lobo hosted her parties there. Villa-Lobos and Isadora Duncan among others attended. Today, the cultural center still plays an active role in the neighborhood by hosting exhibitions and open-air concerts throughout the year.

LARGO DAS NEVES Map p241

End of Rua Progresso

A slice of small-town life in the city, this small square is the gathering point of neighborhood children and families who lounge in the benches by day. At night, the bars surrounding the square come alive with revelers crowding the walks. At times, MPB (Música Popular Brasileira) bands perform to a young crowd here. Largo das Neves is the terminus of the Paula Matos *bonde* line.

LARGO DO GUIMARÃES Map p241

Rua Almirante Alexandrino

The square named after Joaquim Fonseca Guimarães (a local resident whose house became Hotel Santa Teresa just up the road) now forms the center of bohemian Santa Teresa. A festive Carnaval street party originates here, and a number of restaurants, handicrafts and thrift shops lie within a short distance of here.

MUSEU CHÁCARA DO CÉU Map p241

☎ 2507 1932; Rua Murtinho Nobre 93; admission US$3; ⌚ noon-5pm Wed-Mon

The former mansion of art patron and industrialist Raymundo Ottoni de Castro Maya, the museum contains a small but diversified collection of modern art – formerly Ottoni's private collection, which he bequeathed to the nation. In addition to works by Portinari, Di Cavalcanti, Picasso, Matisse and Salvador Dalí, the museum displays furniture and Brazilian maps dating from the 17th and 18th century. Beautiful gardens surround the museum, and a panoramic view of Centro and Baía de Guanabara awaits visitors.

MUSEU DO BONDE Map p241

☎ 2242 2354; Rua Carlos Brant 14; admission free; ⌚ 9am-4:30pm

The tiny one-room Tram Museum at the depot close to Largo do Guimarães offers a history of Rio's tramways since 1865 – when the trams were pulled by donkeys. A few photographs, trip-recorders and conductor uniforms are just about the only objects documenting their legacy. Uplifting music plays overhead. The term *bonde,* incidentally, means just that – bond – indicating the way in which the first electric trams were financed – through public bonds. While you're at the museum, wander down to the old workshop that houses the trams. Cineastes may remember the depot from the opening sequence of the film *Orfeu Negro.*

PARQUE DAS RUINAS Map p241

☎ 2252 1039; Rua Murtinho Nobre 169; admission free; ⌚ 10am-8pm Tue-Sun

Connected to the Museu Chácara do Céu by a walkway, this park contains the ruins of the mansion belonging to Brazilian heiress Laurinda Santos Lobo. Her house was a meeting point for Rio's artists and intellectuals for many years until her death in 1946. Today, the park often stages open-air concerts and performances for children on Sunday mornings (readings, puppet shows). Don't miss the excellent view from the top floor.

LAPA

ARCOS DA LAPA Map p241

Near Av Mem de Sá

The landmark aqueduct dates from the mid-1700s when it was built to carry water from the Carioca River to downtown Rio. In a style reminiscent of ancient Rome, the 42 arches stand 64m high. Today, it carries the famous *bonde* on its way to and from Santa Teresa atop the hill.

CATEDRAL METROPOLITANA Map p241

☎ 2240 2669; Av República do Chile 245; admission free; ⏰ 7am-5:30pm

The enormous cone-shaped cathedral was inaugurated in 1976 after 12 years of construction. Among its sculptures, murals and other works of art, the four vivid stained-glass windows, which stretch 60m to the ceiling, are breathtaking. The **Museu de Arte Sacra** (Museum of Sacred Art) in the basement contains a number of historical items, including the baptismal font used at the christening of royal princes and the throne of Dom Pedro II. The cathedral can accommodate up to 20,000 worshippers.

ESCADARIA SELARÓN Map p241

Stairway btwn Rua Joaquim Silva in Lapa & Rua Pinto Martins in Santa Teresa

An ever-expanding installation, the staircase leading up to the Convento de Santa Teresa from Rua Joaquim Silva became a work of art when Chilean-born artist Selarón decided to cover the steps with colorful mosaics. Originally a homage to the Brazilian people, the 215 steps feature ceramic mosaics in green, yellow and blue. He uses mirrors as well as tiles collected from around the world to create the illustrious effects. A hand-painted sign in English and Portuguese explains Selarón's vision. Recently, the artist has expanded his artistry to include mosaics near the Arcos da Lapa.

FUNDIÇÃO PROGRESSO Map p241

☎ 2220 5070; Rua dos Arcos 24; admission free; ⏰ 9am-6pm Mon-Fri

Once a foundry for the manufacturing of safes and ovens, the building today hosts avant garde exhibitions, performances and its popular samba parties during the summer. It is one of the few buildings in the area that survived the neighborhood redistricting project in the 1950s to widen the avenue.

MONUMENTO NACIONAL AOS MORTOS DA II GUERRA MUNDIAL

Map pp238-9

☎ 2240 1283; Av Infante Dom Henrique 75; admission free; ⏰ 10am-4pm Tue-Sun

This delicate monument to the soldiers who perished in WWII contains a **museum**, a **mausoleum** and the **Tomb of the Unknown Soldier**. The museum exhibits uniforms, medals and documents from Brazil's Italian campaign. There's also a small lake and **sculptures** by Ceschiatti and Anísio Araújo de Medeiros.

MUSEU DE ARTE MODERNA

Map pp238-9

☎ 2240 4944; www.mamrio.org.br in Portuguese; Av Infante Dom Henrique 85; admission US$2.50; ⏰ noon-6pm Tue-Fri, noon-7pm Sat & Sun

At the northern end of Parque do Flamengo, the Museu de Arte Moderna (MAM) is immediately recognizable by the striking postmodern edifice designed by Alfonso Eduardo Reidy. The landscaping of Burle Marx is no less impressive.

After a devastating fire in 1978 that consumed 90% of its collection, the Museu de Arte Moderna is finally back on its feet, and now houses 11,000 permanent works, including pieces by Brazilian artists Bruno Giorgi, Di Cavalcanti and Maria Martins. Curators often bring excellent photography and design exhibits to the museum, and the cinema hosts regular film festivals throughout the year. Check the website for details.

GREATER RIO

Eating p125; Shopping p171

Although visitors tend to stick to the Zona Sul and Centro, Rio's outer regions offer a variety of attractions from sweeping views from the other side of the bay to football rowdiness at Maracanã.

São Cristóvão encompasses the Quinta da Boa Vista, a large park containing the Museu Nacional and the zoo. It's also the site of the football stadium and the Feira Nordestina, one of Brazil's wildest weekend markets. In the 19th century the suburb was the home of the nobility, including the monarchs themselves. It has since become one of the most populous suburbs in Rio.

To the east of Centro lies Rio's lovely bay. Unfortunately, it's too polluted for swimming, but it makes a fine setting for a cruise to either Ilha de Paquetá or Niterói. The bay has a prominent place in Rio's history. In 1502 Portuguese explorers sailed into the bay and, mistaking it for the entrance to a large river, named it Rio de Janeiro (River of January). Even though they were mistaken in their geography, the name stuck and was later extended to the new settlement as a whole. Of course, the history doesn't begin with the Portuguese arrival. The indigenous Tamoio people lived along the shore long before their arrival, and the bay provided much of their sustenance. They were the ones who named the bay 'Guanabara,' which means 'arm of the sea.' In those days it was a tropical wilderness teeming with tapirs and jaguars. Today the wild animals (and much of the aquatic life as well) have disappeared from Baía de Guanabara. Much of its area has also disappeared. Owing to several landfill projects – which created Parque do Flamengo and Aeroporto Santos Dumont – the bay is also disappearing. The best way to experience the bay is to sail around it. Take a ferry ride to Niterói or go on a three-hour cruise (p58).

Orientation

São Cristóvão lies a few metro stops west of Centro, and is bordered by a number of suburbs and favelas, which extend in all directions. Rio and Niterói face each other across the Baía de Guanabara. In addition to the landfill that was added to the bay to create the Aeroporto Santos Dumont and the Parque do Flamengo, there are a number of natural islands. Ilha Fiscal, just off Centro, is among the smallest. The largest is Ilha do Governador, which is the site of the international airport.

SÃO CRISTÓVÃO

FEIRA NORDESTINA Map pp236-7

☎ 3860 9976; Campo de São Cristóvão; ☼ Fri-Sun
This enormous fair (32,000 sq meters with 658 stalls) is not to be missed. The fair showcases the culture from the northeast, with barracas (food stalls) selling Bahian dishes as well as beer and cachaça (cane liquor), which flows in great abundance here. Bands play throughout the weekend – accordion, guitar and tambourine players performing forró, samba groups and comedy troupes, MPB and rodas de capoeira (capoeira circles). The vibrant scene starts around 8pm on Friday and continues nonstop through Sunday evening. (Many club kids stop by here just before sunrise). In addition to food and drink, you can stock up on secondhand clothes, some well-priced hammocks and a wide (and wild) assortment of handicrafts.

JARDIM ZOOLÓGICO Map pp236-7

☎ 2569 2024; Quinta da Boa Vista; admission US$2; ☼ 9am-4:30pm Tue-Sun
Covering over 120,000 sq meters, the zoo at Quinta da Boa Vista has a wide variety of reptiles, mammals and birds – mostly indigenous to Brazil. Special attractions include the large walk-through aviary and the night house, which features nocturnal animals. The monkey house is also a crowd favorite.

MARACANÃ FOOTBALL STADIUM
Map pp236-7

☎ 2568 9962; gate 18, Rua Professor Eurico Rabelo; ☼ 9am-5pm Mon-Fri
Brazil's temple of soccer easily accommodates more than 100,000 people. On certain occasions, such as the World Cup match of 1950 or Pelé's last game, it has squeezed in close to 200,000 crazed fans – although it's now been modified to hold fewer.

If you like sports, if you want to understand Brazil, or if you just want an intense, quasi-psychedelic experience, then by all means go see a game of futebol – preferably a championship game or one between local rivals Flamengo, Vasco, Fluminense or Botafogo. See p150 for details.

There's a sports museum (☼ 9am-5pm Mon-Fri) inside the stadium. It has photographs, posters, cups and the uniforms of Brazilian sporting greats, including Pelé's famous No 10 shirt. There's also a store where you can buy soccer shirts. Enter through gate No 18 on Rua Professor Eurico Rabelo.

MUSEU DO PRIMEIRO REINADO
Map pp236-7

Av Dom Pedro II 293; admission US$2; ☼ 11am-5pm Tue-Fri
Housed in the former mansion of the Marquesa de Santos, this museum depicts the history of the First Reign (the reign of bumbling Dom Pedro I before he was driven out of the country). The collection includes documents, furniture and paintings, but the main attraction is the building and its interior, with murals by Francisco Pedro do Amaral.

MUSEU NACIONAL Map pp236-7

☎ 2568 8262; Quinta da Boa Vista; admission US$1; ☼ 10am-4pm Tue-Sun
This museum and its imperial entrance are still stately and imposing, and the view

from the balcony to the royal palms is majestic. However, the graffitied buildings and unkempt grounds have clearly declined since the fall of the monarchy.

There are many interesting exhibits: dinosaur fossils, saber-toothed tiger skeletons, beautiful pieces of pre-Columbian ceramics from the littoral and high plains of Peru, a huge meteorite, hundreds of stuffed birds, mammals and fish, gruesome displays of tropical diseases, and exhibits on the peoples of Brazil.

The back end of the collection is the most interesting. Rubber gatherers and Indians of the Amazon, lace workers and *jangadeiros* (traditional sailboat fishermen from the northeast), Candomblistas of Bahia, *gaúchos* (residents of Rio Grande do Sul) and *vaqueiros* (cowboys) of the *sertão* (interior) are all given their due.

QUINTA DA BOA VISTA Map pp236-7

☎ 2234 1609; ☼ 9am-5pm
Quinta da Boa Vista was the residence of the Portuguese imperial family until the Republic was proclaimed. Today, it's a large and busy park with gardens and lakes. At weekends it's crowded with soccer games and families from the Zona Norte. The former imperial mansion houses the **Museu Nacional** (opposite) and **Museu da Fauna**. The **Jardim Zoológico** (opposite), Rio's zoo, is 200m away.

BAÍA DE GUANABARA & NITERÓI
ILHA DE PAQUETÁ

☎ ferry 2533 6661, hydrofoil 2533 7524
This tropical island in the Baía de Guanabara was once a very popular tourist spot and is now frequented mostly by families from the Zona Norte. There are no cars on the island. Transport is by foot, bicycle (with literally hundreds for rent) or horse-drawn cart. There's a certain dirty, decadent charm to the colonial buildings, unassuming beaches and businesses catering to local tourism. The place gets crowded at weekends.

Go to Paquetá for the boat ride through Rio's famous bay and to see Cariocas at play – especially during the **Festa de São Roque**, which is celebrated on the weekend following August 16.

Boats leave from near the Praça Quinze de Novembro (Map pp238–9) in Centro. The regular ferry takes an hour and costs US$0.50. The more comfortable – and much quicker – hydrofoil takes only 25 minutes and costs US$5. Ferry service goes from 5:30am to 11pm, leaving every two to three hours. The hydrofoil departs daily at 10am, noon, 2pm and 4pm and returns at 7:40am, 11:40am, 12:30pm, 2:30pm and 4:30pm.

ILHA FISCAL Map pp238-9

☎ 3870 6992; admission US$3; ☼ 1pm, 2:30pm & 4pm Thu-Sun except on the 2nd weekend of month
This eye-catching lime-green, neogothic palace sitting in the Baía de Guanabara looks like something out of a child's fairy tale book. It was designed by engineer Adolfo del Vecchio and completed in 1889. Originally used to supervise port operations, the palace is famous as the location of the last Imperial Ball on 9 November 1889. Today it's open for guided tours three times a day from Thursday to Sunday; tours leave from the dock near Praça Quinze.

MUSEU DO ARTE CONTEMPORÂNEA

☎ 2620 2400; www.macniteroi.com in Portuguese; Mirante da Boa Viagem s/n, Niterói; admission US$1.75; ☼ 11am-7pm Tue-Sun
Designed by Brazil's most famous architect, Oscar Niemeyer, the MAC has been likened to a flying saucer. Its sweeping curvilinear design, however, is much more breathtaking than that. The views from here are splendid. The expositions inside the museum, on the other hand, are a mixed bag. To get to the MAC from the Niterói ferry terminal, turn right as you leave and walk about 50m across to the bus terminal in the middle of the road; a 47B minibus will drop you at the museum door.

NITERÓI

Niterói's principal attraction is the famous Museu do Arte Contemporânea. The cruise across the bay, however, is perhaps just as valid a reason for leaving Rio. Out on the water, you'll have impressive views of downtown, **Pão de Açúcar** (p76) and the other green mountains rising up out of the city; you'll also see planes (quite close) landing and

Sights

GREATER RIO

taking off at Santos Dumont. Try to be on the water at sunset when Centro glows with golden light. The ferry costs about US$0.75 and leaves from Praça Quinze de Novembro in Centro every 15 to 30 minutes; it's usually quite full of commuters. The faster and more comfortable alternative is the jumbo catamaran, which runs every 20 minutes from 7:20am to 8pm and costs US$2. Once you reach the dock, there isn't much to see in the immediate area. It's a busy commercial area, full of pedestrians, and crisscrossing intersections. From here catch a bus to the MAC or to one of the beaches.

PONTE RIO-NITERÓI

The Ponte (bridge) Rio-Niterói (Ponte Pres Costa E Silva) offers spectacular views of Baía de Guanabara. It is 15.5km long, 60m high and 26.6m wide, with two three-lane roads. There's a tollbooth 3km from the Niterói city center.

BARRA DA TIJUCA & WEST OF RIO

Eating p125; Shopping p171; Sleeping p188

Barra is the Miami of Rio, with malls and shopping centers set against the tropical landscape. The beach here is lovely and the city's longest at 15km wide. The commercial area has a different feel to other parts of Rio owing to its fairly recent founding. The middle classes first began moving here in the 1970s, when the situation in urban Rio

seemed as if it had reached boiling point. Cariocas fled crime and the crowded city to live on a gorgeous stretch of sand. Today, Barra is still a safe neighborhood, but the influx of new residents has created crowded conditions once again.

Barra da Tijuca is no longer fashionable. It's too far from anywhere and suffers huge traffic bottlenecks and a chronic shortage of water. The upper classes have begun moving back to Ipanema, Leblon and the traditional Av Osvaldo Cruz area of Flamengo. Barra mostly caters to *emergentes*, the nouveaux riches from the towns west of Rio.

At the western tip of Barra, Recreio dos Bandeirantes is being built up fast. It's full of gated communities, modern shopping centers and giant supermarkets. There are also some fine beaches and a very interesting museum. Beyond this, the region gets less and less urban. Some of Rio's loveliest beaches lie out this way. Further west lies Brazil's gorgeous coastal road, which travels through the region known as the Costa Verde.

Orientation

Barra da Tijuca lies 10km west of Leblon, reached by a scenic stretch along the coast. The major roads that pass through Barra are the east–west Av das Américas and the north–south Av Ayrton Senna. At the intersection of these two roads is the major commercial area, where *shoppings* (shopping malls) bloom like wildflowers. Av Ayrton Senna's southern terminus is the beach (Praia da Barra da Tijuca). Av Sernambetiba

Museu de Arte Moderna (p89)

PARQUE NACIONAL & FLORESTA DA TIJUCA

The Tijuca is all that's left of the Atlantic rain forest that once surrounded Rio de Janeiro. In just 15 minutes you can go from the concrete jungle of Copacabana to the 120-sq-km tropical jungle of the Parque Nacional da Tijuca (Map p249). A more rapid and dramatic contrast is hard to imagine. The forest is an exuberant green, with beautiful trees, creeks and waterfalls, mountainous terrain and high peaks. It has an excellent, well-marked trail system. Candomblistas leave offerings by the roadside, families have picnics and serious hikers climb the 1012m to the summit of **Pico da Tijuca**.

The heart of the forest is the **Alto da Boa Vista** area in the Floresta (Forest) da Tijuca, with many lovely natural and manmade features. Among the highlights of this beautiful park are several waterfalls (**Cascatinha de Taunay**, **Cascata Gabriela** and **Cascata Diamantina**), a 19th-century chapel (**Capela Mayrink**) and numerous caves (**Gruta Luís Fernandes**, **Gruta Belmiro**, **Gruta Paulo e Virgínia**). Also in the park is a lovely picnic spot (**Bom Retiro**) and several restaurants (**Restaurante Os Equilos** and **Restaurante a Floresta**, which is near the ruins of Major Archer's house – **Ruínas do Archer**). A recommended culinary experience is dining at the open-air brunch at the **Museu do Açude** (p126), held the last Sunday of the month.

The park is home to many different bird and animal species, including iguanas and monkeys, which you might encounter on one of the excellent day hikes you can make here (the trails are well-signed). Maps can be obtained at the small artisan shop just inside the park entrance, which is open from 7am to 9pm.

The entire park closes at sunset. It's best to go by car, but if you can't, catch a 221, 233 or 234 bus. Alternatively, take the metro to Saens Peña, then catch a bus going to Barra da Tijuca and get off at Alta da Boa Vista.

The best route by car is to take Rua Jardim Botânico two blocks past the Jardim Botânico (heading east from Gávea). Turn left on Rua Lopes Quintas and then follow the Tijuca or Corcovado signs for two quick left turns until you reach the back of the Jardim Botânico, where you turn right. Then follow the signs for a quick ascent into the forest and past the **Vista Chinesa** (Map pp236–7, get out for a good view) and the **Mesa do Imperador** (Map pp236–7). As soon as you seem to come out of the forest, turn right onto the main road and you'll see the stone columns to the entrance of Alto da Boa Vista on your left after a couple of kilometers. You can also drive up to Alto da Boa Vista by heading out to São Conrado and turning right up the hill at the Parque Nacional da Tijuca signs.

Warning: there have been occasional reports of robbery within the park. Most Cariocas recommend going at weekends when there are more people around. Ask at Riotur (p216) about the present situation.

---

runs along the beach (east–west) – as it heads east it eventually turns into Av Niemeyer; heading west, it leads to Recreio dos Bandeirantes and other beaches.

BOSQUE DA BARRA Map pp236-7

☎ 3325 6519, guided tours 2509 5099; Km 7, Av das Américas (intersection of Av Ayrton Senna), Barra da Tijuca; 🕙 7am-6pm

Covering 500,000 sq meters of salt-marsh vegetation, the park provides a refuge and breeding area for many small birds and animals. The woods have a jogging track and bicycle path.

MUSEU AEROSPACIAL Map pp236-7

☎ 3357 5212; www.musal.aer.mil.br in Portuguese; Av Marechal Fontenele 2000, Campo dos Afonsos; admission free; 🕙 9am-3pm Tue-Fri, 9:30am-4pm Sat & Sun

This museum maintains expositions on Santos Dumont (the Brazilian father of aviation), Air Marshal Eduardo Gomes, the history of Brazilian airmail and the role of Brazil's air force in WWII. There are lots of old planes,

motors and flying instruments. Highlights are replicas of Santos Dumont's planes, the *14 Bis* and the *Demoiselle*. You can also arrange guided visits if you call at least three days in advance.

MUSEU CASA DO PONTAL

☎ 2490 4013; Estrada do Pontal 3295, Recreio dos Bandeirantes; admission US$4, children under 5 free; 🕙 9am-5:30pm Tue-Sun

Owned by French designer Jacques Van de Beuque, this impressive collection of over 4500 pieces is one of the best folk-art collections in Brazil. The assorted artifacts are grouped according to themes, including music, Carnaval, religion and folklore. The grounds of the museum are surrounded by lush vegetation, which alone makes it worth the trip out here.

PARQUE DO MARAPENDI Map pp236-7

Av Sernambetiba, Recreio dos Bandeirantes; 🕙 8am-5pm

At the end of Av Sernambetiba in Recreio dos Bandeirantes, this biological reserve sets aside 700,000 sq meters for study and has a small area for leisure, with workout stations and games areas.

PARQUE ECOLÓGICO MUNICIPAL CHICO MENDES Map pp236-7

☎ 2437 6400; Km 17, Av Jarbas de Carvalho 679, Recreio dos Bandeirantes; ☽ 8:30am-5:30pm

This 400,000-sq-meter park was created in 1989 and named after the Brazilian ecological activist who was murdered for his work. The park protects the remaining sand-spit vegetation from real estate speculators. The facilities include a visitors center and ecological trails leading to a small lake. Animals protected in the park include butterflies, lizards, tortoises and the broad-nosed caiman.

PRAIA DA BARRA DA TIJUCA

Map pp236-7

The best thing about Barra is the beach. It's 12km long, with the lovely blue sea lapping at the shore. The first few kilometers of the eastern end of the beach are filled with bars and seafood restaurants.

The young and hip hang out in front of *barraca* (food stall) No 1 – also known as the *barraca do Pepê*, after the famous Carioca hang-gliding champion who died during a competition in Japan in 1991.

The further out you go, the more deserted it gets, and the stalls turn into trailers. It's calm on weekdays and crazy on hot summer weekends.

RIO WATER PLANET

☎ 2428 9000; Estrada das Bandeirantes 24000, Recreio dos Bandeirantes; admission US$20; ☽ 10am-5pm Sat, Sun & holidays

Rio Water Planet claims to be the biggest aquatic park in Latin America. Waterfalls, artificial beaches (a bit surprising in this part of the world) and lazy rafting rivers are part of the attractions, as are Rio Kart Planet (an open-air kart track), Rio Show Planet (an area for shows) and Rio Circus Planet.

SITIO BURLE MARX

☎ 2410 1412; burlemarx@alternex.com.br; Estrada da Barra de Guaratiba 2019, Guaratiba; ☽ 7am-4pm, by advance appointment only

This huge 350,000-sq-meter estate was once the home of Brazil's most famous landscape architect, Roberto Burle Marx. The estate's lush vegetation includes thousands of plant species, some of which are rare varieties from different corners of the globe. A 17th-century Benedictine chapel also lies on the estate, along with Burle Marx's original farmhouse and studio, where you can see displays of paintings, furniture and sculptures by the talented designer.

TERRA ENCANTADA Map pp236-7

☎ 2421 9369; www.terra-encantada.com.br in Portuguese; Av Ayrton Senna 2800, Barra da Tijuca; adult/child US$12/4; ☽ 2-9pm Thu-Sat, noon-9pm Sun

The Enchanted Land is a large amusement park in Barra. It includes Cabhum, a 64m, 100km/h free fall; Ressaca, a toboggan ride that goes over a waterfall, as well as many other rides.

WET 'N' WILD RIO DE JANEIRO

☎ 2428 9300; Av das Américas 22000, Recreio dos Bandeirantes; admission US$14; ☽ 10am-5pm Wed-Sun & holidays

Although it sounds more like the title of an adult film, Wet 'n' Wild Rio is a water park similar to Rio Water Planet – although its water slides are a bit more radical.

Walking & Cycling Tours

Historic Centro	96
Lagoa to Leme	97
Santa Teresa	100
Urca: the Village by the Sea	101

Walking & Cycling Tours

Rio's tropical climate, its lush, mountainous setting and its glorious location make it an excellent city for power walking, biking or just strolling. We've included a number of options that showcase the city's vibrant blend of old and new, tropical and urban – along with its natural splendor. For those who prefer to take part in an organized walking tour, see p61.

HISTORIC CENTRO

A mélange of historic buildings and young skyscrapers, the center of Rio is an excellent place to discover the essence of the city away from its beaches and mountains. Among the hustle and bustle of commerce, you'll find fascinating museums, atmospheric bars and theaters, open-air bazaars and the colonial-antique stores set near old samba clubs. This tour is best done during the week, when the Centro is at its most vibrant.

WALK FACTS

Start Praça Floriano (metro Cinelândia)
End Praça Floriano
Distance 4km
Duration 3 hours
Fuel stop Bar Luiz (p135)

Start at the **Praça Floriano** 1 (p86), which is where the Cinelândia metro stop is. This plaza is the heart of modern Rio. Praça Floriano comes to life at night when the outdoor cafés are filled with beer drinkers, samba musicians and political debate. The neoclassical **Teatro Municipal** 2 (p129) overlooking the plaza is one of Rio's finest buildings.

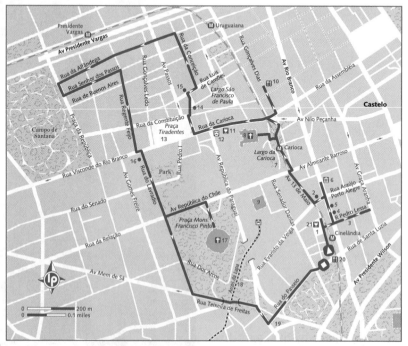

On the east side of Av Rio Branco facing Praça Floriano is the Rua Pedro Lessa, where you can browse through the record and CD stalls at the open-air music market called the **Feira de Música** 3 (p168). Nearby is the **Centro Cultural Justiça Federal** 4 (p83), which often hosts decent exhibitions. The solid **Biblioteca Nacional** 5 (p82) is next door, while north on Av Rio Branco is another striking building, which currently hosts the **Museu Nacional de Belas Artes** 6 (p85). Take a peek or two inside if you're interested in seeing some of Rio's best-known 19th-century painters.

Now cross over Av Rio Branco and walk briefly back toward Praça Floriano. Take a right on Evaristo da Veiga (in front of the Teatro Municipal) and another right onto the pedestrian-only Av 13 de Maio. Cross a street and you're in the **Largo da Carioca** 7, a bustling area with a small market where vendors sell a sunglasses, bootleg CDs, maps, leathergoods and a wide array of items you probably don't really need. Up on the hill is the recently restored **Convento de Santo Antônio** 8 (p84). The original church here was built in 1608.

Gazing at the skyline from the convent, you'll notice the **Petrobras building** 9, whose boxlike metal chassis seems to cast an ominous shadow over the area.

After coming back down from the convent, continue along Av 13 de Maio, then turn right onto Rua da Carioca and left onto Gonçalves Dias before stopping in the **Confeitaria Colombo** 10 (p123) for a dose of caffeine and art nouveau. Head back to Rua da Carioca. Along this street you'll find an array of old shops, a slice of 19th-century Rio. **Bar Luiz** 11 (p135) at number 39 makes a fine stop for a bite or a *chope* (draft beer).

At the end of the block you'll pass the **Cinema Iris** 12, which used to be one of Rio's most elegant theaters, and will then emerge into the hustle of **Praça Tiradentes** 13. Soak up some of the stately ambience. On opposite sides of the square are the Teatro João Caetano and the Teatro Carlos Gomez (p128), and around the corner is the **Centro Cultural Carioca** 14 (p83). Stop in here to see what's on, musically speaking, for the evening. Just across from the theater is the **Real Gabinete Português de Leitura** 15 (p85), Rio's loveliest reading room.

Walk up to Rua da Conceiçao and take a left onto Rua da Alfândega. This will take you into the heart of Saara, a longstanding neighborhood bazaar packed with shops, pedestrians and Lebanese restaurants. Walk, shop and snack as far as Campo de Santana. Make a U-turn there and proceed back along Rua Senhor dos Passos. Take a right on Rua Regente Feijó. When this street ends, take a short left and then a right and head down Rua do Lavradio. This street is famous for its antique shops set in the colorful 19th-century buildings. A number of great nightspots, like **Río Scenarium** 16 (p142), have sprung up on this street, some constructed in brick-lined colonial relics. The mix of samba-jazz and antiques makes a fine setting.

When you reach Av República do Chile, take a left and stop in the **Catedral Metropolitana** 17 (p89) for a break. There, check out the marvelous stained-glass windows. When you leave, head back to Rua do Lavradio for more antique browsing. When you reach Av Mem de Sá, take a left and follow the road around the curve as you pass beneath the **Arcos da Lapa** 18 (p88). This is Rio's big samba center at night, with clubs and old-school bars scattered all over this neighborhood. When you reach the **Largo da Lapa** 19, take a left and walk along Rua do Passeio. You'll have great views of the arches from here. In two more blocks you'll be back to where you started. When you reach Praça Floriano, grab a seat at one of the outdoor tables at **Ateliê Odeon** 20 (p135) or **Amarelinho** 21 (p135), and cool off with a *chope* or fresh-squeezed *suco* (juice), a refreshing end to the walk.

LAGOA TO LEME

It's hard to think of a better setting for a bike ride than the Zona Sul's lovely coastline and its nearby lakeside jewel, Lagoa Rodrigo de Freitas (p64). The mountains rising out of the sea and the white-sand beaches facing them are a big part of the allure of the *cidade maravilhosa* (marvelous city) and you'll be rewarded with a number of panoramic views along this journey. Beaches, bay, Corcovado, Pão de Açúcar (Sugarloaf) and many of Rio's other lush peaks are the backdrop for your ride.

Bring some money for snacks and *agua de coco* (coconut water) – both prevalent along the beach – and a meal at the end of your ride. You'll work up an appetite out in the sun.

Most of this journey follows a bike path separate from the traffic on the street. Sunday is the best day to do this ride, as the road bordering the bike path is closed then – giving you more room to connect to your inner Armstrong.

Begin in the **Parque Brigadeiro Faria Lima 1** on the edge of Lagoa. Conveniently, there's a bike-rental place right there. You can also rent bikes at a number of other places in town (p204).

Once you're on the bike path, follow it north as it loops around the lake. You'll soon pass the **Ilha Piraquê 2**, one of the island country clubs out on the lake. As you make your way east you'll probably see a few egrets. Continue along the path, curving south and pedaling past some of the **Lagoa kiosks 3**. These become crowded at night with Cariocas enjoying the lakeside dining and live music. After your third turn you'll pass another island, the **Ilha dos Caiçaras 4**. In another 500m, exit onto **Rua Mário Ribeiro 5**, but keep your eyes peeled: it's a major street with a bike lane along the north side of the road. Once in this lane, follow it until just beyond Av Bartolomeu Mitre. You'll be riding south down this street, but there's a better crossing one block up. Once you find the crosswalk, head across and stay on the bike path. At Av Bartolomeu Mitre take a right. In a few blocks you'll reach the beach.

From Leblon, start pedaling east along Av Vieira Souto. As you ride along, take note how the crowds change along the beach from **Posto 10 6** (Cariocas who've obviously spent a lot of time at the gym) to **Posto 9 7** (a rather more laid-back crowd not averse to lighting a joint from time to time). When you reach Arpoador, you can pull off the bike path for your first maté (tealike beverage) or *agua de coco* from the stand in the **Praça do Arpoador 8**. You'll need to walk your bike here, as it's usually full of pedestrians. Take a seat under a palm tree and enjoy

RIDE FACTS

Start Parque Brigadeiro Faria Lima
End Parque Brigadeiro Faria Lima
Distance 26km
Duration 3 hours
Fuel stop Arab da Lagoa (p114) or Caipirinha & Filé (p132)

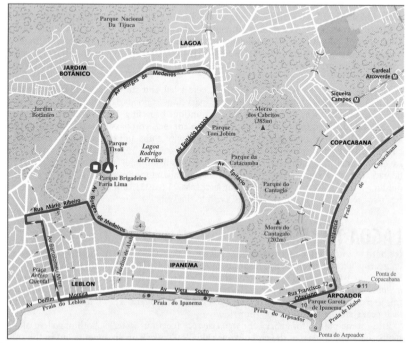

Entrance to Forte de Copacabana (p66)

the fine view west, with Dois Irmãos rising over Leblon. The rock outcropping to your left is **Ponta do Arpoador 9**, which offers decent waves. It's a rare day when there aren't at least a dozen surfers jockeying for good breaks. After your rest, get back on the bike – either pushing your bike along the path through the **Parque Garota de Ipanema 10** (p62), or going back up to Rua Francisco Otaviano, where the bike path continues.

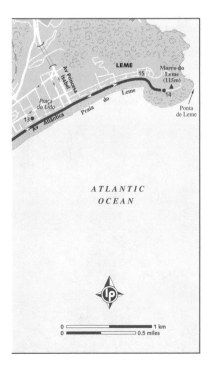

As you continue on the path, you'll pass the **Forte de Copacabana 11** (p66) and will soon have a splendid view of Morro de Leme, which is at the end of the long stretch of sand formed by Copacabana and Leme beaches. At the beginning of Copacabana you'll see the **posto dos pescadores 12** (fishermen's place). If you do this ride early in the morning, it's possible to see the fishermen pulling their nets out of the water. As you continue along the bike path, which is now running parallel with Av Atlântica, be sure to stop for cups of *agua de coco;* there are stands all along the beach.

Although you'll probably be watching the beach, the mountains and the sea, keep an eye out for the whitewashed **Copacabana Palace 13** (p180); it was Copa's first hotel (1923) back when the beach was still a remote getaway from Centro. In Leme the path ends at the **Morro do Leme 14**, where you'll probably see kids fishing off the rocks. Take a break (there's yet another **drink stand 15** here) before starting the return journey, which follows the same route back. If you haven't eaten by the time you return to Lagoa, grab a meal at one of the kiosks.

SANTA TERESA

Colorful colonial buildings, narrow brick-lined streets and sweeping views of downtown are a few of the reasons artists flocked here in the mid-'70s. Today the 'hood is still experiencing a cultural renaissance. You never know what you'll find here: old mansions hosting African drumming, bossa-jazz in a bombed-out building or impromptu music jams. No other neighborhood has quite the energy that Santa Teresa has. Do be careful when exploring this neighborhood, as muggings still occur. Travel in groups, and keep an eye out for pairs of young men on mopeds. We recommend not straying too far off the *bonde* line. The weekends are the liveliest time to visit, but if you plan to take the *bonde* then, travel to the *bonde* station by taxi as Centro is deserted (and dangerous) on Saturdays and Sundays.

Our saunter begins in the small square of **Largo das Neves** 1 (p88), also the end of the *bonde* line. The first part of our walk will follow the tracks, removing the possibility of getting lost among the winding streets.

Above the Largo das Neves are the twin spires of **Igreja de Nossa Senhora das Neves** 2, one of many 19th-century churches in the area. On weekend nights, the Largo becomes the set piece for the music-filled cafés and bars that open onto it.

Start following the tracks. You'll pass through a few curves before reaching an even sharper turn leading to Rua Monte Alegre. If you need a drink, the old-time **Armazém São Thiago** 3 (p136) is a good place to stop. Across the street is **Brechó Arte 70** 4 (p170), a thrift shop worth a browse.

Keep following the tracks and you'll pass **Centro Cultural Laurinda Santos Lobo** 5 (p88). Stop here to take a look at current exhibitions and find out if any concerts are planned. Continue following the tracks, and you'll soon reach the **Bar do Mineiro** 6 (p136), an old-school *boteco* (open-air bar) that's famous throughout Rio for its excellent home cooking.

WALK FACTS

Start *Bonde* (tram) to Largo das Neves (Paulo Matos line)
End Bus 572 from Rua da Lapa to the Zona Sul
Distance 3.5km
Duration 2½ hours
Fuel stop Bar do Mineiro (p136)

Continue down the hill and you'll reach **Largo do Guimarães** 7 (p88), a popular reference point for Santa Teresa bohemians. If you take a left on Rua Carlos Brandt, you can visit the tiny **Museu do Bonde** 8 (p88) for a symphonic journey back to the *bonde*'s once-glorious day in the sun. After checking out the museum and the tram-storage building next door, walk back up to Largo dos Guimarães and head up the little staircase to visit another thrift shop, **Brechó**

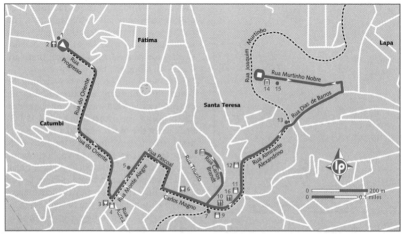

Antigamente 9 (p170). Back on the tracks, you'll notice many more restaurants and shops. Pleasant **Porta Quente** 10 (p125) serves coffee and light snacks. When you continue, you'll pass **La Vareda** 11 (p171) and **Trilhos Urbanos** 12 (p171), both good spots to purchase Brazilian handicrafts.

Keep walking downhill. Soon you'll reach **Curvelo** 13, a *bonde* shelter astride the road. Here you'll turn right (leaving the tracks behind, so get your bearings) onto Rua Dias de Barros. Follow this street until you reach a road branching off to the left (Rua Murtinho Nobre). Follow this all the way around and you will reach the **Museu Chácara do Céu** 14 (p88), with its small collection of modern art, and the **Parque das Ruínas** 15 (p88) next door. Don't miss the splendid views from here. After your trek, grab a cool drink at **Sobrenatural** 16 (p125) before taking the *bonde* back down to Centro.

URCA: THE VILLAGE BY THE SEA

One of Rio's most charming neighborhoods is one of its least explored – and safest (this is one place where you won't have any worries with a camera). The peaceful streets are lined with trees, beautiful houses and lush gardens. Out by the bay, fishermen cast their lines just beyond the rocky shoreline as couples lounge on the seawall, Corcovado framing the scene.

Our walk begins where Rua Marechal Cantuária meets Av São Sebastião. On your left, you'll see **Cassino da Urca** 1, or at least what remains of the once-popular gambling and night spot, where Carmen Miranda and Josephine Baker both performed. Veer to the right along Av São Sebastião, noting the splendid Tudor-style **Instituto Cultural Cravo Albim** 2 against the back of Morro da Urca. The road goes uphill from here. Follow the

WALK FACTS

Start Bus 511 or 512 to Rua Marechal Cantuária
End Praia Vermelha
Distance 4km
Duration 3 hours
Fuel stop Praia Vermelha (p138) or Bar Urca (p119)

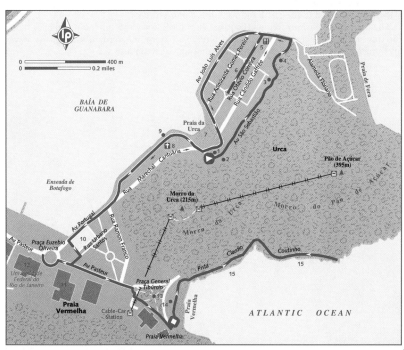

road all the way along; you'll pass **Carmen Miranda's former residence 3** at number 131. You'll also pass beneath the wall that separates the military fort from the neighborhood. High up are **mango trees 4**. If you're lucky, a mango will fall into your hands.

When you get to the end of the street, take the steps down to Av João Luis Alves. From here you'll have splendid views of Corcovado, Parque do Flamengo and the Rio-Niterói bridge as you walk along the bay. Stop for a juice or a plate of fresh fish at **Bar Urca 5** (p119). Then stroll down **Rua Otávio Correira 6** to get a glimpse of the charming houses on this side of Rio. Retrace your footsteps and continue along Av João Luis Alves until you reach **Praia da Urca 7** (p77). You have the option of walking across the sand or taking the road around. Stick to the bay side as the road forks. Look for the small **Igreja de Nossa Senhora do Brasil 8**. Peek inside the small church (the chapel is on the ground floor; the church is upstairs). Note the small Brazilian flag on the Madonna's cloak on your way out – perhaps it really is true that God is Brazilian after all. Facing the church is the floating **statue of São Pedro no Mar 9**. On June 29, St Peter's feast day, the fishermen make a procession across the bay, past the statue, scattering flowers across the water.

> ## TIP
>
> Start your walking tour of Urca in the afternoon, around 3pm. When you finish, you can take the cable car up to Pão de Açúcar for sunset over the city. After coming back down, stop at Praia Vermelha (p138) for drinks and excellent live music by the sea.

Keep going along the avenue, now called Av Portugal, and you'll reach a bridge. To your left is the **Quadrado da Urca 10**, which is a harbor for the poor fishermen. Dozens of tiny fishing boats bob on the sadly polluted water. Keep walking on this street until it ends on Av Pasteur. Urca's most majestic buildings lie along this stretch. Walk up the stairs at **Companhia de Pesquisa de Recursos Minerais 11** (if the lion doesn't scare you off). A little up the road is the neoclassical masterpiece, the **Universidade Federal do Rio de Janeiro 12**. Turn back down Av Pasteur and walk southeast toward Pão de Açúcar. Just beyond the cable-car station is the beautifully laid-out **Praça General Tibúrcio 13**. Keep walking toward the sea and you'll reach the **statue of Chopin 14**, donated to the city by Rio's Polish community.

The last part of the tour follows the paved **Pista Cláudio Coutinho 15** (p77) out and back. Look for tiny *micos* (capuchin monkeys) and birds, and enjoy the verdant setting, the waves crashing against the rocks below and the panoramic views out to sea.

Eating

Ipanema & Leblon	106
Gávea, Jardim Botânico & Lagoa	113
Copacabana & Leme	115
Botafogo & Urca	118
Flamengo	120
Catete & Glória	121
Centro & Cinelândia	122
Santa Teresa & Lapa	124
Barra da Tijuca & Greater Rio	125

Eating

Rio's enchanting scenery is only part of its diverse attractions – numerous restaurants offer yet another way to experience its eclecticism. They can be found in every part of the *cidade maravilhosa* (marvelous city) – along its tree-lined streets, overlooking its beaches, hidden in old colonial buildings, atop skyscrapers or spilling into its pedestrian-filled neighborhoods.

The bountiful coastline, its tropical fruits and Rio's immigrant population add up to some fantastic dining opportunities. Regional cuisines from all over Brazil – Minas Gerais, Bahia and even Amazônia – are represented, and any night of the week connoisseurs can enjoy traditionally prepared Italian, French, German, Japanese and Syrian cuisine.

Ipanema and Leblon are the best places to browse for a memorable meal. There you'll find top-rated chefs, beautifully set dining rooms and the fashion-conscious crowds that fill them. You'll also find excellent restaurants scattered about Copacabana, hidden in the streets of Jardim Botânico and dotting Santa Teresa. Centro also has some choice spots – though it caters largely to the weekday crowds.

Opening Hours

Aside from juice bars, cafés and bakeries, few restaurants open for breakfast (those that do start serving around 7am). Cariocas don't typically order a sit-down meal until noon, which is when most restaurants open. Most restaurants in Centro open only during the week and only for lunch – usually from noon until 3pm. Restaurants in the Zona Sul, with its wealth of culinary options, attract larger dinner crowds than lunch ones. Typically, they don't close until midnight – and some serve until three or four in the morning. Cariocas aren't known for rushing off to eat when the sun goes down. Most restaurants don't pack crowds until 9pm or so. On Saturdays and Sundays, lunch is the big meal of the day – Saturday being the traditional day to linger (sometimes for hours) over *feijoada* (black beans and pork stew).

How Much?

Rio can be light or hard on the wallet, depending on where and what you eat (but mostly where). Juice bars and *botecos* (small, open-air bars) are the cheapest; you can order a *misto quente* (toasted ham-and-cheese sandwich) and juice or a *comida corriente* (a plate of chicken, steak or fish with sides) for around US$5. One budget option is the pay-by-weight restaurants throughout the city These eateries vary in price and quality, but average about US$13 per kilo (a fairly loaded plate will cost US$7).

There are a vast array of midrange dining options; expect to pay between US$10 and US$15 for a main course. *Churrascarias* (traditional barbecue restaurants) offer all-you-can-eat dining options – try to fast for at least six hours before going. Most charge around US$15, with more food than you could possibly imagine (much less *eat*).

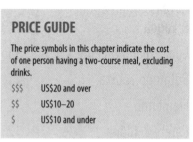

PRICE GUIDE

The price symbols in this chapter indicate the cost of one person having a two-course meal, excluding drinks.

$$$	US$20 and over
$$	US$10–20
$	US$10 and under

To experience the talents of Rio's top chefs, head to Centro by day, where power-lunching executives enjoy masterfully prepared sushi, steak or duck confit in stately environments. By night, restaurants in Leblon and Ipanema – and a handful in Copacabana – compete for annual culinary prizes. A main course in any of these locations will cost between US$18 and US$30. Rio's best restaurants have impressive wine cellars that range far beyond the Argentine, Chilean and Brazilian vintages you'll find at other places.

Booking Tables

Most restaurants accept reservations for both lunch and dinner, so call ahead if you want to avoid a wait. Restaurants that don't accept reservations often have a bar where you can have a drink while you wait for a table.

Unfortunately, when you call to make a reservation, the person who answers the phone is not likely to speak English. Concierges are adept at booking seats for you, but if you're game, have a stab at speaking Portuguese – Brazilians, after all, are known for their patience.

Tipping

In restaurants, a 10% tip is usually included in the bill. When it isn't included – and your waiter will generally tell you if it's not – it's customary to leave 10%. If the service was exceptionally bad or good, adjust accordingly. Tipping in cafés and bars is always appreciated too.

BRAZILIAN DISHES

Acarajé A specialty of Bahia made from peeled brown beans mashed with salt and onions, and then fried in *dendê*. Inside these delicious croquettes is *vatapá*, dried shrimp, pepper and tomato sauce.

Angú A kind of savory cake made with very fine corn flour called *fubá*, mixed with water and salt.

Bobó de camarão Manioc paste cooked and flavored with dried shrimp, coconut milk and cashew nuts.

Camarão á paulista Unshelled fresh prawns (shrimp) fried in olive oil with lots of garlic and salt.

Canja A hearty soup made with chicken broth; often a meal in itself.

Caranguejada Crab cooked whole in seasoned water.

Carne de sol A tasty salt-cured meat, grilled and served with beans, rice and vegetables.

Caruru One of the most popular Brazilian dishes of African origin. Made with boiled okra or other vegetables mixed with grated onion, salt, shrimp, chili peppers and *dendê*. Traditionally, a saltwater fish such as *garoupa* (grouper) is added.

Casquinha de caranguejo or siri Stuffed crab, prepared with manioc flour.

Cozido Any kind of stew, usually with vegetables (such as potatoes, sweet potatoes, carrots and manioc).

Dendê Palm oil; decidedly strong stuff. Many non-Brazilian stomachs can't handle it.

Dourado A scrumptious freshwater fish found throughout Brazil.

Farofa Otherwise known as cassava or manioc flour, it is a legacy of the Indians, for whom it has traditionally been an essential dietary ingredient; it remains a Brazilian staple.

Feijoada The Carioca answer to cassoulet. See p15.

Frango ao molho pardo Chicken pieces stewed with vegetables and covered with a seasoned sauce made from the blood of the bird.

Moqueca A kind of sauce or stew, as well as a style of cooking from Bahia, which is properly prepared in a covered clay pot. Fish, shrimp, oyster, crab or a combination of those are served with a *moqueca* sauce, which is defined by its heavy use of *dendê* and coconut milk, and often contains peppers and onions.

Moqueca capixaba A *moqueca* from Espírito Santo that uses lighter *urucum* (from the seeds of the berrylike fruit of the annatto tree) oil from the Indians instead of *dendê*.

Pato no tucupi Roast duck flavored with garlic and cooked in *tucupi* sauce, which is made from the juice of the manioc plant and *jambu*, a local vegetable. A very popular dish in Pará.

Peixada Fish cooked in broth with vegetables and eggs.

Peixe a delícia Broiled fish usually served in a sauce made with bananas and coconut milk.

Petiscos Appetizers.

Picanha Thin cut of rump steak.

Prato de verão Literally, a 'summer plate,' which is served at many juice stands in Rio. It's basically a fruit salad.

prato feito Literally a 'made plate,' usually a serving of rice, beans and salad, with chicken, fish or beef. Sometimes abbreviated to 'PF'.

Pirarucu ao forno *Pirarucu,* the most famous fish from the rivers of Amazônia, baked with lemon and other seasonings.

Tacacá An Indian dish of dried shrimp cooked with pepper, *jambu*, manioc and much more.

Tutu á mineira A bean paste with toasted bacon and manioc flour, often served with cooked cabbage.

Vatapá A seafood dish with a thick sauce made from manioc paste, coconut and *dendê*. Perhaps the most famous Brazilian dish of African origin.

Xinxim de galinha Pieces of chicken flavored with garlic, salt and lemon. Shrimp and *dendê* are often added.

Groceries & Takeout

Open-air markets abound in the city. Juicy pineapples, mangos, papayas and the plethora of fruits you'll find only in Brazil make fine snacks for the beach. Some markets (p167, p168) – like the Feira Hippie on Sundays in Ipanema – feature fresh-cooked food from Brazil's northeast.

Supermarkets provide another option for self-caterers. The city's most prominent supermarket chain, Zona Sul, is prevalent throughout Ipanema, Leblon and Copacabana. Zona Sul (p113) on Rua Dias Ferreira in Leblon is the best supermarket in Rio, with an excellent assortment of imported cheeses, fresh breads, deli items, salads, and wines and spirits. Nearby is Hortifruti (p111), an indoor fruit and vegetable market. Leblon's Garcia & Rodrigues (p110), which is also a restaurant, stocks a seductive selection of French and Italian wines, cheeses and other deli items. The patisserie and ice-cream counters alone warrant a visit.

Downtown, the gleaming shelves at Lidador (p124) enable commuters to stock up on smoked meats, chocolates and other delicacies before they head off to the suburbs. Lidador also has a small stand in back where you can order a drink, in case the busy streets outdoors have unsettled you.

Per-kilo places all have takeout containers, if you're in a hurry and simply want to grab something freshly cooked, while juice bars also accommodate takeout customers.

One needn't, however, even step off the streets to find sustenance. Throughout town, you'll find vendors selling *agua de coco* (coconut water), available by the cup or by the liter. Look for the vendors advertising their wares as *'bem gelado'* (well chilled) for ice-cold refreshment on a steamy day.

On the beach, you're never more than a stone's throw from drink stands. Many offer caipirinhas, beer and snack food in addition to *agua de coco,* here served straight from the coconut. If you're frolicking in the waves and can't be bothered making the trek up the beach, don't worry. Vendors laden with heavy bags roam the beach till sundown, offering beer, soda, *globos* (a bag of puffed chips), maté (a tealike drink) or *sanduich natural* (a sandwich, filled with ricotta cheese, or salad of chicken or tuna). Others offer *queijo coalho* (hot cheese), which will be cooked on a small stove in front of you and served to you on a stick (with herbs if you prefer). You can also find vendors cooking *churrasco* (roasted meat) – also served on a stick, with or without *farofa* (manioc flour).

IPANEMA & LEBLON

Residents of these twin neighborhoods are blessed with the city's best selection of restaurants, cafés and juice bars. During the day their eateries fill with bronze bodies heading to and from the beach, when the sun goes down, the tree-lined streets form the backdrop to the city's most elegant open-air dining. The trendy new restaurant of the month doesn't always live up to the hype, but there are plenty of time-tested favorites that do.

ALESSANDRO E FEDERICO

Map pp246-7   Pizza $$
☎ 2522 5415; Rua Garcia D'Ávila 151, Ipanema; pizzas US$10-15; ☒ 7pm-2am
Dominated by the wood-burning oven at center stage, this stylish two-story restaurant serves some of Ipanema's best thin-crust pizzas. You'll also find a large wine cellar and a well-dressed neighborhood crowd. Another Alessandro e Federico (☎ 2521 0828; Rua Garcia D'Ávila 134; ☒ 9am-1am)

on the same street specializes in fresh sandwiches and has an inviting front patio.

ANTIQUARIUS Map pp246-7   Portuguese $$$
☎ 2294 1049; Rua Aristídes Espínola 19, Leblon; mains US$29-45; ☒ noon-2am
Serving without a doubt the city's best Portuguese cuisine, Antiquarius is a rewarding but pricey spot to celebrate old-world cuisine with an antique-filled dining room, top-notch service and lovingly prepared dishes. Some particular recommendations include the leg of lamb, the wild boar in red-wine sauce and the Portuguese favorite *bacalhau* (cod), elevated here to the sublime.

ARMAZÉM DO CAFÉ
Map pp246-7   Café $
☎ 2259 0170; Rua Rita Ludolf 87B, Leblon; ☒ 9am-midnight Sun-Thu, to 1am Fri & Sat
Dark-wood furnishings and the fresh-ground coffee aroma lend an authenticity to this Leblon coffeehouse. Connoisseurs

rate the aromatic roasts much higher here than neighboring Cafeína. It also serves waffles, snacks and desserts.

ATAÚLFO Map pp246-7 — Self-serve $

☎ 2540 0606; Av Ataúlfo de Paiva 630, Leblon; sandwiches US$5, mains US$8-12; ☽ 9am-midnight Sun-Thu, to 2am Fri & Sat

The front of the restaurant features a lunch counter where you can grab a quiche, a tasty sandwich or a juice. In back, the narrow restaurant opens up, and you'll encounter a small but excellent self-serve buffet by day – serving salmon with artichoke-and-sun-dried-tomato tagliatelle among other things. At night Ataúlfo serves à la carte.

ATELIÊ CULINÁRIO

Map pp246-7 — Patisserie $

☎ 2239 2825; Rua Dias Ferreira 45, Leblon; desserts from US$4; ☽ 6pm-1am Mon-Fri, 1pm-1am Sat & Sun

This small café offers quiches, salads and empanadas, but it's the desserts that draw most people here. Dense cheesecake with guava sauce or moist chocolate mud cake are best enjoyed at the small tables out front, allowing premium views of the people parade filing past.

AZUL MARINHO Map pp246-7 — Seafood $$

☎ 3813 4228; Av Francisco Bhering, Praia do Arpoador, Ipanema; mains for 2 US$30-36; ☽ noon-midnight

Below the Hotel Arpoador, Azul Marinho serves an excellent range of seafood dishes, and the outdoor tables facing the ocean have the best beachside setting you'll find in the Zona Sul (there's no traffic between you and the sea, only sand). Try the *moqueca,* the shrimp in pumpkin sauce or the lobster filet with hearts of palm.

B! Map pp246-7 — Café $

☎ 2249 4977; Rua Visconde de Pirajá 572, Ipanema; salads US$8-12; ☽ 9am-midnight Mon-Sat, 1pm-midnight Sun

Located on the 2nd floor of the Ipanema branch of the Livraria da Travessa bookstore (p162), this stylish café makes a fine setting for a light lunch. Salads, quiches and chocolaty brownies are served by attentive – and good-looking – staff.

TOP FIVE EAT STREETS

- Rua Barão da Torre, Ipanema – This long, tree-lined street has stylish, time-tested favorites.
- Rua Dias Ferreira, Leblon – A great street for serious culinary browsing, it is packed with award-winning eateries and ever-daring newcomers.
- Rua Garcia D'Avila, Ipanema – One of Ipanema's poshest locales, this is a choice destination for a light meal after window-shopping. Neighboring Rua Aníbal de Mendonça is the runner-up.
- Rua Almirante Alexandrino, Santa Teresa – Perhaps Rio's most picturesque eat street, this one is lined with colorful restaurants offering sushi, pizza, Amazonian cuisine and everything in between.
- Rua Visconde de Caravelas, Botafogo – One of Botafogo's most tranquil streets, it has some decent eating options, and if nothing strikes your fancy, you can always walk one block north to the restaurant-packed Cobal do Humaitá.

BANANA JACK Map pp246-7 — Steak House $

☎ 2521 9055; Rua Jangadeiros 6, Ipanema; mains around US$8; ☽ noon-1am Sun-Thu, to 2am Fri & Sat

Aiming for the American roadhouse experience, Banana Jack lacks the battered pool table and the saucy waitstaff, but it does have thick burgers, juicy Red Angus steaks and plenty of fried fixings and its own microbrew to round out the meal.

BARRA BRASA Map pp246-7 — Churrascaria $$

☎ 2111 5700; Av Afrânio de Melo Franco 131, Leblon; per person US$18-27; ☽ noon-1am

One of Rio's top *churrascarrias,* Barra Brasa features nearly 30 different types of meat as well as sushi, seafood and salads. The beautifully presented all-you-can-eat buffet is set in a dining room with tall ceilings and elegant table settings.

BARRIL 1800 Map pp246-7 — Brazilian $

☎ 2523 0085; Av Vieira Souto 110, Ipanema; mains US$6-9; ☽ 11am-3am

Overlooking Ipanema beach, this open-sided restaurant is an informal place to grab a quick bite before hitting the surf. The good-value lunch buffet (US$8 per kilo) features the usual Brazilian favorites – fish, roasted meat, salad, fresh fruit – while at night Barril offers an à la carte menu.

BAZZAR Map pp246-7 — Eclectic $$

☎ 3202 2884; Rua Barão da Torre 538, Ipanema; mains US$12-18; ⏲ noon-midnight Mon-Thu, to 2am Fri & Sat, 10am-6pm Sun
Set on a peaceful, tree-lined street, this nicely designed restaurant serves a wide variety of cuisine, making it a good spot if you're not sure what you're in the mood for, but want something dazzling. Top choices are grilled *namorado* (a type of perch) with whole-grain rice, citrus and pesto, and lamb with polenta and mushrooms.

BIBI CREPES Map pp246-7 — Crêperie $

☎ 2259 4948; Rua Cupertino Durão 81, Leblon; crepes US$5-8; ⏲ noon-1am
This small, open-sided restaurant attracts a young, garrulous crowd who come to enjoy the more than two dozen sweet and savory crepes available. There are plenty of straight-forward options as well as creative choices like salmon with cream cheese. There are also decent salads – you choose up to 15 toppings. Come early to beat the lunchtime crowds. Bibi Crepes also has a branch in Copacabana (☎ 2513 6000; Rua Miguel Lemos 31).

BIBI SUCOS Map pp246-7 — Juice Bar $

☎ 2259 4298; Av Ataúlfo de Paiva 591, Leblon; juice US$2; ⏲ 9am-1am
Among Rio's countless juice bars, Bibi Sucos is a long-standing favorite. You'll find over 40 different varieties, and a never-ending supply of the favorite *açaí* (juice made from an Amazonian berry). Sandwiches will quell greater hunger pangs.

CAFÉ SEVERINO Map pp246-7 — Café $

☎ 2239 5294; Rua Dias Ferreira 417, Leblon; mains US$7-13; ⏲ 9am-midnight Mon-Sat, 10am-midnight Sun
In the back of the Argumento bookshop (p158), this charming café is a cozy place to hide away with a book or a new friend. In addition to coffees and lighter fare – sandwiches, salads and desserts – it's justly famed for its tasty crepes (try the salmon with Gruyère).

CAFEÍNA Map pp246-7 — Café $

☎ 2521 2194; Rua Farme de Amoedo 43, Ipanema; sandwiches US$4-7; ⏲ 8am-11:30pm
In the heart of Ipanema, this inviting café (and its sidewalk tables) is a fine spot for having a cup of java while watching the city stroll by. In addition to strong coffee and a lively mixed crowd, you'll find sand-wiches, salads and some very rich desserts.

CARLOTA Map pp246-7 — Eclectic $$

☎ 2540 6821; Rua Dias Ferreira 64, Leblon; mains US$18-25; ⏲ 7pm-midnight Tue-Fri, 1pm-midnight Sat & Sun
This award-winning restaurant has an intimate ambience that sits just right with the delicate cuisine. The small but ever-changing menu features elements from traditional Portuguese cooking (like the cod recipes) as well as Eastern influences (salmon sashimi, shiitake dishes). Regardless, inventive chef Carla Pernambuco always creates some memorable meals.

CARPACCIO & CIA Map pp246-7 — Seafood $

☎ 2511 4094; Rua Prudente de Moraes 1838, Ipanema; carpaccio US$9-13; ⏲ 5pm-2am Mon-Thu, to 3am Fri, noon-3am Sat & Sun
Those who like their meat on the rare side – extremely rare – should visit this late-night spot in Ipanema. Offering over 60 varities of tender, raw slices, Carpaccio & Cia has smoked salmon and octopus for more conservative palates. Its open-air patio is also enjoyed by those who simply want to drink. In addition to beer, sake and exotic caipirinhas with a twist (infused violets or berries) are top sellers here.

CASA DA FEIJOADA

Map pp246-7 — Feijoada $$
☎ 2247 2776; Rua Prudente de Moraes 10B, Ipanema; feijoada US$17; ⏲ noon-midnight
Admirers of Brazil's historic *feijoada* needn't wait until Saturday to experience the meaty meal. At this 15-year-old institution any day is fine to sample the rich black-bean and salted-pork dish. Served with the requisite orange slices, *farofa* and grated kale (cabbage), it goes nicely with a caipirinha.

CELEIRO Map pp246-7 — Salads $

☎ 2274 7843; Rua Dias Ferreira 199, Leblon; salads US$8-14; ⏲ 10am-5:30pm Mon-Sat
This casual spot on one of Leblon's main restaurant strips packs crowds during lunchtime. Celeiro is mostly famed for its salad bar, though the small eatery serves

excellent soups, pastries and quiches. Get there early to avoid the rush.

CHAIKA Map pp246-7
Fast Food $

☎ 2267 3838; Rua Visconde de Pirajá 321, Ipanema; lunch specials US$4; ☺ 9am-1am

One of Ipanema's classics, this popular, low-key restaurant features a stand-up bar in front for quickly devoured hamburgers, pastries and sodas. The sit-down restaurant in back offers a bigger menu – *panini,* salads and pancakes – and the staff'll still bring your selection to you in a hurry.

CHEZ PIERRE Map pp246-7
Eclectic $$

☎ 3687 2010; Rua Farme de Amoedo 34, Ipanema; mains from US$10; ☺ noon-midnight

On the ground floor of the Ipanema Plaza, this trim modern bistro serves tasty soups, salads, pastas, sandwiches and innovative hot plates (like shrimp-filled pastries). The front patio is a relaxing place to indulge.

CHOCOLATRAS Map pp246-7
Patisserie $

☎ 3204 4141; Av Ataúlfo de Paiva 1321, Leblon; ☺ noon-11:30pm

Chocolate lovers, take note. This small, homey café serves over a dozen desserts showcasing the dark, addictive element in one form or another. In addition to cakes, tarts, pies and brownies, Chocolatras serves *salgados* (bar snacks) and other refreshments for the chocolate-intolerant.

COLHER DE PAU Map pp246-7
Patisserie $

☎ 2274 8295; Rua Rita Ludolf 90, Leblon; desserts US$3-5; ☺ 10am-7:30pm

Cakes and pies are displayed in such a way that their magnetic powers exert a force that would be foolish to resist. The branch at Ipanema (☎ 2523 3018; Rua Farme de Amoedo 39) also serves quiches, salads and sandwiches and is worth investigating.

DA SILVA Map pp246-7
Portuguese $$

☎ 2521 1289; Rua Barão da Torre 340, Ipanema; plates US$10-20; ☺ 11:30am-2am

Da Silva puts on a fine buffet for those who want to sample excellent Portuguese cuisine without all the fussiness. Lamb stew, pork tenderloin and delicate desserts all make regular appearances at the lunchtime self-serve per-kilo buffet – and on the nightly à la carte menu.

TOP FIVE BRAZILIAN – DISH BY DISH

- Espirito Santa (p125) – Heavenly *tambaqui* (a large Amazonian fish) and other Amazonian cuisine – the best this side of the Rio Amazonas.
- Juice Co (p111) – Rio's best *suco* (juice), served without sugar.
- Petronius (p112) – Rio's best Saturday *feijoada.*
- Porção Rio's (p120) – The best *churrasco* (barbecued meat) with stunning views to match those juicy cuts.
- Yorubá (p119) – Serving delectable *moqueca* and Bahian cuisine fit for the gods.

DELÍRIO TROPICAL
Map pp246-7
Salads $

☎ 3201 2977; Rua Garcia D'Ávila 48, Ipanema; salads US$4-6; ☺ 8am-10pm Mon-Sat, to 9pm Sun

Famed for its salads, Delírio Tropical serves 16 varieties each day along with a few soups and hot dishes (veggie burgers, grilled salmon) if you're famished. The open layout has a pleasant, casual vibe and two stories, with big windows overlooking the street.

DOCE DELÍCIA Map pp246-7
Brazilian $$

☎ 2249 2970; Rua Dias Ferreira 48, Leblon; mains US$9-18; ☺ noon-11pm

Doce Delícia has a small but loyal following that is sold on the restaurant's innovative Eastern design concept. Restaurant goers create their own salads from over 40 ingredients on the menu. Feeling daring? Go for the pumpkin, jerked meat and leeks. The only limit is your imagination, *cara.* In Ipanema there's a second branch of Doce Delícia (☎ 2259 0239; Rua Aníbal de Mendonça 55, Ipanema; mains US$9-18; ☺ noon-11pm).

EMPÓRIO ARABE
Map pp246-7
Middle Eastern $

☎ 2512 7373; Av Ataúlfo de Paiva 370, Leblon; savory pies US$1-2; ☺ noon-8pm Mon-Sat

There are only a few tables inside this tiny restaurant in Leblon, but most people stop by just long enough to down a quick bite from the counter facing the sidewalk. Triangular pies filled with chicken, spinach or ricotta make for a quick bite on your way back from the beach.

Eating

IPANEMA & LEBLON

FELLINI Map pp246-7 — Self-serve $$

☎ 2511 3600; Rua General Urquiza 104, Leblon; per kg US$17; ⏱ 11:30am-4pm & 7:30pm-midnight

One of Leblon's top buffet restaurants, Fellini has an enticing selection of dishes: salads, pastas, grilled fish and shrimp, a sushi counter and the hallowed roast-meat counter. Fellini's modest dining room attracts a mix of hungry patrons – tourists, neighborhood folk and the beautiful crowd included (this is still Leblon, after all folks).

FONTES Map pp246-7 — Vegetarian $

☎ 2512 5900; Rua Visconde de Pirajá 605D, Ipanema; mains around US$5; ⏱ 11am-10pm Mon-Sat, noon-8pm Sun

Hidden in a nondescript shopping plaza, this tiny, low-key restaurant is worth seeking out if you're after a decent vegetarian meal. The menu changes daily but features shiitake-filled manioc pastries, green salads, roasted eggplant and the like. On Saturday, the rich, smoked-tofu *feijoada* always draws a crowd.

FRATELLI Map pp246-7 — Italian $

☎ 2259 6699; Av General San Martin 983, Leblon; mains US$9-15; ⏱ 6pm-2am Mon-Fri, noon until last customer Sat & Sun

On a quiet street in Leblon, Fratelli's large glass windows frame families and young couples enjoying a fine neighborhood restaurant. It's the food, however, that ought to be on display: creamy linguini with *langosta* (lobster), polenta with porcini and Brie and plump tortellini all pair nicely with Fratelli's decent wine selections.

GALANI Map pp246-7 — Italian $$

☎ 2525 2525; Av Vieira Souto 460, Ipanema; mains US$15-20; ⏱ 6:30am-6pm

Set on the 23rd floor of Ipanema's Caesar Park hotel (p174), Galani has handsome views of the beach and equally captivating cuisine, like the expertly prepared shrimp risotto. You can also catch an excellent breakfast here before an early flight.

GALETO DO LEBLON

Map pp246-7 — Brazilian $$

☎ 2294 3997; Rua Dias Ferreira 154, Leblon; mains US$12-17; ⏱ 11am-3am

One of the pioneers on this street, Galeto do Leblon has been around for over 35 years. Although a recent renovation has

---

TOP FIVE IPANEMA & LEBLON EATS

- Bazzar (p108)
- Carlota (p108)
- Gero (below)
- Sushi Leblon (p112)
- Zazá Bistrô Tropical (p113)

---

created an airy, modern feel, with glass windows around the outside, Galeto still serves the traditional Brazilian dishes that have made it such a neighborhood favorite over the years. On Saturdays, stop in for excellent *feijoada*.

GARCIA & RODRIGUES

Map pp246-7 — French $$

☎ 3206 4100; Av Ataúlfo de Paiva 1251, Leblon; mains US$15-24; ⏱ 8am-midnight Sun-Thu, to 1am Fri & Sat

Serving French food with a Brazilian accent (like roast veal à la Pantanal), Garcia & Rodrigues remains popular with Gallic expats in the city. Its two floors provide an elegant dining experience, though you can also sit in the café in front if you simply want a quick bite. Behind the glass counters surrounding the tiled floor, you'll find breads and cheeses, a good wine selection, homemade ice cream and good-looking desserts.

GERO Map pp246-7 — Italian $$

☎ 2239 8158; Rua Aníbal de Mendonça 157, Ipanema; mains US$16-28; ⏱ noon-4:30pm & 7pm-1am Mon-Fri, noon-2am Sat, to midnight Sun

Elegance is the spice of choice at this handsome Ipanema favorite on posh Aníbal de Mendonça. It's hard to go wrong with anything chef Rogerio Fasano puts his hand to, but favorites are tuna *tartare*, risottos, raviolis and fine desserts.

GULA GULA Map pp246-7 — Brazilian $

☎ 2259 3084; Rua Aníbal de Mendonça 132, Ipanema; mains US$9-18; ⏱ noon-midnight Sun-Thu, to 1am Fri & Sat

Founded over 20 years ago, Gula Gula still remains popular in Ipanema – which counts for a lot in a neighborhood ever in search of the new. Quiches and salads are tops at this casual spot, but those in search of heartier fare can opt for grilled meats or other Brazilian dishes. For dessert, the rich chocolate mousse doesn't disappoint. Order it *quente* (hot).

HORTIFRUTI Map pp246-7   Fruit Market
☎ 2512 6820; Rua Dias Ferreira 57, Leblon; ⏰ 8am-8pm Mon-Sat, to 2pm Sun
Leblon's popular indoor produce market features a wide variety of fruits and vegetables, as well as a small juice bar.

JUICE CO Map pp246-7   Eclectic $
☎ 2294 0048; Av General San Martín 889, Leblon; mains US$7-18; ⏰ noon-midnight
This stylish two-story restaurant serves much more than just tasty, freshly squeezed juices. In an überdesigned lounge-like setting, you can sample a wide range of fare – focaccia sandwiches, salads, risottos, grilled fish and roast meats, any of which can be paired nicely with one of 60 juice concoctions.

KILOGRAMA Map pp246-7   Self-serve $$
☎ 2512 8220; Rua Visconde de Pirajá 644, Ipanema; per kg US$14; ⏰ 11am-11pm Mon-Sat, to 7pm Sun
A mix of young and old converge on this excellent lunch buffet during the day. There's a vague art-modern glow to the place, giving it a splash of style – which is a rarity among *a quilo* (self-serve per-kilo) restaurants. Kilograma features lots of fresh fruits and salads, good cheeses, roast meats and sushi.

KURT Map pp246-7   Patisserie $
☎ 2294 0599; Rua General Urquiza 117B, Leblon; pastries US$2-5; ⏰ 8am-6pm Mon-Fri, to 5pm Sat
Entering a true patisserie should delight all of your senses, and Kurt does just that. The flaky strudels and palm-sized tortes with strawberries and kiwifruit lie illuminated behind the glass counter. The smell of cappuccino hangs in the air as classical music plays overhead. A few round tables then set the stage for the most rewarding sensory experience: tasting these delicate cakes and pastries.

L'ASSIETTE Map pp246-7   French $
☎ 2227 1477; Rua Visconde de Pirajá 18, Ipanema; mains around US$7; ⏰ noon-9pm
This cute bistro just off the beaten path has a small menu of French specialties, and

the three-course meals are good value for US$9. Popular dishes are crepes, smoked salmon on baguettes and salad *niçoise*. Wines are available by the glass.

MIL FRUTAS Map pp246-7   Ice Cream $
☎ 2521 1384; Rua Garcia D'Avila 134A, Ipanema; ice cream US$3-4; ⏰ 10:30am-1am Mon-Fri, 9:30am-1am Sat & Sun
On chic Rua Garcia D'Avila (next door to Rio's only Louis Vuitton store), Mil Frutas serves tasty ice cream that showcases fruits from the Amazon and abroad. *Jaca* (jackfruit), lychee and *açaí* are among the several dozen varieties – all of which are best enjoyed on the tiny shade-covered patio out front.

MUSTAFÁ Map pp246-7   Middle Eastern $
☎ 2540 7299; Av Ataúlfo de Paiva 1174, Leblon; hummus US$2-4; ⏰ noon-8pm Mon-Sat, to 7pm Sun
It's easy to walk right by this small takeout counter in Leblon, but if you have a craving for fresh pita bread, tabbouleh, hummus or kibbe, that would be a serious mistake. In business for over 33 years, Mustafá is a favorite among Leblon residents.

Ice cream delights at Mil Frutas (above)

NAM THAI Map pp246-7 — Thai $$

☎ 2259 2962; Rua Rainha Guilhermina 95B, Leblon; mains US$11-19; ☽ 7pm-1am Mon, 11:30am-4pm & 7pm-1am Tue-Fri, noon-1am Sat, to 11pm Sun,
Thai cuisine is a rarity in Rio, which makes charming Nam Thai even more of a star. The French colonial interior is a cozy setting for the eclectic Thai cooking. Favorites are squid salad and spicy shrimp curry with pineapple. No less intoxicating are Nam Thai's tropical drinks, like the *caipivodca de lychee* (lychee vodka caipirinha).

NEW NATURAL Map pp246-7 — Vegetarian $

☎ 2287 0301; Rua Barão da Torre 167, Ipanema; lunch specials US$6; ☽ 7am-11pm
Featuring an excellent vegetarian lunch buffet, New Natural was the first health-food restaurant in the neighborhood. Fill up on fresh pots of soup, rice, veggies and beans for less than US$7.

NIK SUSHI Map pp246-7 — Japanese $$

☎ 2512 6446; Rua Garcia D'Ávila 83, Ipanema; meals US$10-17; ☽ 11:30am-midnight Tue-Sat, 1-11pm Sun
This simple but stylish Japanese restaurant has earned many loyal customers for its decent prices and delicately prepared dishes. Grilled items are available but are not as popular as the sushi – owing largely to the all-you-can-eat sushi lunches (US$12) and dinners (US$16).

OSTERIA DELL'ANGOLO

Map pp246-7 — Italian $$
☎ 2259 3148; Rua Paul Redfern 40, Ipanema; mains US$16-22; ☽ noon-4pm & 6pm until last customer Mon-Fri, 6pm until last customer Sat & Sun
Northern Italian cuisine is prepared and served with consummate skill. You'd be hard pressed to find fault with fresh pastas, seafood, and much-lauded risottos – the squid risotto in ink sauce in particular. President Lula, among other notable visitors, once dined in the elegant but understated Osteria.

PETRONIUS Map pp246-7 — Feijoada $$$

☎ 2525 2525; Av Vieira Souto 460, Ipanema; feijoada buffet US$40; ☽ 6:30am-6pm
Rio's best *feijoada* is served at this pleasant restaurant overlooking the beach on the 2nd floor of the Caesar Park hotel. The rich cuisine is expertly prepared, without a lot of extra fat, and you can sample nearly a dozen varieties of pork dishes. A live samba band lends a festive atmosphere to the feasting.

PLATAFORMA Map pp246-7 — Churrascaria $$

☎ 2274 4022; Rua Adalberto Ferreira 32, Leblon; mains US$15-25; ☽ noon until last customer
This restored *churrascaria* still draws a garrulous mix of politicians, artists and tourists. Dark, mellow woods in the dining room match the tones of the roast meats traveling from table to table. Also in this complex is the Bar do Tom (p137), with live bossa nova, and downstairs is the Plataforma Show – the over-the-top Carnaval show for tourists.

POLIS SUCOS Map pp246-7 — Juice Bar $

☎ 2247 2518; Rua Maria Quitéria 70, Ipanema; juices US$1.50-3; ☽ 7am-midnight
One of Ipanema's favorite spots for a dose of fresh-squeezed vitamins, this juice bar facing the Praça Nossa Senhora (NS) de Paz has dozens of flavors, and you can pair those tangy beverages with sandwiches or *pão de queijo* (cheese-filled rolls).

QUADRUCCI Map pp246-7 — Italian $$

☎ 2249 2301; Rua Dias Ferreira 233, Leblon; mains US$15-24; ☽ noon-1am Mon-Sat, to 7pm Sun
Boasting a charming wooden patio, this Italian restaurant serves decent plates in a handsome but low-key setting. Start off with a tuna seviche before moving on to tagliatelli with lamb and artichoke sauce or tortellini with basil pesto. Strudels and tortes finish off the proceedings nicely.

QUITANDA VEGETAL

Map pp246-7 — Vegetarian $$
☎ 2249 2301; Rua Dias Ferreira 135, Leblon; mains around US$11; ☽ noon-6pm Mon-Sat
This simple vegetarian eatery serves light and healthy meals, including salads, sandwiches and soups. After dining on the patio in front, you can have a browse inside the tiny adjoining health-food store.

SUSHI LEBLON Map pp246-7 — Japanese $$

☎ 2512 7830; Rua Dias Ferreira 256, Leblon; mains US$18; ☽ noon-4pm & 7pm-1:30am Mon-Sat, 1:30pm-midnight Sun
Leblon's top sushi destination boasts a zen-like ambience with a handsome, darkwood

sushi counter setting the stage for succulent cuisine. In addition to sashimi and sushi, you'll find grilled *namorada* (white fish) with passionfruit *farofa*, sea-urchin seviche and refreshing sake to complement the meal.

TALHO CAPIXABA

Map pp246-7   Sandwiches $

☎ 2512 8760; Av Ataúlfo de Paiva 1022, Leblon; mains US$8-16; ⏰ 7am-9pm Mon-Sat, 8am-8pm Sun
This tiny deli and grocery store is one of the city's best spots to put together a takeout meal. In addition to pastas, salads and antipastos, you'll find some of the city's best sandwiches. At weekends, to accommodate the crowds, Talho Capixaba puts a few tables out on the sidewalk for customers to enjoy the tasty bites alfresco.

VEGETARIANO SOCIAL CLUB

Map pp246-7   Vegetarian $

☎ 2294 5200; Rua Conde Bernadotte 26L, Leblon; mains around US$8; ⏰ noon-5:30pm
Vegetarians interested in sampling Brazil's signature dish should visit this inviting spot on Saturday when tofu *feijoada* is served. The small menu changes regularly, and features salads, soups and *sucos* (juices), like rose-petal juice or guarana with mint and ginger. The café also serves organic wine.

VIA SETE Map pp246-7   Eclectic $$

☎ 2512 8100; Rua Garcia D'Ávila 125, Ipanema; mains US$8-15; ⏰ noon-midnight
This restaurant on upscale Garcia D'Ávila serves a good selection of salads and sandwich wraps, as well as heartier fare like grilled tuna steak and a high-end cheeseburger (covered with mushrooms, thyme and a red-wine sauce). The pleasant front-side patio is a prime spot for sipping smooth tropical cocktails while practicing the discreet art of people-watching.

ZAZÁ BISTRÔ TROPICAL

Map pp246-7   French-Thai $$

☎ 2247 9101; Rua Joana Angélica 40, Ipanema; mains US$14-22; ⏰ 7:30pm-midnight Sun-Wed, to 1:30am Fri & Sat
French-colonial decor and delicately spiced cuisine await those venturing inside this charming converted house in Ipanema. Inventive combinations like pumpkin-and-chestnut risotto or sesame-battered tuna

with wasabi cream enhance the seductive mood inside. Upstairs, diners lounge on throw pillows, while candles glow along the walls. You can also dine on the porch out front – everything here is organic.

ZONA SUL SUPERMARKET

Map pp246-7   Supermarket $

☎ 2259 4699; Rua Dias Ferreira 290, Leblon; ⏰ 24hr 7am Mon-midnight Sun
A Rio institution for 44 years, Zona Sul supermarket has branches all over the city. The one in Leblon is the best of the bunch, with fresh-baked breads, imported cheeses, olives, French Bordeaux, prosciutto and many other delicacies.

ZUKA Map pp246-7   Eclectic $$

☎ 3205 7154; Rua Dias Ferreira 233, Leblon; mains US$13-22; ⏰ 7pm-1:30am Mon, noon-4pm & 7pm-1:30am Tue-Fri, 1:30pm-1:30am Sat & Sun
This trendy spot continues to draw crowds with its ever-inventive dishes. Tuna foie gras in thyme or the smoked duck with caramelized pineapple are excellent, though you'll want dessert – skewers of fruit in sake or chocolate soufflé.

GÁVEA, JARDIM BOTÂNICO & LAGOA

The backdrop to some of Rio's most charming dining rooms is the placid surface of Lagoa Rodrigo de Freitas. On warm nights at the small open-air restaurants perched along the lake, live music fills the air as diners eat, drink and stroll along the lakeshore path. The hotspots for cuisine and live music are the Parque dos Patins on the west side and Parque do Cantagalo on the east side.

Gávea's top culinary spot is around Praça Santos Dumont, while Jardim Botânico's thickest concentration of eateries is on Rua JJ Seabra and Rua Pacheco Leão.

00 (ZERO ZERO) Map pp246-7   Brazilian $$

☎ 2540 8041; Planetário da Gávea, Av Padre Leonel Franca 240, Gávea; mains from US$13; ⏰ 8pm until late
Housed in Gávea's planetarium, 00 is a sleek restaurant-lounge that serves Brazilian cuisine with Asian and Mediterranean overtones. Jerked beef and leek-tapioca rolls or

filet mignon with puree of *arracacha* (a root vegetable that is something of a cross between carrot and celery) are best enjoyed on the open-air veranda. After dinner, have a few cocktails and stick around: some of Rio's best DJs spin at parties here (p143).

ARAB DA LAGOA

Map pp246-7   Middle Eastern $$

☎ 2540 0747; Parque dos Patins, Av Borges de Medeiros, Lagoa; platter for 2 US$22; ◷ 10am-1am Sun-Thu, to 2:30am Fri & Sat

One of the lake's most popular outdoor restaurants, serving traditional Middle Eastern specialties like hummus, baba ghanoush, tabbouleh, kibbe and tasty thin-crust pizzas. The large platters for two or more are good for sampling the tasty varieties. During the day, it's a peaceful refuge from the city, while at night you can hear live samba, *choro* (romantic, intimate samba) or jazz from 9pm (cover charge US$2).

BOTECO 66 Map pp246-7   French $$

☎ 2266 0838; Av Alexandre Ferreira 66, Lagoa; mains US$15-26; ◷ noon-midnight

A small outdoor garden lends a rustic air to this French bistro, which is run by the same chef that owns Olympe. A couples' favorite, the vibe always remains casual. Good choices include filet mignon with gorgonzola and potato *galette* (thick pancake).

BRASEIRO DA GÁVEA

Map pp246-7   Brazilian $

☎ 2239 7494; Praça Santos Dumont 116, Gávea; plates US$6-12; ◷ 11am-1am Mon-Thu, to 3am Fri & Sat

This family-style eatery serves up large portions of its popular steak with *farofa,* pot roast or fried chicken. On weekends, the open-air spot fills with the din of conversation and the aroma of fresh *chope* (draft beer) drifting by. A younger crowd takes over at night and into the early morning.

DOM JOÃO Map pp246-7   Eclectic $$$

☎ 3874 2819; Rua Pacheco Leão 836, Jardim Botânico; mains US$15-25; ◷ 7:30pm-1:30am Mon-Wed, to 2:30am Thu-Sat, noon-5:30pm Sun

Overlooking the Botanical Gardens, this stately restaurant serves excellent fusion cuisine in a lovely 19th-century building. On the 1st floor, you'll find a casual patio

and a bar serving lighter fare, while upstairs you'll be greeted with elegant table service and lovely park views. A changing menu features delightful combinations, including risotto, grilled fish, steak and delectable appetizers.

GUIMAS Map pp246-7   Eclectic $$

☎ 2259 7996; Rua José Roberto Macedo Soares 5, Gávea; mains US$14-25; ◷ noon-1am

A classic Carioca *boteco* with a creative flair, Guimas has been going strong for almost 20 years. Trout with leeks or the honey-roast duck with pear rice go nicely with the superfine *caipivodcas* (caipirinhas made with vodka instead of *cachaça*). The small but cozy open-air restaurant attracts a more colorful mix of diners as the night progresses.

MISS TANAKA Map pp246-7   Japanese $$

☎ 3205 7322; Rua Pacheco Leão 758, Jardim Botânico; mains US$11-19; ◷ 6pm-midnight Mon-Thu, to 2am Fri, noon-2am Sat, to midnight Sun

This charming Japanese restaurant wows diners with the warm welcome, the cozy ambience and the outstanding dishes. You'll find not only exquisite sushi rolls and sashimi, but creative dishes like spicy shrimp-and-coconut croquettes, grilled crayfish with sweetened soy and *acarajapa* (fried bean cake with various fruit curries).

OLYMPE Map pp246-7   Eclectic $$$

☎ 2539 4542; Rua Custódio Serrão 62, Lagoa; mains US$26-31; ◷ 7:30pm-midnight Mon-Thu & Sat, noon-4pm & 7pm-midnight Fri

One of Rio's best chefs, Claude Troisgros continues to dazzle guests with unforgettable meals at his award-winning restaurant. Originally from France, Troisgros mixes the old-world with the new in dishes like heart-of-palm salad with fresh octopus and red snapper covered with foie gras and asparagus tempura. The setting is in a lovely house on a quiet tree-lined street.

QUADRIFOGLIO Map pp246-7 Italian $$

☎ 2294 1433; Rua JJ Seabra 19, Jardim Botânico; plates US$12-20; ✆ noon-3:30pm & 7:30pm-midnight Mon-Thu, noon-3:30pm & 7:30pm-1am Fri, 7:30pm-1am Sat, noon-5pm Sun

A charming Italian spot famed for exotic raviolis like its *ravioli de maça ao creme e semente de papoula* (apple ravioli with cream-and-poppy-seed sauce), Quadrifoglio has long been a neighborhood favorite – ever since it opened.

SUSHINAKA LIGHT

Map pp246-7 Japanese $$

☎ 2247 9479; Facing Av Epitácio Pessoa 3330, Parque do Cantagalo, Lagoa; mains from US$13; ✆ noon-1am

On the east shore of the lake, this outdoor sushi spot is one of several relaxed restaurants where you can enjoy a meal alfresco. Traditional sushi and sashimi fill the menu along with teriyaki salmon and a few other hot plates.

COPACABANA & LEME

Copacabana has many culinary gems, from venerable five-star institutions atop stunning beachfront hotels to charming old bistros dating from the mid-20th century. In general, you will encounter less culinary experimentation here, but if you're looking for excellent traditional cuisine – both Brazilian and international – you will find plenty of delectable options in Copacabana.

Dozens of restaurants line Av Atlântica, offering sweeping views across the curving shoreline. Unfortunately, the panorama is much better than the food on this strip – with a few exceptions of course. Things get seedy here at night, and if you're looking for an escort, you're in the right spot. If you're looking for good cuisine, however, go elsewhere. The narrow roads crisscrossing Av NS de Copacabana all the way from Leme to Arpoador contain many fine establishments – and many mediocre ones. Do some exploring, trust your instincts and *bom proveito* (happy eating).

TOP FIVE COPACABANA & LEME EATS

- Amir (below)
- Copa Café (p116)
- La Trattoria (p117)
- Le Pré Catalan (p117)
- Marius Crustáceos (p117)

AMIR Map pp244-5 Middle Eastern $$

☎ 2275 5596; Rua Ronald de Carvalho 55C, Copacabana; mains US$10-14; ✆ noon-11pm Sun-Thu, to midnight Fri & Sat

A cozy air pervades this small, casual restaurant near the beach. As you step inside, you'll notice the handsomely dressed waiters in embroidered vests, and heavenly aromas wafting from the kitchen. Delicious platters – hummus, *kaftas* (spiced meat patty), falafel, kibbe and salads – are the best way to experience Amir's riches.

AZUMI Map pp244-5 Japanese $$

☎ 2541 4294; Rua Ministro Viveiros de Castro 127, Copacabana; plates US$10-20; ✆ 7pm-midnight Tue-Thu & Sun, to 1am Fri & Sat

Some claim Azumi is the bastion of traditional Japanese cuisine in the city. This laid-back sushi bar certainly has its fans – both in the nisei community and from abroad. Azumi's *sushiman* (sushi chef) masterfully prepares delectable sushi and sashimi, though tempuras and soups are also excellent. Be sure to ask what's in season.

BAKERS Map pp244-5 Patisserie $

☎ 3209 1212; Rua Santa Clara 86B, Copacabana; sandwiches US$3-6; ✆ 9am-8pm

One of the best places for flaky croissants, banana Danishes, strudels and other fresh-baked treats. There are also deli sandwiches (try the turkey breast and provolone).

CAFÉ FLEURI Map pp244-5 Eclectic $$$

☎ 3873 8881; Le Meridien, Av Atlântica 1020, Copacabana; lunch buffet US$23-32; ✆ noon-3:30pm & 7-11pm Mon-Fri, 12:30-5pm & 7-11pm Sat & Sun

Excellent cuisine in a more casual setting than its big brother upstairs (Le Saint Honoré; p117). Amid a dining room with a vaguely country-kitchen air, Fleuri's chefs put on elegant lunch buffets. Cuisines vary: Spanish

(Monday), French (Tuesday), Italian (Wednesday), Asian (Thursday), Bahian (Friday), *feijoada* (Saturday) and brunch (Sunday).

CARRETÃO Map pp244-5 Churrascaria $$
☎ 2542 2148; Rua Ronald de Carvalho 55, Leme; all-you-can-eat US$12; ☯ 11:30am-midnight
It's all about the meat at this decent but inexpensive *churrascaria* in Leme. With several branches throughout the city, including an Ipanema **Carretão** (☎ 2267 3965; Rua Visconde de Pirajá 112), this popular chain serves up consistently good cuts – and heaps of them. There's also a small salad bar, and you can order sides from the menu at no added charge.

CERVANTES Map pp244-5 Brazilian $
☎ 2275 6147; Av Prado Júnior 335B, Copacabana; sandwiches US$5-8; ☯ noon-4am Tue-Thu, to 5am Fri & Sat, to 3am Sun
A Copacabana institution, the late-night Cervantes gathers a broad mix of Cariocas who come to feast on Cervantes' trademark meat-and-pineapple sandwiches. Its waiters are famed for their fussiness, along with their quickness to the tap when your *chope* runneth dry. Around the corner (Rua Barato Ribeiro 7), Cervantes' stand-up *boteco* serves up tasty bites in a hurry.

CIPRIANI Map pp244-5 Italian $$$
☎ 2545 8747; Copacabana Palace Hotel, Av Atlântica 1702, Copacabana; mains US$25-35; ☯ 12:30-3pm & 7pm-1am Mon-Sat, 12:30-4pm & 7pm-1am Sun
On a candlelit patio beside the Palace's pool, Cipriani serves fine northern Italian cuisine to a well-dressed, largely non-Brazilian crowd. Signature dishes such as the gnocchi, the sirloin with port sauce, and the smoked scallops all meet their mark. For dessert, tiramisu and chocolate mousse are both good options. The dress code is once again in force, so leave your Havaianas at home.

CONFEITARIA COLOMBO
Map pp244-5 Café $
☎ 3201 4049; Forte de Copacabana, Praça Coronel Eugênio Franco, Copacabana; mains US$6-13; ☯ 10am-8pm Tue-Sun
Far removed from the hustle and bustle of Av Atlântica, this handsome café offers truly magnificent views of Copacabana beach. At the outdoor tables, you can sit beneath shady palm trees, enjoying cappuccino, salads, quiche or crepes as young soldiers from the fort file past. To get there, you'll have to pay admission (US$1) to the **Forte de Copacabana** (Copacabana fort; p66), but it's well worth the price. There's also a Confeitaria Colombo worth a visit in Centro (p123).

COPA CAFÉ Map pp244-5 Eclectic $$
☎ 2235 2947; Av Atlântica 3056, Copacabana; mains US$9-18; ☯ 7pm-2am Tue-Sun
This stylish new two-story restaurant facing Copacabana beach brings some much-needed life to the aging restaurant strip along Av Atlântica. The black wood floors, white bar stools, trim open layout and ambient electronic music make a nice setting for fresh fish, steak and high-end burgers.

DON CAMILLO Map pp244-5 Italian $$
☎ 2225 5126; Av Atlântica 3056, Copacabana; mains US$10-18; ☯ noon-2am
The wandering street musicians and carnavalesque street parade lend a festive air to this beachfront Italian spot. Pastas are flavorful, and hearty seafood dishes won't disappoint. With many desserts to choose from, you may have a tough time deciding how to finish that meal.

KILOGRAMA Map pp244-5 Self-serve $$
☎ 3202 9050; Av Nossa Senhora de Copacabana 1144, Copacabana; per kg US$14; ☯ noon-10pm Mon-Sat, noon-7pm Sun
One of Rio's most reliable per-kilo chains recently opened a convenient Copacabana branch; it's a decent option for a satisfying meal without the wait. While the ambience is lacking in this massive dining room, you'll find a good selection of salads, meats, seafood and desserts.

LA FIORENTINA Map pp244-5 Italian $$
☎ 2543 8465; Av Atlântica 458A, Leme; mains US$15-22; ☯ noon-2am
One of Leme's classic Italian restaurants, La Fiorentina attracted Rio's glitterati in the '60s. Today, its beach-facing outdoor tables draw a loyal, mostly neighborhood crowd, who come to feast on the delectable dishes. In addition to delicate pizzas, La Fiorentina serves an excellent shrimp risotto.

LA TRATTORIA Map pp244-5 Italian $

☎ 2255 3319; Rua Fernando Mendes 7A,
Copacabana; mains US$8-18; ⏰ noon-1am
Old photos, simple furnishings, hearty
dishes and the constant din of conversation
have made this trattoria a neighborhood
favorite for almost 30 years. Shrimp dishes
are the Italian family's specialty – they've
won over many diners with their *espaguete
com camarão e óleo tartufado* (spaghetti
with shrimp and truffle oil).

LE BLÉ NOIR Map pp244-5 Crêperie $

☎ 2287 1272; Rua Xavier da Silveira 15A,
Copacabana; mains US$8-12; ⏰ 7pm-1am Wed-Thu
& Sun, to 2am Fri & Sat
Flickering candles and subdued conversation make this restaurant a real date-pleaser.
Le Blé Noir offers over 50 different varieties
of crepe, and pairs rich ingredients like
shrimp and artichoke hearts or Brie, honey
and toasted almonds. Call for a reservation
or wait and enjoy a cocktail on the patio.

LE PRÉ CATALAN

Map pp244-5 French $$$
☎ 2525 1232; Level E, Sofitel Rio de Janeiro, Av
Atlântica 4240, Copacabana; mains from US$30;
⏰ 7:30-11pm Mon-Sat
Neck-and-neck with Le Saint Honoré, Le
Pré Catalan is often rated Rio's best French
restaurant. The art-deco dining room sets the
stage for chef Roland Villard's award-winning
dishes with a tropical infusion.

LE SAINT HONORÉ

Map pp244-5 French $$$
☎ 3873 8888; 37th fl, Le Meridien, Av Atlântica
1020, Copacabana; mains US$22-35; ⏰ 7:30pm-
1am Mon-Sat
In a lavish dining room overlooking the
coast, Le Saint Honoré does its best to
dazzle you with culinary pyrotechnics. Chef

TOP FIVE – INTERNATIONAL CUISINES

- Amir (p115) – Best Middle Eastern
- Antiquarius (p106) – Best Portuguese
- Gero (p110) – Best Italian
- Miss Tanaka (p114) – Best Japanese
- Olympe (p114) – Best French

Dominique Oudin prepares delicate slices
of heaven – scallop carpaccio, caramelized
roast duck – while his *sous chef* delivers the
coup de grâce with hot raspberry soufflé.
Given the decadent display of food that will
arrive at your table, you will have to dress
accordingly: jacket and tie are required.

LOPE'S CONFEITARIA

Map pp244-5 Brazilian $
Av NS de Copacabana 1334, Copacabana; lunch
plates US$5; ⏰ 7am-midnight
Lope's is like a vision of 1950s Rio – chicken
roasting on the sidewalk out front, aged
black-and-white photos along the walls,
simple tables scattered around the large,
elliptical lunch counter. A noisy lunch
crowd still fills the chairs, with no-nonsense
service hurrying them along. The food
hasn't changed much over the years –
portions are large, grease is plentiful and
the dessert shop lies just next door.

LUCAS Map pp244-5 German $

☎ 2521 4705; Av Atlântica 3744, Copacabana;
mains US$8-13; ⏰ 10am-2am
Classic German cooking with a view of the
beach? We're clearly not in Regensburg,
but the *kassler* (pork loin), frankfurters and
strudel might as well have been made in
the old country. A handful of Cariocas and
many tourists frequent this indoor-outdoor
restaurant.

MARIUS CARNES

Map pp244-5 Churrascaria $$$
☎ 2104 9002; Av Atlântica 290B, Leme; per person
US$39; ⏰ noon-midnight
In addition to the wide array of roast meats
carried from table to table, this Leme
churrascaria features a lavish buffet table.
Oysters in the half shell, sushi and grilled
vegetables with herbs all seem too lovely
to eat. But somehow the garrulous crowd
overcome their aesthetic inhibitions, and
get down to serious eating.

MARIUS CRUSTÁCEOS

Map pp244-5 Seafood $$$
☎ 2104 9002; Av Atlântica 290A, Leme; per person
US$57; ⏰ noon-midnight
Although the price of Marius' all-you-can-
eat seafood buffet has reached astronomi-
cal heights, that hasn't stopped diners from

packing the restaurant most nights of the week. Aquatic decoration and many shades of blue create a 20,000-leagues-under-the-sea-like ambience – matched by an astonishing array of mouth-watering seafood. If you have a weakness for tuna, lobster, scallops and the like, this is the place to indulge.

PEIXE VIVO Map pp244-5 — Seafood $$
☎ 2255 9225; Rua Tonelero 76, Copacabana; mains US$13-20; ☽ noon-midnight
This old-fashioned restaurant may not have the flash of other places, but the seafood here is reliably decent. Among the top picks are stuffed crab, codfish cakes, and *bobó de camarão* (manioc, coconut milk and dried shrimp stew).

SERAFINA Map pp244-5 — Italian $
☎ 2256 5565; Rua Figueiredo de Magalhães 28, Copacabana; mains US$6-10; ☽ 8am-11pm Tue-Thu, to 1am Fri & Sat, to 9pm Sun
A few paintings adorn the walls of this cheerful eatery just off the beach. Here the decor matches the cooking: simple but successful. Grilled fish, risottos, pastas and lighter fare like sandwiches draw a largely local crowd.

SHIRLEY Map pp244-5 — Spanish $
☎ 2275 1398; Rua Gustavo Sampaio 610, Leme; mains US$9-18; ☽ 11am-12:30am
The aroma of succulent paella hangs in the air as waiters hurry to and from the kitchen, bearing platefuls of fresh seafood. Some critics say Shirley isn't what it used to be, but crowds still pack this simple Leme restaurant on weekends (making reservations advisable). In addition to paella, the mussel-vinaigrette appetizer or the octopus and squid in ink are also recommended. One dish easily serves two.

SIRI MOLE & CIA Map pp244-5 — Brazilian $$
☎ 2267 0894; Rua Francisco Otaviano 50, Copacabana; mains US$14-21; ☽ 7pm until last customer Mon, noon until last customer Tue-Sun
Understated elegance is the key to Siri Mole & Cia's longstanding success – both in ambience and in the perfectly prepared seafood. Among the favorites are *moqueca de siri mole* (spicy, soft-shell-crab stew), *acarajé* (mussels in broth) and the grilled fish.

TEMPERARTE Map pp244-5 — Self-serve $
☎ 2267 1149; Av NS de Copacabana 266, Copacabana; plates US$6-13; ☽ 11am-2:30pm Mon-Sat
One of the neighborhood's best pay-by-weight restaurants, the casual Temperarte has a good selection of salads, roast meats, vegetables and sushi, as well as ample dessert offerings.

TRAITEURS DE FRANCE
Map pp244-5 — French $$
☎ 2548 6440; Av NS de Copacabana 386B, Copacabana; mains US$10-14; ☽ 10am-7pm Mon-Thu, to 11pm Fri & Sat
Step into this pleasant café and restaurant for an escape from the busy traffic. In front, you'll find a variety of tempting baked goods, perfect for a quick takeout for the beach, while the restaurant in back offers salmon crepes, quiches, and grilled meats. Opt for the three-course special for US$12.

YONZA Map pp244-5 — Crêperie $
☎ 2521 4248; Rua Miguel Lemos 21B, Copacabana; crepes US$4-7; ☽ 10am-midnight Tue-Fri, 6pm-midnight Sat & Sun
Surfboards and Japanese anime superhero posters create the ambience at this *crêperie* in an otherwise empty stretch of Copacabana. A young crowd flocks here at night to fill up on hearty platefuls of crepes. The simple *quejo e tomate* (cheese and tomato) does just fine.

BOTAFOGO & URCA

Botafogo has a sparse selection of restaurants, and Urca, untouched by commercial development, has even fewer. Diners looking for something off the beaten path shouldn't overlook these areas. Splendid offerings await – great views, live music, or simply that inexplicable allure of finding that splendid but largely undiscovered place.

ADEGA DO VALENTIM
Map pp242-3 — Portuguese $$
☎ 2541 1166; Rua da Passagem 178, Botafogo; mains US$12-19; ☽ noon-1am
Bacalhau (cod) in 12 ways is the specialty at this old-fashioned Portuguese restaurant. Jocular old waiters also serve other favorites: baked rabbit, roast suckling pig, octopus, the list goes on…

Eating

BOTAFOGO & URCA

BAR URCA
Map pp242-3   Brazilian $

☎ 2295 8744; Rua Cândido Gaffré 205, Urca; lunch specials US$5-10; ⊙ 11am-5pm

This upstairs spot has a nice view of the bay along with a fresh sea breeze to cool things off. The food is a straightforward affair: *bobó de camarão* (shrimp-and-coconut stew), grilled fish and squid aren't winning any culinary awards, but they're reliably decent.

CARÊME BISTRÔ
Map pp242-3   French $$

☎ 2537 2274; Rua Visconde de Caravelas 113, Botafogo; mains US$15-25; ⊙ 8pm until last customer Tue-Sat

This French bistro does everything right to make sure its fans keeps coming back. In an intimate but unpretentious space, attentive waiters bring plates of marinated snapper, braised rabbit, and apple-and-nut risotto (among other vegetarian offerings). Don't neglect the small but excellent wine list.

EMPORIUM PAX
Map pp242-3   Brazilian $

☎ 2559 9713; 7th fl, Praia de Botafogo 400, Botafogo; mains US$8-14; ⊙ noon-midnight

One of many eateries at Botafogo Praia Shopping (p166), Emporium Pax is a statelier affair than the adjoining food court and offers spectacular views of Pão de Açúcar and Baía de Guanabara. As well as salads, pastas and tasty desserts, the lunch bufet draws in the shopping and film-goers.

GAROTA DA URCA
Map pp242-3   Brazilian $

☎ 2541 8585; Rua João Luís Alves 56, Urca; mains from US$8; ⊙ 11am until last customer

Overlooking the small Praia da Urca, this neighborhood restaurant serves standard Brazilian fare at decent prices. The weekday lunch specials are good value, and you can enjoy views over the bay from the open-air veranda. By night, a more garrulous crowd meets here for steak and *chope*.

KOTOBUKI
Map pp242-3   Japanese $$

☎ 2550 9713; 7th fl, Praia de Botafogo 400, Botafogo; mains US$12-20; ⊙ noon-midnight

On the 7th floor of Botafogo Praia Shopping, Kotobuki serves fresh sushi in an elegantly set dining room. Although this is inside a mall, the fabulous view of Pão de Açúcar is far from pedestrian.

LIVRARIA PREFÁCIO
Map pp242-3   Café $

☎ 2527 5699; Rua Voluntários da Pátria 39, Botafogo; sandwiches US$4-7; ⊙ 10am-10pm Mon-Fri, 2-10pm Sat & Sun

In the back of the small arts-oriented bookshop of the same name, this café, with its exposed brick walls and atmospheric lighting, makes the perfect hideaway on those rare rainy days. The menu features *bruschetta* (crusty bread with tomato and basil), salads, sandwiches – vegetarian, *croque monsieur* (toasted ham-and-cheese sandwich) – and desserts, and the café fills with diners killing time before catching a film at the cinema next door. The café hosts occasional book signings and art openings.

PIZZA PARK
Map pp242-3   Pizza $

☎ 2537 2602; Cobal do Humaitá, Rua Voluntários da Pátria 446, Botafogo; pizzas US$8-16; ⊙ noon-1am

One of many restaurants inside the market, the very low-key Pizza Park serves over 25 different varieties of tasty thin-crust pizzas. Expect a lively crowd to descend on this and neighboring spots most nights, with live music never far away – like at **Espirito do Chopp** (p134).

STRAVAGANZE
Map pp242-3   Pizza $$

☎ 2535 0591; Rua Visconde de Caravelas 121, Botafogo; pizzas US$12-17; ⊙ 6pm-midnight

This small, elegant restaurant serves piping-hot pizzas cooked in a wood-burning oven. Fresh ingredients and excellent variety along with attentive service make this one of Rio's top pizza picks.

YORUBÁ
Map pp242-3   Bahian $$

☎ 2541 9387; Rua Arnaldo Quintela 94, Botafogo; mains for 2 US$35; ⊙ 7-11pm Wed-Fri, 2-10pm Sat, noon-6pm Sun

Yorubá looks as if it's always prepared for the imminent arrival of an *orixá* (spirit or deity). Leaves lie scattered across the floor as candle flames flicker on the walls. Young waiters in red aprons stand at attention while something mystical transpires in the kitchen. Plates here are simply heavenly: plump shrimp and rich coconut milk blend to perfection in *bobó de camarão,* and the *moqueca* is simply outstanding.

ZIN Map pp242-3 — Brazilian $

☎ 2559 6430; 8th fl, Praia de Botafogo 400, Botafogo; mains US$7-12; ☉ noon-8:30pm
Boasting the same views as Emporium Pax, Zin also has an outdoor veranda – perfect for breezy eating in the summertime. Zin caters to hurried shoppers and offers them tasty Brazilian bites like roast meats, shrimp dishes and a range of dessert offerings.

FLAMENGO

One of Rio's oldest neighborhoods, Flamengo has its share of historic restaurants, scattered among its tree-lined streets. Flamengo's ongoing gentrification ensures that new restaurants are constantly being added to the mix. Rua Marquês de Abrantes is one of the best streets in which to wander and see old and new vying for attention. On weekend nights, the sidewalks grow crowded with people eating, drinking and flirting, all of which Cariocas do quite well.

ALHO E ÓLEO Map pp242-3 — Brazilian $$

☎ 2558 3345; Rua Buarque de Macedo 13, Flamengo; plates US$15-22; ☉ noon until last customer
Impeccable service, a stately air and innovative dishes make Alho e Óleo a top choice for lunching execs trying to cut a deal. In the evening, older couples hold court as the chef churns out lobster in tangerine sauce or duck tortellini with fresh mushrooms.

BELMONTE Map pp242-3 — Brazilian $

☎ 2552 3349; Praia do Flamengo 300, Flamengo; mains US$6-13; ☉ 7am until last customer
One of the classic *botecos* in Rio, Belmonte is a vision of Rio from the '50s. Globe lights hang overhead as patrons steel their nerves with *cachaça* (cane liquor) or Pepsi from the narrow bar. Meanwhile, unhurried waiters make their way across the intricate tile floors, carrying plates of trout or steak sandwiches. And history repeats itself.

CHURRASCARIA MAJÓRICA

Map pp242-3 — Churrascaria $$
☎ 2285 6789; Rua Senador Vergueiro 11, Flamengo; mains from US$12; ☉ noon-midnight Tue-Thu, to 1am Fri & Sat
A true *gaúcho* (person from Rio Grande do Sul) would chuckle at the kitschy cowboy accoutrements inside this restaurant. He'd shut his trap, however, once his plate of steak arrived. Meat is very serious business at Majórica, and if you're seeking an authentic *churrascaria* experience, look no further.

LAMAS Map pp242-3 — Brazilian $$

☎ 2556 0799; Rua Marquês de Abrantes 18A, Flamengo; mains US$10-20; ☉ 8am-2:30am Sun-Thu, to 4am Fri & Sat
This classic Brazilian restaurant opened in 1874, and has fans from all over. In spite of the mileage, dishes here hold up well, and those omniscient waiters in starched white coats will tell you what's hot in the kitchen. You can't go wrong with grilled *lingüiça* (sausage) or filet mignon with garlic.

PORCÃO RIO'S

Map pp242-3 — Churrascaria $$$
☎ 2554 8535; Av Infante Dom Henrique, Flamengo; all-you-can-eat US$23; ☉ 11:30am-midnight Sun-Thu, to 1am Fri & Sat
Set in the Parque do Flamengo with a stunning view of Pão de Açúcar, Porcão Rio's has been gradually moving up the charts in the *churrascaria* ratings. Some claim it's the best in the city; others are content just to go for the view. Whatever the case, you're in for an eating extravaganza. Call a few days in advance to book that table by the window.

Step back to the '50s at Belmonte (left)

SENAC BISTRÔ Map pp242-3 Brazilian $$

☎ 3138 1540; Rua Marquês de Abrantes 99, Flamengo; mains US$10-16; ✆ 11:30am-4pm Sun-Thu, 11:30am-4pm & 7pm-midnight Fri & Sat

On the bottom floor of an old mansion built 100 or so years ago, Senac serves tasty plates of seared tuna, shrimp *moqueca* and other Brazilian specialties. In spite of the splendid exterior, the decor inside is a bit lacking. The chocolate cake, however, makes up for any ambience issues. It comes warm and oozing decadence.

TACACÁ DO NORTE

Map pp242-3 Amazonian $

☎ 2205 7545; Rua Barão do Flamengo 35R, Flamengo; tacacá US$4; ✆ 9am-10pm Mon-Sat, to 7pm Sun

In the Amazonian state of Pará, people order their *tacacá* late in the afternoon from their favorite street vendor. The dish is usually served from a gourd bowl. In Rio, you don't have to wait until the sun is setting. The fragrant soup of manioc paste, *jambu* (a Brazilian vegetable) leaves and fresh and dried shrimp isn't for everyone. But then again, neither is the Amazon. For the faint of heart, this simple lunch counter also offers fruit juices and a handful of daily specials like *pirarucu* (a kind of fish) from Amazônia.

CATETE & GLÓRIA

As the twin rulers of Rio's budget-hotel kingdom, Glória and Catete offer plenty of inexpensive eateries. A stroll down Rua Catete will lead past half a dozen counters serving the same uninspiring brand of lunch special. Those on a tight budget can still eat well, while those looking for something fancy usually skip the area though there are some exciting upscale choices here.

AMAZÓNIA Map pp242-3 Brazilian $$

☎ 2557 4569; upstairs, Rua do Catete 234, Catete; mains US$10-14; ✆ 11am-midnight

Don't be fooled by the name. The only thing Amazonian about this place is the size of the portions. Traditional Brazilian cuisine, however, comes in many forms at this simple restaurant: try the juicy steak, tasty grilled chicken with creamed-corn sauce or *feijão manteiga* (butter-simmered beans).

BISTRÔ JARDINS

Map pp242-3 Italian $$

☎ 2558 2673; Parque do Catete, Rua do Catete 153, Catete; mains US$7-10; ✆ 9:30am-6pm

Behind the Museu da República, this handsome outdoor café overlooking the Catete gardens offers a verdant respite from the chaotic streets. In addition to breakfast, the bistro serves light lunch fare – sandwiches, salads, quiches and pastas.

CASA DA SUÍÇA Map pp238-9 Swiss $$

☎ 2509 3870; Rua Cândido Mendes 157, Glória; mains US$17-26; ✆ noon-3pm & 7pm-midnight Mon-Fri, 7pm-1am Sat, noon-4pm & 7-11pm Sun

Tucked inside the Swiss Embassy, this cozy restaurant serves top-notch steak *tartare*, though it specializes in flambés and fondues. The Casa da Suíça creates an almost tangible aura of sensuality – perhaps due to those open fires flaring inside. After dinner, you can hear live music at the St Moritz bar.

CATETE GRILL Map pp242-3 Self-serve $

☎ 2285 3442; Rua do Catete 239, Catete; plates US$5-10; ✆ 11am-midnight Mon-Sat, to 11pm Sun

One of the newer restaurants in Catete, the Catete Grill has won over the neighbohood with its excellent buffet – served all day. It also offers ice creams – *a quilo* (by the kilo), of course.

ESTAÇÃO REPÚBLICA

Map pp242-3 Self-serve $

☎ 2225 2650; Rua do Catete 104, Catete; plates US$5-10; ✆ 11am-midnight Mon-Sat, to 11pm Sun

Estação's buffet table is a neighborhood institution, featuring an extensive selection of salads, meats, pastas and vegetables. It's easy to indulge without breaking the bank. Sundays are family affairs here.

TABERNA DA GLÓRIA

Map pp238-9 Brazilian $

☎ 2265 7835; Rua do Russel 32A, Glória; mains US$8-13; ✆ 11:30am-1am Sun-Thu, to 2am Fri & Sat

On a small plaza in the heart of Glória, this large outdoor eatery serves decent Brazilian staples, and in abundance – most dishes here serve two. The *feijoada* on Saturday still draws crowds, and if you're not up for a big meal, appetizers and ice-cold *chope* are a good way to enjoy the open-air ambience.

Eating

CATETE & GLÓRIA

CENTRO & CINELÂNDIA

Catering to Rio's workday crowds, Centro offers a wide variety of restaurants, from divey diners to haute cuisine, sushi bars and French bistros to juice bars and *churrascarias*. Most restaurants open only for lunch and on weekdays. Many pedestrian-only areas throughout Centro (like Rua do Rosario) are full of restaurants, some spilling onto the sidewalk, others hidden on upstairs floors, all of which make restaurant-hunting something of an art. Areas worth exploring include Travessa do Comércio just after work, when the restaurants and cafés fill with chatter; another early-evening gathering spot is Av Marechal Floriano, full of snack bars specializing in fried sardines and beer. Cinelândia, just behind the Praça Floriano, features a number of open-air cafés and restaurants. Most Cariocas stop for the ice-cold *chopes* and a few appetizers.

ARTE TEMPERADA

Map pp238-9   French $$
☎ 2253 2589; rear entrance of Casa França-Brasil, Rua Visconde de Itaboraí 78, Centro; mains US$11-17; ⏰ 11am-4pm Mon-Fri
Hidden in a tiny alley behind the Casa França-Brasil, this charming restaurant serves delicious Franco-Brazilian cuisine without the fuss. Some top choices are the crepes, the bouillabaisse, and the chicken breast served with passionfruit sauce and polenta. You can also opt for the two-course plate of the day (US$9).

ATELIÊ ODEON Map pp238-9   Brazilian $
☎ 2240 0746; Praça Floriano, Cinelândia; mains US$8-12; ⏰ noon-10pm Mon-Fri
Next to the art house cinema of the same name, the Ateliê Odeon serves up decent Brazilian fare on its open-air terrace to a festive crowd. Ateliê opens onto the Praça Floriano, which is a lively gathering spot on weekday evenings. At weekends, it stays opens during film screenings next door.

ATRIUM Map pp238-9   Brazilian $$
☎ 2220 0193; Paço Imperial, Praça Quinze de Novembro 48, Centro; mains around US$17; ⏰ 11:30am-3:30pm Mon-Fri
A stately dining room in the Paço Imperial, Atrium serves power-lunching business execs and those simply wanting a taste of

Eating

CENTRO & CINELÂNDIA

TOP FIVE CENTRO & CINELÂNDIA EATS

- Arte Temperada (left)
- Ateliê Odeon (left)
- Brasserie Rosário (below)
- Cais do Oriente (opposite)
- Confeitaria Colombo (opposite)

decadence. The lamb with rosemary-and-mushroom risotto would have brought a smile to the face of Dom Pedro I (who once gazed out these same windows a little less than 200 years ago).

BAR LUIZ Map pp238-9   German $
☎ 2262 6900; Rua da Carioca 39, Centro; mains US$9-15; ⏰ 11am-11:30pm Mon-Sat
Bar Luiz first opened in 1887, making it one of the city's oldest *cervejarias* (pubs). A festive air fills the old saloon as diners get their fill of traditional German cooking (potato salad and smoked meats), along with ice-cold drafts – including dark beer – on tap.

BEDUÍNO Map pp238-9   Middle Eastern $
☎ 2524 5142; Av Presidente Wilson 123, Centro; mains US$7-10; ⏰ 6am-midnight Mon-Fri
You'll always find a lunchtime crowd at this low-key restaurant east of Cinelândia. Reliably good food and excellent prices are Beduíno's keys to success, with 30 different traditional Middle Eastern dishes to choose from. Favorites include grilled *kafta,* lamb stew, and rice and lentils.

BISTRÔ DO PAÇO Map pp238-9   Self-serve $
☎ 2262 3613; Paço Imperial, Praça Quinze de Novembro 48, Centro; mains around US$10; ⏰ 11am-7:30pm Mon-Fri, noon-7pm Sat & Sun
On the ground floor of the Paço Imperial, this informal restaurant offers a tasty assortment of quiches, salads, soups and other light fare. Save room for the delicious pies and cakes.

BRASSERIE ROSÁRIO
Map pp238-9   French $$
☎ 2518 3033; Rua do Rosário 34, Centro; mains from US$11; ⏰ 8am-8pm Mon-Fri, 10am-5pm Sat
Set in a handsomely restored 1860s building, this atmospheric bistro has a hint of

Paris about it. The front counters are full of croissants, *pain au chocolat* (chocolate croissant) and other baked items, while the restaurant menu features roast meats and fish, soups, baguette sandwiches and the like. Old American jazz plays overhead.

CAFÉ DO RODRIGUES

Map pp238-9   Café $$
☎ 3231 8015; Travessa de Ouvidor 17, Centro; lunch US$6-9; ⊗ 9am-8pm Mon-Fri, 10am-1pm Sat

Inside the charming Centro branch of the Livraria da Travessa bookstore (p169), Café do Rodrigues is a suitable setting for philosophical conversation when the world – or the humidity – has worn you down. Browse for books, then peruse your finds over a *torta do palmito* (heart-of-palm quiche), a hearty soup or a flavorful salad.

CAIS DO ORIENTE Map pp238-9   Eclectic $$
☎ 2203 0178; Rua Visconde de Itaboraí 8, Centro; mains US$12-20; ⊗ noon-4pm Mon, to midnight Tue-Sat

Brick walls lined with tapestries stretch high to the ceiling in this almost-cinematic 1870s mansion. Set on a brick-lined street, hidden from the masses, Cais do Oriente blends West with East in dishes like sesame tuna. On Friday and Saturday nights, live bands perform in the restaurant (US$10 cover; see p138).

CASA CAVÉ Map pp238-9   Patisserie $
☎ 2221 0533; Rua Sete de Setembro 137, Centro; pastries from US$2; ⊗ 9am-7pm Mon-Fri, to 1pm Sat

Set with beautiful tile floors and marble tabletops, this simple, historic coffeehouse (c 1860), lures in passersby with its glass shop windows full of tempting desserts. Inside, diners gather at the long, narrow counter, sipping hot coffee served by kind-hearted waitstaff.

CEDRO DO LÍBANO

Map pp238-9   Lebanese $
☎ 2224 0163; Rua Senhor dos Passos 231, Centro; mains US$6-13; ⊗ 11am-5pm

White plastic chairs and tables covered by white tablecloths might make you feel like you stumbled into someone's wedding reception at this dining spot in the heart of Saara. But in fact, the white decorating this 70-year-old Lebanese institution has more

to do with the purity of the Lebanese cooking: kibbe, *kaftas*, lamb – tender portions of perfection.

CONFEITARIA COLOMBO

Map pp238-9   Patisserie $$
☎ 2232 2300; Rua Gonçalves Dias 34, Centro; desserts/mains from US$3/12; ⊗ 8am-8pm Mon-Fri, 10am-5pm Sat

Stained-glass windows, brocaded mirrors and marble countertops create a lavish setting for coffee or a meal. Dating from the late 1800s, the Confeitaria Colombo serves desserts befitting the elegant decor. The restaurant overhead serves traditional Brazilian cuisine for those wanting to further soak up the splendor. There's also a Confeitaria Colombo in Copacabana (p116).

DITO & FEITO Map pp238-9   Self-serve $
☎ 2222 4016; Rua do Mercado 19, Centro; meals US$7-12; ⊗ 11am-4pm Mon-Fri

Set in an atmospheric 19th-century mansion near Praça Quinze, this three-story restaurant serves a popular weekday lunch buffet. Although it's not the best per-kilo place in Rio, it's a good spot for a quick, inexpensive meal in between dipping into the nearby museums. At night Dito & Feito becomes a popular bar and nightclub (p136).

Cais do Oriente (left) will tempt your taste buds

EÇA Map pp238-9 — French $$

☎ 2524 2399; Basement, Av Rio Branco 128,
Centro; mains US$17-28; noon-4pm Mon-Fri
The well dressed cut deals over beautifully
presented dishes at this classic of French
eclectic cuisine. Among the offerings,
breast of duck with lime confit has earned
Eça its admirers, as has the fine chocolate
soufflé for dessert. Our only complaint:
eating at Eça, with its polished walls and
artful lighting, is not unlike eating inside a
museum – which is, perhaps, just the point,
given chef Frédéric De Maeyer's artful
combinations.

LIDADOR Map pp238-9 — Liquor Store & Deli $

☎ 2533 4988; Rua da Assembléia 65, Centro;
9am-8pm Mon-Fri
Gleaming bottles stretch high to the ceiling
of this well-stocked liquor cabinet. Founded
in 1924, Lidador also sells a range of smoked
meats, chocolates and imported goods. A tiny
area in the back serves as an informal pub.

RANCHO INN Map pp238-9 — French $

☎ 2263 5197; 2nd fl, Rua do Rosário 74, Centro;
mains US$7-14; 11:30am-3:30pm Mon-Fri
Exposed brick and tall windows lend a
vaguely Parisian air to this charming lunchtime spot. In addition to offerings like *caprese
raviolini* (tomato-and-mozzarella ravioli) and
snapper with basil and almonds, the salads
and quiches are *muito gostoso* (very tasty).

RESTAURANTE ALBAMAR

Map pp238-9 — Seafood $$
☎ 2240 8378; Praça Marechal Âncora 186, Centro;
mains US$12-24; 11:30am-6pm Tue-Sun
The green gazebo structure perched over
water offers excellent views of the Baía de
Guanabara and Niterói. The seafood has its
fans, but it's not nearly as outstanding as
the view. The *peixe brasileira* (fish in coconut
milk) is one of the most popular dishes.

SANTA TERESA & LAPA

As one of the most charming neighbor-
hoods of Rio, Santa Teresa, not surprisingly,
has a range of attractive dining spots. Great
views, historic ambience and live music
are a few of the ingredients that make the
neighborhood's regional and international
restaurants such an attraction. The biggest

swath of restaurants stretch on either side
of Largo dos Guimarães. Although Lapa is
known more for its samba than its cuisine,
a handful of restaurants lies scattered in the
area, many catering to the young crowds
heading to the bars.

APRAZÍVEL Map p241 — Brazilian $$

☎ 3852 4935; Rua Aprazível 62, Santa Teresa;
mains US$13-22; 8pm until last customer Thu,
noon-midnight Fri & Sat, 1-6pm Sun
Hidden on a windy road high up in Santa
Teresa, Aprazível offers beautiful views and
a lush garden setting. Brazilian fare with a
twist showcases plates of succulent quail
and salmon with mango chutney. Wednesday nights are dedicated to live *choro*
(US$5 cover).

BAR BRASIL Map pp238-9 — German $

☎ 2509 5943; Av Mem de Sá 90, Lapa; mains
US$9-18; 11:30am-11pm Mon-Fri, to 4pm Sat
According to legend, this German restaurant went by the name Bar Adolf until
WWII. Although the name has been Bra-
zilianized, the cuisine is still prepared in
the same tradition as it was back before
the war. Sauerkraut, wursts, lentils and an
ever-flowing tap quench the appetites and
thirsts of the sometimes-rowdy Lapa crowd.

BAR DO ERNESTO Map pp238-9 — Brazilian $

☎ 2509 6455; Largo da Lapa 41, Lapa;
mains US$8-17; 11:30am-1am Mon-Sat
For years Ernesto has been a popular spot
for the patrons and musicians who come
here after a concert next door at Sala Cecília
Meireles (p128). The menu features fine
Brazilian fare as well as pastas, pizzas and
desserts.

BAR DO MINEIRO Map p241 — Brazilian $

☎ 2221 9227; Rua Paschoal Carlos Magno 99,
Santa Teresa; mains US$8-15; 11am-2am Tue-
Thu, to 4am Fri & Sat, to 8pm Sun
Photographs of old Rio cover the walls of
this old-school *boteco* in the heart of Santa
Teresa. Lively crowds have been filling this
spot for years to enjoy traditional Minas
Gerais dishes. *Feijoada* is tops on Saturdays.
Other good anytime dishes include *carne
seca* (dried meat with spices) and *lingüiça*
(pork sausage). Strong caipirinhas will help
get you in the mood.

ENCONTRAS CARIOCAS

Map pp238-9   Pizza $

☎ 2221 0028; Av Mem de Sá 77, Lapa; pizzas US$6-16; ⏰ 6pm-5am Wed-Sun

This late-night pizza parlor is a good place to stop in while exploring Lapa's live music scene. Featuring a wide variety of ingredients (such as shiitake mushrooms, sun-dried tomatoes and jerked beefs), Encontras Cariocas serves tasty pies amid an atmosphere of old-fashioned charm – high wooden ceilings, brick walls and warm lighting.

ESPIRITO SANTA Map p241   Amazonian $

☎ 2508 7095; Rua Almirante Alexandrino 264, Santa Teresa; mains US$9-18; ⏰ noon-5pm Tue-Wed, to midnight Thu-Sat, to 7pm Sun

Opened in 2005 and one of our favorite new restaurants, Espirito Santa is set in a beautifully restored mansion in Santa Teresa. Take a seat on the back terrace with its sweeping views or inside the charming, airy dining room, and feast on rich, expertly prepared meat and seafood dishes from the Amazon.

MARIZÉ GOURMET

Map pp238-9   Lighter Fare $

☎ 2221 0919; Av Mem de Sá 82, Lapa; sandwiches US$2-6; ⏰ 8am-8pm Mon-Wed, to 3am Thu & Fri, 8pm-3am Sat

This airy two-story restaurant is suited to samba-club-goers. You'll find exposed brick walls, big windows from which to watch the street action and tasty salads, sandwiches and *salgados* (bar snacks). Our favorites: *bobó de camarão* and the vegetarian sandwich (roasted peppers and eggplant).

MIKE'S HAUS Map p241   German $$

☎ 2509 5248; Rua Almirante Alexandrino 1458A, Santa Teresa; mains US$10-16; ⏰ 11:30am-midnight Tue-Sun

Mike's Haus has German pub atmosphere with traditional cooking and cold glasses of imported Weizenbier. Although plates are small here, the place remains a popular gathering spot for expats and Cariocas on Friday and Saturday night.

NOVA CAPELA Map pp238-9   Portuguese $

☎ 2252 6228; Av Mem de Sá 96, Lapa; mains US$8-15; ⏰ 11am until last customer

Like Bar Brasil next door, Nova Capela dates from the beginning of the 20th century.

It stays open late into the evening, and fills with a noisy mix of artists, musicians and party kids. Legendarily bad-tempered waiters serve up big plates of traditional Portuguese cuisine. The *cabrito* (goat) is among the best examples of this dish you'll encounter in Rio.

PORTA QUENTE Map p241   Pizza $

☎ 2509 5152; Rua Almirante Alexandrino 470, Santa Teresa; pizzas US$7-14; ⏰ noon-midnight Mon-Sat

This pleasant café near the *bonde* stop serves decent thin-crust pizzas, salads and lighter fare. If you're staying in Santa Teresa, the café also delivers inside the neighborhood.

SANSUSHI Map p241   Japanese $$

☎ 2224 4658; Rua Almirante Alexandrino 382, Santa Teresa; meals US$11-20; ⏰ 7pm-midnight Tue-Fri, 1pm-midnight Sat, to 8pm Sun

This tiny sushi spot on Santa Teresa's main strip attracts a loyal local following with its delectable sushi and sashimi (36 varieties) as well as teriyaki and other hot dishes.

SOBRENATURAL Map p241   Seafood $

☎ 2224 1003; Rua Almirante Alexandrino 432, Santa Teresa; mains US$8-14; ⏰ 11:30am-midnight Mon-Sat

The exposed brick and old hardwood ceiling set the stage for feasting on the *frutas do mar* (seafood). Lines gather on weekends for the grilled fish and *moqueca*. During the week, stop by for the US$3 to US$4 lunchtime specials.

BARRA DA TIJUCA & GREATER RIO

Other parts of Rio offer some of the city's more rustic dining experiences. Outside the city limits one can find open-air spots overlooking the coast – beautiful views complemented by fresh seafood.

BARREADO Map pp236-7   Seafood $$$

☎ 2442 2023; Estrada dos Bandeirantes 21295, Vargem Grande; lunch for 2 US$35-50; ⏰ noon-11pm Tue-Sat, noon-8pm Sun

In a lush setting west of Barra, this rustic spot serves fresh Brazilian seafood with a

Eating

BARRA DA TIJUCA & GREATER RIO

wildly eclectic twist. Meals are prepared in the wood-burning oven, and pumpkin is the serving vehicle of choice. You can order it filled with rich delicacies like shrimp with *catupiry* (a kind of cheese), scampi, or lobster and mango. For those who'd rather save the pumpkins for Halloween, *vatapá* (a Bahian seafood dish made with manioc paste, coconut milk and *dendê*) and roast meats are also excellent choices.

BIRA
Seafood $$

☎ 2410 8304; Estrada da Vendinha 68A, Barra de Guaratiba; mains US$17-25; ⏱ noon-midnight Mon-Sat

Splendid views of Baía de Marambaia await diners who make the trek to Bira, about 45 minutes outside the city. On a breezy wooden deck, diners can partake in the flavorful, rich seafood emerging from the kitchen. *Moquecas,* sea bass, shrimp, crabmeat pastries – all are prepared with doting tenderness.

MUSEU DO AÇUDE
Map p249   Brunch $$$

☎ 2492 2119; Estrada do Açude 764, Tijuca Forest; brunch US$19; ⏱ 12:30-4pm last Sun of the month Mar-Nov

Once a month, the museum hosts a gastronomic festival, with brunch in a lovely mansion in the Tijuca forest. There's often live music, adding to the charm of the natural setting. If you happen to be around, don't miss it.

TIA PALMIRA
Seafood $$$

☎ 2410 8169; Caminho do Souza 18, Barra de Guaratiba; prix-fixe lunch US$24; ⏱ 11:30am-5pm Tue-Fri, to 6pm Sat & Sun

On weekends, Cariocas feast on seafood at this simple open-air eatery overlooking the coast. A venerable destination for 40 years, Tia Palmira keeps its fans coming back for its exquisite seafood *rodizio* (all-you-can-eat barbecue dinner). Plate after plate of *vatapá,* crabmeat, grilled fish, shrimp pastries and other fruits of the sea come to your table until you can eat no more.

Entertainment

Performing Arts   128

Drinking   129
  Ipanema & Leblon 129
  Gávea, Jardim Botânico & Lagoa 131
  Copacabana & Leme 133
  Botafogo & Urca 134
  Flamengo 135
  Centro & Cinelândia 135
  Santa Teresa & Lapa 136

Music & Dance   137
  Live Music 137
  Big Venues 143

Nightclubs   143

Cinema   147

Entertainment

The cultural capital of Brazil, Rio boasts an astounding array of entertainment options. Few places, in fact, can rival the dynamism of Rio's live music circuit – from its samba clubs to its jazz bars – with open-air cafés, lounges and nightclubs all adding to the mix. Meanwhile, the bar scene here is practically a Carioca institution, with ice-cold *chope* (draft beer), fun, mixed crowds and a spontaneous, festive air being the virtues of the ideal Rio *boteco* (neighborhood bar). If you need to take a break from the heady nightlife scene, there's plenty more on hand, including theater, dance, film and even the occasional opera.

Going out in the city requires little in the way of slick attire. Most men put on jeans and a clean T-shirt and perhaps comb their hair. Meanwhile, the *garotas* (girls) put a bit more effort into their wardrobes: a skirt, heels and a fun and sexy top are the mode du jour.

If you can read a bit of Portuguese, there are a number of handy sources for getting a handle on what's going on about town. Pick up the *Veja Rio* insert in *Veja* magazine, which comes out each Sunday and can be found at newsstands throughout the city. Thursday and Friday editions of *O Globo* and *Jornal do Brasil* also have extensive entertainment sections. The Rio Festa website (www.riofesta.com.br) lists the top picks for shows, clubs and happy hours each week.

Tickets & Reservations

TICKETMASTER
☎ 0300 789 6846; www.ticketmaster.com.br in Portuguese; ⏰ 9am-8pm Mon-Sat
This international company sells tickets to shows at Claro Hall in Barra da Tijuca and the Teatro Municipal in Centro. Tickets can be purchased over the phone or online (you'll need Portuguese) or at Modern Sound (p165).

TICKETRONICS
☎ 0300 789 3350; www.ticketronics.com.br in Portuguese; Modern Sound, Rua Barata Ribeiro 502, Copacabana; ⏰ 9am-9pm Mon-Fri, to 8pm Sat
Tickets for a wide range of shows, concerts and dance performances can be purchased through Ticketronics either over the phone or through a distributor like Modern Sound.

PERFORMING ARTS

Concerts, live performances, plays and musicals are among the daily events happening somewhere around town. For a rough idea of what's on, pick up Riotur's quarterly *Rio Guide* available at any office of Riotur (p216). If you speak a bit of Portuguese, you can also find up-to-the-minute arts and entertainment listings online through Terra Guides (http://cidades.terra.com.br/rio in Portuguese).

ARTE SESC CULTURAL CENTER
Map pp242-3
☎ 3138 1020; Rua Marquês de Abrantes 99, Flamengo
Housed in one of Flamengo's lovely old mansions, Arte Sesc has occasional classical recitals throughout the year. It also hosts panel discussions on various art and cultural topics.

ESPAÇO BNDES Map pp238-9
☎ 2277 7757; Av República do Chile 100, Centro
Weekly concerts are held at this Centro venue throughout the year. Featuring a mix of popular and classical music, BNDES in the past has featured musicians exploring symphonic pop, as well as other experimental groups playing samba-jazz.

SALA CECÍLIA MEIRELES Map pp238-9
☎ 2224 3913; Largo da Lapa 47, Lapa; ⏰ 1-6pm ticket office, 7:30pm concerts
Lapa's splendid early-20th-century gem hosts orchestral concerts throughout the year. Lately, the repertoire has included contemporary groups, playing both *choro* (romantic, intimate samba) and classical.

TEATRO CARLOS GOMES Map pp238-9
☎ 2232 8701; Rua Pedro I, 22, Centro
Facing the Praça Tiradentes, the large Teatro Gomes stages avant-garde dance shows

and experimental theater. The theater seats 600; tickets for events here can be purchased through Ticketronics.

TEATRO DO CENTRO CULTURAL BANCO DO BRASIL Map pp238-9

☎ 3808 2000; Rua Primeiro de Março 66, Centro
In addition to its exhibitions, this large cultural center in downtown Rio has two stages and a cinema. Film, dance and musical events are usually coordinated with current exhibits: the recent African art exhibit, for instance, featured musicians from Cameroon and films from the African diaspora.

TEATRO LAURA ALVIM Map pp246-7

☎ 2267 1647; Av Vieira Souto 176, Ipanema
Across from the beach in Ipanema, this small center stages plays and hosts classical and other live-music styles. It also has art openings and a cinema. Stop in to see what's on.

TEATRO MUNICIPAL Map pp238-9

☎ 2299 1711; Praça Floriano, Cinelândia
This gorgeous art-nouveau theater provides the setting for Rio's best opera, ballet and symphonic concerts. Tickets are available at the box office or at **Ticketronics** (opposite). The Municipal seats 2400, and sight lines are generally quite good.

DRINKING

Cariocas have no shortage of options when it comes to enticing bars and lounges. For those looking for a bit of flash, Leblon and Ipanema are good – though Leblon boasts classic watering holes too. You'll find a more youthful bar scene in Gávea and Jardim Botânico, while a good place for a date is around the Lagoa kiosks. Copacabana has a mix of brash newcomers and old favorites. Botafogo is known for its bars. Centro's colorful, open-air bars are great options on weeknights, when the narrow colonial streets make a charming backdrop for a beer among friends. You'll find similarly atmospheric digs in Santa Teresa. At the opposite end of the spectrum is Barra da Tijuca, home to large entertainment complexes with bars, discos and restaurants all in one shopping-mall-like structure.

BAR D'HOTEL Map pp246-7
☎ 2172 1100; 2nd fl, Marina A[...]
Moreira 696, Leblon; ⊙ 6p[...]
The waves crashing [...]
part of the backg[...]
rich bar overlo[...]
narrow bar i[...]
who gath[...]
tropica[...]
amb[...]

- Best [...]
  De[...]
- Bes[...]
- Bes[...]
- Bes[...]
- Best happy hour – **Seu Martin** (p131)
- Best dance floor – **00** (p143)
- Best people-watching – **Melt** (p147)
- Best live music – **Carioca da Gema** (p139) and **Democráticus** (p141) among many other favorites. See p137 for more.

IPANEMA & LEBLON

While Ipanema has some enticing options, Leblon is the undisputed champ of the *boteco*, with a dash of stylish lounges thrown in as well. A particularly good place to wander is along Av General San Martin.

ACADEMIA DA CACHAÇA Map pp246-7

☎ 2239 1542; Rua Conde de Bernadotte 26G, Leblon; ⊙ noon-1am Sun-Thu, to 2am Fri & Sat
Although *cachaça* (cane liquor) has a bad reputation in some parts, here the fiery liquor is given a respect it nearly deserves. Along with tasty, inexpensive meals, this pleasant indoor-outdoor spot serves dozens of varieties of *cachaça,* and you can order it straight, with honey and lime, or disguised in a fruity caipirinha. For a treat (and/or a bad hangover), try the passion-fruit *batida* (*cachaça* and passion-fruit juice).

BAR 121 Map pp246-7

☎ 2274 1122; Av Niemeyer 121, Vidigal; ⊙ 5pm-1am
With sweeping views of the beaches Bar 121 is a lovely spot to take in the sunset. The dexterous bartender creates tasty cocktail combinations for an upscale crowd as the weekend nears. Live bossa nova and MPB *(Música Popular Brasileira)* bands (9pm Thu, 10pm Fri & Sat) draw a mix of Brazilians and tourists. The bar is inside the Sheraton hotel (p178).

...l Suites, Av Delfim
...n-2am
...on the shore are just
...round of this texture-
...king Ipanema Beach. The
...s like a magnet for the style set,
...er in the intimate space to enjoy
...l drinks to the backdrop of sea and
...ient electronic music.

BOTEQUIM INFORMAL Map pp246-7
☎ 2259 6967; Rua Humberto de Campos 646,
Leblon; ☾ noon-1am Tue-Sun

This charming neighborhood bar is hidden
away on a quiet, tree-lined street and it
makes a fine detour before or after hitting
one of the many restaurants nearby. Here
you'll find open seating on the front patio
and a small, cozy bar inside. Although beer
is the beverage of choice, the bar also
serves inventive cocktails and tasty *petiscos*
(appetizers).

BRACARENSE Map pp246-7
☎ 2294 3549; Rua José Linhares 85B, Leblon;
☾ 7am-midnight Mon-Sat, 9am-10pm Sun

Opened in 1948, Bracarense is a classic Carioca watering hole, famous for its simple,
unpretentious ambience and its heavenly
salgados (bar snacks). A steady stream of
neighborhood regulars enjoys over 20
varieties of the snacks (try the *aipim com
camarão* – cassava with shrimp) to the
accompaniment of icy-cold *chope*.

CANECO 70 Map pp246-7
☎ 2294 1180; Av Delfim Moreira 1026, Leblon;
☾ 11am-4am

Facing the beach, the large open-air Caneco
70 is one of Leblon's traditional after-beach
hangouts. The fresh breeze, well-chilled
beers and hum of conversation make a nice
prelude to the evening (or the morning, as
the case may be).

COBAL Map pp246-7
☎ 2239 1549; Rua Gilberto Cardoso, Leblon;
☾ closed Mon

Leblon's flower-and-produce market
features a number of open-air bars and
restaurants. A vibrant, youthful air pervades
this place, and it's a major meeting spot in
the summer.

CONVERSA FIADA Map pp246-7
☎ 2512 9767; Av Ataúlfo de Paiva 900B, Leblon;
☾ noon-2am

'Conversa Fiada,' which can mean chit-
chat or nonsense depending on the con-
text, is an apt title for this lively Leblon
bar. With its deep red walls, an open-sided
setting and a laid-back crowd it's earned
a place among the top neighborhood
botecos.

DEVASSA Map pp246-7
☎ 2259 8271; Rua General San Martin 1241,
Leblon; ☾ 5pm-5am

Serving perhaps Rio's best beer, Devassa
makes its own creamy brews, before
offering them up to festive crowds at its
two-floor *chopperia* (beer hall). Top picks:
sarará (wheat beer), *ruiva* (pale ale) and
mulatta (a mix of dark and light beer with
a shot of coffee). An occasional MPB band
adds to the din on the upstairs level.

BAR BITES

If you're heading home from the beach, but can't be
bothered with a sit-down meal, go Carioca and grab
a few bites (and a *chope*) at the *boteco* (neighborhood
bar). Bars in Brazil offer a wide variety of snacks and
appetizers. Here are some items you are most likely
to find.

Batida A strong mixed drink made with *cachaça* (a
rumlike cane liquor) and fruit juice, usually passion
fruit or lime.

Bolinhos de bacalhau Deep-fried codfish balls, usually served with sauce.

Bolinhos de queijo Crispy deep-fried cheese balls.

Caipirinha The national drink of Brazil; a strong
mixed drink made with limes, sugar and *cachaça*.

Chope Light pilsner draft beer.

Coxinha Pear-shaped cornmeal balls filled with fried
chicken. They are eaten as a snack, but a few of these
will fill most people up fast.

Misto quente A hot ham-and-cheese sandwich.

Pão de queijo A slightly gooey cheese bread, baked
into bite-sized biscuits; the biscuits so popular in
Brazil that a whole franchise was launched on their
success (naturally named Pão de Queijo).

Paste A crispy pastry filled with cheese or meat.

Salgado Any savory pastry filled with cheese or meat;
types include *pasteis* (turnovers), *coxinhas*, *bolinhos
de queijo* and *bacalhau*. Most bars offer a variety of
salgados. Sometimes they are on the menu under
tira-gostos (appetizers).

Entertainment

DRINKING

EMPÓRIO Map pp246-7

☎ 2267 7992; Rua Maria Quitéria 37, Ipanema; ☾ noon-2am

A young mix of Cariocas and gringos stirs things up over cheap cocktails at this battered old favorite in Ipanema. A porch in front overlooks the street – a fine spot to stake out when the air gets too thick with cigarette smoke or bad '80s music.

GAROTA DE IPANEMA Map pp246-7

☎ 2523 3787; Rua Vinícius de Moraes 49, Ipanema; mains US$5-10 ☾ 11am-2:30am

During its first incarnation, this small, open-sided bar was called the Bar Veloso. Its name and anonymity disappeared once two scruffy young regulars – Tom Jobim and Vinícius de Moraes – penned the famous song here that changed history (and the name of the street, too). Today, you'll find plenty of tourists here, but little inspiration aside from the ice-cold *chope.*

GUAPO LOCO Map pp246-7

☎ 2294 2915; Rua Rainha Guilhermina 48, Leblon; ☾ 7pm-midnight Mon, to 4am Tue-Fri, noon-4am Sat, to midnight Sun

This colorful Mexican restaurant and bar is one of Leblon's livelier spots for the under-30 crowd. Things get rowdier as the night progresses, helped along no doubt by the wide variety of tequilas on hand. Guapo Loco also serves decent quesadillas, tacos and fajitas if hunger strikes after working the tiny dance floor.

JILÓ Map pp246-7

☎ 2274 6841; Av General San Martin 1227, Leblon; ☾ 6pm-2am Mon-Fri, noon-2am Sat & Sun

This lively open-sided bar opened in 2005, adding a splash more color to an already festive street. Creamy *chope,* a tasty appetizer menu and the inviting, informal ambience have paved the way for its popularity, with the bar and its sidewalk tables packed on weekend nights.

JOBI Map pp246-7

☎ 2274 0547; Av Ataúlfo de Paiva 1166, Leblon; ☾ 9am until last customer

A favorite since 1956, Jobi has served a lot of beer in its day, and its popularity hasn't waned. The unadorned *botequim* (bar with table service) still serves plenty; grab a seat by the sidewalk and let the night unfold. If hunger beckons, try the tasty appetizers (jerked beef or codfish croquettes are tops).

LORD JIM Map pp246-7

☎ 2259 3047; Rua Paul Redfern 63, Ipanema; ☾ 6pm-2am Mon-Thu, 6pm-3am Fri, 1pm-3am Sat & Sun

Something of a novelty for Cariocas, Lord Jim is one of several English-style pubs scattered about the Zona Sul. Darts, English-speaking waiters and all the requisite expat beers – Guinness, Harps, Bass, Foster's etc – are on hand to complete the ambience. The pub hosts quiz nights on Wednesdays.

SEU MARTIN Map pp246-7

☎ 2274 0800; Av General San Martin 1196, Leblon; ☾ 1pm-1am Tue-Thu, to 2am Fri & Sat, noon-midnight Sun

This small, inviting bar in Leblon is an intimate setting for a drink. Jazz plays overhead as young friends and couples work their way through cocktails and conversation. Seu Martin also serves delicious appetizers and sandwiches. Try the shrimp croquettes.

SHENANIGAN'S Map pp246-7

☎ 2267 5860; Rua Visconde de Pirajá 112A, Ipanema; ☾ 6pm-3am Mon-Fri, 2pm-3am Sat, to 2am Sun

Overlooking the Praça General Osorio, Shenanigan's is a fairly recent addition to Ipanema's growing pub scene. And it's no small success: through the smoke hanging overhead, the beautiful waitstaff shuttles between tables *packed* full of Cariocas and sunburnt gringos. The exposed brick walls, pool table and mix of spoken languages all contribute to the dark and pubby ambience Shenanigan's aims for.

GÁVEA, JARDIM BOTÂNICO & LAGOA

Gávea and Jardim Botânico have a youthful population that comes out en masse to the bars along Rua JJ Seabra; meanwhile there's almost always a fun crowd packing the bars facing Praça Santos Dumont. The lakeside kiosks, which offer both live music and the backdrop of Lagoa and Redeemer, fill with couples on warm summer nights.

BAR LAGOA Map pp246-7

☎ 2523 1135; Av Epitácio Pessoa 1674, Lagoa; ᕀ 6pm-2am Mon, noon-2am Tue-Sun

With a view of the lake, Bar Lagoa is one of the neighborhood's classic haunts. Founded in 1935, this open-air spot hasn't changed all that much since then: the bar still has surly waiters serving the excellent beer to ever-crowded tables, and in spite of its years, a youthful air pervades the old bar.

CAIPIRINHA & FILÉ Map pp246-7

☎ 3204 2485; Parque dos Patins, Av Borges de Medeiros, Lagoa; live-music charge US$2; ᕀ 5pm-midnight Tue-Fri, 11am-2am Sat & Sun

True to its name, the fairly new Caipirinha & Filé serves some tasty varieties of the potent spirit: passion fruit, guava and pineapple are a few of the addictive caipirinhas that you can enjoy in the fine open-air setting facing the lake. Live MPB bands perform nightly at 8pm.

CAROLINE CAFÉ Map pp246-7

☎ 2540 0705; Rua JJ Seabra 10, Jardim Botânico; ᕀ 6pm-3am Sun-Thu, to 4am Fri, 7pm-4am Sat

A mix of couples and groups of friends out for the night (pre- or post-clubs) fills Caroline Café most nights of the week. The sexy young crowd milling around the tables inside and out makes this place a bit sceney at times.

BEST NEIGHBORHOOD BARS

For the classic *boteco* experience, drop in on one of the following old-school haunts:

- Botafogo – **Bar do Belmiro** (p134) and **Champanharia Ovelha Negra** (p134)
- Copacabana – **Bip Bip** (p137) and **Cervantes** (opposite)
- Centro – **Via XV Botequim** (p136)
- Flamengo – **Belmonte** (p135)
- Gávea – **Hipódromo Up** (right)
- Ipanema – **Vinícius Piano Bar** (p139) and **Garota de Ipanema** (p131)
- Lagoa – **Bar Lagoa** (above)
- Leblon – **Jobi** (p131) and **Botequim Informal** (p130)
- Santa Teresa – **Bar do Mineiro** (p136) and **Armazém São Thiago** (p136)
- Urca – **Praia Vermelha** (p138)

DA GRAÇA Map pp246-7

☎ 2249 5484; Rua Pacheco Leão 780, Jardim Botânico; ᕀ 6pm-1:30am Tue-Thu, noon-1:30am Fri & Sat

New in 2005, the colorful Da Graça is one of Jardim Botânico's liveliest bars. The decor is festive and kitsch: rising up to the tall ceilings are walls draped with shimmery fabric; brightly hued lamps decorate the entrance. On weekends, the sidewalk tables and the inside of the bar gather a loud but fun crowd.

DRINK CAFÉ Map pp246-7

☎ 2239 4136; Parque dos Patins, Av Borges de Medeiros, Lagoa; live-music charge US$2; ᕀ 5pm-2am Mon, 9am-2am Tue-Sun

One of a handful of lively, open-air restaurants along the lake, the Drink Café is one of the most charming spots to hear live jazz and bossa nova. Besides the peaceful setting and decent tunes, Drink Café has a small menu featuring German specialties.

HIPÓDROMO UP Map pp246-7

☎ 2274 9720; Praça Santos Dumont 108, Gávea; ᕀ 8am-3am

In an area more commonly referred to as Baixo Gávea, Hipódromo is one of several bars in the area responsible for the local residents' chronic lack of sleep. A young college-age crowd celebrates here on Monday, Thursday and Sunday nights.

JOTA BAR Map pp246-7

☎ 3874 6835; Rua Jardim Botânico 595, Jardim Botânico; ᕀ noon-3am

This sleek, trim bar features DJs most nights (beginning at 10pm), a young, fairly hip crowd and a talented group of bartenders. If Jota Bar doesn't suit, you'll find several other decent bars just around the corner.

SATURNINO Map pp246-7

☎ 3874 0064; Rua Saturnino de Brito 50, Jardim Botânico; ᕀ 6pm-2am Sun-Wed, to 3am Thu-Sat

Another newcomer to the scene, Saturnino was quick to become a neighborhood favorite. In a large room with high ceilings and touches of tropical decor, the stylish 20-something crowd mingles over *chope* and fruity cocktails (that could use a touch more alcohol). The open-sided patio in front is a particularly fine vantage point for people-watching.

Entertainment

DRINKING

SITIO LOUNGE Map pp246-7

☎ 2274 2226; Rua Marquês de São Vicente 10, Gávea; ⏱ 8pm-2am Tue-Thu, to 3am Fri & Sat

Blazing the trail in Gávea's fledgling lounge scene, Sitio is a sleek space that treads the line between pretension and style. The cocktails, ambient sounds (mixed by a changing crew of house and drum 'n' bass hands) and attractive staff draw a broad mix to the bar.

SKY LOUNGE Map pp246-7

☎ 2219 3133; Av Borges de Medeiros 1426, Lagoa; ⏱ 9pm-3am Wed-Sat

This beautifully designed lounge is a stylish but informal place for a drink, with a glass rooftop lending an open feel to the place. DJs spin house and techno to a young Zona Sul crowd. The open-air patio is a particularly enticing in the moonlight.

COPACABANA & LEME

While Av Atlântica has plenty of open-air bars and restaurants, the strip unfortunately gets rather seedy after dark. There are some gems hidden in these once-idolized streets, but you'll have to seek them out.

ALLEGRO

Map pp244-5

☎ 2548 500

Sound record

admission fre

This small

cabana fea

p165 for m

CERVAN

☎ 2275 61

⏱ noon-4am Tue-Thu, to 5am Fri & Sat, to 5am Sun.

This Copacabana institution is as renowned for its meaty sandwiches as it is for the characters who eat them – at least at four in the morning. Not surprisingly, Cervantes also has excellent *chope*, making it a reliable haunt after the bars give you the boot. See also p116.

COPA CAFÉ Map pp244-5

☎ 2235 2947; Av Atlântica 3056, Copacabana; ⏱ 7pm-2am Tue-Sun

One of Copacabana's best new bars, Copa Café has sleek contemporary design, a satisfying menu and plenty of tasty drink concoctions. See also p116.

Entertainment

DRINKING

Hard to believe, but there's room for live music too at Allegro Bistrô Musical (above)

...bana Palace hotel, Av
...acabana; ⊙ noon-11pm
...n't swing the US$300-a-
..., you can still soak up some of
...dence that the Palace delivers in
... The poolside bar offers dozens of
...ptuous libations on a lovely outdoor ter-
...ace, a setting suitable for young duchesses
and weary travelers alike. If you're looking
for something more stately, head inside to
the elegant **piano bar** (⊙ 4pm-midnight).

HORSE'S NECK Map pp244-5

☎ 2525 1232; Sofitel Rio de Janeiro, Av Atlântica
4240, Copacabana; ⊙ 5pm-1am
Formerly a British-style pub, this place has
been reborn as a creature from Africa, with
leopards being the animal of choice when
it comes to the print on seat cushions and
wall hangings. Just like before, it's still a
quiet, peaceful place to grab a drink, with
an inviting balcony overlooking the ocean.

SINDICATO DO CHOPP Map pp244-5

☎ 2523 4644; Av Atlântica 3806, Copacabana;
⊙ 11am-3am
A Copacabana institution, this open-air
bar looks out on the wide avenue, with
the beach in the background. Owing to its
breezy location, it attracts a wide mix of
people, all playing a part in Copa's inim-
itable street theater. The food isn't so hot
here, but the beers are icy cold and the
ocean is, well, right there. A second **Sindicato
do Chopp** (Av Atlântica 514) in Leme also
overlooks the beach.

SKYLAB BAR Map pp244-5

☎ 2525 1500; 30th fl, Rio Othon Palace, Av Atlântica
3264, Copacabana; ⊙ 7pm-midnight
It's all about the view at this bar in the
Rio Othon Palace. From 30 floors up, the
coastline unfolds, allowing a glimpse of the
cidade maravilhosa at its most striking.

BOTAFOGO & URCA

If you're seeking out lively, authentic Carioca bars, Botafogo is the place to look, with
fun, mixed crowds and none of the pretense
you may encounter in bars further south.
Rua Visconde de Caravelas is a good place
to browse the pub scene. Untouched Urca

remains fairly nightlife-starved, though it
does hide one of our favorite places to hear
live music (Praia Vermelha, p138).

AURORA Map pp242-3

☎ 2539 4756; Rua Capitão Salomão 43, Botafogo;
⊙ 11am-midnight Mon-Thu, to 2am Fri & Sat,
to 9pm Sun
This classic *boteco* is 100% Carioca. Here
you'll find a comfortable, roomy bar with
a lively, talkative crowd spilling onto the
sidewalk tables out front. If you're in the
mood for a meal, traditional Brazilian fare is
available – including *feijoada* on Friday and
Saturday.

BAR DO BELMIRO Map pp242-3

☎ 2539 1354; Rua Conde de Irajá, Botafogo;
⊙ 7am-2:30am Mon-Fri, to 10pm Sat
Serving up endless pints of Brahma *chope*
to a chatty crowd, this casual bar is a good
place to meet the locals. Bar do Belmiro
hosts live *chorinho* (romantic, intimate
samba) bands, generally from Wednesday
to Friday, starting around 8pm (cover US$2).

BOTEQUIM Map pp242-3

☎ 2286 3391; Rua Visconde de Caravelas 184, Botafogo; ⊙ 11:30am-1am Sun-Thu, to 2am Fri & Sat
Another of Botafogo's great neighborhood
bars, Botequim is an old-school, down-at-
the-heels watering hole serving a friendly
crowd. The menu has plenty of appetizers
and more substantial dishes, if you need
something to accompany those *chopes*.

CHAMPANHARIA OVELHA NEGRA
Map pp242-3

☎ 2226 1064; Rua Bambina, Botafogo; ⊙ 5-11pm
Mon-Fri
One of Rio's best happy-hour scenes, Ovelha
Negra draws a mix of locals who come for
the lively conversation and the 40 different
varieties of champagne and *prosecco* (Italian
sparkling white wine) – the specialties of the
house. It's a tiny bar, opened in 2005, but
with a classic *boteco* feel.

ESPIRITO DO CHOPP Map pp242-3

☎ 2266 5599; Cobal do Humaitá, Rua Voluntários
da Pátria 446, Botafogo; ⊙ 9am-2:30am Sun-Wed,
to 4am Thu-Sat
One of many open-air venues in the Cobal,
Espirito do Chopp fills up its plastic tables

PARTY ON THE MOUNTAIN

One of Rio's best summer-long parties is the annual Noites Cariocas, held atop Pão de Açúcar. Boasting fabulous views of the city, the mountaintop gathers a festive crowd who come for dancing and revelry as Brazil's top DJs and bands take the stage. In recent years, performers like Jorge Benjor, Gilberto Gil and Kid Abelha have all made an appearance. From mid-November to early February, Noites Cariocas are held on Friday and Saturday night, from 9:30pm to 4am. Admission is US$42 (US$32 for students), which includes the price of the cable-car ride. See the Noites Cariocas website for more details: http://oinoitescari-ocas.oi.com.br in Portuguese.

most nights with a festive, low-key crowd. The beer flows in abundance here, and there's always music nearby – either here or at one of the neighboring bars.

GAROTA DA URCA Map pp242-3

☎ 2541 8585; Rua João Luís Alves 56, Urca; ⏱ 11am until last customer

A neighborhood crowd gathers in the evening at this low-key spot over *chope* and *salgados*. See p119.

FLAMENGO

BELMONTE Map pp242-3

☎ 2552 3349; Praia do Flamengo 300, Flamengo; ⏱ 7am until last customer

One of Flamengo's ultraclassic *botecos,* Belmonte serves up well chilled *chope* until late into the night. See p120 for more details.

CENTRO & CINELÂNDIA

Lined with low-key open-air bars, Travessa do Comércio is highly recommended as a place for grabbing a drink on weekday evenings. Another choice after-work spot is at the bars along Praça Floriano.

AMARELINHO Map pp238-9

☎ 2240 8434; Praça Floriano 55, Cinelândia; ⏱ 11am until last customer

Easy to spot by its bright *amarelo* (yellow) awning, Amarelinho has a splendid setting on the Praça Floriano. Yellow-vested waiters serve plenty of *chope* here, wandering

among the crowded tables, with the Teatro Municipal (p86) in the background. Amarelinho is a popular lunch spot but packs even bigger crowds for that oh-so-refreshing after-work brew.

ARCO DO TELES Map pp238-9

☎ 2242 9589; Travessa do Comércio 2, Centro; ⏱ noon-10pm Mon-Thu, 7am-2am Fri

Hidden in a narrow lane leading off Praça Quinze de Novembro, the Arco do Teles is one of several charming open-air bars on the colonial Travessa do Comércio. The scenic lane is a popular meeting spot and a festive air arrives at workday's end as Cariocas fill the tables spilling onto the street.

ATELIÊ ODEON Map pp238-9

☎ 2240 0746; Praça Floriano, Cinelândia; ⏱ noon-10pm Mon-Fri

A lunch and after-work crowd gathers at this pleasant open-air bistro on the edge of Praça Floriano. See p122 for more details.

BAR LUIZ Map pp238-9

☎ 2262 6900; Rua da Carioca 39, Centro; ⏱ 11am-11:30pm Mon-Sat

Well over 100 years old, this saloon and dining spot serves some of the city's best brew. See p122 for more details.

BECO DA SARDINHA Map pp238-9

Largo de Santa Rita, Centro; ⏱ 5-10pm Mon-Fri

See Centro's quirkier side at this longstanding happy-hour favorite. After work, crowds fill the tables of this open-air spot as bar owners serve fried sardines – with beer of course – continuing a tradition begun in the 1960s.

CHOPP DA LAPA Map pp238-9

☎ 2224 9358; Av Mem de Sá 17, Lapa; ⏱ 6pm until last customer Tue-Thu, 11am until last customer Sat & Sun

Just past the Passeio Público (p85), this classic bar has outside seating with an excellent view of the Arcos da Lapa (p88). It attracts a diverse bunch – old artists, shop owners, musicians, prostitutes and the odd ones you can't pin down – and the crowd tends to get more colorful as the night progresses. Note well: the food isn't so hot here, so stick to the drinks.

DITO & FEITO Map pp238-9

☎ 2509 1407; Travessa do Comércio 7, Centro;
🕑 11:30am-3:30pm & 6pm until last customer
Mon-Fri

Another popular bar on atmospheric Travessa do Comércio, Dito & Feito has dozens of outdoor tables for enjoying warm nights and ice-cold beer to move things along. Stop in early as this is usually an after-work (weekday) affair.

ESCH CAFÉ Map pp238-9

☎ 2507 5866; Rua do Rosário 107, Centro;
🕑 noon-10pm Mon-Fri

The smoky twin of the Leblon Esch Café (p138), this Esch offers the same selection of Cuban cigars from its humidor. Its dark-wood interior features stuffed leather chairs, a decent food-and-cocktail menu, and jazz throughout the week, usually Tuesday to Thursday, from 7pm to 9pm.

VIA XV BOTEQUIM Map pp238-9

☎ 2222 4016; Travessa do Comércio 15, Centro;
🕑 5pm-midnight Mon-Fri

One of numerous bars lining an old pedestrian lane just off Praça Quinze, this informal bar gathers a garrulous Centro set, meeting for a drink when the workday is done. The ambience comes from the historic street itself, as the best seating is outside. *Cerveja* (beer) is the drink of choice.

SANTA TERESA & LAPA

Two of Rio's most atmospheric neighborhoods are still rough around the edges, so take care when visiting here. Lapa is at its wildest during the weekends – which can be a bit much at times (Thursday is our favorite night). Santa Teresa's bar scene is sprinkled about, though Largo das Neves with its tiny plaza and open-sided bars is a must in the area.

ADEGA FLOR DE COIMBRA Map pp238-9

☎ 2224 4582; Rua Teotônio Regadas 34, Lapa;
🕑 noon-midnight Mon-Sat

In the same building that was once the home of Brazilian painter Cândido Portinari, the Adega Flor de Coimbra has been a bohemian haunt since it opened in 1938. Back in its early days, leftists, artists and intellectuals drank copiously at the slim old bar looking out on Lapa. Today, it draws a mix

of similar types, who drink wine and sangria with Adega's tasty *bolinhos de bacalhau* (codfish croquettes) or *feijoada*.

ARMAZÉM SÃO THIAGO Map p241

☎ 2232 0822; Rua Áurea 26, Santa Teresa;
🕑 11am-11pm Mon-Sat, to 6pm Sun

Part grocer, part bar, this hole-in-the-wall drinking establishment features a few stand-up tables and a counter. It doesn't look like much, and the neighborhood regulars would probably say it isn't – between sips of their beers – which is part of its charm. The crowds pack this place on weekends, with revelers spilling onto the sidewalks.

BAR DO MINEIRO Map p241

☎ 2221 9227; Rua Paschoal Carlos Magno 99, Santa Teresa; 🕑 11am-2am Tue-Thu, to 3am Fri & Sat, to midnight Sun

Famous for its Minas Gerais cuisine, Bar do Mineiro is one of Santa Teresa's most traditional *botecos* – and an excellent place for a drink while catching up on the local gossip. See p124 for more details.

CAFÉ NEVES Map p241

☎ 2221 4863; Largo das Neves 11, Santa Teresa;
🕑 6pm until last customer Tue-Sat

Small but charming, Café Neves is one of Santa Teresa's gems. It faces out onto Largo das Neves, with the occasional tram rattling by in the early evening. The open-sided bar draws a vibrant mix as the weekend nears.

COSMOPOLITA Map pp238-9

☎ 2224 7820; Travessa da Mosqueira 4, Lapa;
🕑 11am-10pm Mon-Fri, to 6pm Sat & Sat

Behind the stained-glass doors of this 1906 saloon, patrons gather about the long bar as the street scene unfolds outside. Cosmopolita is a fine setting in which to daydream over a few cocktails before hitting the samba clubs up the street.

GOIA BEIRA Map p241

☎ 2232 5751; Largo das Neves 13, Santa Teresa;
🕑 6pm-midnight Sun-Thu, 7:30pm-2am Fri & Sat

Another handsome bar on Largo das Neves, Goia Beira is a small, intimate spot serving a range of tasty *cachaças*. The open-air scene gets lively on weekends, with an occasional band playing out on the square.

MIKE'S HAUS Map p241

☎ 2509 5248; Rua Almirante Alexandrino 1458A, Santa Teresa; ⏲ 11:30am-midnight Mon-Sat

This German-style pub attracts a mix of expats and Cariocas, weekend nights. It's a bit off the beaten path, so plan on sticking around a while before moving on. See p125 for more details.

SIMPLESMENTE Map p241

☎ 2508 6007; Rua Paschoal Carlos Magno 115, Santa Teresa; ⏲ 7pm-3am Mon-Sat

One of Santa Teresa's long-standing favorites, Simplesmente is just that – a simple place without much decor – where the ambience is provided by the patrons rather than the furniture. A young, boho neighborhood crowd keeps things going until late – especially at weekends.

MUSIC & DANCE

Summarizing Rio's contemporary musical landscape is quite simple: Rio has one of the best music scenes on the planet. Encapsulating the diversity of its music, on the other hand, is rather difficult in a city with so much to offer. Samba, jazz, bossa nova, MPB, rock, hip-hop, reggae, electronic music and the fusions among them are a big part of the picture. Brazil's many regional styles – *forró* (traditional Brazilian music from the northeast), *chorinho*, *pagode* (relaxed and rhythmic samba) – are no less a contributor.

Rio's burgeoning and ever-evolving scene showcases its quality in diverse settings. Venues range from megamodern concert halls seating thousands to intimate samba clubs in edgy neighborhoods. Antiquated colonial mansions, outdoor parks overlooking the city, old-school bars, crumbling buildings on the edge of town and hypermodern lounges facing the ocean are all part of the mix.

LIVE MUSIC

Although straight-up bossa nova isn't much in fashion today in Rio, there are plenty of places to hear other styles from Brazil's rich musical heritage. Informal, laid-back settings like the ones that follow showcase some of the city's best talents. Those looking to dance should check out Samba Clubs (p139). For more information on Brazilian music, see p33.

ALLEGRO BISTRÔ MUSICAL
Map pp244-5

☎ 2548 5005; www.modernsound.com.br; Modern Sound, Rua Barata Ribeiro 502, Copacabana; admission free; ⏲ 9am-9pm Mon-Fri, to 8pm Sat

This small café in Copacabana's excellent music store Modern Sound (p165) features live music most nights of the week. Jazz and MPB groups play to a mix of Cariocas, predominantly aged 30 and up. Most groups play from 5pm to 9pm, though Allegro periodically becomes a lunchtime venue (1pm to 5pm). The more popular groups attract a large audience, with people spilling out into the store. Reservations are available if you want to be sure to snag that table by the piano.

BAR DO ERNESTO Map pp238-9

☎ 2509 6455; Largo da Lapa 41, Lapa; admission US$3.50

This rather simple *boteco* beside the Sala Cecília Meireles attracts a lively mixed crowd to its *roda de samba* (samba show or party) on Friday nights. The action usually gets going around 11:30pm.

BAR DO TOM Map pp246-7

☎ 2274 4022; Churrascaria Plataforma, Rua Adalberto Ferreira 32, Leblon; admission US$10-30; ⏲ 9pm-2am Fri & Sat

A mix of Cariocas and tourists – but mostly tourists – fill this downstairs space at Plataforma in Leblon. The 350-seat bar has excellent acoustics and hosts a range of top musicians performing MPB, bossa nova, tango and jazz. It opens only for shows.

BIP BIP Map pp244-5

☎ 2267 9696; Rua Almirante Gonçalves 50, Copacabana; admission free; ⏲ 6:30pm-1am

For years, Bip Bip has been one of the city's favorite spots to catch a live *roda de samba*. Although the ambience isn't much to speak of – just a storefront with a few battered tables –as the evening progresses, the tree-lined neighborhood becomes the backdrop to serious, improvised jam sessions with music and revelers spilling out onto the sidewalk. The schedule at the time of writing was samba on Sunday, *chorinho* on Tuesday, and bossa nova on Wednesday. The music usually begins around 8pm.

There's always time to relax and play, Bar Bip Bip (p137)

CAIS DO ORIENTE Map pp238-9
☎ 2233 2531; Rua Visconde de Itaboraí 8, Centro; cover US$12

On the 2nd floor of this 1870s mansion in Centro, excellent jazz, bossa nova and MPB groups perform throughout the year. Most shows happen on Friday or Saturday night; call or stop in to see what's on. Most shows start around 10pm. See also p123.

CLAN CAFÉ Map pp242-3
☎ 2558 2322; Rua Cosme Velho 564, Cosme Velho; admission free; 🕙 6pm-1am Tue & Wed, to 1:30am Thu & Fri, 1pm-2am Sat

Set against the hillside of Corcovado, the basically unmarked door of Clan Café hides a large open-air patio covered with abundant greenery. Slow-paced waiters shufle between the many tables as talented musicians fill the air with sound. Tuesdays belong to *chorinho,* while MPB rules on Wednesday, and jazz on Saturday. The music starts around 9pm.

ESCH CAFÉ Map pp246-7
☎ 2512 5651; Rua Dias Ferreira 78, Leblon; 🕙 noon until last customer

Billing itself as the House of Havana, Esch offers a blend of Cuban cigars and jazz. The dark-wood interior combined with the well-dressed over-30 crowd will probably make you feel like you're stepping into a Johnnie Walker photo shoot. Groups perform throughout the week – weekdays around 7pm, weekends around 2pm.

FAR UP Map pp242-3
☎ 2266 5599; Cobal do Humaitá, Rua Voluntários da Pátria 446, Botafogo; admission US$2-6; 🕙 9pm-2am Tue-Thu, to 5am Fri & Sat

Featuring live music most nights of the week, Far Up is a good destination if you're hanging out in Botafogo. The program leans toward rock and MPB, although the Tuesday-night karaoke session mixes things up.

MISTURA FINA Map pp246-7
☎ 2537 2844; www.misturafina.com.br in Portuguese; Av Borges de Medeiros 3207, Lagoa; shows US$5-10; 🕙 noon until last customer

Both a restaurant and a concert space, Mistura Fina attracts a wide mix of people to dine and take in the music. The piano bar plays for the restaurant downstairs, while jazz, MPB and samba are staged upstairs. With a view of Lagoa, the outdoor veranda becomes particularly lively during happy hour. For the latest show schedules check out the website.

PARQUE DAS RUINAS Map p241
☎ 2252 1039; Rua Murtinho Nobre 169, Santa Teresa; admission free

This scenic park overlooking downtown has live jazz concerts throughout the year. Music ranges from jazz to regional Brazilian. Schedules change regularly, but there are often events on Sunday afternoon.

POINT DA LAPA Map pp238-9
Rua Joaquim Silva 11, Lapa; admission free; 🕙 7pm-2am Thu-Sat

One of Lapa's classic samba spots, this tiny bar has excellent live groups playing to a cheerful crowd. The outdoor seating and informal setting are an unbeatable mix. Marcio, the friendly owner, hails from Minas Gerais; to get the night started, ask him for a tasty *cachaça* from his home region. Friday nights are particularly good nights to catch live samba.

PRAIA VERMELHA Map pp242-3
☎ 2275 7292; Praça General Tibúrcio, Urca; cover US$3; 🕙 11:30am-midnight

Perched over the beach of the same name, Praia Vermelha has gorgeous views of Pão de Açúcar looming overhead. By night, jazzy MPB bands play from 6pm onward, making for an enviable open-air setting. The food, unfortunately, is less spectacular. Steer clear of the limp pizzas and stick to beer and cocktails.

SEVERYNA Map pp242-3
☎ 2556 1296; Rua Ipiranga 54, Laranjeiras; admission free; ⏰ 11:30am-2am
At night this broad, simple dining hall (c 1950) forms the backdrop to northeastern rhythms. Large percussive groups perform *xote* (a 2/4 dance style derived from the polka), *forró* and *chorinho*, among other styles, to a sometimes-packed house. Shows begin at 8:30pm.

TEATRO RIVAL PETROBRAS Map pp238-9
☎ 2524 1666; www.rivalbr.com.br in Portuguese; Rua Álvaro Alvim 33, Cinelândia; admission US$8-15
Near Praça Floriano, this 450-seat hall has become a popular spot for some of the city's up-and-coming groups as well as veteran musicians. Four or five nights a week, Teatro Rival hosts MPB, *pagode*, samba, *chorinho* and *forró* groups. Tickets for events here can be purchased through Ticketronics (p128).

TOCA DO VINÍCIUS Map pp246-7
☎ 2247 5227; www.tocadovinicius.com.br in Portuguese; Rua Vinícius de Moraes 129, Ipanema; ⏰ 9am-9pm Mon-Fri, 10am-9pm Sat & Sun
This small CD-and-record shop hosts live *choro*, samba and bossa nova throughout the year. In summer, Toca stages several shows a week in its intimate space. Most start around 7pm. Stop by to see what's on.

VINÍCIUS PIANO BAR Map pp246-7
☎ 2523 4757; Rua Prudente de Moraes 34, Ipanema; admission US$5-15
Billing itself as the 'temple of bossa nova,' Vinícius Piano Bar has been an icon in the neighborhood since 1989. The indoor-outdoor tables make a fine setting to listen to decent bossa nova – although it's mostly tourists filling those seats since bossa nova isn't very popular anymore among Cariocas.

Samba Clubs

Gafieiras (dancehalls) are rising from the ashes of a once-bombed-out neighborhood and reinvigorating it with an air of youth, samba and an artistic edge. The neighborhood in question is Lapa, and after years

and years of neglect it is returning to its roots as center stage of Rio's nightlife. In the '20s and '30s, Lapa was a major destination for the bohemian members of society, who were attracted to its decadent array of cabaret joints, brothels and *gafieiras*. Today, its crumbling buildings hide beautifully restored interiors leading to rooms with broad dance floors. Atop the long stages, a crowd of musicians weaves together the seductive rhythms of samba. Although not all the spots mentioned below are in Lapa – and not all of them can be technically classed as *gafieiras* either – they all reconnect with Rio's era of fallen splendor.

ASA BRANCA Map pp238-9
☎ 2224 9358; Av Mem de Sá 17, Lapa; admission US$4-10; ⏰ 10pm-3am Tue-Sun
Near the Arcos da Lapa, Asa Branca is one of the more traditional Lapa nightspots, attracting an older crowd that packs its large smoky dance floor. In addition to some of the best *forró* in the city, the club also hosts DJs spinning a wide variety of styles.

CARIOCA DA GEMA Map pp238-9
☎ 2221 0043; Av Mem de Sá 79, Lapa; admission US$6-8; ⏰ 6pm-2am Mon-Wed, to 3am Thu & Fri, 9pm-4am Sat
Although it's now surrounded by clubs, Carioca da Gema was one of Lapa's pioneers when it opened in 2000. This small, warmly lit club still attracts some of the city's best samba bands, and you'll find a festive, mixed crowd filling the dance floor most nights. Current favorites are Monday and Friday.

CARIOLAPA Map pp238-9
☎ 2509 7418; Av Mem de Sá 61, Lapa; admission US$5-7; ⏰ 7pm-2am Tue-Thu, to 4am Fri & Sat
This charming, informal bar opened in 2005, adding yet another lively music spot to Mem de Sá. Samba, *choro* and MPB concerts are held most nights in the two-story Cariolapa, with DJs playing through the *madrugada* (wee hours) on Fridays and Saturdays.

CASA DE MÃE JOANA Map pp238-9
☎ 2531 9435; Av Gomes Freire 547, Lapa; admission US$6-10; ⏰ 7pm-1am Tue-Thu, to 3am Fri, 9pm-3am Sat
This near-sacred São Cristóvão club was transferred to Lapa back in 2001. Although

the address has changed, lovers of samba still have much to celebrate here, with top-notch groups, a cozy bohemian setting, and an always-full dance floor at the foot of the stage.

CASA ROSA Map pp242-3

☎ 9363 4645; Rua Alice 550, Laranjeiras; admission US$3-7; ◷ 11pm-5am Fri & Sat, 7pm-2am Sun
In the first decades of the 20th century, Casa Rosa was one of the city's most famous brothels in Rio's 'red light' area. Times have changed somewhat and today the demure Pink House is one of Rio's best nightspots. It has a large outdoor patio between several dance floors, where different bands play throughout the night. Surprisingly, there's also a thrift shop here, open until about 3am. The rest of the party keeps going until dawn. Saturday is the best night to go, though Casa Rosa's new Sunday *roda de samba* party also draws its fans – a good mix of Cariocas.

CASARÃO CULTURAL DOS ARCOS

Map pp238-9
☎ 2509 5166; Av Mem de Sá 23, Lapa; admission US$5-10; ◷ 11pm-3am Fri & Sat
A creatively decked-out place with old costumes on the walls, antique refrigerators and a red telephone booth, the Casarão gathers young and seriously dance-focused crowds to its jam sessions.

CENTRO CULTURAL CARIOCA

Map pp238-9
☎ 2252 6468; www.centroculturalcarioca.com.br in Portuguese; Rua do Teatro 37, Centro; ◷ 7pm-2am Mon-Fri, 8:30pm-3am Sat
This theater (p83) on Praça Tiradentes books top samba groups all year. Groups perform daily except on Sunday. To find out who's playing, check the website. The center also hosts ongoing exhibitions and gives dance lessons (see p156 for more details).

SAMBA DA MESA Carmen Michael

On Friday nights, Rio's samba community congregates in front of the faded colonial facades of Rua do Mercado under a canopy of tropical foliage to play *samba da mesa xote* (literally, samba of the table). On the worn cobblestones, a long table stands, altarlike. Around it the musicians sit and the crowd gyrates, paying homage to their favorite religion. *Samba da mesa* in Rio today is a grassroots movement of musicians and appreciators passionately committed to keeping their music on the street and in an improvised form.

It typically involves a table, at least one *cavaquinho* (small, ukelele-like instrument) player, an assortment of *tambores* (drums) and any number of makeshift instruments like coke cans, knives and forks that will make a rattle. The standard of the music can be outstanding, and it is not uncommon to catch sight of a samba *bamba* (big-name samba performer) keeping the beat for the group or belting out one of its tunes. Depending on which bohemians have blown through for the night, you might even catch a duel, where two singers will pit their wits against each other in a battle of rhymes. It is a challenge of the intellect, and the topics include everything from love to poverty to the opponent's mother. Even if you speak some Portuguese, you probably won't understand the slang and local references, but the delight of the crowd is infectious.

Street samba has taken a battering from the commercialization of music and space, the rising popularity of funk in the favelas and the police clampdown on 'noise pollution' in public spaces. However, for those still interested in a little piece of bohemian Rio, there are several established places that support free improvised street music. On Friday nights, Rua do Mercado and **Travessa do Comércio** (p135) near Praça Quinze in Centro attract the younger radical chic set. On Sunday and Tuesday nights, a tiny bar in Copacabana, **Bip Bip** (p137), caters for hard-core *sambistas* (samba dancers). If you're around on December 2, Dia de Samba, then you can join the samba train bound for Otavio Cross with the rest of Rio's samba community. The musicians disembark in the dusty backstreets of this working-class suburb, which is transformed every year into a labyrinth of makeshift bars and stages that host a 24-hour marathon of *samba da mesa*.

Impromptu street gatherings in Rio are more elusive at other times and finding them can sometimes resemble the mad scramble of trying to locate an illegal rave in the Western world. But it's an unforgettable experience if you find one. There are few fixed places for these parties, and they move from one week to the next. The *bairro* (neighborhood) of Lapa, in particular Rua Joaquim Silva, generally has something going on, but if not, keep your ears open for the unmistakable sound of the *samba bateria* (percussive-style samba) – follow that sound and you will find a party. Pay heed to the local etiquette: ensure you do not talk over the music, use cameras with a flash or sit down unless you are a contributing musician.

SAMBA SCHOOLS & SHOWS

Starting in August and September, most big samba schools, in preparation for Carnava[...] public. A samba school *(escola de samba)* is a professional troupe that performs in the sam[...] These are large dance parties, not specific lessons in samba, although you may learn to samb[...] typically charge between US$2 and US$5 at the door, and you'll be able to buy drinks there. Ma[...] in the favelas, so use common sense when going.

You can set up a visit to one or more samba schools through a travel agent. It's always best to call to c[...] is going to be rehearsal. Following is a list of the samba schools, contact information and rehearsal days – th[...] for tourists are generally Salgueiro and Mangueira.

Beija-Flor (☎ 2791 2866; www.beija-flor.com.br in Portuguese; Praçinha Wallace Paes Leme 1025, Nilópolis) Rehearsals begin in September and are held every Thursday at 8pm.

Caprichosos de Pilares (☎ 2592 5620; www.caprichosos.com.br in Portuguese; Rua Faleiros 1, Pilares) Rehearsals begin in August and are held every Saturday at 10pm.

Grande Rio (☎ 2775 8422; www.granderio.org.br in Portuguese; Rua Almirante Barroso 5-6, Duque de Caixas) Rehearsals begin in July and are held every Friday at 11pm.

Imperatriz Leopoldinense (☎ 2560 8037; www.imperatrizleopoldinense.com.br in Portuguese; Rua Professor Lacê 235, Ramos) Rehearsals begin in August and are held every Sunday at 7pm.

Mangueira (☎ 2567 4637; www.mangueira.com.br in Portuguese; Rua Visconde de Niterói 1072, Mangueira) Rehearsals begin in August and are held every Saturday at 10pm. This is one of the better samba schools for tourists to visit, but it gets packed close to Carnaval.

Mocidade Independente de Padre Miguel (☎ 3332 5823; Rua Coronel Tamarindo 38, Padre Miguel) Rehearsals begin in August and are held every Saturday at 10pm.

Porta da Pedra (☎ 3707 1518; www.gresuportadapedra.com.br; Av Lúcio Tomé Feteiro 290, São Gonçalo) Rehearsals begin in September and are held every Friday at 10pm.

Portela (☎ 2489 6440; www.gresportela.com.br in Portuguese; Rua Clara Nunes 81, Madureira) Rehearsals begin in August and are held every Friday at 10pm.

Rocinha (☎ 3205 3303; www.academicosdarocinha.com.br in Portuguese; Rua Bertha Lutz 80, São Conrado) Rehearsals begin in September and are held every Saturday at 10pm.

Salgueiro (☎ 2238 5564; www.salgueiro.com.br in Portuguese; Rua Silva Teles 104, Andaraí) Rehearsals begin in August and are held every Saturday at 10pm. This is another good choice for tourists.

Tradição (☎ 3350 5668; Estrada Intendente Magalhães 160, Campinho) Rehearsals begin in August and are held every Friday at 8pm.

Unidos da Tijuca (☎ 2516 4053; www.unidosdatijuca.com.br in Portuguese; Clube dos Portuários, Rua Francisco Bicalho 47, Cidade Nova) Rehearsals begin in September and are held every Saturday at 10pm.

Vila Isabel (☎ 2578 0077; www.gresunidosdevilaisabel.com.br in Portuguese; Av Blvd 28 de Setembro 382, Vila Isabel) Rehearsals begin in September and are held every Saturday at 11pm.

Viradouro (☎ 2628 7840; www.unidosdoviradouro.com.br in Portuguese; Av do Contorno 16, Barreto, Niterói) Rehearsals begin in September and are held every Saturday at 10pm.

DAMA DA NOITE Map pp238-9

☎ 2508 6219; www.damadanoite.com.br in Portuguese; Av Gomes Freire 773, Lapa; admission US$6-8; ☺ 7pm-2am Thu & Fri, 9pm-3am Sat
This 1907 mansion hosts excellent samba shows during the week. An outdoor patio, several bars and a *crêperie* (not to be missed) lie scattered about the three-story building. Check Dama's website for show listings or to reserve a table (recommended).

DEMOCRÁTICUS Map pp238-9

☎ 2252 4611; Rua do Riachuelo 91, Lapa; admission US$3-5; ☺ 10pm-3am Wed-Sat, 8pm-midnight Sun
Murals line the foyer walls of this 1867 mansion. The rhythms filter down from above. Follow the sound up the marble staircase and out into a large hall filled with tables, an enormous dance floor, and a long stage covered with musicians. A wide mix of Cariocas gathers here to dance, revel

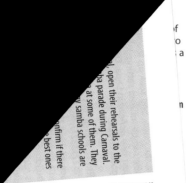

...play here and the club's old-city charm, it's not surprising that Elite has one of the more popular dance floors on weekend nights.

ESTRELA DA LAPA Map pp238-9
☎ 2507 6686; Av Mem de Sá, Lapa; admission US$5-10; 🕑 6pm-1am Wed & Thu, to 3am Fri, 7pm-3am Sat
One of Lapa's latest installments, this handsome samba club is set in a restored 19th-century mansion. Estrela da Lapa has an eclectic music scene and hosts bands playing *choro*, blues and hip-hop. Shows begin at 9pm, followed by a DJ who keeps the dance floor going until late.

ESTUDANTINA CAFÉ Map pp238-9
☎ 2507 8067; Praça Tiradentes 79, Centro; admission US$3-5; 🕑 11pm-3:30am Thu-Sat
Overlooking the Praça Tiradentes, this old dance hall packs large crowds on the weekend who enjoy excellent samba bands. The open-air veranda provides a nice spot to cool off if you've danced yourself into a sweat.

MANGUE SECO CACHAÇARIA
Map pp238-9
☎ 3852 1947; Rua do Lavradio 23, Lapa; admission US$5-6; 🕑 11am-3pm Mon, to 1am Tue-Sat
Set in a street lined with a mix of antique shops and bars, the two-story Mangue Seco has a casual bar and restaurant on the first floor and a *cachaçaria* (cachaça bar) on the 2nd floor. Sample over 100 different brands of the fiery stuff while listening to live *choro*, bossa nova or samba bands (starting at 8pm Tuesday to Thursday and 10pm Friday and Saturday).

RÍO SCENARIUM Map pp238-9
☎ 3852 5516; www.rioscenarium.com.br in Portuguese; Rua do Lavradio 20, Lapa; admission US$7-9; 🕑 6:30pm-2am Tue-Thu, 7pm-3am Fri & Sat
One of Rio's loveliest nightspots, Río Scenarium has three floors, each lavishly decorated with antiques. Balconies overlook the stage on the 1st floor, with dancers keeping time to the jazz-infused samba, *choro* or *pagode* filling the air. Río Scenarium has had much press outside of Brazil, and today it has a local-to-foreigner ratio of 50:50.

SACRILÉGIO Map pp238-9
☎ 2222 7345; Av Mem de Sá 81, Lapa; admission US$6-8; 🕑 7pm-1am Tue-Thu, to 3am Fri, 8pm-3am Sat
Next door to Carioca da Gema (p139), Sacrilégio is another major spot for catcing live

Río Scenarium (above) is big on atmosphere

bands in an intimate setting. The outdoor garden makes a fine spot for imbibing a few cold *chopes* while the music filters through the windows. In addition to samba, Sacrilégio hosts *choro, forró* and MPB bands.

TEATRO ODISSÉIA Map pp238-9

☎ 2224 6367; Av Mem de Sá 66, Lapa; admission US$5-10; 🕑 9pm-3am Tue-Sat
This newly opened three-story Lapa club features live music shows and DJs, with a relaxed area upstairs if you need a break from the sounds. You'll find plenty of samba, and MPB and rock make an occasional appearance at the club.

BIG VENUES

In addition to small bars and clubs, Rio has a few large concert halls that attract Brazilian stars like Gilberto Gil and Milton Nascimento, as well as well-known international bands stopping off in Rio on world tours. Citywide music festivals include October's Rio Jazz Festival (p11) and January's Rock in Rio Festival. In addition to the venues below, during the summer (December to February) concerts take place on the beaches of Ipanema, Copacabana, Botafogo, Barra da Tijuca and on the Marina de Glória.

ARMAZEM DO RIO Map pp238-9

☎ 2213 0826; Armazem No 5, Av Rodrigues Alves, Cais do Porto
Just north of Centro, on the docks of Rio, the Armazem hosts concerts, parties and cultural events throughout the year. You can find listings for upcoming events in *Veja Rio*.

CANECÃO Map pp242-3

☎ 2105 2000; www.canecao.com.br in Portuguese; Av Venceslau Brás 215, Botafogo
Near the Rio Sul Shopping (p166), Canecão holds big-venue music concerts – rock, MPB, hip-hop – throughout the year. Tickets are available at Ticketronics outlets or at the Canecão box office (cash only).

CIRCO VOADOR Map pp238-9

☎ 2533 5873; www.circovoador.com.br in Portuguese; Rua dos Arcos, Lapa; admission US$5-15
In a curvilinear building behind the Arcos da Lapa, this brand-new theater hosts a wide

range of music. The acoustics here are excellent, and after a show, you'll find plenty of other musical options in the area. Check the website to see what's on. You can also take classes in *capoeira*, dance or yoga here.

CLARO HALL Map pp236-7

☎ 2156 7300; Av Ayrton Senna 3000, Barra da Tijuca
Rio's largest concert house hosts big-name performers. As well as music shows, it hosts ballets, operas and an occasional circus. The Hall, which seats around 6000, is in the Via Parque Shopping Center (p172) in Barra. Purchase tickets through Ticketmaster (p128).

FUNDIÇÃO PROGRESSO Map pp238-9

☎ 2220 5070; www.fundicao.org; Rua dos Arcos 24, Lapa; admission US$5-15
This former foundry in Lapa hides one of Rio's top music and theater spaces. A diverse range of shows is staged here, which include big-name acts like Manu Chao and Caetano Veloso as well as theater, video arts and ballet. The foundation is one of Lapa's premier arts institutions, and you can study dance and *capoeira* or even circus arts here.

NIGHTCLUBS

Rio's vibrant dance scene isn't limited to its samba clubs. DJs spin a variety of beats – from house and hip-hop to more uniquely Brazilian combinations like electro-samba and bossa-jazz. In addition to Brazilian DJs, Rio attracts a handful of vinyl gurus from New York, Los Angeles and London to spin at bigger affairs. Flyers advertising dance parties and raves (pronounced *hah*-vees) can be found in some boutiques in Ipanema and Leblon, and in the surf shops in Galeria River (p165) by Praia Arpoador. Most clubs give a discount if you've got a flyer.

00 (ZERO ZERO) Map pp246-7

☎ 2540 8041; Planetário da Gávea, Av Padre Leonel Franca 240, Gávea; admission US$7-13; 🕑 10pm-4am Fri & Sat, 7pm-2am Sun
Housed in Gávea's planetarium, 00 is a restaurant by day, sleek lounge by night. A mix of Cariocas joins the fray here, though they mostly tend to be a fashion-literate, Zona Sul crowd. Playground, 00's Sunday party, has quite a following among house fans – gay and straight. In addition to rotating parties, the club also hosts CD-release parties.

Entertainment   NIGHTCLUBS

GAY RIO *Dan Littauer*

As one of the world's most exciting cities, Rio has been attracting queers since the beginning of the 20th century. Gay balls date as far back as the 1930s, and Carnaval celebrations have long given gays a chance to dress up, dance and meet. The gay balls have become an institution – the most famous is Gala Gay at Scala, a fabulous *festa* that attracts worldwide attention and is televised live throughout Brazil. Turma OK, the second-longest-running gay and lesbian club in the world, is still alive and kicking in Rio. Indeed, Rio has been a Mecca for gay and lesbian tourists since the 1950s. At that time, the place to see and be seen was the beach right in front of Copacabana palace (still a gay beach, which now attracts an older crowd), while nights were spent in the clubs of Copacabana and Centro.

Nowadays the GLBT (gay, lesbian, bisexual, transgender) scene, especially for visitors, is in Ipanema, with the gay beach (at the end of Rua Farme de Amoedo; look for the rainbow flag) at center stage. Rua Farme de Amoedo, where the girl of Ipanema has been brushed aside by muscle boys (humorously nicknamed 'barbies'), is the queerest street of Rio.

Having said all this, the Carioca definition and idea of a 'gay friendly' area is very different from, say, the Castro, Old Compton Street, or the Marais where there are clearly demarcated area for GLBT businesses. Rainbow flags are still a rarity in Rio, and people prefer mixing to exclusivity. Remember that most of the 30-something crowd grew up beneath a dictatorship that was not exactly gay friendly, and it's only the younger generation that is beginning to openly assert its sexual identity.

Nightlife

For all the latest parties about town, check out www.gbrazil.com. Here's a quick rundown of our top nightlife picks:

Monday This is among the quieter evenings in town as Cariocas recover from weekend partying. If you've just arrived, spend time on Rua Farme de Amoedo; Bofetada is a good choice of venue. Girls can head to La Girl for a decent line up of DJs.

Tuesday One option is to hang around Posto 6 bars and then move on to Le Boy's Xtravaganza, the best party in town on Tuesday. If not in the mood for dancing, head to the open-air bars around Lapa, where, on steamy summer nights the area hosts many pre-Carnaval parties – all of them gay friendly.

Wednesday You can take in the ambient music at the Copa or at **Copa Café** (p116), followed by a drag show at Le Boy. If you want just to relax, opt instead for one of Rio's best lounges or restaurants: **Bar d'Hotel** (p130), **Zazá Bistrô Tropical** (p113), **Gero** (p110), 00 (p113) and many others.

Thursday A great night to go out: around midnight, leave Rua Farme de Amoedo and walk one block to Galeria Café. You can have a drink at the bar outside or go straight to the excellent party inside, where DJs spin '70s and '80s records. Another option is Dama de Ferro, for excellent house music. In Copacabana, top choices for '80s music are Le Boy or the Copa. Girls can check out La Girl.

Friday This is the day for Lapa, a queer-friendly neighborhood with a fabulous atmosphere. After checking out the street party on Rua Joaquim Silva, you have many choices: for a fun, trashy night, Cabaret Casanova puts on a hilarious drag show. You can also go to Star Club, to the Buraco da Lacraia party that plays almost every imaginable musical style; the club has a pool table, karaoke and pub. If you'd rather stay in the Zona Sul then try Le Boy, Galeria Café, Dama de Ferro, Fosfobox, the Copa, Blue Angel (p146) and others. If you prefer a mature crowd, head to La Cueva.

Saturday Hang around Baixo Leblon, a gay-friendly, bohemian part of Leblon with lots of bars and restaurants that stay open late. This is usually the best night for partying. Try Galeria Café with its groovy house tunes or Dama de Ferro for the country's best funk, electro and house DJs. Fosfobox attracts lovers of electronic music. Le Boy has its biggest night. Head to La Girl for a girls' night.

Sunday Hang out at the beach, where you'll see seemingly every Carioca enjoying the seaside. Afterward, go to Rua Farme de Amoedo and spend time at Bar Bofetada (which incidentally translates as big slap in your face!) with the barbies. The best club tonight is **00** (zero zero, p143), where you can also enjoy a yummy dinner and relax in the lounge. Le Boy is popular with the barbies on this night.

Venues

Bar Bofetada (Map pp246–7 ☎ 2227 6992; Rua Farme de Amoedo 87A, Ipanema) This place is frequented by gay guys enjoying a glass of beer after the beach. It's a good place to watch the boys doing the catwalk up and down Rua Farme de Amoedo.

Cabaret Casanova (☎ 2221 6555; Av Mem de Sá 25, Lapa; ☼ Fri & Sat) This is one of Rio's oldest clubs, featuring a good mixed crowd, drag queens and slightly trashy music.

Casa da Lua (☎ 2247 4652; Rua Barão da Torre 240A, Ipanema) This lesbian bar is in a leafy part of Ipanema and serves great drinks.

Cine Ideal (☎ 2252 3460; www.cineideal.com.br in Portuguese; Rua da Carioca 62, Centro; ☽ Fri & Sat) An old movie theater, and now an electronic music club, Ideal has an outdoor terrace with views of old Rio.

Copa (☎ 2256 7412; www.thecopa.com.br; Rua Aires Saldanha 13A, Copacabana; ☽ Fri & Sat) This restaurant, bar and dance club is a relaxed hangout, attracting an 'intellectual' crowd of guys and girls aged 30 and up.

Dama de Ferro (Map pp246–7; ☎ 2247 2330; www .damadeferro.com.br in Portuguese; Rua Vinícius de Moraes 288, Ipanema; ☽ Tue-Sat) This club boasts one of the best electronic-music scenes in town.

Fosfobox (Map pp244–5 ☎ 2548 9478; www .fosfobox.com.br in Portuguese; basement level, loja 22A, Rua Siqueira Campos 143, Copacabana; ☽ Tue-Sun) This small underground club has live alternative bands, a mixed crowd, and easygoing ambience.

Galeria Café (☎ 2523 8250; www.galeriacafe.com.br; Rua Teixeira de Mello 31, Ipanema; ☽ Thu-Sat) This bar with a very mixed crowd has lovely decor.

La Cueva (☎ 2521 4999; www.boatelacueva.com; basement, Rua Miguel Lemos 51, Copacabana; ☽ Tue-Sun) This small club caters mostly for bear crowds and the more mature on weekends, but throws great parties on weekdays, especially Tuesdays.

La Girl (Map pp244–5 ☎ 2247 8342; www.lagirl .com.br in Portuguese; Rua Raul Pompéia 102, Copa-cabana; ☽ Mon, Fri & Sat) This lesbian club has a great atmosphere.

Le Boy (Map pp244–5 ☎ 2513 4993; www.leboy .com.br in Portuguese; Rua Raul Pompéia 102, Copa-cabana; ☽ Tue-Sun) Open since 1992, Le Boy is Rio's gay temple. There are theme nights with drag shows and go-go boys. Girls pay more to get in.

Space Club (☎ 2434 0984; Av Sernambetiba 5750, Barra da Tijuca; ☽ Fri & Sat) Cool club in the west part of the city has beautiful boys and tribal music.

Star Club (Buraco Da Lacraia; ☎ 2242 0446; Rua André Cavalcante 58, Lapa; ☽ Thu-Sat) This wicked place has entertained people for over 12 years. You'll find glamorous and trashy visitors, bizarre drag shows, karaoke, a dark room and other attractions.

Turma OK (Rua do Resende 43, Centro; ☽ Thu & Fri) The oldest club in South America has lots of trashy music (and we mean that in the kindest way) and attracts people from all over Rio – and the rest of the world. Not surprisingly, it gets very animated around Carnaval time.

BARONNETI Map pp246-7

☎ 2522 1460; Rua Barão da Torre 354, Ipanema; admission US$5-15; ⊙ 11pm-5am Tue-Sun

One of Ipanema's only nightclubs, Baronneti has a sleek and trim interior with a choice of two dance floors. Given its prime Zona Sul location, you'll find a young, well-heeled crowd here. Eclectic DJs and fruity cocktails keep the fans returning again and again.

BLUE ANGEL Map pp244-5

☎ 2513 2501; Rua Júlio de Castilhos 15B, Copacabana; admission US$2-4; ⊙ 10pm-2am Wed-Sat

At night the blue light comes on and Rio's freethinkers converge at the Blue Angel. A mixed crowd arrives weeknights, while weekends belong to the boys, indicated in part by the small shrine to Marlene Dietrich above the bathrooms – the line outside full of eager G-boys is another. It's a rather cozy bar, and on weekends there's not much room for dancing – although the DJs spin a good mix.

BOMBAR Map pp246-7

☎ 2249 2161; Av General San Martin 1011, Leblon; admission US$7-15; ⊙ 10pm-4am Mon-Sat

This popular Leblon nightclub attracts a festive, well-dressed neighborhood crowd to fill the upstairs dance floor as DJs spin a wide mix of electronica. Downstairs is a cozy, well-designed bar, which is the perfect spot for mingling among the mostly Zona Sul crowd.

BUNKER 94 Map pp244-5

☎ 3813 0300; Rua Raul Pompéia 94, Copacabana; admission US$5-10; ⊙ 11:30pm-3am Thu-Sun

Featuring big parties throughout the week, Bunker 94 is one of Copacabana's big draws. Its three rooms feature different music and you'll find an eclectic mix of Cariocas and tourists against the backdrop of hip-hop, acid jazz, rock, trance and deep house – among other selections. Weekends get crowded – come early and stake out a spot before the masses converge (around 1am).

CASA DA MATRIZ Map pp242-3

☎ 2266 1014; www.casadamatriz.com.br in Portuguese; Rua Henrique de Novaes 107, Botafogo; admission US$5-10; ⊙ 11:30pm-5am Mon & Thu-Sat

Artwork lines this avant-garde space in Botafogo. With numerous rooms to explore (lounge, screening room, dance floors) this old two-story mansion embodies the creative side of the Carioca spirit. Check the website for party listings – click 'festas.'

CINE IDEAL Map pp238-9

☎ 2221 1984; Rua da Carioca 64, Centro; admission US$7-12; ⊙ 11:30pm-6am Fri & Sat

This enormous downtown club hosts some of the city's best parties on the weekends. Here you'll find a fun, mixed crowd and top DJs spinning house, jungle, trance, with ample space for dancing and other rooms for lounging, including an open-air sky terrace.

BAILE FUNKS Tom Phillips

It's long past midnight and the streets in the Zona Norte community of Cidade Alta are filling. The sports hall is crammed with local youths – there for the community's weekly 'baile.' On stage the DJ hammers out a blend of Rio's bass-heavy funk music, around him a troupe of dancers wiggling simultaneously through impossibly complex moves. Security men from the neighborhood's resident drug gang – the Comando Vermelho – hover around the dance floor, in case of trouble.

Bailes (literally a 'dance' or 'ball') sprung out of the Carioca favelas during the 1970s, and since then their popularity has skyrocketed. Some 100,000 people attend parties like this each weekend in and around the city, in nightclubs, sports centers and on street corners.

The baile's increasing profile has been accompanied by controversy. Many criticize the music's sexually explicit lyrics, which some say encourage underage sex and violence against women.

The movement's infamy is compounded by its ties to the drugs trade – many of the parties are funded by Rio's traficantes (drug traffickers), keen to ingratiate themselves with locals.

These days the music is undeniably part of the mainstream, with the city's wealthy playboyzada (playboys) dancing alongside people from the favela. Rio's politicians are even trying to regulate the parties for the first time. Tour guides have begun to include the bailes on their itineraries. Most tours visit the Castelo das Pedras venue, which holds some 10,000 people.

CLUB SIX Map pp238-9

☎ 2510 3230; Rua das Marrecas 38, Lapa; admission US$10-20; ⏰ 11pm-6am Fri & Sat

Near the Arcos da Lapa, Club Six is perhaps Rio's only nightclub built to resemble a castle. Three dance floors, five bars and a number of lounge spots lie scattered about the building, with DJs spinning house, hip-hop, trance and MPB till daybreak.

FOSFOBOX Map pp244-5

☎ 2548 7498; Rua Siqueira Campos 143, Copacabana; admission US$5-10; ⏰ 11pm-4am Wed-Sat, 10pm-3am Sun

This subterranean club is hidden under a shopping center near the metro station. Good DJs spin everything from funk to glam rock, and the crowd here is one of the more eclectic in the club scene.

MELT Map pp246-7

☎ 2249 9309; Rua Rita Ludolf 47, Leblon; admission US$7-12; ⏰ 10pm-4am Mon & Thu-Sat, 11pm-4am Tue & Wed

The sinewy Melt club gathers a young, attractive crowd in its candlelit downstairs lounge, sipping brightly colored elixirs. Upstairs, DJs break beats over the dance floor, with the occasional band making an appearance. At the time of writing, Thursday night was the best night to go, though keep an eye out for Melt's excellent electro-samba parties.

More than one way to break the ice – try Melt (above)

CINEMA

Rio is one of Latin America's most important film centers. The market here is remarkably open to foreign and independent films, documentaries and avant-garde cinema. This isn't to say that mainstream Hollywood films are in short supply. The latest Hollywood blockbusters get ample screening space here – particularly in the shopping centers throughout town. Cultural centers, museums and old one-screen theaters, have substantially more diverse offerings. Most films are shown in the original language with Portuguese subtitles. Family movies and cartoons are usually dubbed. On weekends theaters get crowded, so buy your ticket early. Prices range from US$6 to US$8 per ticket, with matinee prices Monday through Thursday. For extensive listings and times pick up a copy of *O Globo*, *Jornal do Brasil* or *Veja Rio*.

CASA DA CULTURA LAURA ALVIM

Map pp246-7

☎ 2267 1647; Av Vieira Souto 176, Ipanema

Facing the beach, the charming Laura Alvim cultural center screens foreign (of the non-Hollywood variety) and independent flicks. Its small screening room seats 72.

CASA FRANÇA-BRASIL Map pp238-9

☎ 2253 5366; Rua Visconde de Itaboraí, Centro

Housed in the *Casa França-Brasil* (p82), the small 53-seat theater shows French films and an occasional independent classic.

ESPAÇO LEBLON Map pp246-7

☎ 2511 8857; store 101, Rua Conde de Bernadotte 26, Leblon

A one-screen theater in Leblon, Espaço shows foreign and independent films. In the same complex, there are a number of restaurants and cafés, making a perfect prelude to the cinema.

ESPAÇO MUSEU DA REPÚBLICA

Map pp242-3

☎ 3826 7984; Museu da República, Rua do Catete 153, Catete

The screening room in the dramatic Museu da República (p80) shows films you aren't likely to encounter elsewhere. The focus is world cinema – both contemporary and classic films.

RIO DE JANEIRO INTERNATIONAL FILM FESTIVAL

The Rio film fest is one of the biggest in Latin America. Over 200 films from all over the world are shown at some 35 theaters in Rio, with occasional open-air screenings on Copacabana Beach. The festival runs for 15 days from the last week of September to the first week of October. For films and locations, check the multilingual www.festivaldorio.com.br.

ESPAÇO UNIBANCO DE CINEMA
Map pp242-3

☎ 3221 9221; Rua Voluntários da Pátria 35, Botafogo

This two-screen cinema in Botafogo shows a range of films – Brazilian, foreign, independent and the occasional Hollywood film. It has a lovely café inside, as well as a used record-and-book shop with a number of works focusing on the film arts.

ESTAÇÃO BOTAFOGO Map pp242-3

☎ 2226 1988; Rua Voluntários da Pátria 88, Botafogo

One block from Espaço Unibanco, this small three-screen theater shows a mix of Brazilian and foreign films. The small café in front is a good place to grab a quick *cafézinho* (small black coffee) before the movie.

ESTAÇÃO IPANEMA Map pp246-7

☎ 2540 6445; Rua Visconde de Pirajá 605, Ipanema

On the 1st floor of a small shopping complex in Ipanema, Estação Ipanema screens popular contemporary films from Brazil and abroad. Its single theater seats 140.

ESTAÇÃO PAÇO Map pp238-9

☎ 2529 4829; Paço Imperial, Praça Quinze de Novembro 48, Centro

This small one-room screening theater (seats 64) in the Paço Imperial doesn't offer much in the way of state-of-the-art cinema viewing. However, the excellent selection of foreign and independent films makes up for the technological shortcomings.

ODEON BR Map pp238-9

☎ 2262 5089; Praça Mahatma Gandhi 5, Cinelândia

Rio de Janeiro's landmark cinema is a remnant of the once flourishing moviehouse scene that gave rise to the name Cinelândia. The restored 1920s film palace shows independent films, documentaries and foreign films and hosts the gala for prominent film festivals. Next door, Ateliê Odeon (p122) opens around weekend screenings.

PALÁCIO Map pp238-9

☎ 3221 9292; Rua do Passeio 40, Cinelândia

The two-screen Palácio shows first-run Hollywood films in an aging building across the street from Praça Mahatma Gandhi.

ROXY Map pp244-5

☎ 3221 9292; Av Nossa Senhora de Copacabana 945

Copacabana's only cinema is a good retreat when the weather sours. On three screens here, the Roxy shows the usual films on wide release.

TEATRO LEBLON Map pp246-7

☎ 3221 9292; Av Ataúlfo de Paiva 391, Leblon

Leblon's popular theater has two screens showing the latest Hollywood releases.

UCI – NEW YORK CITY CENTER
Map pp236-7

☎ 2432 4840; New York City Center, Av das Americas 5000, Barra da Tijuca; ◷ 1-10pm Mon-Fri, 11am-midnight Sat & Sun

Brazil's largest megaplex features 18 different screening rooms complete with large, comfortable chairs and stadium seating. Films are screened constantly (every 10 minutes on weekends).

Activities

Watching Sports 150
Horse Racing 150
Soccer 150

Outdoor Activities 151
Climbing 151
Cycling 152
Diving 152
Fishing 152
Hang Gliding 153
Hiking 153
Paddle Boating 154
Volleyball & Other Beach Sports 154
Walking & Jogging 154

Health & Fitness 156
Dancing 156
Gyms 156
Yoga 156

Activities

Rio's lush mountains and glimmering coastline just cry out for attention, and there are hundreds of ways to experience their magic on a sun-drenched afternoon. If you can't tear yourself away from the shore, there are plenty of ways to amuse yourself, including surfing, honing your volleyball game, joining a pickup soccer match or trying your hand at *frescobol* (game played on the beach with two wooden racquets and a rubber ball). Nearby, palm-lined paths offer spots for jogging, hiking, walking and cycling. While the mountain backdrops are fine to jog past, they are also the setting for some of the city's unique adventures: you can climb up them, hang-glide down from them or go hiking in the forests that surround them. For something a little different, you can take a dance class, go scuba diving off the islands near Rio, go fishing or stretch those sunburned gams at a yoga class. And for those who'd rather take their sport sitting down, there's always Maracanã, the world's largest football stadium.

> ## TOP FIVE REASONS TO LEAVE YOUR BEACH TOWEL
>
> - Rock-climb up the face of Pão de Açúcar (Sugarloaf) with **Akelá** (opposite).
> - Bike the shoreline **path** (p152) from Lagoa to Leme.
> - Go hang gliding off **Pedra Bonita** (p153).
> - Take an afternoon cruise along the **Baía de Guanabara** (p58) .
> - Surf amazing breaks off **Prainha** (p155).

WATCHING SPORTS

HORSE RACING

JÓQUEI CLUBE Map pp246-7

☎ 2512 9988; www.jcb.com.br in Portuguese; Jardim Botânico 1003, Gávea; ⊙ 6:15-11pm Mon, 4-11pm Fri, 2-8pm Sat & Sun

One of the country's loveliest racetracks, with a great view of the mountains and Corcovado, the Jóquei Clube (Jockey Club) seats 35,000 and lies on the Gávea side of the Lagoa Rodrigo de Freitas opposite Praça Santos Dumont. Local race fans are part of the attraction – it's a different slice of Rio life.

Tourists are welcome in the members' area, which has a bar overlooking the track. Races are held on Monday, Friday, Saturday and Sunday. The big event is the Brazilian Grand Prix (the first Sunday in August).

SOCCER

MARACANÃ FOOTBALL STADIUM

Map pp236-7

☎ 2568 9962; Av Maracanã, São Cristóvão; admission US$3-10; Ⓜ Maracanã

Nearly every Brazilian child dreams of playing in Maracanã, Rio's enormous shrine to

soccer. Matches here rate among the most exciting in the world, and the behavior of the fans is no less colorful. The devoted pound huge samba drums as their team takes the field, and if things are going badly – or very well – fans are sometimes driven to sheer madness. Some detonate smoke bombs in team colors, while others launch beer bottles, cups full of urine or dead chickens into the seats below. Enormous flags spread across large sections of the bleachers as people dance in the aisles (known to inspire a goal or two).

Games take place year round and can happen any day of the week. Rio's big four clubs are Flamengo, Fluminense, Vasco da Gama and Botafogo. Although many buses run to and from the stadium, the metro is safer and less crowded on game days. The safest seats in the stadium are on the lower level *cadeira* (seats), where the overhead covering protects you from descending objects. The ticket price is US$5 for most games. For more information on the stadium, see p90.

ESTÁDIO SÃO JANUÁRIO

Rua General Almério de Moura 131, São Cristóvão

Don't be put off by the fact that dictator-cum-president Getúlio Vargas used to hold his rallies here in the 1940s. The lively stadium in the Zona Norte neighborhood of Vasco da Gama has undergone some renovation since a stand collapsed here during a game in 2000.

ESTÁDIO DE CAIO MARTINS
Rua Presidente Backer, Niterói
This small 12,000-capacity ground in the nearby city of Niterói is currently home to the newly promoted club Botafogo.

ESTÁDIO EDSON PASSOS
Rua Cosmorama 200, Edson Passos
América's pint-sized stadium can hold 6000, making for some lively packed stands.

OUTDOOR ACTIVITIES
Climb, hike, surf or hang glide your way across Rio's enticing land- and seascapes. For those seeking more than just a taste of the outdoors, take a class and become an expert in your sport of choice.

CLIMBING
Rio is the center of rock climbing in Brazil, with 350 documented climbs within 40 minutes of the city center. Climbing in Rio is best during the cooler months of the year (April to October); during the summer, the tropical sun heats up the rock to ovenlike temperatures and turns the forests into saunas. People climb during the summer, but usually only in the early morning or late afternoon when it's not so hot.

A number of agencies offer climbing and hiking tours (see p60). Rio also has several well-organized climbing clubs, which have weekly meetings to discuss outings. The clubs, which welcome outsiders, also have something of a social component for those interested in mingling with Cariocas.

ANIMUS KON-TIKIS
☎ 2295 0086; www.animuskontikis.com.br; rock climbs/hikes US$55/23
Led by the intrepid and multilingual rock climber Akelá, who quickly established himself as the guide of choice when scaling the face of Pão de Açúcar. Although his climbs are challenging, beginners are welcome to join. Food, water and all the gear for the journey (including shoes and helmets) are provided. Along the way you'll have stunning views over the ocean, and you'll reach the summit just before sunset. You will then return to terra firma by cable car. Tours typically begin at 11am, and include one hour of hiking and four to six hours of rock climbing, depending on the route. Akelá also leads hiking tours through Floresta da Tijuca.

CENTRO EXCURSIONISTA BRASILEIRA Map pp238-9
CEB; ☎ 2252 9844; www.ceb.org.br in Portuguese; 8th fl, Av Almirante Barroso 2, Centro; ☒ office 2-6pm Mon-Fri, meetings 7pm Thu
Founded in 1919, CEB sponsors day hikes and weekend treks (with camping). It also

CAPOEIRA
The only surviving martial art native to the new world, *capoeira* was invented by Afro-Brazilian slaves about 400 years ago. In its original form, the grappling martial art developed as a means of self-defense against the slave owners. Once the fighting art was discovered, it was quickly banned and *capoeira* went underground. The slaves, however, continued to hone their fighting skills; they merely did it out of sight, practicing secretly in the forest. Later the sport was disguised as a kind of dance, allowing them to practice in the open. This is the form that exists today.

Capoeira, which is referred to as a *jogo* (game), is accompanied by hand clapping and the plucking of the *berimbau*, a long single-stringed instrument. Initially the music was used to warn fighters of the boss' approach; today it guides the rhythm of the game. Fast tempos dictate the players' exchange of fast, powerful kicks and blows, while slower tempos bring the pace down to a quasi dance. The *berimbau* is accompanied by the *atabaque*, a floor drum, and a *pandeiro*, a Brazilian tambourine.

The movements combine elements of fighting and dancing, and are executed (at least by the highly skilled) as fluid and circular, playful and respectful. *Capoeira's* popularity has spread far beyond Brazil's borders (there's even a *capoeira* club in Serbia). You can see musicians and spectators arranged in the *roda de capoeira* (*capoeira* circle) at the weekly **Feira Nordestina** (p90) in São Cristóvão. Unfortunately, there aren't any special *capoeira* clubs for visitors; most gyms, however, offer classes.

arranges trips further out, such as two-week hikes across Ushuaia in Southern Argentina. The club plans its activities at its weekly meeting, a good spot to have a chat with the laid-back enthusiasts. Its office is open during the week for people who want to stop in, say hello and take a look at the bulletin board, which lists upcoming excursions – as does the website.

CLUBE EXCURSIONISTA CARIOCA
Map pp244-5

CEC; ☎ 2255 1348; www.carioca.org.br in Portuguese; Ste 206, Rua Hilário de Gouveia 71, Copacabana; ☽ meetings 8:30pm Thu

Although CEC is 50 years old, it's still going strong. Typically, CEC arranges hikes and technical climbs, although from time to time it organizes rappelling and rafting. The club is also involved in preservation and education efforts, and gives five-week courses on basic mountaineering.

CYCLING

Rio has over 74km of bike paths, making cycling an excellent way to get some exercise. There are bike paths around Lagoa Rodrigo de Freitas (p64), along Barra da Tijuca and

on the oceanfront from Leblon to Leme which then goes to Flamengo and into the center. In the Tijuca forest, a 6km bikeway runs from Cascatinha to Açude. If you don't mind traffic, a bike is an excellent way to discover the city. On Sundays the beach road – from Leblon to Leme – is closed to cars, as is the road through Parque do Flamengo (p78). See the Directory (p204) for details on where to hire bikes.

DIVING

CALYPSO Map pp238-9

☎ 2542 8718, 9939 5997; www.calypsobrasil.com.br in Portuguese; Ste 502, Rua México 111, Centro

Calypso offers courses (up to Dive Master) in waters near Rio. The company also offers excellent excursions for certified divers to Arraial do Cabo and Angra dos Reis, among other spots. Those looking to do diving further afield should consider one of Calypso's affordably priced excursions to Fernando Noronha, a lovely island in the northeast.

DIVE POINT Map pp246-7

☎ 2239 5105; www.divepoint.com.br; Shop 4, Av Ataúlfo de Paiva 1174, Leblon

Scuba divers can rent equipment or take classes from Dive Point. It also offers diving courses, and dive tours around Rio's main beaches and Ilha Cagarras (the island in front of Ipanema), as well as the premier dive spots in Angra dos Reis, Búzios.

MAR DO RIO Map pp238-9

☎ 2225 7508; www.mardorio.com.br in Portuguese; Marina da Glória, Av Infante Dom Henrique, Glória

One of several dive operators in the Marina da Glória, Mar do Rio offers two-tank dives on Saturdays and Sundays, departing at 8:30am and returning at 2:30pm (US$70). It also offers night dives twice a month. Less-experienced divers can opt for one of the courses, including a five-day PADI-certified basic course (US$375).

FISHING

MARLIN YACHT CHARTERS Map pp238-9

☎ 2225 7434; loja (level) A1, Marina da Glória, Av Infante Dom Henrique, Glória

Those who have their own equipment should look into hiring a boat. The Marina

Take a break from the saddle and exercise

da Glória has a number of outfits, although Marlin Yacht Charters often has the largest fleet.

UNIVERSIDADE DA PESCA Map pp238-9
☎ 2240 8117, 9949 2363; www.upesca.com.br in Portuguese; Ste 502, Rua México 111, Centro
Universidade da Pesca offers a wide range of fishing tours – from day trips around Baía de Guanabara and Ilha Cagarras to week-long adventures in the Amazon. Trips include professional instructors and multilingual guides.

HANG GLIDING
If you weigh less than 100kg (about 220lb) and have a spare US$80 to spend, you can do the fantastic hang glide off 510m Pedra Bonita – one of the giant granite slabs that tower above Rio – onto Pepino beach in São Conrado. No experience is necessary. We've been assured that the winds are very safe here and the pilots know what they are doing. Guest riders are secured in a kind of pouch which is attached to the hang glider.

Naturally, hang gliding flights are one of those activities that are at the mercy of weather and wind conditions. During summer you can usually fly on all but three or four days a month, and conditions during winter are even better. If you fly early in the day, you will have more flexibility to accommodate unforeseen weather delays. The cheapest, but probably not the safest, way to arrange a flight is to go to the far end of Pepino beach on Av Prefeito Mendes de Moraes, where the flyboys hang out at the Vôo Livre (hang gliding) club (below). Be aware that their levels of experience vary. During the week, you might get a flight for around US$60. Travel agents can book tandem flights, but they add their own fee; to cut out the middlemen, call direct.

ASSOCIAÇÃO BRASILEIRO DE VÔO LIVRE Map pp236-7
☎ 3322 0266; www.abvl.com.br in Portuguese; Av Prefeito Mendes de Moraes, São Conrado
If you've had a taste of hang gliding, and you think you've found your calling, the Associação Brasileiro de Vôo Livre (Brazilian Association of Hang Gliding) offers classes in the sport.

CLUBE ESPORTIVO ULTRALEVES
Map pp236-7
☎ 2441 1880; Av Embaixador Abelardo Bueno 671, Jacarepaguá; ☽ 8am-sunset Tue-Sun
Ultra-leve (ultra light) flights are more comfortable than hang gliders, but you have to listen to the motor. The trips leave from the Aeroclube do Jacarepaguá. The club has some long-range ultra lights that can stay up for more than two hours. Fifteen-minute flights cost around US$30. Courses are also available.

JUST FLY
☎ 2268 0565, 9985 7540; www.justfly.com.br
Paulo Celani is a highly experienced tandem flyer with over 6000 flights to his credit. His fee includes picking you up from and dropping you off at your hotel.

SUPERFLY
☎ 3322 2286, 9982 5703; Casa 2, Estrada das Canoas 1476, São Conrado
Founder Ruy Marra has more than 25 years of flying experience and is an excellent tandem glider pilot. Regarded as one of the best in Rio, Ruy is also the person to see if you want to paraglide (gliding with a special parachute).

TANDEM FLY
☎ 2422 6371, 2422 0941; www.riotandemfly.com.br
Three experienced pilots run this flight outfit, and they'll arrange pick up and drop off at your hotel. They also give lessons for those wanting to learn how to fly solo.

HIKING
Rio is good for hiking and offers some outstanding nature walks. Visitors can hike one of the many trails through Floresta da Tijuca (p93) or head to one of the three national parks within a few hours of the city.

In recent years there's been a boom in organized hikes around the city, including hikes through wilderness areas around Corcovado, Morro da Urca and Pão de Açúcar, and of course Tijuca. It's advisable to go with a guide for a number of obvious reasons, getting lost and getting robbed being at the top of the list. Group outings can also be a great way to meet Cariocas. For more information on hiking outfits, turn to p60.

TOP FIVE HIKES

Ringed with tropical rainforest, Rio has plenty of in-spiring places in which to get a dose of the tropic's natural wonders. Here's a rundown of the city's best hikes, courtesy of Juliana Botafogo of Tangará Ecological Hikes (p60):

Corcovado Heavy hike to one of Rio's icons, with lovely views. It's steep, but highly rewarding.

Pedra Bonita Easy hike along a sunny trail; there's not much vegetation, but the views are worth it. You'll see part of Alto da Boa Vista and all of São Conrado, plus the islands off Rio's coast.

Pedra da Gávea Heaviest hike in Rio, but the sacrifice is worth it. Some rock-climbing skills needed.

Primatas Waterfall Easy hike less than one hour from Jardim Botânico. Gorgeous trail, interesting vegetation and a chance to spot monkeys.

Tijuca Peak Moderate hike to the highest place in the city: simply breathtaking views.

PADDLE BOATING

Those who've always dreamed of paddling a swan boat around the Zona Sul's largest lake can do just that on the Lagoa Rodrigo de Freitas (p64). Boat hire (US$10 per half hour) is available on weekends on the east shore near the Parque do Cantagalo.

VOLLEYBALL & OTHER BEACH SPORTS

Volleyball is Brazil's second-most popular sport (after soccer). A natural activity for the beach, it's also a popular spectator sport on TV. A local variation of volleyball you'll see on Rio's beaches is *futevôlei* – played without using hands. Good luck!

Usually played on the firm sand at the shoreline, *frescobol* involves two players, each with a wooden racquet, hitting a small rubber ball back and forth as hard as possible.

ESCOLINHA DE VÔLEI Map pp246-7

☎ 9702 5794; www.dudanet.eng.br/pele in Portuguese; Ipanema beach

Those interested in improving their game – or just meeting some Cariocas – should pay a visit to Pelé de Ipanema. Pelé, who speaks English, has been hosting volleyball classes for 10 years. Lessons are in the morning

(from about 6:30am to 9am) and in the afternoon (2pm to 9pm), ranging from one to two hours. He currently charges around US$25 for the month and you can come as often as you like. Look for his large Brazilian flag on the beach near Rua Garcia D'Ávila. Pelé's students are a mix of Cariocas and expats, who then meet for games after honing the fundamentals.

WALKING & JOGGING

Splendid views and the sounds of the ever-present ocean nearby are just two of the features of the many good walking and jogging paths of the Zona Sul. The Parque do Flamengo (p78) has plenty of paths stretching between city and bay. Further south the Lagoa Rodrigo de Freitas (p64) has a 7.5km track for cyclists, joggers and rollerbladers. At the lakeside Parque do Cantagalo you can rent bicycles, tricycles or quadricycles. The favorite option is the seaside path from Leme to Barra da Tijuca. Sunday is the best day to go, as the road is closed to traffic but open to the city's many outdoor enthusiasts.

Closed to bicycles but open to walkers and joggers is the Pista Cláudio Coutinho, between the mountains and the sea at Praia Vermelha in Urca. It's open from 7am until 6pm daily.

There's more to Brazil's beaches than just lounging about

SURF CITY *Thomas Kohnstamm*

When people think of Rio, Carnaval, music and swimsuit fashion come to mind. Yet quietly in the shadow of these attractions is the fact that Rio is also one of the best urban surf destinations in the world. It deserves a seat in the pantheon of the great surf cities, alongside Los Angeles, Honolulu and Sydney.

It is true that Brazil's best surfing is found further afield, in the smaller city of Florianopolis or on the remote islands of Fernando de Noronha. However, Rio is one of the few places on the planet where you can choose from nearly 50 surfable breaks in the afternoon, then take a quick shower and head out for an evening among the dynamism and energy of 6.2 million people.

The major beach spots along Copacabana and Ipanema cough up a few feeble rollers (mainly at Postos 5 and 6 on Copacabana, Postos 9 and 10 on Ipanema). These waves are generally better for body boarding than for surfing. For the classic, and often ridiculously crowded, Rio surf experience head to Arpoador and Diabo – both on the point of land that separates Copacabana from Ipanema. These spots pump fast, hollow beach breaks to the left and to the right. The biggest trick is jockeying for position among the aggressive squadrons of local watermen (and a few waterwomen). If you are a beginner, we suggest that you wait for the thinner crowds on weekday mornings, when there is less of a risk of dropping in on a wave already claimed by some macho Carioca.

Many surfers are turned off by the lack of waves on the major beaches and the packed conditions at Arpoador and Diabo. To find the real beauty of Rio surfing, you need to look beyond the obvious. Waves lick the shores of greater Rio from the excellent Itacoatiara break in Niterói, across the main beaches to Barra da Tijuca (check out Postos 3, 5 and 7) and continue all the way out to the Marambaia sandbar.

Most of the best waves are at the beaches to the west of Barra da Tijuca. Just past Barra and Recreio (about 30km from downtown Rio) is Macumba beach, which is also known as CCB (Camping Clube do Brasil). It is a top-notch beach with a variety of waves that cater to different types of surfers. The left end wave is ideal for long boarding, while the other breaks tend to be fast and hollow and can create barrels on a strong day. Macumba's sandy bottom makes it safer for wipeout-prone beginners and intermediates.

The next stop after Macumba is gorgeous Prainha (little beach). There is both a long right and a long left coming off either side of the bay with a grab bag of waves rolling down the middle. The beach is an attractive destination in itself and is backed by a virgin-forest preserve. While the right end wave can rise up to 3m on a powerful swell, the middle waves are accessible to intermediates (and often beginners). The only drawback is that the spot can get crowded. If the number of surfers becomes an issue, skip along to the next beach, Grumari. It is not always as good as Prainha, but usually offers more space.

For a less urban experience that's just a short overnight trip from Rio, go up the coast to Saquarema or down to Ilha Grande. Saquarema is about 100km from the city and serves up clean and consistent waves from Itauna to Vila beach (3km from town). Even if the surf is nonexistent in Rio, chances are there will be something to ride at Saquarema. This tranquil escape from the city has a sandy bottom, fast and powerful waves, and is suitable for all levels of surfers. You might even be tempted to stay a few days.

If it is natural beauty that you are seeking, head down to Ilha Grande and hike the trail across the island to the white crescent of Lopes Mendes beach. Crystalline right breaks peel along the southern end of the beach against a backdrop of lush tropical forest. The western end of the island has a few lesser-known waves that can be accessed by water taxi, an experience in itself.

For more information, check out www.wannasurf.com, which has finely detailed information on most of the major waves around Rio, or www.riosurfpage.com.br, which has a few photographss and gives an overview of Rio surfing.

For boards and other gear, check out **Galeria River** (p165; www.galeriariver.com.br in Portuguese).

For transportation that allows you to bring your board, try **Surfbus** (☎ 2539 7555), a brightly painted vehicle that travels four times daily (beginning at 7am) from Largo do Machado, to Prainha, with stops at beaches along the way (US$2).

For classes, try the following:

Escolinha de Surf Barra da Tijuca (☎ 3209 0302; 1st kiosk after Posto 5, Av Sernambetiba, Barra da Tijuca beach) This surfing school is run by a former professional champion Brazilian surfer. Young surfers aged five and up are supervised by a team of lifeguards. It's open every day.

Escolinha de Surf Paulo Dolabella (☎ 2490 4077; Ipanema beach in front of Rua Maria Quitéria) Although you'll have to ask around to find him, Paulo gives private lessons to those looking to learn. In the past, those who have taken lessons from him have said that Arpoador is a good place to learn. Lessons typically cost US$10 per hour; or sign up for a month for US$50.

HEALTH & FITNESS

DANCING

Given samba's resurgence throughout the city, it's not surprising there are a number of places where you can learn the moves. You can also find places to study *forró* (dance accompanied by the traditional, fast-paced music from the northeast), salsa and even the tango. A dance class is a good setting to meet other people while getting those two left feet to step in time.

ANTONIO CARIOCA Map pp244-5

☎ 2522 1142; contato@antoniocarioca.com.br; Level P, Rua Aires Saldanha 48, Copacabana
Inside the Rio Roiss hotel, this small dance studio offers a surprising range of classes in ballroom dancing, samba, *forró*, tango, salsa and belly dancing. Most classes are taught by the cheerful Antonio Carioca, who has over 15 years of experience as a teacher and performer.

CASA DE DANÇA CARLINHOS DE JESUS Map pp242-3

☎ 2541 6186; www.carlinhosdejesus.com.br in Portuguese; Rua Álvaro Ramos 11, Botafogo
At this respected dance academy in Botafogo, Carlinhos and his instructors offer evening classes in samba, *forró*, salsa and hip-hop. On Friday nights open dance parties for students and guests are sometimes held. One of Botafogo's colorful **bloco parties** (p26) begins from here during Carnaval.

CENTRO CULTURAL CARIOCA

Map pp238-9
☎ 2252 6468; www.centroculturalcarioca.com.br in Portuguese; Rua Sete de Setembro 237, Centro; 11am-8pm Mon-Fri
The cultural center offers one-hour classes in samba, ballroom dancing, and the sensual lambada. Most classes meet twice a week and cost from US$40 to US$60 for a six-week course. The large dance hall hosts parties on Friday at which samba bands perform.

CLAUDIO AFFONSO Map pp238-9

☎ 2221 8116; www.claudioaffonso.com.br in Portuguese; Rua do Ouvidor 37, Centro; 1-month class US$20-35
Set in an atmospheric old building near Travessa do Comércio, this studio offers a range of classes (samba, tango, bolero, swing) from Monday through Friday. Most classes are run across one month (US$20–US$35), though you can also arrange private lessons (US$15 per hour) if you want a crash course.

NÚCLEO DE DANÇA Map pp238-9

☎ 2221 1011; Rua da Carioca 14, Centro
A large upstairs spot on the edge of Lapa, Núcleo de Dança gives classes on *forró*, tango, salsa and samba. Instructor Marcia Pinheiro is flexible, and you can often drop in and join a class. Most are held around noon – so stop in to see what's on.

GYMS

Many hotels in Rio feature small workout centers with, perhaps, an adjoining sauna, but for those looking for a more intensive workout there are other options:

BODY TECH Map pp246-7

☎ 2529 8898; Rua General Urquiza, Leblon; 6am-11pm Mon-Fri, 9am-9pm Sat, 9am-2pm Sun
Body Tech has gyms all over the Zona Sul, which offer a full range of services: swimming pool, free weights and cardio machines and classes such as dance, gymnastics and spinning. The best of the bunch is the three-story Leblon branch, but there are also a couple of Body Techs in **Ipanema** (Map pp246–7; Rua Barão de Torre 577, Rua Gomes Carneiro 90) and one in **Copacabana** (Map pp244–5; Av NS de Copacabana 801).

YOGA

Yoga's popularity is on the rise in Rio, though there is a shortage of places where you can simply pop in for a class. Those around on Sunday can take a free class at 10am in Parque da Catacumba (Map pp246–7) in front of Lagoa Rodrigo de Freitas.

YÔGA CENTER Map pp246-7

☎ 2323 6775; www.uni-yoga.org; Rua Visconde de Pirajá 8, Ipanema
On the eastern edge of Ipanema, this peaceful center offers morning, afternoon and evening classes with friendly instructors (some of whom speak English). This is a good place to meet other yoga aficionados and find out about upcoming yoga events.

Shopping

Ipanema & Leblon   158

Gávea, Jardim Botânico
& Lagoa   164

Copacabana & Leme   164

Botafogo & Urca   166

Flamengo, Laranjeiras
& Cosme Velho   166

Centro & Cinelândia   167

Santa Teresa & Lapa   170

Barra da Tijuca & Greater Rio   171

Shopping

Rio has some enticing options when it comes to shopping. Whatever your weakness – you'll find it abundance in Rio and probably at lower prices than you'd pay at home. The hunting ground for top fashion designs (both Brazilian and international) is boutique-filled Ipanema. You'll also find music stores, bookshops, chocolate shops and plenty of cafés (sometimes inside the stores) in which to unwind along the way.

For something a little different, head to Centro, where bargains abound in the narrow pedestrian streets around Saara (p81). Centro also boasts the city's largest antique market, Praça do Mercado Feira de Antiguidades (p168), open on Saturdays. Copacabana's shops, just like the residents that shop in them, are a pretty diverse bunch, and you'll find everything from wine to soccer jerseys, with a mix of shoe stores, surf shops and record stores (including Modern Sound, the city's best, p165). Lapa and Santa Teresa have a mix of thrift shops and a few handicraft shops scattered along the old streets.

Shoppings (malls) are popular in Rio, and are good places to hide away when bad weather arrives. In addition to window shopping, most *shoppings* have restaurants (some with panoramic views) and movie theaters. Barra da Tijuca is the kingdom of shopping malls, each offering something slightly different than the one next door – one even services its 4.8km of stores with a monorail.

No matter where you are in Rio, you're probably not far from an open-air market. Fruit and vegetables dominate, but you'll also find markets selling used CDs and records, furniture and clothing.

Opening Hours

Most stores in Centro open from 9am to 6pm Monday to Friday. A few open on Saturday, usually from 9am to 1pm. In the Zona Sul stores typically open from 10am to 6pm Monday through Friday, though some stay open until 8pm or 9pm. On Saturday the shopping hours run from 10am to 2pm. Only a few of the big shopping malls open on Sunday – from about 3pm to 8pm.

Consumer Taxes

Most stores list their prices with the tax already included. So what you see on the price tag is the total price you'll pay for the goods.

Bargaining

Bargaining is uncommon in the shops of Rio, but if you buy on the street or at the markets it's quite a different story. Bargain as hard and as much as you can, but don't be surprised if the seller won't meet you halfway. Some vendors will simply be happy to watch you walk away if you don't meet their asking price.

IPANEMA & LEBLON

AMSTERDAM SAUER

Map pp246-7   Jewelry & Accessories
☎ 2512 1132; www.amsterdamsauer.com; Rua Garcia D'Ávila 105, Ipanema; 🕑 9:30am-2:30pm Mon-Fri, 10am-2pm Sat
Well known for its impressive collection of precious stones, Amsterdam Sauer also sells finely crafted jewelry. Watches, pens, wallets and other accessories are available too. Visitors can also check out the **museum** (p62) while they are here.

ANTONIO BERNARDO

Map pp246-7   Jewelry
☎ 2512 7204; Rua Garcia D'Ávila 121, Ipanema; 🕑 10am-8pm Mon-Fri
Designer-goldsmith Antonio Bernardo has garnered attention for his lovely bracelets, earrings and necklaces. His boutiques in Rio, include one in **Forum de Ipanema** (p162).

ARGUMENTO Map pp246-7   Books
☎ 2239 5294; Rua Dias Ferreira 417, Leblon; 🕑 9am-midnight Mon-Sat, 10am-midnight Sun
One of Leblon's fine neighborhood bookstores, Argumento stocks a small but decent

TOP RIO SOUVENIRS

- CDs – Rio is one of the world's best places to expand your music collection. Don't overlook local favorites like *sambista* (samba singer) Teresa Cristina.
- *Cachaça* – Connoisseurs rate the smooth Germana as one of the best brands.
- Swimwear – You may not be able to take the beach home, but you can at least flaunt your new tan in a tiny *sunga* (Speedo) or *fio dental* (string bikini).
- *Maracatu* drum – If you don't think the massive northeastern instrument will fit on your coffee table, consider the smaller, gentler *cavaquinho* (small ukelele-like instrument). Maracatu Brasil (p167) and Casa Oliveira (p167) are the best places to look.
- Havaianas – At less than US$6 a pair, you can buy these for every relative.
- Favela paintings – You can find some fantastic art-naïf works for sale on Rocinha's main street, and help support the local community besides.
- Soccer jersey – Forget the well-known yellow label. Try to score a jersey for one of Rio's teams – Flamengo, Fluminense or Vasco da Gama.
- Folk art – Tap into Brazil's rich handicraft traditions at stores like O Sol (p164), Brumada (p166), Empório Brasil (p160) and Brasil & Cia (below).

selection of foreign-language books and magazines. The charming café in back is a perfect place to disappear with a book – or a new friend.

BOCA DO SAPO Map pp246-7   Books & Music
☎ 2287 5207; Rua Visconde de Pirajá 12D, Ipanema; 🕑 10am-8pm Mon-Fri, 10am-7pm Sat, 1-7pm Sun
This charming used-book and -record shop is a good place to browse on a rainy day – or when the sun gets to be too much. Indie rock, *Música Popular Brasileira* (MPB), samba and funk are well represented in the music department.

BRASIL & CIA Map pp246-7   Handicrafts
☎ 2267 4603; Rua Maria Quitéria 27, Ipanema; 🕑 10am-7pm Mon-Sat, 10am-4pm Sun
This new handicrafts shop sells colorful works in papier-mâché, porcelain and glass, showcasing Brazil's rich artisan traditions. Figurines, wooden boxes, dolls and other crafts were made by artists from Pernambuco and Alagoas. Perfect for keepsakes of your travels.

CHEZ BONBON Map pp246-7   Chocolates
☎ 2521 4243; Rua Visconde de Pirajá 414, Ipanema; 🕑 9am-7pm Mon-Fri, 10am-2pm Sat
This small chocolate shop tucked away in a little gallery of stores sells decadent truffles and solid chocolates. It's a popular stopping point between shops…for obvious reasons.

CONTEMPORÂNEO
Map pp246-7   Clothing & Accessories
☎ 2287 6204; Rua Visconde de Pirajá 437, Ipanema; 🕑 9am-8pm Mon-Sat
A glowing boutique reminiscent of something you'd find in the center of Soho – better yet Nolita (it's the fashionistas' neighborhood of choice in New York). See the work of Brazil's best up-and-coming designers here. It also hosts parties from time to time.

DA CONDE Map pp246-7   Books
☎ 2274 0359; store 125, Rua Conde de Bernadotte 26, Leblon; 🕑 11am-midnight Mon-Sat
Secreted inside a tiny shopping plaza, this little multilevel bookstore stocks a small selection of English-language titles (including some Lonely Planet titles that are practically antiques or collector's items). You'll also find CDs, DVDs and a cozy café and lounge on the 2nd floor that hosts occasional book signings.

DAQUI Map pp246-7   Clothing & Accessories
☎ 2529 8576; Av Ataúlfo de Paiva 1174, Leblon; 🕑 9am-8pm Mon-Fri, 9am-4pm Sat
This tiny boutique is a fun place for a quick stop-off – perhaps en route to Mustafá (p111) next door. Here you'll find handmade jewelry, purses, colorfully designed clothes and curiosities for the home, including tiny mirrors and seductively shaped pencils.

ELIANE CARVALHO
Map pp246-7   Clothing & Accessories
☎ 2540 5438; Rua Dias Ferreira 242, Leblon; 🕑 2-7:30pm Tue-Fri, 10am-6:30pm Sat & Sun
Featuring tile floors and a cozy ambience, this boutique sells elegant handmade bags and purses, pillows, jewelry and even tiny lamps. After browsing, be sure to sample some of the good breads and jams in the charming café inside.

Shopping

IPANEMA & LEBLON

EMPÓRIO BRASIL

Map pp246-7   Handicrafts

☎ 2512 3365; store 108, Rua Visconde de Pirajá 595, Ipanema; ⏰ 10am-6pm Mon-Fri, 10am-4pm Sat

Hidden in the back of a small shopping center, Empório Brasil sells some of Rio's loveliest objets d'art. Works here showcase both the talents and fibers of the country – jewelry, vases, instruments, baskets and an ever-changing array of works produced by Brazilian artists and artisans.

ESCADA Map pp246-7   Antiques

☎ 2274 9398; Av General San Martin 1219, Leblon; ⏰ 5-10pm Mon-Sat

One step inside this rambling antique shop, and you'll just know there's some treasure hidden within. The only problem is that it may not fit in your suitcase. Chandeliers, papier-mâché sculptures, along with antique rings, rugs, little statues and countless other objects litter the interior of this store. Peer beneath the dust and you might find a gem.

ESCH CAFÉ Map pp246-7   Cigars

☎ 2512 5651; Rua Dias Ferreira 78, Leblon; ⏰ noon until last customer

This restaurant-bar is also the 'house of the Havana,' which means if you have a taste for the Cubans, this is your place. The humidor is stocked with a decent selection, which you can enjoy there over a glass of port, or a few blocks away on the beach (admiring a sunset).

FLORESTAS Map pp246-7   Beauty & Cosmetics

☎ 2227 0417; www.florestas.com.br; store 207, Av Visconde de Pirajá 414, Ipanema; ⏰ 10am-7pm Mon-Fri, 10am-1pm Sat

This inviting store sells beauty products derived from sustainable sources – plants, vegetable oils, flowers and fruits – found only in Brazil. Among the selections are a facial mask made from Amazonian white clay, a hand cream enriched with *babassu* nut oil, and gift sets containing spa products made from Amazonian berries.

FORUM Map pp246-7   Shopping Center

☎ 2521 7415; www.forum.com.br; Rua Barão da Torre 422, Ipanema; ⏰ 10am-6pm Mon-Fri, 10am-2pm Sat

Much vaunted Brazilian designer Tufi Duek has set up his wildly designed flagship store

CLOTHING SIZES

Measurements approximate only, try before you buy

Women's Clothing

Aus/UK	8	10	12	14	16	18
Europe	36	38	40	42	44	46
Japan	5	7	9	11	13	15
USA	6	8	10	12	14	16

Women's Shoes

Aus/USA	5	6	7	8	9	10
Europe	35	36	37	38	39	40
France only	35	36	38	39	40	42
Japan	22	23	24	25	26	27
UK	3½	4½	5½	6½	7½	8½

Men's Clothing

Aus	92	96	100	104	108	112
Europe	46	48	50	52	54	56
Japan	S		M	M		L
UK/USA	35	36	37	38	39	40

Men's Shirts (Collar Sizes)

Aus/Japan	38	39	40	41	42	43
Europe	38	39	40	41	42	43
UK/USA	15	15½	16	16½	17	17½

Men's Shoes

Aus/UK	7	8	9	10	11	12
Europe	41	42	43	44½	46	47
Japan	26	27	27½	28	29	30
USA	7½	8½	9½	10½	11½	12½

on a peaceful, tree-lined street just up from the main avenue. Here you'll find elegant, beautifully made pieces from his men's and women's collections – which have secured his reputation among high-end retailers in both São Paulo and New York.

GILSON MARTINS Map pp246-7   Accessories

☎ 2227 6178; Rua Visconde de Pirajá 462, Ipanema; ⏰ 10am-8pm Mon-Fri, 10am-4pm Sat

Designer Gilson Martins turns the Brazilian flag into a fashion statement in his flag-ship store in Ipanema. In addition to glossy handbags, wallets and other accessories, the shop sports a gallery in back with ongoing exhibitions – usually dealing with outsider fashion.

H STERN Map pp246-7   Jewelry & Accessories

☎ 2259 7442; hstern@hstern.com.br; Rua Garcia D'Ávila 113, Ipanema; ⏰ 8:30am-6:30pm Mon-Fri, 8:30am-2pm Sat

The famous jeweler H Stern has an array of finely crafted jewelry, watches and other accessories for sale. At the company's head-quarters you can also take a tour of the H Stern **gem museum** (p62).

INTERSTUDIO Map pp246-7 — Arts & Crafts

☎ 2511 1237; Rua Visconde de Pirajá 595, Ipanema; ☯ 10am-7pm Mon-Fri, 10am-4pm Sat
This small Ipanema shop sells some beautifully made art pieces. You'll find works in colored glass, wooden boxes, paintings and some intriguing papier-mâché objets d'art. Nearly everything here comes from Brazil (Minas and Recife in particular). Worldwide shipping available for bigger pieces.

IPANEMA.COM

Map pp246-7 — Clothing & Accessories
☎ 2227 1288; Rua Prudente de Moraes 237c, Ipanema; ☯ 10am-7pm Mon-Fri, 10am-4pm Sat
Featuring local and international designers, Ipanema.com focuses on men – though it also has women's wear. A good spot if you need a new look in a hurry – for that special night out.

ISABELA CAPETO

Map pp246-7 — Women's Clothing
☎ 2540 5232; Rua Dias Ferreira 45B, Leblon; ☯ 10am-8pm Mon-Fri, 10am-3pm Sat
One of Brazil's rising young stars, Isabela Capeto creates beautifully handmade pieces with seductive lines and a masterful use of color. All of her pieces are embroidered and feature add-ons of vintage lace, sequins or fabric trims. A good place to see some of the dresses and skirts that have earned her accolades from *O Globo, Vogue* and others.

JULIANA FARO

Map pp246-7 — Clothing & Accessories
☎ 2294 4393; Rua Visconde de Pirajá 611, Ipanema; ☯ 10am-7pm Mon-Fri, 10am-2pm Sat
Hidden inside a tiny shopping plaza, this small store sells young, hip women's fashions as well as handbags and accessories. In the same complex, you'll find a handsome jewelry shop and the popular *pão de queijo* (cheese-filled roll) snack stand.

KOPENHAGEN Map pp246-7 — Chocolates

☎ 2511 1112; Av Ataúlfo de Paiva 1025, Leblon; ☯ 10am-7pm Mon-Fri, 10am-2pm Sat
Serving up tasty bonbons and other decadent chocolate treats, Kopenhagen has

TOP FIVE SHOPPING STRIPS

- Av Ataúlfo de Paiva, Leblon – Boutiques selling haute couture sprinkled among cafés, bookshops and restaurants.
- Av Nossa Senhora (NS) de Copacabana, Copacabana – Packed during the week, this strip is lined with shops selling everything from chocolates to soccer balls, with plenty of street vendors hawking their wares along the sidewalks.
- Rua do Lavradio, Lapa – Rows of antique stores mixed with hypermodern furniture shops, along with a few cafés and bars – sometimes inside the stores.
- Rua Visconde de Pirajá, Ipanema – Ipanema's vibrant shopping strip has boutiques, shopping centers and scores of dining and coffee-sipping options.
- Senhor dos Passos, Centro – One of the main streets coursing through the Middle Eastern bazaar–like Saara, with clothing and curio shops spilling onto the street.

been satisfying children and chocoholics since 1928. There's a tiny café on hand if you can't resist the temptation to devour those cognac-filled truffles right there. There's another store in **Copacabana** (Map pp244–5; ☎ 2521 5949; Av NS de Copacabana 583; ☯ 9am-8pm Mon-Fri, 10am-7pm Sat & Sun).

LETRAS E EXPRESSÕES

Map pp246-7 — Books & Music
☎ 2521 6110; Rua Visconde de Pirajá 276, Ipanema; ☯ 8am-midnight
One of Ipanema's growing assortment of bookshops, Letras e Expressões carries a decent selection of foreign-language books from architectural tomes to fiction and travel books (Lonely Planet titles notwithstanding). It also has a variety of English-language magazines and an Internet café (Café Ubaldo), which is nice for sipping cappuccino and sending envy-worthy missives back home. There is also a 24-hour location in **Leblon** (Map pp246–7; Av Ataúlfo de Paiva 1292).

LIDADOR Map pp246-7 — Wine & Spirits

☎ 2512 1788; Av Ataúlfo de Paiva 1079, Leblon; ☯ 10am-8pm Mon-Fri, 10am-5pm Sat
One of Leblon's best wine shops, Lidador stocks a decent variety of good Chilean and

161

Argentinean wines as well as vintages from Europe and beyond. *Cachaças,* rums and even Brazilian wines are available if you're looking for something with a little more bite.

LIVRARIA DA TRAVESSA

Map pp246-7 — Books & Music

☎ 2249 4977; Rua Visconde de Pirajá 572, Ipanema; ꔄ 9am-midnight Mon-Sat, 1pm-midnight Sun

One of a growing chain of bookstores around the city, Livraria da Travessa has a small selection of foreign-language books and periodicals. Upstairs it has a good music collection – most of which you can listen to by scanning the discs under the headphone stations. After browsing stop in at B! (p107) for tasty salads, quiches and desserts.

LUKO Map pp246-7 — Clothing & Accessories

☎ 2540 0589; store 111, Rua Visconde de Pirajá 547, Ipanema; ꔄ 10am-7pm Mon-Fri, 10am-4pm Sat

This charming boutique has an eclectic collection of youthful women's couture. Slim, beaded necklaces and bracelets, silk scarves, form-fitting tops and skirts and slinky lingerie are among the pieces you'll find here. Rumor has it that Luko is a great favorite among TV production companies looking for pieces for their actors.

MBR Map pp246-7 — Women's Shoes

☎ 2549 0805; store 227, Rua Visconde de Pirajá 414, Ipanema; ꔄ 10am-8pm Mon-Fri, 10am-3pm Sat

MBR, we suspect, is some kind of code word for 'popsicle.' How else to explain the pink walls, the curved red and yellow displays, and the shoes themselves, painted in an array of cheery and fun colors? MBR also sells sunglasses and hats, though it's the heels and sandals that bring in the young neighborhood patrons. A second store is in Copacabana (Map pp244–5; ☎ 2549 0805; Av NS de Copacabana 664).

MIXED Map pp246-7 — Clothing & Accessories

☎ 2259 9544; www.mixed.com.br in Portuguese; Rua Visconde de Pirajá 476, Ipanema; ꔄ 10am-8pm Mon-Fri

One of Rio's premier boutiques, Mixed actually originated in São Paolo. Ipanemans, however, love it as their own. The shoes and platforms, blouses and pants sold here aim to capture the essence of Carioca sensuality. And they do it quite well.

BUILDINGS OF BOUTIQUES

Lovely shops abound in Ipanema and Leblon, though they're not always obvious to the eye. Some of the best finds are hidden away in shopping plazas like these:

Forum de Ipanema (Map pp246-7; Rua Visconde de Pirajá 351, Ipanema; ꔄ 10am-8pm Mon-Sat) Top stores here include Via Milano shoes; Yes, Brazil apparel; and Bum Bum and Salinas (both selling men's and women's swimwear).

Galeria Ipanema Secreta (Map pp246-7; Rua Visconde de Pirajá 371, Ipanema; ꔄ 10am-8pm Mon-Sat) Featuring a number of elegant designs, including the comely handbags of Dani Carvalho.

Ipanema 2000 (Map pp246-7; Rua Visconde de Pirajá 547, Ipanema; ꔄ 10am-8pm Mon-Fri) Ipanema's fashion-conscious shoppers flock to this store gallery in search of something new for the after-office soiree – or the upcoming trip to Búzios.

Rio Design Center (Map pp246-7; ☎ 3206 9100; Av Ataúlfo de Paiva 270, Leblon; ꔄ 10am-10pm Mon-Fri, 10am-8pm Sat, 3-9pm Sun) Four floors of galleries and stores, most dedicated to home decor.

MUSICALE Map pp246-7 — Music

☎ 2540 5237; Rua Visconde de Pirajá 483, Ipanema; ꔄ 10am-7pm

This small music shop has narrow aisles, but you'll come across some real finds if you brave the elbow jousting at Musicale. Used and new CDs are organized somewhat by category, and you can listen to any used CD at one of the decks up front.

NO MEIO DO CAMINHO

Map pp246-7 — Art & Home Furnishings

☎ 2294 1330; Av General San Martin 1247, Leblon; ꔄ 10am-7pm Mon-Fri, 10am-2pm Sat

Showcasing the work of talented Brazilian artisans, No Meio do Caminho has two floors full of pottery, vases, ceramics and woodwork. Decorative items here are more akin to art pieces – and are priced accordingly. No Meio do Caminho will ship anywhere.

OSKLEN Map pp246-7 — Clothing

☎ 2227 2911; Rua Maria Quitéria 85, Ipanema; ꔄ 10am-7pm Mon-Fri, 10am-2pm Sat

One of Brazil's hottest labels in recent years. The fashions here are light and playful with subdued colors. The company was started in 1988 by outdoor enthusiast Oskar Metsavaht, the first Brazilian to scale Mont Blanc.

OZ
Map pp246-7 · Art & Home Furnishings

☎ 3204 0754; store 302, Rua Visconde de Pirajá 580, Ipanema; 🕙 10am-7pm Mon-Fri, 10am-2pm Sat

Complete with ruby-red heels and a yellow-brick road of sorts, Oz is a playful send-up of the old Dorothy story. T-shirts are the specialty here and, not surprisingly, come in whimsical designs that may be just the item needed for a casual night out in Rio.

PANO NOSSO
Map pp246-7 · Clothing & Accessories

☎ 2511 3800; store 103, Rua Visconde de Pirajá 595, Ipanema; 🕙 10am-7pm Mon-Fri, 10am-2pm Sat

One of Rio's most colorful stores, Pano Nosso is filled with brightly hued pillow-cases, silk-encased Havaianas, cheery hand-bags, willowy dresses and dozens of other fabric-draped items that we couldn't identify but were drawn to nonetheless. Fabric designers shouldn't miss this dreamlike store.

TEARGAS
Map pp246-7 · Men's Clothing

☎ 2267 6598; store 201, Rua Visconde de Pirajá 444, Ipanema; 🕙 10am-7pm Mon-Fri, 10am-3pm Sat

Daring men's fashions are for sale at this innovative store and design studio in Ipanema. Stylized T-shirts (including one bearing the company logo, a gas mask), intricately embroidered button-downs, sleek jackets, pants and jeans are suitable not just for the mass demonstration, but for the posh after-party as well.

TOCA DO VINÍCIUS
Map pp246-7 · Music

☎ 2247 5227; www.tocadovinicius.com.br; Rua Vinícius de Moraes 129, Ipanema; 🕙 9am-9pm Mon-Fri, 10am-9pm Sat & Sun

Bossa nova fans shouldn't miss this store. In addition to its ample CD selection of contemporary and old performers, Toca do Vinícius sells music scores and composition books. Upstairs a tiny museum displays memorabilia of the great songwriter and poet Vinícius de Moraes. Occasional concerts in the afternoon fill this neighborhood with smooth bossa sounds.

URUCUM ART & DESIGN
Map pp246-7 · Home Decor

☎ 2540 9990; Rua Visconde de Pirajá 605, Ipanema; 🕙 10am-8pm Mon-Fri, 10am-5pm Sat

This small, trim shop is in the same complex as the cinema Estação Ipanema (p148) Make your choice from the vases, block prints, playful sculptures, pottery and other artworks for sale.

Shopping

IPANEMA & LEBLON

So many enticing period choices – but will they fit in your luggage bag?

163

VALE DAS BONECAS

Map pp246-7   Clothing & Accessories

☎ 2523 1794; Rua Farme de Amoedo 75C, Ipanema; ◷ 10am-8pm Mon-Fri, 10am-2:30pm Sat
Youthful street fashion is the focal point at this small Ipanema boutique. Local designers play with color and material here – not always successfully. But if you're looking for something a little edgy, the Vale das Bonecas (Valley of the Dolls) is a fine destination.

WÖLLNER OUTDOOR

Map pp246-7   Clothing & Accessories

☎ 2512 6531; Rua Visconde de Pirajá 511, Ipanema; ◷ 10am-9pm Mon-Fri
The great outdoors, and the shirt and shorts you'll need to enjoy it, seem to be the inspiration of Wöllner. Clothes feature rugged styles, nicely cut – though not always so interesting. Once you've browsed the selections, grab a *cafézinho* (small black coffee) and a window seat in the café and watch the day go by.

WORLD MAP Map pp246-7   Shoes

☎ 2523 0154; Rua Vinícius de Moraes 121B, Ipanema; ◷ 10am-7pm Mon-Fri, 10am-2pm Sat
Brazil is known for producing excellent, high-quality footwear at much lower prices than you'll find in the US or Europe. One of several shops where you can tap into this market is World Map, with a good mix of casual and sporty shoes for men and women (you'll also find sandals in the women's department). There are branches throughout town, including one in **Leblon** (Map pp246–7; ☎ 2511 3050; Rua Dias Ferreira 482).

GÁVEA, JARDIM BOTÂNICO & LAGOA

O SOL Map pp246-7   Handicrafts

☎ 2294 5099; Rua Corcovado 213, Jardim Botânico; ◷ 9am-6pm Mon-Fri, 9am-1pm Sat
O Sol is run by Leste-Um, a nonprofit social-welfare organization. This delightful store displays the works of regional artists and sells Brazilian folk art in clay, wood and porcelain. It also sells baskets and woven rugs.

TOP FIVE RECORD STORES

- Feira de Música (p168) – During the week browse through bins of records and CDs at this open-air market in Centro.
- Modern Sound (opposite) – One of Brazil's largest music stores stocks an impressive selection, with lots of staff recommendations, top Rio artists and imports. Live music shows are staged here daily.
- Plano B (p171) – An underground favorite among local DJs, Plano B has new and used records and CDs, as well as a tattoo parlor in back.
- Toca do Vinícius (p163) – Bossa nova's smooth grooves live on in this shop dedicated to old and new artists of the genre. Upstairs, Vinícius' fans can get a glimpse of his life's work in the small museum dedicated to him.
- Musicale (p166) – The excellent selection of used CDs here makes stopping in a must.

SHOPPING DA GÁVEA

Map pp246-7   Shopping Center

☎ 2274 9896; Rua Marquês de São Vicente 52, Gávea; ◷ 10am-10pm Mon-Sat, 3-9pm Sun
Shopping da Gávea touts itself as the preferred mall of artists and intellectuals, although we couldn't discern whether the shoppers here were sculptors or gym coaches. There are 200 stores, four performance theaters and numerous restaurants, including La Pasta Gialla, Brazil's bruschetta capital with 29 different types.

VIT Map pp246-7   Antiques

☎ 2294 2410; Rua JJ Seabra 18, Jardim Botânico; ◷ 10am-6pm Mon-Fri, 10am-3pm Sat
In a small but flourishing block in Jardim Botânico, this rambling antiques shop is a fun place for browsing while checking out the neighborhood. You'll find old globes, furniture from the '30s to the '60s, stylized lamps, vases, crockery and other curios from the past.

COPACABANA & LEME

ARTE BRASILIS Map pp244-5   Handicrafts

☎ 2513 1238; Av NS de Copacabana 1313, Copacabana; ◷ 9am-6pm Mon-Sat
One of Copacabana's few decent handicraft stores, Arte Brasilis sells colorful wall hangings, wooden carvings, place settings and other handmade objects from Minas Gerais

and the northeast. There are better places to shop for souvenirs, but this one is convenient if you're based in Copacabana.

DE SALTO ALTO Map pp244-5   Thrift Shop
☎ 2223 2589; store 44, Rua Siqueira Campos 143, Copacabana; ⏰ 10am-7pm Mon-Fri, 10am-2pm Sat
Not far from the subway station, this small colorful thrift shop sells clothes, hats, jewelry, shoes, records and books. While the '70s era is well represented by the rayon and polyester shirts, you might also stumble across some vintage skirts, dresses and outerwear from much earlier.

GALERIA RIVER
Map pp244-5   Shopping Center
Rua Francisco Otaviano 67, Arpoador; ⏰ 10am-6pm Mon-Sat
Surf shops, skateboard and Rollerblade outlets, and shops selling beachwear and fashions for young nubile things fill this shopping gallery in Arpoador. Shorts, bikinis, swim trunks, party attire and gear for outdoor adventure are in abundance. The shops here – like Ocean Surf Shop – are a good place to inquire about board rentals,

which c
intereste
should s
trekking-
about co

MARIA [
☎ 2235 43.
⏰ 10am-1(
This tiny sh
handcrafte
Brazil. Woo
mals such a ___ ___ ___ carved in the side, tiny clay pots and sculptures in stone are among the simple, art-naïf pieces.

MODERN SOUND Map pp244-5   Music
☎ 2548 5005; www.modernsound.com.br; Rua Barata Ribeiro 502, Copacabana; ⏰ 9am-9pm Mon-Fri, 9am-8pm Sat
One of Brazil's largest music stores, Modern Sound makes a fine setting for browsing through the many shelves of samba, electronica, hip-hop, imports, classical and dozens of other well-represented categories. The small café in the store features live jazz daily.

Modern Sound (above) is a must for all types of music and there's live jazz too.

erde.com.br in
...acabana 630, Copacabana;
..., 9am-2pm Sat
...health-food retailer, Mundo
...organic products (including
... – bar-type snacks – and other
...s besides), jams made from Amazo-
...n fruits and other assorted goods. The
sun-care products are usually cheaper here
than in pharmacies – and much better for
your skin.

MUSICALE Map pp244-5   Music
☎ 2267 9607; Av NS de Copacabana 1103C,
Copacabana; ☽ 10am-8pm Mon-Sat
One of Rio's top used-CD stores, Musicale
doesn't have racks and racks of CDs like
Modern Sound, but its selection is quite
good. In keeping with the neighborhood
that surrounds the store, a diverse bunch
shops here – club kids, old samba soft-
ies, expats trapped in the '80s – which is
reflected in the range of albums for sale.
Musicale also buys and trades CDs.

BOTAFOGO & URCA

ARTÍNDIA Map pp242-3   Handicrafts
☎ 2286 8899; Museu do Índio, Rua das Palmeiras
55, Botafogo; ☽ 9:30am-5:30pm Tue-Fri, 1-5pm
Sat & Sun
Inside the grounds of the Museu do Índio,
Artíndia sells a variety of indigenous handicrafts – masks, musical instruments, toys,
pots, baskets and weapons. Regional artists,
mostly from northern tribes, craft objects
using native materials like straw, clay, wood
and feathers.

BOTAFOGO PRAIA SHOPPING
Map pp242-3   Shopping Center
☎ 2559 9880; Praia de Botafogo 400, Botafogo;
☽ 10am-10pm Mon-Sat, 3-10pm Sun
Botafogo's large shopping center has
dozens of stores, featuring Brazilian and
international designers to suit every style –
and clothe every part of the body. The 3rd
floor's the best – for top designers check
stores like Philippe Martins, Giselle Martins,
Osklen, Equatore and more whimsical shops
like d-xis. The mall also has a cinema and
several top-floor restaurants, such as Pax
(p119) and Zin (p120), with panoramic views.

LIVRARIA PREFÁCIO
Map pp242-3   Books & Music
☎ 2527 5699; Rua Voluntários da Pátria 39, Botafogo; ☽ 10am-10pm Mon-Fri, 2-10pm Sat & Sun
This charming bookshop stocks a small
selection of foreign titles as well as music.
And perusers need not go hungry or thirsty
while they browse for titles: a slender bar
in front delivers refreshing glasses of chope
(draft beer), while seating upstairs and in
the café (p119) in back offers heartier fare.
The bookshop hosts an occasional poetry
reading or record-release party

RIO OFF-PRICE SHOPPING
Map pp242-3   Shopping Center
☎ 2542 5693; Rua General Severiano 97, Botafogo;
☽ 10am-10pm Mon-Sat, 3-9pm Sun
Near Rio Sul Shopping, Rio Off-Price Shopping is something of a factory outlet center.
It has many of the same stores as other
malls – domestic and international designers – but prices are about 20% lower. It also
has two cinemas and meal options (mostly
fast food).

RIO SUL SHOPPING
Map pp242-3   Shopping Center
☎ 2545 7200; www.riosul.com.br in Portuguese;
Rua Lauro Müller 116, Botafogo; ☽ 10am-10pm
Mon-Sat, 3-10pm Sun
The biggest shopping center you can reach
without heading to Barra, Rio Sul has over
400 shops, featuring both the prominent
and the obscure, cinemas, restaurants
and – at least on weekends – overwhelming
crowds.

FLAMENGO, LARANJEIRAS & COSME VELHO

BRUMADA Map pp242-3   Handicrafts
☎ 2558 2275; Rua das Laranjeiras 486, Laranjeiras;
☽ 10am-6pm Mon-Sat
Handicrafts from all over Brazil – but particularly the northeast are here at Brumada.
Wooden figurines, porcelain dolls, brightly
hued tapestries, indigenous art and hand-
woven baskets make up the bulk of what's
on sale, but there's also a handful of paintings, antiques and colonial furniture. Colorful carvings and ceramics – giraffes, horses,
soldiers – make nice gifts for children.

FARMERS MARKETS

The *feiras* (markets) that pop up in different locations throughout the week are the best places to shop for fruit and vegetables. For an authentic slice of home-grown Carioca commerce, nothing beats wandering through and taking in the action.

Cobal do Humaitá (Map pp242–3; ☎ 2266 1343; Rua Voluntários da Pátria 446, Botafogo; ☒ 7am-4pm Mon-Sat) The city's largest farmers' market sells plenty of flowers, veggies and fruits; there are also cafés and restaurants on hand for those looking for a bit more.

Cobal de Leblon (Map pp246–7; ☎ 2239 1549; Rua Gilberto Cardoso, Leblon; ☒ 7am-4pm Mon-Sat) Smaller than Humaitá's market, the Cobal de Leblon makes a fine setting for stopping to smell the flowers – or the *maracujá* (passionfruit) – before settling down to a meal at one of the cafés there.

Copacabana feiras by day Wednesday on Rua Domingos Ferreira, Thursday on Rua Belford Roxo and Rua Ronald de Carvalho, Sunday on Rua Decio Vilares.

Ipanema feiras by day Monday on Rua Henrique Dumont, Tuesday on Praça General Osório and Friday on Praça NS da Paz.

Leblon feiras by day Thursday on Rua General Urquiza.

JEITO BRASILEIRO Map pp242-3 Handicrafts
☎ 2205 7636; Rua Ererê 11A, Cosme Velho; ☒ 9am-6pm Mon-Fri, 9am-4pm Sat, 9am-1pm Sun
Next to the Corcovado train terminal in Cosme Velho, Jeito Brasileiro has a wide selection of handicrafts from all over the country, including folk art made by members of the Camucim tribe.

MARACATU BRASIL
Map pp242-3 Percussion Instruments
☎ 2557 4754; www.maracatubrasil.com.br; Rua Ipiranga 49, Laranjeiras; ☒ 10am-6pm Mon-Sat
You can't miss the lime-green building that houses this small percussion store and workshop. Inside, you can buy an *afoxê* (a gourd shaker with beads strung around it), conga and bongo drums, tambourines and other Brazilian percussion instruments. Upstairs is a drum clinic, where you can study a number of styles with local musician-teachers. See p79 for more details.

PÉ DE BOI Map pp242-3 Handicrafts
☎ 2285 4395; Rua Ipiranga 55, Laranjeiras; ☒ 9am-7pm Mon-Fri, 9am-1pm Sat
Traditional artisan handicrafts feature at Pé de Boi. Works in wood and ceramic as well as tapestries, sculptures and weavings showcase the talent of artists from Amazô-nia, Minas Gerais and the south. The shop also has works made by indigenous artists from further afield: Peru, Guatemala and Ecuador.

CENTRO & CINELÂNDIA
CASA OLIVEIRA
Map pp238-9 Musical Instruments
☎ 2325 8109; Rua da Carioca 70, Centro; ☒ 10am-6pm Mon-Fri
One of several excellent music shops on Rua da Carioca, Casa Oliveira sells all the pieces that make up the rhythm section of Carnaval *baterias* (percussion sections). If *forró* (trad-itional, fast-paced music from the northeast) is more your speed, you can also purchase a variety of mandolins as well as accordions and electric guitars.

EDITORA GEOGRÁFICA J PAULINI
Map pp238-9 Maps
☎ 2220 0181; loja (level) K, Rua Senador Dantas 75, Centro; ☒ 10am-6pm Mon-Fri
This small shop on the way to the *bonde* (tram) station sells a decent selection of maps: national road maps as well as topo-graphical, physical and nautical maps. It has a small selection of maps of other major Brazilian cities, in addition to Rio maps.

EMPÓRIO MUSICALE
Map pp238-9 Music
☎ 2252 9714; Rua Sete de Setembro, Centro; ☒ 10am-6pm Mon-Fri
This is an LP-lover's dream. You'll find bins and bins of old records covering the full spectrum of Brazilian music. You can un-earth some gems of classic samba, MPB and funk. CD users have less to celebrate, with a rather paltry selection.

ESCH CAFÉ Map pp238-9 Cigars
☎ 2507 5866; Rua do Rosário 108, Centro; ☒ noon-10pm Mon-Fri
Centro's branch of the 'house of the Havana' is just as stocked with the fruit of

MARKETS FOR THE MASSES

Av Atlântica Fair (Map pp244–5; Av Atlântica near Rua Djalma Ulrich, Copacabana; ⏰ 7pm-midnight) Paintings, drawings, jewelry, clothing and a fair bit of tourist junk make up this Copacabana market. It's located on the median along Av Atlântica.

Babilônia Feira Hype (Map pp246–7; ☎ 2267 0066; www.babiloniahype.com.br; Jóquei Clube, Rua Jardim Botânico 971, Jardim Botânico; admission US$2; ⏰ 2-10pm Sat) A festival atmosphere pervades this popular weekend fair at the Jockey Club. Young crowds mill through the clothing, sunglasses and jewelry stalls as live bands play nearby. There are also places to get your fortune read by 'místicos' (psychics) or receive a henna tattoo. Food stalls (of the fried-sausages-and-beer variety) litter the fairgrounds.

Feira de Música (Map pp238–9; Rua Pedro Lessa, Centro; ⏰ 9am-5pm Mon-Fri) On weekdays, next to the Biblioteca Nacional, record and CD stalls line the small lane. You'll find everything from American indie rock to vintage Brazilian funk, and most vendors will let you listen to any of their discs for sale – new or used.

Feira do Rio Antigo (Map pp238–9; ☎ 2224 6693; Rua do Lavradio, Centro; ⏰ 10am-6pm 1st Sat of month) Although the Rio Antiques Fair happens just once a month, don't miss it if you're in town. The colonial buildings become a living installation as the whole street fills with antiques and music – samba and MPB bands – creating a fine ambience.

Feira Nordestina (Map pp236–7; ☎ 3860 9976; Campo de São Cristóvão, São Cristóvão; ⏰ 10am-4pm Tue-Thu, nonstop 10am Fri to 10pm Sun) For details see p90.

Hippie Fair (Map pp246–7; Praça General Osório, Ipanema; ⏰ 9am-5pm Sun) The Zona Sul's most famous market, the Hippie Fair (aka Feira de Arte de Ipanema) has lots of artwork, jewelry, handicrafts and leather goods plus the occasional piece of furniture for sale. A stall in the southeast corner of the plaza sells tasty northeastern cuisine. Don't miss it.

Photography and Image Fair (Map pp242–3; ☎ 2558 6350; Museu da República, Rua do Catete 153, Catete; ⏰ 9am-5pm last Sun of month) Works from amateur and professional photographers are for sale at this once-monthly market in the verdant Parque do Catete. There's also a multimedia room which hosts workshops, talks and slide projections.

Praça do Lido Market (Map pp244–5; Praça do Lido, Copacabana; ⏰ 8am-6pm Sat & Sun) Copacabana's response to Ipanema's widely popular Hippie Fair, this weekend affair features handicrafts and souvenirs, soccer jerseys, a few jewelry stands and, from time to time, a man selling amazing slices of chocolate cake.

Praça do Mercado Feira de Antiguidades (Map pp238–9; Praça do Mercado; ⏰ 9am-5pm Sat) This antique market next to the Niterói ferry terminal has a vast array of antique and not-so-antique finds – silverware, carpets, pocket watches, jewelry, typewriters, records and art-deco and art-nouveau items. You can find nearly anything out here, making it a browser's paradise.

Praça Santos Dumont Antique Fair (Map pp246–7; Praça Santos Dumont, Gávea; ⏰ 9am-5pm Sun) Small but substantial, Gávea's antique fair features jewelry, records, watches, dinnerware, books and other odds and ends.

Praça Quinze Handicrafts Fair (Map pp238–9; Praça Quinze de Novembro, Centro; ⏰ 8am-6pm Thu-Fri) This street fair near the Imperial Palace features craftsmen selling their works of leather, wood, porcelain, glass and silver. There are also stalls with regional Brazilian fare.

Shopping Cassino Atlântico Antiques Fair (Map pp244–5; Av Atlântico 4240, Copacabana; ⏰ 11am-7pm Sat) Inside an air-conditioned shopping center, this antique fair consists of three floors of blown glass, sculpture, carpets, silverware and jewelry. Pieces are in much better condition here, which is clearly reflected in the prices. A tearoom and live music help bring on the mood.

Don't miss Zona Sul's Hippie Fair (above)

the Cuban vine – or the leaf, rather – as **Leblon's** (p160). The end of the Carioca workday (from 5pm onward) is a lively time to stop by, and you can always move on – with smokes in hand of course. Esch is also a bar; see p136.

EXPAND WINE STORE
Map pp238-9   Wine & Liquors

☎ 2220 1887; Av Erasmo Braga 299B, Centro; ⏰ 9am-8pm Mon-Fri

This well-stocked wine shop is a great place to buy a few bottles while out exploring Centro. Chile, Argentina and 11 other countries are represented among the vintages. The 2nd floor has a wine bar where you can taste those velvety Malbecs and Merlots.

H STERN Map pp238-9   Jewelry

☎ 2524 2300; Av Rio Branco 128, Centro; ⏰ 10am-6pm Mon-Fri

The jewelry giant's branch in Centro has an ample selection of exquisite pieces, without the flash of Zona Sul locations. If gazing at all those diamonds makes you salivate, move it downstairs to **Eça** (p124) and sample some of the neighborhood's best cuisine.

LIVRARIA DA TRAVESSA
Map pp238-9   Books & Music

☎ 3231 8015; Travessa de Ouvidor 17, Centro; ⏰ 9am-8pm Mon-Fri, 10am-1pm Sat

Livraria da Travessa, hands down, wins Centro's most-charming-bookstore award. The location, tucked off the narrow alley Travessa de Ouvidor, accounts for a large part of it, then there's the knowledgeable sales staff, the bistro, and the light falling just so across the shelves. A second **Livraria da Travessa** (Map pp238–9; Av Rio Branco 44) has a decent café overlooking the store.

LIVRARIA IMPERIAL
Map pp238-9   Books & Music

☎ 2533 4537; Praça Quinze de Novembro 48, Centro; ⏰ 9am-8pm Mon-Fri, 9:30am-2pm Sat

Bossa nova plays overhead at this charming bookstore–music shop. In addition to new and used books (including a selection of foreign-language titles), Livraria Imperial sells a handful of old prints and postcards, and a less extensive collection of CDs covering bossa, samba, *chorinho* (romantic, intimate samba) and rock and pop. You can also find a selection of Lonely Planet titles.

LOJA NOVO DESENHO
Map pp238-9   Eclectic

☎ 2524 2290; Av Infante Dom Henrique 85, Centro; ⏰ noon-6pm Tue-Fri, noon-7pm Sat & Sun

This 'Store of New Design' sells pure eye candy – and lives up to its name. Some of Rio's best modern designs are here (created by some of the country's best industrial designers no less). And you'll find whimsical two-dimensional vases, surreal clock faces, sleek coiled lamps and other clever works.

NOVA LIVRARIA LEONARDO DA VINCI Map pp238-9   Books

☎ 2533 2237; Av Rio Branco 185, Centro; ⏰ 9am-7pm Mon-Fri, 9am-noon Sat

With one of Rio's best foreign-language book collections, da Vinci also has a wide range of art and photography books, as well as coffee-table books about Rio's history and architecture. It's one floor down – follow the spiral ramp. A decent coffee shop is nearby.

SUB & SUB
Map pp238-9   Diving, Climbing & Hiking

☎ 2509 1176; subsub.com.br; sobreloja (first flight up), Rua da Alfândega 98, Centro; ⏰ 10am-6pm Mon-Fri

Sub & Sub has an array of gear for outdoor adventure: climbing and mountaineering, diving, snorkeling, camping and hiking. The knowledgeable staff can also recommend courses for those interested in learning a new craft.

TABACARIA AFRICANA
Map pp238-9   Tobacco & Cigars

☎ 2509 5333; Largo do Paço 38, Centro; ⏰ 9am-5pm Mon-Fri

The sweet fragrance of pipe tobacco is embedded in the walls and furniture of this tiny shop facing the Praça Quinze. Regulars sit at the table in front slowly drawing on the pick of the day while the afternoon drifts by, smokelike. In back, the glass jars contain a variety of flavors and aromas. Let the shopkeeper put a mix together for you.

UNIMAGEM Map pp238-9   Photography

☎ 2507 7745; Rua dos Andradas 29, Centro; ⏰ 9am-6pm Mon-Fri, 9am-noon Sat

The choice of professional photographers in the city, Unimagem has a good selection of new and used cameras (SLRs, TLRs, point-and-shoot) as well as all the accessories (tripods, film, paper). It also runs a superb developing lab: black-and-white, color and slides. And it can provide a one-hour developing service for both slide and color film.

SANTA TERESA & LAPA
ALFONSO NUNE'S ANTIQUARIO

Map pp238-9   Antiques

☎ 2232 2620; Rua do Lavradio 60, Lapa; ⏰ 9am-7pm Mon-Fri, 9am-3pm Sat

The old colonial edifice features an excellent selection of antiques – from tables and chairs to chandeliers and glassware. Discerning collectors will want to give the shop a good look over before proceeding to the other antique stores lining Lavradio.

ARQUITETURA & DECORAÇÃO

Map pp238-9   Antiques

☎ 2507 6873; Rua do Lavradio 34, Lapa; ⏰ 9am-6pm Mon-Sat

One of Rua do Lavradio's most magical antique shops, with a small assortment of antiques ranging from heavy 1930s pieces

to sleek, trim designs from the 1960s. Unfortunately, most of what's for sale is furniture, and you may have difficulty squeezing the Oscar Niemeyer *poltrona* (armchair) into your suitcase. Sharing the space is a small art gallery.

BRECHÓ ANTIGAMENTE

Map p241   Thrift Shop

☎ 2220 1878; Rua Almirante Alexandrino 428, Santa Teresa; ⏰ 3-8pm Thu-Sun

One of Santa Teresa's better-stocked secondhand shops, Brechó Antigamente sells costume jewelry as well as clothes and attracts a wide mix of local residents. *Brechós,* incidentally, are secondhand stores, which come and go in this neighborhood.

BRECHÓ ARTE 70 Map p241   Thrift Shop

☎ 2221 3205; Rua Monte Alegre 337, Santa Teresa; ⏰ 10:30am-9pm Tue-Sat, 2-9pm Sun

Brechó Arte 70 features several racks of secondhand clothes as well as a few antique pieces such as teapots and costume jewelry – for sale from time to time. Depending on your luck, you can come across some good finds here.

Strolling through the backstreets of Santa Teresa

WILD RUBBER Cassandra Loomis

Amazon Life, Rio's most ecologically minded company, may lie some 3000km from the Amazon, but the forest plays a vital role in the company's products. Amazon Life's founders, Maria Beatriz Saldanha Tavares and João Augusto Fortes, were inspired by environmental activist and martyr Chico Mendes. Mendes brought attention to rubber tappers who were losing their livelihood as the Amazon was cleared for farmland. Tavares and Fortes worked with local communities of rubber tappers, and soon Treetap, a wild rubber, was born. In addition to giving the local Indian communities an income, it has helped to preserve their lands, owing to the creation of extraction reserves. In the summer the villages make Treetap, and in the winter they transport the product by canoe, then barge, to Rio. Treetap is now much in demand by environmentally responsible companies. Giant, the largest European bicycle company, ordered 10,000 bags made from Treetap; Hermès, the French fashion king, has used the wild rubber in the production of accessories. To see some of Amazon Life's products, order products online or visit the store in **Ipanema** (☎ 2511 7686; www .amazonlife.com; Av Visconde de Pirajá 499).

CASA DO BRAZÃO Map pp238-9   Antiques
☎ 2232 12670; Rua do Lavradio 60, Lapa;
🕑 10am-6pm Tue-Fri, 10am-2pm Sat
One Lavradio's atmospheric antique shops, Casa do Brazão offers the usual assortment of wooden tables and chairs, chandeliers, lamps and other fragments from the past piled in heaps about this rambling shop.

LA VAREDA Map p241   Handicrafts
☎ 2222 1848; www.lavareda.hpg.com.br in Portuguese; Rua Almirante Alexandrino 428, Santa Teresa; 🕑 10am-9pm Tue-Sun, 1-9pm Mon
On the *bonde* line near Largo do Guimarães, La Vareda stocks a colorful selection of handicrafts and from local artists and artisans. Pottery, furniture, paintings, handmade dolls and tapestries cover the interior of the old store. You can also purchase stationery and prints highlighting historic Santa Teresa.

PLANO B Map pp238-9   Music & Tattoos
☎ 2507 9860; Rua Francisco Muratori 2A, Lapa;
🕑 10am-7pm Mon-Wed, 10am-10pm Thu & Fri, noon-10pm Sat & Sun
Only in Lapa will you encounter a place where you can pick through bins of old jazz records and new electronic mixes before stepping into the back room to get a tattoo down your arm, inspired perhaps by that old Elza Soares song playing overhead. Plano B also has a decent selection of CDs, and the young staff can advise – if samba-funk eludes you.

RASGANDO PANO
Map p241   Clothing & Accessories
☎ 2232 1389; Rua Santa Cristina 181A, Santa Teresa; 🕑 11am-8pm Tue-Sun
Down the hill from La Vareda, Rasgando Pano features a small selection of women's clothing and accessories, bags and pillows. Many items for sale are imported from India or show traces of Indian influences.

TRILHOS URBANOS
Map p241   Handicrafts
☎ 2242 3632; Rua Almirante Alexandrino 402A, Santa Teresa; 🕑 10am-7pm Tue-Sat
Vying for attention near La Vareda, Trilhos Urbanos also stocks a small but interesting assortment of handicrafts. Works by local artists and artisans are for sale – photographs, picture frames, paintings and works in metal.

BARRA DA TIJUCA & GREATER RIO
BARRA SHOPPING
Map pp236-7   Shopping Center
☎ 3089 1000; www.barrashopping.com.br in Portuguese; Av das Américas 4666, Barra da Tijuca; 🕑 10am-10pm Mon-Sat, 3-10pm Sun
Rio's largest mall (and one of the biggest in South America) is an easy place to shop away a few hours or days. Some 30 million shoppers pass through Barra's doors each year. Over 500 stores clutter the 4km-long stretch of stores, along with five movie screens, a children's parkland and a wealth of dining options.

CLUBE CHOCOLATE
Map pp236-7   Eclectic
☎ 3322 3733; store 202, São Conrado Fashion Mall, Estrada da Gávea 899, São Conrado; 🕑 noon-midnight Sun-Fri, 10am-midnight Sat
This innovative store is definitely not to be missed on any serious shopping itinerary.

Amid a spacious, handsomely designed boutique you can browse through clothing designs of Marc Jacobs, Prada, Paul Smith and all the fashionable top Brazilian stylists. You can also have a bite at the French bistro or sample some of the latest CDs, books and gadgets.

RIO DESIGN CENTER

Map pp236-7   Shopping Center

☎ 2461 9999; www.riodesign.com.br in Portuguese; Av das Américas 7770, Barra da Tijuca; ◷ 10am-10pm Mon-Fri, 10am-8pm (stores), 11am-midnight (restaurants) Sat, 3-10pm Sun

This architecturally rich center features a number of excellent home-furnishing stores selling designer lamps, vases, decorative pieces and furniture. It also has some very good restaurants and a few art galleries.

SÃO CONRADO FASHION MALL

Map pp236-7   Shopping Center

☎ 3083 0300; Estrada da Gávea 899, São Conrado; ◷ 10am-10pm

Rio's most beautiful mall features all the big names – Armani, Versace, Louis Vuitton – and all of Brazil's most recognizable designers. It's located in the posh neighborhood of São Conrado, near the Hotel Intercontinental.

VIA PARQUE SHOPPING

Map pp236-7   Shopping Center

☎ 2421 9222; www.shoppingviaparque.com.br in Portuguese; Av Ayrton Senna 3000, Barra da Tijuca; ◷ 10am-10pm Mon-Sat, 3-10pm Sun

With 280 stores, six movie theaters and abundant restaurants, this is the heart of Rio's consumer culture. It's also home to one of the big concert arenas, Claro Hall.

Sleeping

Ipanema & Leblon	174
Copacabana & Leme	179
Botafogo & Urca	184
Flamengo	185
Catete & Glória	186
Centro & Cinelândia	187
Santa Teresa	188
Barra da Tijuca & West of Rio	188

Sleeping

In preparation for the 2007 Pan American Games in Rio, hoteliers have made some modest improvements to the badly out-of-date designs afflicting so many of the city's digs. While much work has yet to be done, in the last few years some charming boutique hotels and bed-and-breakfasts have opened, and some of the old classics have received a lovely makeover. By and large, most hotel rooms are in high-rises near the beach (Copacabana has the lion's share), and range from lavishly designed suites to dingy overpriced boxes. It's wise to shop around.

It's also wise to reserve ahead: you can save 30% just by booking in advance. Hotel rates rise during the summer months (December through February), particularly for New Year's Eve and Carnaval. Most places (including hostels) will only book in four-day blocks around these holidays.

Keep in mind that many hotels add a combined 15% service and tax charge. The cheaper places don't generally bother with this.

IPANEMA & LEBLON

Ocean views and access to some of Rio's loveliest beaches, restaurants and bars make Ipanema and Leblon a magnet for those travelers seeking the best of Rio. Although many more hotels litter the beaches of Leme and Copacabana, there are abundant lodging options here, from boutique hotels to serviced apartments, with plenty of straightforward standards in between. Prices here are generally much higher than elsewhere, though it's still possible to find affordable – if rather modest – lodging.

ARPOADOR INN Map pp246-7   Hotel $$
☎ 2523 0060; www.riodejaneiroguide.com/hotel/arpoador_inn.htm; Rua Francisco Otaviano 177, Ipanema; s/d standard US$86/96, deluxe US$173/192; ⌘
Overlooking Praia do Arpoador (Arpoador beach), this battered six-story hotel is the only one in Ipanema or Copacabana that doesn't have a busy street between it and the beach. The rooms are small and worn, with dirty carpeting and little ambience, but the 'deluxe' rooms have glorious ocean views. (We strongly suggest you don't even consider staying in any of the other rooms.)

CAESAR PARK Map pp246-7   Hotel $$$
☎ 2525 2525; www.caesar-park.com; Av Vieira Souto 460, Ipanema; d/ste from US$275/540; ⌘ ⌑ ⌬
The Caesar Park breathes opulence; it's apparent from the moment you catch sight of a classical pianist playing in the foyer. The rooms are sizable, with a warm, cozy feel and have artwork on the walls, flat-screen TVs, high-speed Internet connections and ocean views (in the deluxe rooms). **Petronius** (p112) serves a legendary *feijoada* (black-bean and pork stew) on Saturday.

CASA 6 IPANEMA Map pp246-7   Hostel $
☎ 2247 1384; www.casa6ipanema.com; Rua Barão da Torre 175, Ipanema; dm/d US$21/55; ⌑
A simple hostel on what is now Ipanema's hostel row, Casa 6 offers accommodation

either in a private double room or in one of the six-bed dorm rooms. The quarters are a bit tight, but the beach is just a few blocks away.

CHE LAGARTO IPANEMA

Map pp246-7   Hostel $

☎ 2512 8076; www.chelagarto.com; Rua Paul Redfern 48, Ipanema; dm/d US$20/60
Part of a small empire of hostels in the Zona Sul, Che Lagarto's new Ipanema branch is a popular budget spot for those young travelers who want to be close (two blocks) to the beach. It's a five-story hostel, with basic rooms and not much common space – aside from the pricey bar on the 1st floor.

EVEREST RIO Map pp246-7   Hotel $$

☎ 2525 2200; www.everest.com.br; Rua Prudente de Moraes 1117, Ipanema; d from US$95; ⌗
Another of Ipanema's elegant high-rise hotels, the Everest Rio features nicely decorated rooms ranging from small to spacious, professional service and an enviable location. All the rooms have carpeting, large windows that let in plenty of light and modernized bathrooms with bathtubs. Deluxe here means more space (the view is the same), and a queen-size bed.

TOP FIVE SLEEPS

- Cama e Café (p188) – Best B&B experience.
- Ipanema Beach House (p176) – Best penny-pincher.
- Le Meridien (p182) – Best restaurant – Le Saint-Honoré.
- Marina All Suites (p177) – Best interior design.
- Sofitel Rio de Janeiro (p184) – Best pools.

HOTEL PRAIA IPANEMA

Map pp246-7   Hotel $$$

☎ 2141 4949; www.praiaipanema.com; Av Vieira Souto 706, Ipanema; s/d from US$150/170; ⌗ ⌗
With a view of Ipanema Beach, this popular 16-story hotel offers trim, comfortable rooms, each with a balcony. The design is sleek and modern, with off-white tile floors, recessed lighting and artwork on the walls. Sstretch out on the molded white lounge chairs next to the rooftop pool. The bar has a view, and there's a small fitness center.

HOTEL SAN MARCO

Map pp246-7   Hotel $

☎ 2540 5032; www.sanmarcohotel.net; Rua Visconde de Pirajá 524, Ipanema; s/d US$65/70; ⌗
Like the Vermont up the road, it's all about location if you stay at the San Marco. A

Lounging by the pool at opulent Caesar Park (left)

coffin-sized elevator carries you up to the rooms, which are small, dark and cramped, with faded green duvets and tile floors. The beach, however, is just two blocks away.

HOTEL VERMONT

Map pp246-7   Hotel $

☎ 2522 0057; hoteisvermont@uol.com.br; Rua Visconde de Pirajá 254, Ipanema; s/d from US$57/78; 🔀

One of the few nonluxury hotels in Ipanema, the Hotel Vermont offers guests no-frills accommodations in a high-rise a few blocks from the beach. Although the place received a slight makeover in recent years, the rooms are still on the shabby side, with tile floors, elderly bathrooms and poor lighting.

IPANEMA BEACH HOUSE

Map pp246-7   Hostel $

☎ 3202 2693; www.ipanemahouse.com; Rua Barão da Torre 485, Ipanema; dm/d US$18/55; 🖳

A lovely hostel, the Ipanema Beach House is set in a converted two-story house with six- and nine-bed dorms (with three-tiered bunk beds). There are private rooms, indoor and outdoor lounge spaces, a small bar and a beautiful pool.

IPANEMA FLAT HOTEL RESIDÊNCIA

Map pp246-7   Serviced Apartments $$

☎ 2523 1292; fax 2287 9844; Rua Gomes Carneiro 137, Ipanema; s/d US$82/90; 🔀 🖳

This place is suffering from a bad case of style envy: cheaply furnished rooms are seriously short on style and just aching to get some. Still, the simple apartments have kitchens, balconies (no view) and bland but clean bedrooms at reasonable prices for the area.

IPANEMA HOTEL RESIDÊNCIA

Map pp246-7   Serviced Apartments $$

☎ 2523 3682; www.ipanemahotel.com.br; Rua Barão da Torre 192, Ipanema; d US$130-157; 🔀 🖳

Set on one of Ipanema's lovely tree-lined streets, this high-rise hotel has large apartments with tile floors, kitchen units with sparsely furnished lounge areas and pleasantly furnished bedrooms. Although the rooms are short on charm, this place is a good option if you want more space but still want to be in a great neighborhood.

IPANEMA INN

Map pp246-7   Hotel $$

☎ 2523 6092; arpoador@unisys.com.br; Rua Maria Quitéria 27, Ipanema; s/d standard US$105/116, superior US$123/136; 🔀

Ipanema Inn is a simple hotel with nice touches. The pleasant rooms have wood-block prints on the walls, off-white tile floors and modern bathrooms with big tubs. Front-facing rooms (superiores) don't have ocean views, but if you lean far enough out the window, you get a glimpse of the glistening sea. Ipanema Inn has friendly, multilingual staff.

IPANEMA PLAZA

Map pp246-7   Hotel $$$

☎ 3687 2000; www.ipanemaplazahotel.com; Rua Farme de Amoedo 34, Ipanema; s/d/ste from US$158/174/289; 🔀 🖳

One of the nicest hotels, the 18-story Plaza in Ipanema features nicely decorated rooms with tile floors, a muted color scheme and sizable windows to let in the tropical rays. You'll also find broad, comfortable beds, spacious bathrooms (all with tubs) and a lovely rooftop pool. Some rooms overlook the ocean, while others face the outstretched arms of Cristo Redentor.

IPANEMA SWEET

Map pp246-7   Serviced Apartments $$

☎ 2551 0488; soniacordeiro@globo.com; Rua Visconde de Pirajá 161, Ipanema; apt from US$95; 🔀 🖳

Modern, furnished apartments with kitchen, lounge and balcony (no view) are good value here. All rooms are different, but the best have cozy touches like an Oriental carpet, artwork or stylish furniture. Guests also have access to two outdoor pools, a sauna and a laundry in the building. The mix of Brazilians and international visitors who stay here consistently rate the place highly.

IPANEMA TOWER

Map pp246-7   Hotel $$$

☎ 2247 7033; www.ipanematower.com; Rua Prudente de Moraes 1008, Ipanema; ste US$177-220; 🔀 🖳

Along one of Ipanema's main thoroughfares, the all-suites Ipanema Tower has large, fully furnished apartments with pressed-wood floors, a balcony (some with ocean views), small kitchen, living room and bedroom. While the furnishings are far from opulent, they're cozy enough, with a decent kitchen table and a few pieces of modern artwork on the walls.

IPANEMA WAVE HOSTEL

Map pp246-7   Hostel $

☎ 2227 6458; wavehostel@yahoo.com.br; No 5, Rua Barão da Torre 175, Ipanema; dm US$16; 🖳 Popular with surfers and a youthful, laid-back crowd, the intimate Wave Hostel has wood floors and well-maintained common areas. Because of its size, if you want to snag a bed in one of the four-bed dorms, book early. The highlight here is, of course, lovely Ipanema beach, which is just three blocks away.

LEBLON OCEAN HOTEL RESIDÊNCIA

Map pp246-7   Serviced Apartments $$

☎ 2158 8282; Rua Rainha Guilhermina 117, Leblon; apt from US$130; 🖳 🖳 This all-suites hotel has a range of spacious, simply furnished suites, all with kitchen units and small balconies. There's also a small indoor pool and sauna, and Rio's best restaurants (and a handful of bars) are just outside the door. The only catch is that you have to book a minimum of five days.

LIGHTHOUSE HOSTEL

Map pp246-7   Hostel $

☎ 2522 1353; www.thelighthouse.com.br; No 20, Rua Barão da Torre 175, Ipanema; dm/d US$18/55; 🖳 🖳 Along with a handful of other budget spots on this quiet lane, the Lighthouse has an easy-going vibe and clean, simple rooms that attract a good mix of backpackers. Accommodations consist of eight-bed dorm rooms and one stylish private double (with a fold-out sofa to sleep three).

MAR IPANEMA Map pp246-7   Hotel $$

☎ 3875 9190; www.maripanema.com.br; Rua Visconde de Pirajá 539, Ipanema; d from US$120; 🖳 This is a decent midrange option in Ipanema. The rooms feature a trim, modern design with decent beds, good lighting, tidy wooden floors and an inviting color scheme. The downside is the lack of a view, which is hardly relevant if you plan to spend your day out enjoying the city.

MARGARIDA'S POUSADA

Map pp246-7   Hotel $

☎ 2239 1840; margaridacaneiro@hotmail.com; Rua Barão da Torre 600, Ipanema; s/d/apt from US$37/55/115; 🖳 For those seeking a smaller, cozier atmosphere than the high-rise hotels can provide, this excellently located Ipanema guest house is a good option. You'll find a range of rooms in a small two-story house, with a bigger private apartment available for rent in a building nearby. In the works is a lovely new guest house for Jardim Botânico.

MARINA ALL SUITES

Map pp246-7   Boutique Hotel $$$

☎ 2172 1001; www.marinaallsuites.com.br; Av Delfim Moreira 696, Leblon; ste US$245-675; 🖳 🖳 🖳 Marina All Suites has beautifully decorated rooms, doting service and all the creature comforts you can imagine. As per the name, it's all suites here, meaning you'll have between 420 and 800 sq feet between the comfy bedroom and living room, in which to stretch out. The best rooms in the ocean-front hotel have splendid views of the shoreline, and other attractions are the trendy **Bar D'Hotel** (p130), the lovely top-floor pool and the onsite cinema that you can rent out.

MARINA PALACE Map pp246-7   Hotel $$$

☎ 2172 1001; www.hotelmarina.com.br; Av Delfim Moreira 696, Leblon; d standard/deluxe/ste from US$192/203/290; 🖳 🖳 🖳 Occupying a privileged position overlooking Praia do Leblon, the 26-story Marina Palace has arange of rooms, the best of which have a trim, contemporary look with artwork on the walls, sizable beds, flat-screen TVs, and DVD and CD players. At the bottom end of the scale you'll find similar features but darker carpeting (a tad worn) and poorer lighting. Deluxe rooms face the ocean and add more space to the equation. The Marina has top-notch service and a top-floor bar and restaurant with 360-degree views.

MONSIEUR LE BLOND

Map pp246-7   Serviced Apartments $$

☎ 2239 4598; www.redeprotel.com.br in Portuguese; Av Bartolomeu Mitre 325, Leblon; ste from US$143; 🖳 A five-minute walk from Praia de Leblon, Monsieur Le Blond combines the service of a hotel with the convenience of an apartment. The colorful accommodations are all comfortably furnished with small kitchens, combined living-dining areas and balconies – some with fine views. The pool, which gets direct sunlight only part of the day, makes a fine place for sunbathing and mingling with the mostly Brazilian clients.

PARTHENON QUEEN ELIZABETH
Map pp246-7   Hotel $$$

☎ 3222 9100; www.accorhotels.com.br; Av Rainha Elizabeth 440, Ipanema; s/d from US$153/180; 🛇 🖭

This fairly new hotel offers trim and tidy suites, with pressed-wood floors, big windows and light, muted colors. Some rooms have balconies, and the upper two floors (eight and nine) have slightly better views (though you still won't see the ocean). There's also a pool, which is unfortunately surrounded by tall buildings.

RIO UNIVERSE
Map pp246-7   Boutique Hotel $$$

www.riouniverse.com.br; Av Vieira Souto 80, Ipanema
Scheduled to open in late 2006 or early 2007, the Rio Universe promises to be the city's highest-profile hotel since the

opening of the Copacabana Palace in 1923. It's designed by French architect Philippe Starck, one of the world's best-known contemporary designers. The launch of his Ipanema hotel follows on the heels of his first project in Latin America, designing the much lauded Faena Hotel and Universe in Buenos Aires. Unlike other boutique hotels the überdesigner has worked on, the Rio Universe will receive Starck's total imprint from top to bottom. Starck chose Rio as the site for his work because of its energy, sensuality and beauty, a combination that he often tries to achieve in his own work.

RITZ PLAZA HOTEL
Map pp246-7   Serviced Apartments $$

☎ 2540 4940; fax 2294 1890; Av Ataúlfo de Paiva 1280; ste s/d US$110/147; 🛇
Still a secret, the Ritz Plaza is a stylish all-suites hotel in one of Rio's most desirable areas. Here you'll find top-notch service, handsome, spacious rooms and a relaxed atmosphere that gives the place a boutique feel. The one- or two- bedroom suites all have kitchen units, balconies – some with partial ocean views – art on the walls, good lighting and spotless bedrooms. Considering the high quality of the rooms, the proximity of the beach (three blocks) and the draw of the neighborhood (the city's top restaurants pack the street behind the hotel), this place is excellent value.

SHERATON Map pp246-7   Hotel $$$
☎ 2274 1122; www.sheraton-rio.com; Av Niemeyer 121, Vidgal; d from US$160; 🛇 🖳 🖭
The Sheraton is a true resort hotel, with large, peaceful grounds. Every room has a balcony, facing either Leblon and Ipanema or verdant greenery. The rooms are nicely furnished in a cozy, contemporary style, and if you stay out here you'll enjoy a nearly private beach in front, tennis courts, swimming pools and a good health club. The main drawback is that it's a bit far from the action.

SOL IPANEMA Map pp246-7   Hotel $$
☎ 2525 2020; www.solipanema.com.br; Av Vieira Souto 320, Ipanema; s/d standard US$127/138, deluxe US$150/167; 🛇 🖭
Occupying a prime plot of real estate facing Ipanema beach, the tall, slender Sol Ipanema features well-renovated rooms decorated in warm hues, with dark wood furnishings and

Take in a 360-degree view from Marina Palace (p177)

RIO'S LOVE MOTELS

Living in such a crowded city, Cariocas sometimes have a terrible time snatching a few moments of privacy. For those living with their parents or sharing a tiny apartment with roommates, an empty stretch of beach, a park bench, a seat in the back of the café are all fine spots to steal a few kisses, but for more…progressive action, Cariocas take things elsewhere – to the motel, aka the *love* motel.

Love motels aren't so much a Carioca oddity as they are a Brazilian institution. They are found in every part of the country, usually sprouting along the outskirts of cities and towns. Some are designed with lavish facades – decked out to resemble medieval castles, Roman temples or ancient pyramids – while others blend more discreetly into the surrounding landscape. Regardless of the exteriors, the interiors are far removed from the 'less is more' design philosophy. Mirrors cover the ceiling while heart-shaped, vibrating beds stretch beneath them. Rose-tinted mood lights, Jacuzzis, televisions loaded with porn channels, dual-headed showers and a menu on the bedside table featuring sex toys guests can order to the room – all these come standard in most love motels. Such places scream seediness in the west. In Brazil, however, they're not viewed as anything out of the ordinary. People need a place for their liaisons – they might as well have a laugh and a bit of fun while they're at it. The motels are used by young lovers who want to get away from their parents, parents who want to get away from their kids and couples who want to get away from their spouses. They are an integral part of the nation's social fabric, and it's not uncommon for Cariocas to host parties in them.

Most motels rent rooms by the hour, though some give discounted prices for four-hour blocks or offer lunchtime specials. In Rio many of them are out on the roads that lead to the city, such as Av Brasil in the Zona Norte and Av Niemeyer between Leblon and São Conrado. There are a few, however, scattered about Centro, Flamengo and Botafogo.

The quality of the motels varies, reflecting their popularity across social classes. The most lavish are three-story suites with a hot tub beneath a skylight on the top floor, a sauna and bathroom on the 2nd floor, and the garage underneath (allowing anonymity). They come standard with all the other mood-enhancement features mentioned earlier. For the best suites, expect to pay around US$150 for eight hours and more on weekends. Standard rooms cost quite a bit less, and Cariocas claim that an equally fine time can be had there.

For those interested in checking out this cultural institution, there are a number of motels in the Zona Sul, particularly along Av Niemeyer just west of Leblon, including **Sinless** (☎ 2512 9913; www.sinless.com.br; Av Niemeyer 214, Vidigal; r for 6 hr from US$28), **Shalimar** (☎ 3322 3392; www.hotelshalimar.com.br; Av Niemeyer 218, Vidigal; r for 6 hr from US$25) and **Bambina** (Map pp242–3; ☎ 2507 2037; www.bambinahotel.com.br; Rua Bambina 65, Botafogo; ste for 6 hr from US$52).

---

good lighting. Standard rooms are roughly the same size as the deluxe rooms, though the latter face the ocean, meaning you can hear the waves crashing on the shore as you drift off to sleep.

VISCONTI Map pp246-7   Serviced Apartments $$
☎ 2523 0400; www.promenade.com.br; Rua Prudente de Moraes 1050, Ipanema; ste from US$146;

The Visconti has stylish modern apartments (wood floors, stuffed leather furniture, modular lamps) with small kitchens, living-dining rooms, balconies and bedrooms. It's on a residential, tree-lined street a block from the beach. Your neighbors will mostly be Brazilians.

COPACABANA & LEME

Copacabana has more hotels than any other neighborhood in Rio de Janeiro. The area bordered by Av Atlântica from Leme to Forte de Copacabana is lined with them, while Copacabana's backstreets offer accommodations as well. The quality and price vary considerably here – which suits the range of backpackers, tour groups, business travelers, families and horny teenagers who all find their way here. During New Year's Eve this is the best place to be. If you have a beach view, you'll be able to see the fireworks from your window (which will be adequately reflected in your bill).

ACAPULCO Map pp244-5   Hotel $
☎ 2275 0022; www.acapulcocopacabanahotel .com.br; Rua Gustavo Sampaio 854, Leme; s/d from US$66/76;

The Acapulco hotel lies just a short stroll – one block from the immortalized Copacabana beach, and its recent renovations have made it an attractive and fairly priced option. All rooms have a neat look about them with pressed-wood floors and colorful duvets and curtains.

179

APA HOTEL Map pp244-5 — Hotel $
☎ 2548 8112; www.apahotel.com.br; Rua República do Peru 305, Copacabana; s/d US$55/70; ✕
The Apa would be one of Copacabana's most stylish hotels were the year 1973. Unfortunately, times have changed, but the anointed style of Apa's 52 rooms lives on. Here you'll find tile floors, balconies (in most rooms), decent lighting and fair prices.

ATLANTIS COPACABANA HOTEL
Map pp244-5 — Hotel $$
☎ 2521 1142; www.atlantishotel.com.br in Portuguese; Rua Bulhões de Carvalho 61, Copacabana; s/d from US$107/128; ✕ ⊠
On the border between Copacabana and Ipanema, Atlantis's rooms are short on style and cheaply furnished, though ongoing renovations may improve things. Rooms above the 9th floor have fine views, and there's a modest pool and sauna on the roof.

AUGUSTO'S COPACABANA
Map pp244-5 — Hotel $$
☎ 2547 1800; www.augustoshotel.com.br; Rua Bolívar 119, Copacabana; s/d/tr US$81/91/115; ✕ ⊠
Augusto's is a straightforward hotel with fair prices. The rooms here have a light and airy feel, and modern bathrooms. Some rooms have balconies, although the only way you'll see the ocean is to step onto them and look to the right. It's not close to the beach.

CHE LAGARTO Map pp244-5 — Hostel $
☎ 2256 2778; www.chelagarto.com; Rua Anita Garibaldi 87, Copacabana; dm with/without YHI card US$15/18, d US$46; ⊠
A current favorite among young backpackers, Che Lagarto attracts a rowdy crowd that gathers on the tiny front patio for beer and caipirinhas most nights. It's a good place for meeting young partyers, but the quarters are very tight here.

COPACABANA HOTEL RESIDÊNCIA
Map pp244-5 — Serviced Apartments $$
☎ 2548 7212; www.copahotelresid.com.br; Rua Barata Ribeiro 222, Copacabana; s/d without balcony US$91/115, s/d with balcony US$105/163; ✕ ⊠
The Copacabana Hotel Residência is an excellent choice for those seeking a bit more space. The clean, well-maintained suites here all have small kitchen units and lounge rooms with good natural lighting. and are good value for money. Keep in mind that busy Barata Ribeiro is awfully noisy; try to snag a top-floor apartment.

COPACABANA PALACE
Map pp244-5 — Hotel $$$
☎ 2548 7070; www.copacabanapalace.com.br; Av Atlântica 1702, Copacabana; d from US$371; ✕ ⊠ ⊠
Rio's most famous hotel, the Palace has hosted heads of state, rock stars and

Seems everyone who is anyone has stayed at the Copacabana Palace (above)

other prominent personalities. The dazzling white facade dates from the 1920s, when it became a symbol of the city. Today it is again the premier hotel of Rio – following a massive face-lift. The Palace rooms range from antique-filled superiors to gorgeous suites with balconies and parquet floors. There's also a lovely pool, excellent restaurants and service fit for royalty (Princess Di stayed here, as did Queen Elizabeth).

COPACABANA PRAIA HOSTEL

Map pp244-5   Hostel $

☎ 2547 5422; Rua Tenente Marones de Gusmão 85, Copacabana; dm/s/d/apt US$12/32/46/46
A few steps away from a small park, on a tranquil street, this unsignposted hostel gathers its share of budget travelers with some of the cheapest beds in Copacabana. You'll also find simple furnished apartments for rent at excellent prices.

COPACABANA PRAIA HOTEL

Map pp244-5   Hotel $$

☎ 2522 5646; www.copacabanapraiahotel.com.br; Rua Francisco Otaviano 30, Copacabana; d US$96; 🔀 🖳
The 11-story Copacabana Praia is an aging, generic hotel in Arpoador, within walking distance of both Ipanema and Copacabana beaches. The simple rooms have decent beds, carpeting, and balconies. Book a top-floor room for the partial sea view.

DESIGN HOTEL PORTINARI

Map pp244-5   Hotel $$

☎ 3222 8800; www.hotelportinari.com.br; Rua Francisco Sá 17, Copacabana; d from US$135; 🔀
One of Rio's newest additions, this stylish 13-story hotel demonstrates real design smarts. The rooms have tile floors, artful lighting and big windows, and each floor is decorated in a different style. Our only objection is that the rooms can seem a little stark after a while. The top-floor restaurant is set with tropical plants and boasts fine views through the floor-to-ceiling windows.

EXCELSIOR COPACABANA HOTEL

Map pp244-5   Hotel $$$

☎ 2195 5800; www.windsorhoteis.com.br; Av Atlântica 1800, Copacabana; d from US$175; 🔀 🖳
Overlooking Copacabana beach, this all-glass high-rise has handsomely appointed modern rooms with big windows that either face the crashing waves or provide a lateral beach view. Wood floors and rather sober oranges and browns set the stage in the lower-end rooms. Upper-category digs have brighter, cheerier colors, a bit more space and those fabled ocean views.

HOTEL ASTORIA COPACABANA

Map pp244-5   Hotel $

☎ 2545 9090; www.astoria.com.br; Rua República do Peru 345, Copacabana; d US$72; 🔀 🖳
Yet another of Copacabana's glass-and-steel high-rises, this 11-story hotel has small, clean rooms with tile floors and east-facing windows that let in a decent amount of sunlight. Cheery duvets add some color to the otherwise cookie-cutter design. The pool is small but decent enough for a refreshing dip during the day.

HOTEL DEBRET Map pp244-5   Hotel $$

☎ 2522 0132; www.debret.com; Av Atlântica 3564, Copacabana; d standard/deluxe US$100/135; 🔀
Boasting fine views of Copacabana beach, the Debret has a range of rooms that varies in quality from fair to fairly cramped. It has a cozy lobby and simply furnished rooms with pressed-wood floors. The corner rooms are the best, with plenty of light, twin armchairs and a tiny desk. By all means pay extra for rooms with the ocean view; they're among the best you'll find at this price.

TOP FIVE HOTEL BARS

- Copacabana Palace (opposite) – The elegant, old-world setting at the **Poolside Bar** (p134) will dazzle any date.
- Hotel Praia Ipanema (p175) – Lovely beach views, a fairly hip crowd and decent music warrant the trip to this well-located spot.
- Marina All Suites (p177) – At the **Bar D'Hotel** (p130) a stylish Zona Sul crowd gathers over tropical cocktails to the backdrop of waves crashing on Ipanema beach.
- Marina Palace (p177) – A fun nonpretentious crowd gets festive over stiff drinks at the outdoor Bar da Praia in Leblon.
- Sofitel Rio de Janeiro (p184) – Grab a *cerveja* (beer) inside the wildly decorated **Horse's Neck bar** (p134) or step onto the terrace for stellar views of Copacabana beach.

HOTEL RIO INTERNACIONAL

Map pp244-5   Hotel $$$

☎ 2546 8000; www.riointernacional.com.br; Av Atlântica 1500, Copacabana; s/d from US$161/195;

The Rio Internacional had a total overhaul in 2004, which transformed it into one of Copacabana's top beachfront hotels. The rooms have a light and airy feel, and are painted in cool, elegant tones (mint is a favorite). Large white duvets, light hardwoods, stylish furnishings and simple artwork all complement each other nicely. Big windows let in lots of natural light, and most rooms have balconies.

HOTEL SANTA CLARA

Map pp244-5   Hotel $

☎ 2256 2650; www.hotelsantaclara.com.br; Rua Décio Vilares 316, Copacabana; s/d front US$60/67, s/d back US$55/60

Along one of Copacabana's most peaceful streets, this simple three-story hotel has some charming, old-fashioned features, and it's a nice alternative to the high-rises found elsewhere in the neighborhood. The upstairs rooms are best, with wood floors, antique bed frames, a writing desk and a balcony.

HOTEL TOLEDO Map pp244-5   Hotel $

☎ 2257 1990; fax 2257 1931; Rua Domingos Ferreira 71, Copacabana; mini/s/d US$32/55/67

A block from the beach, the Toledo offers low prices for those who don't need many creature comforts. The rooms need an update, but they're clean and adequately furnished. The Toledo also has some closet-sized singles (minis).

HOTEL VILAMAR Map pp244-5   Hotel $$

☎ 3461 5601; www.hotelvilamarcopacabana.com.br; Rua Bolívar 75, Copacabana; s/d US$89/100;

Less than five years old, the 15-story Hotel Vilamar is set on a quiet street in Copacabana. Inside this fair-priced place, you'll find inviting rooms with pressed-wood floors, cheery duvets and big windows affording decent natural light.

LE MERIDIEN Map pp244-5   Hotel $$$

☎ 3873 8888; www.rio.lemeridien.com; Av Atlântica 1020, Leme; d US$215-260;

One block back from Praia do Leme, the four-star Le Meridien rises up 37 stories in all its decadent glory. Here you'll find crisply dressed staff, an elegant lobby, excellent restaurants, and modern rooms ranging in size and style from small and cozy to large and lavish. Le Meridien still ranks among Rio's top hotels.

LUXOR COPACABANA

Map pp244-5   Hotel $$

☎ 2545 1070; www.luxorhoteis.com.br; Av Atlântica 2554, Copacabana; d standard/deluxe US$116/175;

Smack in the heart of Copacabana, this beachfront property has decent service, but its rooms need a serious update. The quality varies from gloomy standards to roomier superiors to deluxes with better furnishings and ocean views. All rooms have balconies.

MAR PALACE Map pp244-5   Hotel $$

☎ 2132 1500; www.hotelmarpalace.com.br; Av NS de Copacabana 552, Copacabana; s/d US$81/96;

On Copacabana's busiest road, this sleek glass-and-steel high-rise building hides trim, modest-sized rooms with faux-wood floors and large windows overlooking the street. There's a tiny pool and a sauna on the top floor, as well as a workout room with views of Cristo Redentor.

MIRAMAR PALACE HOTEL

Map pp244-5   Hotel $$$

☎ 2195 6200; reservas.miramar@windsorhoteis .com.br; Av Atlântica 3668, Copacabana; d standard/ deluxe US$186/261;

Overlooking Copacabana beach, the Miramar Palace Hotel has sizable, comfortable rooms with wood floors, bright curtains and big bathrooms. The windows allow ample light, and, as elsewhere in Copacabana, only the deluxe rooms have ocean views. Our only reservation with this place is that the price doesn't quite match the quality.

OLINDA OTHON CLASSIC

Map pp244-5   Hotel $$

☎ 2257 1890; www.othon.com.br; Av Atlântica 2230, Copacabana; d standard/deluxe/ste US$82/93/230;

Set in a handsome white building overlooking Copacabana beach, the Olinda Othon is indeed a classic. Its oversized marble lobby,

Sleeping   COPACABANA & LEME

complete with chandeliers, oriental carpets and grand piano, has an old-world charm, although its rooms are in varying states of decay. The best rooms face the ocean and cost only marginally more than superiors, so by all means book one. Renovations are underway, which will drive up prices considerably.

ORLA COPACABANA

Map pp244-5   Boutique Hotel $$

☎ 2525 2425; www.orlahotel.com.br; Av Atlântica 4122, Copacabana; d US$135-170; ✖ 🔊

Despite the 13-story building, the Orla Copacabana, which opened in 2001, has something of a boutique hotel feel. Its stylish, understated rooms, artfully lit lobby and beach-facing location make it a top pick in Copacabana. The standards are too cramped to recommend, so we suggest you try to snag one of the chic deluxe rooms that have more space and that desirable ocean view.

PARTHENON ARPOADOR

Map pp244-5   Boutique Hotel $$$

☎ 3222 9600; www.accorhotels.com.br; Rua Francisco Otaviano 61, Copacabana; ste s/d US$154/178; ✖ 🔊

The all-suites Parthenon Arpoador opened in 2003, which makes it one of Rio's newest hotels. It's also one of its most stylish. Suites have sleek white leather sofas that open into beds, modern kitchenettes, TVs with a stereo and a DVD player, ambient lighting and comfortable bedrooms. All rooms have balconies, although there's no view. The long, slim swimming pool is designed for swimming laps, not for lounging.

PLAZA COPACABANA

Map pp244-5   Hotel $$$

☎ 2195 5500; www.windsorhoteis.com; Av Princesa Isabel 263, Copacabana; s/d from US$173/191; ✖ 🔊

Another generic luxury hotel brought to you by the Windsor group, the six-year-old Plaza is a slender, polished high-rise located two blocks from Praia do Leme. Rooms here are clean and comfortable with bright curtains and subdued carpeting, though the price for all this seems excessive.

POUSADA GIRASSOL

Map pp244-5   Hotel $

☎ 2549 8344; www.girassolpousada.com.br; Travessa Angrense 25A, Copacabana; s/d/tr US$44/55/64

One of two small *pousadas* (guest houses) on a quiet lane off the busy Av Nossa Senhora (NS) de Copacabana, Girassol, with its cleaner quarters and lower prices, is the better choice. You'll find simple en-suite rooms with wood floors and adequate ventilation. There are some better-value places in Copacabana, but this place is fine at a pinch.

PREMIER COPACABANA HOTEL

Map pp244-5   Hotel $

☎ 2548 8581; www.premier.com.br; Rua Tonelero 205, Copacabana; d standard/deluxe US$75/100; ✖ 🔊

One of the neighborhood's better-value hotels, the Premier Copacabana has comfortable, modern rooms painted in cool, subdued colors. While busy Tonelero isn't the best location in Copacabana, it's just a short walk to the beach, and the metro station is right across the road.

REAL PALACE HOTEL

Map pp244-5   Hotel $$

☎ 2541 4387; www.realpalacehotelrj.com.br; Rua Duvivier 70, Copacabana; d US$82; ✖ 🔊

Set on a quiet street a few blocks from Copacabana's famous beach, this simple 13-story hotel has small, and sparsely furnished rooms at reasonable prices. Tiles (of the faux-wood variety) cover the clean-swept floors, and the rooms all get decent light. On the rooftop there's a small pool, though it lies in shadows for most of the day.

RESIDENCIAL APARTT

Map pp244-5   Serviced Apartments $

☎ 2522 1722; www.apartt.com.br; Rua Francisco Otaviano 42, Copacabana; ste from US$63; ✖

One of Rio's cheapest all-suites hotels, this old-fashioned place doesn't have much charm about it. Instead you'll find basic one-bedroom suites with small kitchen units, a gloomy little lounge room (with cable TV) and a bedroom with adequate natural lighting. Breakfast is included in the price (served until 1pm).

Sleeping

COPACABANA & LEME

RIO BACKPACKERS Map pp244-5   Hostel $
☎ 2236 3803; www.riobackpackers.com.br;
Travessa Santa Leocádia 38, Copacabana; dm/d
US$14/41; 🖳
Young backpackers flock to this popular,
three-story hostel in Copacabana. Although
the rooms are a bit small, they're clean
and nicely maintained, and the house has
plenty of choice spots in which to relax and
meet other travelers.

RIO GUESTHOUSE Map pp244-5   Hotel $$
☎ 2521 8568; www.rioguesthouse.com; Rua
Francisco Sá 5, Copacabana; d US$81-205; 🔡
On the top floors of a high-rise overlooking
Copacabana beach, this small guest house
offers excellent rooms in a cozy setting –
topped only by the warm welcome you'll
receive throughout your stay. Inside this
split-level penthouse you'll find antique
furnishings, colorful artwork, and an outdoor
patio with gorgeous views over Copacabana.

RIO OTHON PALACE Map pp244-5   Hotel $$$
☎ 2525 1500; www.hoteis-othon.com.br; Av
Atlântica 3264, Copacabana; d standard/deluxe
US$232/253; 🔡 🖭
Facing Copacabana beach, this is no longer
one of Rio's top hotels, owing to its dated
decor. Beyond the marble lobby you'll find
a bevy of near-identical rooms, each with
thin blue carpeting, wood and faux brick
details along one wall and a balcony – the
rooms' most redeeming feature. There's
also a rooftop pool, a sauna and a workout
room.

RIO ROISS HOTEL Map pp244-5   Hotel $$
☎ 2521 1142; rioroiss.com.br; Rua Aires Saldanha 48,
Copacabana; s/d from US$78/105; 🔡
Like dozens of other hotels in Copacabana,
Rio Roiss needs to modernize its look. Its
rooms are decent enough – good beds and
wood finishes – but you'll feel like you're
stepping back in time at the Rio Roiss.
Rooms in the luxo category have partial sea
views and are more spacious (though lacking in furniture to fill the space).

ROYAL RIO PALACE Map pp244-5   Hotel $$
☎ 2122 9292; www.royalrio.com; Rua Duvivier 82,
Copacabana; s/d from US$107/118; 🔡 🖭
Not far from the beach, this shiny glass-and-
steel high-rise, which opened in 2004, offers
comfortable, modern rooms and decent

amenities. This pleasant if nondescript hotel
is a reasonable second option if your dream
Ipanema or Copacabana pad falls through.
Although the name 'Royal Rio' is a bit of
a stretch, the rooms here aren't half-bad.
You'll find nicely designed spaces with sizable windows and a pleasant top-floor pool.

SOFITEL RIO DE JANEIRO
Map pp244-5   Hotel $$$
☎ 2525 1232; www.sofitel.com; Av Atlântica 4240,
Copacabana; d US$315-380; 🔡 🖭 🖭
One of Rio's most expensive hotels, Sofitel
does its best to dazzle visitors with its lav-
ishness. The excellent service, comfortable
rooms, two lovely pools and beachfront
location have earned many fans – even
more since renovations. All of the rooms
have balconies and are tastefully furnished.
The deluxe rooms and suites have ocean
views.

BOTAFOGO & URCA
Botafogo and Urca are among the least-
explored neighborhoods by foreign visitors.
There aren't many accommodations in the
area to draw them here, but there are abun-
dant opportunities to experience authen-
tic Rio – its tree-lined streets, old-school
botecos (neighborhood bars) and hidden
restaurants – if you do stay here.

CARIOCA EASY HOSTEL
Map pp242-3   Hostel $
☎ 2295 7805; www.cariocahostel.com.br; Rua Mare-
chal Cantuária 168, Urca; dm/d US$18/50; 🖳 🖭
Set against the backdrop of Pão de Açú-
car (Sugarloaf), this charming hostel is a
laid-back place that attracts a good mix of
international travelers. In addition to clean-
swept dorm rooms, several private rooms
and lounge space, there's also a tiny swim-
ming pool in back for taking in a bit of sun.
It's a short bus ride to Copacabana beach.

O VELEIRO   B&B $
☎ 2554 8980; www.oveleiro.com; d US$50-80
A lovely rustic house, O Veleiro is surrounded
by remnants of Atlantic forest. It's reached
by a short walk on an old colonial cobble-
stone road, with a fine view of Cristo Reden-
tor. The owners prefer not to include the
address in guidebooks, so for more informa-
tion, visit their website.

LONG-TERM RENTALS

If you're planning to stay in Rio for longer than a few nights, you should consider renting an apartment. There are a number of agencies dedicated to tracking down short-term hires for foreigners, and it's a fairly straightforward affair. As is the case for hotels, prices rises during Carnaval and New Year's – though there's almost always something available. Prices start at around US$50 per night.

Blame it on Rio 4 Travel (Map pp244–5; ☎ 3813 5510; www.blameitonrio4travel.com; Rua Xavier da Silveira 15B, Copacabana) This popular agency rents many types of apartments; it also rents cell phones and provides many other services.

Copacabana Holiday (Map pp244–5; ☎ 2542 1525; www.copacabanaholiday.com.br; Rua Barata Ribeiro 90A, Copacabana) Specializing in Copacabana, this agency rents apartments for a minimum of three days.

Fantastic Rio (Map pp244–5; ☎ 2543 2667; www.fantasticrio.hpg.ig.com.br; Apt 501, Av Atlântica 974, Leme) Multilingual Peter Corr of Fantastic Rio rents a range of apartments from modest one-bedrooms to spacious four-bedrooms with beach views.

Rio Apartment Services (☎ 2247 3194; www.rioapartmentservices.com) In the rental business for over 10 years, this reliable agency lists dozens of places for hire on its website. Airport transportation is available.

Rio Apartments (Map pp246–7; ☎ 2235 7180; www.rioapartments.com; Ste 301, Rua Farme de Amoedo 76, Ipanema) This highly professional outfit offers a wide selection of apartments in the Zona Sul, and can arrange cell phone rental, airport transport and more.

Yvonne Reimann (Map pp244–5; ☎ 2227 0281; Apt 605, Av Atlântica 4066, Copacabana) Yvonne rents a range of apartments in the area – some with local phone service. She speaks French, German and English.

FLAMENGO

Although decent beaches are far from Flamengo (the water at Praia do Flamengo is too polluted for swimming), the area has its appeal. One of Rio's oldest neighborhoods, it attracts visitors who are seeking a more authentically Carioca experience – its neighborhood feel, traditional bars and youthful inhabitants adding to the charm. Flamengo's other big draw is its range of decent accommodations at much lower prices than those found in Copacabana or Ipanema.

HOTEL FERREIRA VIANA

Map pp242-3   Hotel $

☎ 2205 7396; Rua Ferreira Viana 58, Flamengo; d from US$34; ⊠

Not the nicest place in the area but the Hotel Ferreira Viana is at least cheap. Your *reais* will buy you a small, dark room with tile floors. Some rooms are better than others so take a peek before you commit.

HOTEL FLÓRIDA Map pp242-3   Hotel $$

☎ 2195 6800; www.windsorhoteis.com; Rua Ferreira Viana 81, Flamengo; d from US$115; ⊠ 🖳 🖳
Flamengo's best hotel, the 10-story Flórida has a range of comfortable if uninspiring rooms. All are renovated, with pressed-wood floors and modern bathrooms. The best rooms have huge beds, balconies and Jacuzzi bathtubs. The pool has decent views (including Pão de Açúcar), and there's a workout center and sauna, but for the money most people would rather stay by the beach.

HOTEL PAYSANDU Map pp242-3   Hotel $

☎ 2558 7270; www.paysanduhotel.com.br; Rua Paissandu 23, Flamengo; s/d/tr US$54/60/75; ⊠
Set on a quiet street lined with imperial palm trees, the Paysandu is an affordable although still-decent option in Flamengo. The hotel's best rooms feature high ceilings, good natural light and space to stretch out.

HOTEL REGINA Map pp242-3   Hotel $

☎ 3289 9999; www.hotelregina.com.br; Rua Ferreira Viana 29, Flamengo; d US$55-60; ⊠
Undergoing renovation at the time of research, the Hotel Regina has a range of rooms to choose from. The best have wood floors, a roomy feel and receive adequate natural light. At the lower end of the scale the rooms were gloomy, cramped quarters that may be much improved by the time you visit.

MENGO PALACE HOTEL

Map pp242-3   Hotel $$

☎ 2556 5343; mengohotel@infolink.com.br; Rua Corrêa Dutra 31, Flamengo; ste s/d US$70/88; 🕮

Offering some of the more affordable suites in Rio, Mengo Palace is a clean, modern hotel with a forlorn air about it. The suites are small with pressed-wood floors, carpeting on the walls and Jacuzzi bathtubs big enough for two.

CATETE & GLÓRIA

Budget hotels sprout like weeds from the crumbling buildings on either side of the Catete metro station. Although the exteriors of many of these hotels suggest that they're unpolished gems, once inside you realize that this is rarely the case. Many of these hotels need work – and lots of it. So if you don't mind roughing it, you'll be able to take advantage of the city's cheapest accommodations. That said, both Catete and Glória have some excellent places to stay, and like Flamengo you'll pay much less than you would further south. Catete is already Rio's unofficial Gringolândia, and if you're looking to hook up with other backpackers, this area is a good start.

FLAMENGO PALACE Map pp242-3   Hotel $

☎ 2557 7552; hotelflamengopalace.cjb.net; Praia do Flamengo 6, Flamengo; s/d from US$63/70; 🕮

Trapped in the '70s, the Flamengo Palace has bare rooms with simple furnishings and an odd touch here and there – like wooden-framed oval mirrors and wild curtain patterns. *Luxo* rooms have excellent views of the bay but are noisier.

GLÓRIA Map pp238-9   Hotel $$$

☎ 2555 7373; www.hotelgloriario.com.br; Rua do Russel 632, Glória; d US$155-260; 🕮 💻

A grand 1920s hotel, Glória still retains the aura of its past. There are red carpet hallways, old paintings, antique fixtures and a liberal use of brass throughout the palatial hotel. If you plan to stay here, note that there are two parts to the hotel: the old part with aging but atmospheric rooms (some in a sorry state), and the new wing with trim, modern, fairly bland rooms. At the very top end, you'll find antique-filled rooms with wood floors, marble bathrooms and glorious views of the bay.

HOTEL MONTERREY Map pp242-3   Hotel $

☎ 2265 9899; Rua Arturo Bernardes 39, Catete; s with shared bathroom US$18, s/d with private bathroom US$24/32

Short of sleeping in the metro station, you can't find much cheaper lodging than the Hotel Monterrey. Rooms here are basic: a small bed, a TV, a table, a fan and maybe a window, but the place is fairly clean, and the owner is a kind-hearted old soul.

HOTEL NOVO MUNDO

Map pp242-3   Hotel $$

☎ 2265 2369; www.hotelnovomundo-rio.com.br; Praia do Flamengo 20, Flamengo; d US$100-150; 🕮

With its proximity to Centro, the Hotel Novo Mundo attracts a large percentage of business travelers. Its rooms range from small, rather dour standards to large furnished suites with balconies overlooking the bay or the lush Catete gardens next door.

HOTEL RIAZOR Map pp242-3   Hotel $

☎ 2225 0121; hotelriazor1@hotmail.com; Rua do Catete 160, Catete; s/d US$21/28; 🕮

The lovely colonial facade of the Riazor hides battered quarters short on style. The equation is very simple here: bed, bathroom, TV, air-conditioning, and a door by which to exit the room and explore the city. You'll find a mix of travelers and lost souls at Hotel Riazor.

Glória (left) has the red carpet ready for guests

HOTEL RIO CLARO Map pp242-3   Hotel $

☎ 2558 5180; Rua do Catete 233, Catete;
s/d US$23/30; ❄

The bare-bones Rio Claro is the best of the
budget hotels for those looking to sleep
on the cheap. The no-nonsense rooms and
bathrooms all have white tile floors, air-
conditioning and half-decent beds. Plenty
of backpackers are around.

HOTEL TURÍSTICO Map pp238-9   Hotel $

☎ 2557 7698; fax 2558 9388; Ladeira da Glória 30,
Glória; s/d US$25/30

On a quiet street near the Igreja da NS da
Glória do Outeiro, the Turístico offers spar-
tan accommodations that attract few international travelers. Some rooms get decent
natural light, while others are dark and grim,
so see a few rooms before committing.

IMPERIAL HOTEL Map pp242-3   Hotel $

☎ 2556 5212; www.imperialhotel.com.br; Rua
do Catete 186, Catete; d from US$55; ❄ 🖳

The Imperial Hotel is an excellent choice
for Catete. The lovely white building has
only three stories but goes back endlessly
to reveal a new crop of recently renovated
rooms and suites. Some rooms are too dark
for our tastes, while others have better
natural lighting and that all-important
Jacuzzi tub.

CENTRO & CINELÂNDIA

Centro and Cinelândia cater mostly to Brazilian business travelers with small expense
accounts. Aside from its proximity to excellent lunch spots, pedestrian shopping areas
and a few noteworthy street Carnavals, the
area doesn't offer many attractions. Centro
is deserted after 10pm during the week and
remains pretty barren over the weekends,
making it an unsafe area to linger. However, if it's business you're here for or you
just feel some indescribable urge to stay in
Centro, there are some options.

AMBASSADOR HOTEL

Map pp238-9   Hotel $

☎ 2299 2870; fax 2220 4783; Rua Senador
Dantas 25, Centro; s/d US$35/50; ❄ 🖳

This high-rise hotel has quirky style: trim
furniture with nice lines and a few art-deco
fixtures are scattered among rooms full of
angry brown curtains and clinical-looking

AIRPORT ACCOMMODATIONS

At the international airport there are two hotels.
The better of the two is the **Rio Luxor Aeroporto**
(☎ 2468 8998; www.luxor-hotels.com.br; d US$120,
day use US$65). Situated on the 3rd floor of the air-
port, the 64 rooms here are comfortably furnished,
with cable TV, modern bathrooms and 24-hour room
service. There's also a bar in the hotel. The **Hotel
Pousada Galeão** (☎ /fax 3398 3848; d from US$85)
is on the 1st floor of international arrivals. Rooms are
small but comfortably furnished – lots of dark wood
in the interior.

beds. Carpets are worn, but the bathrooms
are clean, and the price is hard to beat.

CENTER HOTEL Map pp238-9   Hotel $

☎ 2296 6677; www.centerhotel.com.br in
Portuguese; Av Rio Branco 33, Centro; s/d from
US$55/65; ❄

This 12-story hotel on busy Rio Branco is a
good midrange option for those wishing to
stay in Centro. Rooms are clean and comfortable with unique features, like carved
wood headboards and artwork on the
walls, in some. Higher floors have decent
views of downtown.

GUANABARA PALACE

Map pp238-9   Hotel $$

☎ 2216 1313; www.windsorhoteis.com; Av Presi-
dente Vargas 392, Centro; d US$122-160; ❄ 🖳 🖳

Centro's nicest hotel has clean, modern
rooms with hardwood furnishings and
nice views of Baía de Guanabara. Some of
the rooms feel a little cramped, although
there's abundant space on the rooftop,
with a pool and bar and spectacular views
of the bay. There's also a small fitness
center on site.

ITAJUBÁ HOTEL Map pp238-9   Hotel $

☎ 2210 3163; itajubahotel.com.br; Rua Álvaro
Alvim 23, Cinelândia; s/d/tr weekdays US$43/52/68,
weekends US$36/43/60

If you're looking for monastic simplicity,
Itajubá is the place for you. Rooms are
sparse but clean, and the beds are neither
good nor bad. The service here is decent,
and each room has a TV, refrigerator and
telephone. The two-toned wood floors are
a nice feature.

SANTA TERESA

Although accommodations are still sparse in the Montmartre of the tropics, some of the more unusual options are here, just a short tram ride from Centro. Santa Teresa attracts a broad mix of travelers (some later become expats) seeking the artistic heart of Rio. Vibrant restaurants and bars and its proximity to the samba clubs in Lapa add to Santa Teresa's appeal, though you'll want to take care when walking around here.

CAMA E CAFÉ Map p241   B&B $

☎ 2221 7635; www.camaecafe.com; Rua Progresso 67, Santa Teresa; d from US$45

Run by three young Santa Teresans dedicated to rejuvenating the area, Cama e Café is a bed-and-breakfast network that links travelers with local residents. There are some 50 houses to choose from: by location, comfort level or shared interests – art, music, dogs – with their host(s). It's a brilliant way to experience one of the city's most charming neighborhoods. Choices range from modest to lavish, with a decent breakfast and sizable rooms with private bathrooms common to all. See Cama e Café's website.

CASA ÁUREA Map p241   B&B $

☎ 2242 5830; www.casaaurea.com.br; Rua Áurea 80, Santa Teresa; d US$36-55

Set on a quiet street, this handsome two-story house has been converted into a simple guest house that remains one of the neighborhood's better-kept secrets. It's within a short walking distance of the *bonde* (tram) as well as the best restaurants and bars. Casa Áurea's best feature is the large private garden behind the house.

RIO HOSTEL Map p241   Hostel $

☎ 3852 0827; www.riohostel.com; Rua Joaquim Murtinho 361, Santa Teresa; dm US$16-18, d US$50-55; ✷ 🖳 🖳

The Rio Hostel provides travelers with a home away from home. The spacious lounge, backyard patio with pool, ping-pong room and kitchen for guests all add to the charm of this hidden gem. The rooms are clean, and there are two attractive private rooms for couples. The hostel overlooks downtown Rio and lies along the *bonde* line. It can be a bit tricky to find – if you reach Curvelo Sq (the first major *bonde* stop),

you've gone too far. Disembark and walk 200m back down the hill.

BARRA DA TIJUCA & WEST OF RIO

A number of pleasant options lie west of Leblon. If you stay in Barra, you'll need a car to get around, but once there, you'll be able to enjoy some of Rio's most seductive beaches far from the tourist crowds.

ATLÂNTICO SUL

Map pp236-7   Hotel $$

☎ 2490 2050; www.atlanticosulhotel.com.br; Rua Professor Armando Ribeira 25, Recréio dos Bandeirantes; d from US$95; ✷ 🖳

Overlooking the beach, the high-rise Atlântico Sul is at the far end of Barra da Tijuca and has a fine pool, decent apartments and a lot of vacationing Brazilians. It's on the corner of Av Sernambetiba

CASA DEL MAR Map pp236-7   Hotel $$

☎ 2158 6999; www.promenade.com.br; Av Sernambetiba 5740, Barra da Tijuca; ste s/d from US$120/160; ✷ 🖳

This lovely all-suites hotel features stylish, modern furnishings spread between the living-dining area and the bedroom. The locationis excellent and the pool enticing.

INTERCONTINENTAL

Map pp236-7   Hotel $$$

☎ 3323 2200; Av Preifeito Mendes de Morais 222, São Conrado; d from US$200; ✷ 🖳 🖳

Framed by a gorgeous beachfront to the south and the towering peak of Pedra Bonito to the west, the monolithic Intercontinental has excellent facilities (including three swimming pools) and nicely furnished rooms, all with balconies. You'll be far from the heart of Rio – although the hotel runs a complimentary bus shuttle.

PRAIA LINDA Map pp236-7   Hotel $$

☎ 2494 2186; www.hotelpraialinda.com.br; Av Pepê, Barra da Tijuca; d from US$100; ✷

Facing the Praia do Pepê, if you're staying in Barra this is the pick of the bunch. Rooms are clean and comfortable, though the beach and ocean views are the big draw here.

Excursions

Islands 191
National Parks 191
Beaches 191
Towns 191
Drives 191

Búzios   97

Paraty   192

Ilha Grande   195

Petrópolis   199

Visconde De Mauá   201

Excursions

Breathtaking beaches, mountain retreats and island getaways are just a few hours' drive from the city. The geographical diversity within Rio de Janeiro state (roughly the size of Switzerland) provides a wondrous setting for adventure, from hiking and camping to surfing, kayaking and rock climbing. Those who just want to enjoy the beauty – whether in a picturesque colonial plaza or on a white-sand beach – have plenty of options.

The city of Rio and the giant Baía de Guanabara, which has 131km of its own coastline and 113 islands, divide the coast into two regions: the Costa Verde (Green Coast, to the west) and the Costa do Sol (Sun Coast, to the east). Along the Costa Verde, mountains meet the sea, and there are hundreds of islands and beaches, with forests lining the interior. East of the city lies the Costa do Sol, where the mountains begin to rise further inland. The littoral is filled with lagoons and swampland. Stretching away from the coast are plains that extend about 30km to the mountains.

North of Rio lies mountains covered in Atlantic rainforest, with cooler temperatures than in the city. Several towns in the area provide superb hiking and climbing opportunities.

ISLANDS

Two hours west of the city, joff the verdant Costa Verde, is one of the country's most beautiful islands. Ilha Grande (p195) has dozens of untouched beaches and lush, rainforest-covered hills, which provide splendid hikes. The lack of cars ensures a mellow, laid-back stay.

NATIONAL PARKS

Resplendent national parks set in the mountains offer abundant hiking and trekking options for those seeking a dose of nature after the city. North of Rio, the fantastic peaks of the Parque Nacional da Serra dos Órgãos (p200) make a lovely backdrop to hikes in the area. West of Rio lies one of Brazil's loveliest national parks, the Parque Nacional de Itatiaia (p202), packed with waterfalls, pristine lakes and dramatic mountain peaks.

BEACHES

Búzios (p197) may no longer be the tiny fishing village it was back in the 1960s, but its beaches haven't changed much since then. Over a dozen lovely stretches of sand can be found in the area, and, by night, the bayside promenade offers plenty of diversions among the many outdoor restaurants and bars. Beautiful beaches also lie near Paraty (p192), while Arraial do Cabo (p198) and surfer-favorite Saquarema (p198) draw their share of visitors.

TOWNS

In a cool mountain climate, Petrópolis (p199), with its canals, landscaped parks and city squares, has a European air. Its palaces and museums are good places in which to soak up some history. Or head west along the coast to Paraty (p192), a perfectly preserved colonial town, whose colorful buildings and cobbled streets hide some of the state's culinary gems. Northwest of Rio, the village of Visconde de Mauá (p201) and its surroundings are set in a lush alpine area, with idyllic streams, waterfalls, and cozy chalets scattered along country lanes.

DRIVES

The Costa Verde provides the setting for one of the country's most spectacular drives. The panoramic road hugs the coast's edge as it winds its way past lush peaks, beaches and colonial settlements.

PARATY

☎ 24

The striking colonial town of Paraty is one of the gems of Rio state. Picturesque old churches and brightly hued stone buildings line the cobbled streets, with the lush green mountains and deep blue sea adding even more splendor to the historic city. On summer weekends, Paraty's plazas, sidewalk cafés and open-air restaurants come to life as visiting crowds feast on fresh seafood to the backdrop of live music.

Formerly a region populated by Guianás Indians, Paraty first emerged as a European settlement when Portuguese from São Vicente arrived in the 16th century. Paraty's boom time began in the 17th century when gold was discovered in Minas Gerais, and the port became an important link as the riches were shipped back to Portugal. Until 1954, the only access to Paraty was by sea. You can still find a few old-timers around town who fondly remember those days of Paraty's remoteness.

In addition to the 17th-century town's culinary and historical attractions, you'll find striking natural beauty in the surrounding countryside, with steep, forested mountains plunging right down into the sea, and a varied coastline replete with dozens of pristine beaches and islands. Strolls through forest or along the shore, sea kayaking, horse riding, and walking treks along the old gold road are just a few of the ways to fill a sunny day in Paraty.

Paraty's newest attraction is the excellent **Casa da Cultura** (p194), which has a fascinating permanent exhibition that includes interviews with and stories from local residents (in audio and video format), as well as relics from Paraty's past. All exhibits are in both English and Portuguese.

A 20-minute walk north of town, **Forte Defensor Perpétuo** (p194) commands a fine view over the bay. It was built in 1703 (and rebuilt in 1822) to defend against pirate raids on the gold pipeline that ran to Minas Gerais. The fort is located on the Morro da Vila Velha, the hill past Praia do Pontal.

A visit to the town's old churches provides a glimpse of the complexities of 18th-century life: two were built for whites, one for blacks and a fourth for freed mulattos (persons of mixed black and white ancestry).

Built by slaves in 1725, the **Igreja Nossa Senhora do Rosário** (p194) served as the city's black parish. Its two wooden, gilt-trimmed side altars showcase the talents of early 19th-century wood-carvers. Note also the black St Benedict holding the Christ child to the left of the altar, the stone pulpit carved into the wall, and the pineapple-like chandelier base in the roof – a symbol of prosperity. An old burial ground lies beneath the church floorboards.

Overlooking the lush Praça da Matriz, the **Matriz Nossa Senhora dos Remédios** (p194) is a fine stone church with handsome tiled floors, wedding cake–style alcoves and a row of glass-encased saint figures peering down at would-be worshippers. Paraty's settlement began around the time builders first erected the church. In 1646, the benefactor Maria Jácome de Melo donated the land between the rivers on two conditions: that a chapel dedicated to Our Lady be built and that no harm come to the Indians residing there. Sadly, the second demand was ignored.

TRANSPORT

Distance from Rio 261km

Direction West

Travel Time Four hours

Car From the Zona Sul, head north on Av D Infante Henrique, which follows the curve of the bay as it goes north to Centro and eventually links up with Av Presidente Kubitschek. Look for signs to merge onto Av Brasil; this turns into BR 101, which leads all the way out to Paraty.

Bus Buses (US$17) depart eight times daily between 5am and 9pm from Novo Rio bus station in Rio.

TRAVEL TIP

Paraty is renowned for its *cachaça* (cane liquor). To see a selection or sample the goods, visit **Empório da Cachaça** (☎ 3371 6329; Rua Dr Samuel Costa 22) or **Toca da Cachaça** (☎ 3371 1310; Rua da Matriz 9).

Excursions

PARATY

PARTYING IN PARATY

The city by the sea has a calendar packed full with colorful festivals. Among the biggest events is Paraty's **Festa do Divino Espírito Santo**, which features all sorts of merrymaking that revolves around the *fólios*, musical groups that go door to door, singing and joking. The vibrant festival begins nine days before Pentecostal Sunday (the seventh Sunday after Easter).

Festas Juninas are held throughout June, when the town becomes the stage for music, street parties and folk dancing such as the *xiba* (a circle clog dance) and the *ciranda* (a *xiba* with guitar accompaniment). The final festival is on June 29 with a maritime procession to **Ilha do Araújo**, one of the islands near Paraty. From Friday to Sunday on the third weekend in August, Paraty hosts its popular **Festa da Pinga** (*pinga* is a more polite term for *cachaça*, the fiery sugarcane spirit). Local distilleries are on hand to dazzle (or at least intoxicate) festival goers with their rare spirits.

The **Festa de Nossa Senhora (NS) dos Remédios** takes place on September 8, with street processions and religious celebrations.

The city also attracts a crowd to its **Carnaval**, when revelers cover themselves in mud and dance wildly through the streets.

Freed mulattos worshipped in the **Igreja Santa Rita dos Pardos Libertos** (p194). It houses a tiny museum of sacred art and some fine woodwork on the doorways and altars.

Facing the sea, the small, white **Capela de Nossa Senhora das Dores** (p194) gathered the colonial white elite. Dating from 1800 but renovated in 1901, the church hides a fascinating cemetery in the inner courtyard. It opens only sporadically.

Paraty has 65 islands and 300 beaches in its vicinity. The first beach you'll reach walking north of town (just across the canal) is Praia do Pontal, which can get a little murky at times. A handful of open-air restaurants lines its shore. The cleaner and relatively secluded Praia do Forte lies a quick walk north from there. Another 2km further north is Praia do Jabaquara, a spacious beach with great views, shallow waters and a small restaurant overlooking the sand.

For visits to the less accessible sands, schooner tours depart daily, making stops at several beaches; book through **Paraty Tours** (p194). An alternative is to hire one of the small motorboats at the port. Local boatmen know some great spots in the region and will happily take you for the right price (plan on US$20 per hour).

The best of both worlds – colonial buildings dot the Paraty waterfront while would-be fishermen bask in the sun

Sights & Information

Capela de Nossa Senhora das Dores (Rua Dr Pereira)

Casa da Cultura (☎ 3371 2325; Rua Dona Geralda 177; admission US$6; ☻ 10am-6:30pm Sun, Mon & Wed, 1pm-9:30pm Fri & Sat)

Centro de Informações Turísticas (☎ 3371 1222; Av Roberto Silveira; ☻ 9am-9pm) It distributes good maps of the area (as does Paraty Tours, next door) and maintains updated information on hotels and restaurants in the area. For good online information, visit www.eco-paraty.com and www.paraty.com.br.

Forte Defensor Perpétuo (☻ 24hr, arts center 9am-noon & 1:30-5pm Wed-Sun) The fort also houses an arts center.

Igreja Nossa Senhora do Rosário (cnr Rua Samuel Costa & Rua do Comércio; admission US$1; ☻ 9am-noon & 1:30-5pm Tue-Sat, 9am-3pm Sun)

Igreja Santa Rita dos Pardos Libertos (Rua Santa Rita; admission US$1; ☻ 9am-noon & 1:30-3pm Wed-Sun)

Matriz Nossa Senhora dos Remédios (Cnr Rua da Matriz & Rua da Capela; admission US$1; ☻ 9am-noon & 1:30-5pm Wed-Sat, 9am-3pm Sun)

Paraty Tours (☎ 3371 1327; www.paratytours.com.br; Av Roberto Silveira 11; ☻ 9am-8pm) One of several tour companies in town, Paraty Tours is a good source of information and offers a range of tours, including schooner tours, and kayaking, biking, horse riding and diving trips. It's at the colonial end of town. Paraty Tours also rents bikes.

Eating

Academia de Cozinha (☎ 3371 6468; Rua Dona Geralda 288; all-included dinner US$60) A mix of theater and haute cuisine, the Academia de Cozinha stages cooking shows in Portuguese and English. Guests learn about the regional cuisines, watch chef Yara Castro Roberts in action, then enjoy the fruits of her labor. The price of dinner includes cocktails, wine, desserts and a wide variety of other fare.

Café Paraty (☎ 3371 1464; Rua do Comércio 253; mains US$12-28; ☻ 9am-midnight) This long-standing favorite serves a variety of Brazilian fare amid old-world splendor. Decent bossa-nova musicians perform most summer nights.

Margarida Café (☎ 3371 2441; Praça do Chafariz; mains from US$14) This charming restaurant serves tasty seafood dishes and thin-crust pizzas, enjoy them in the spacious lounge area or inner courtyard. Live music most nights.

Refúgio (☎ 3371 2447; loja (shop) 4, Rua Fresca, Praça do Porto; mains from US$18) Refúgio's candlelit interior and scenic location near the docks make it sound like the setting for a *novela* (soap opera), but don't let that deter you from experiencing the delicious seafood specialties.

Sleeping

Hotel Coxixo (☎ 3371 1460; www.hotelcoxixo.com.br; Rua do Comércio 362; d from US$85) Featuring spacious rooms and a lovely inner courtyard (complete with swimming pool and palm trees), the Hotel Coxixo is good value for Paraty. Some rooms could use some modernization.

Hotel Solar dos Gerânios (☎ /fax 3371 1550; Praça da Matriz 2; s/d from US$22/34) This colonial hotel overlooking the Praça da Matriz features wood and ceramic sculptures, heavy rustic furniture and *azulejos* (Portuguese tiles). Some rooms have balconies, so check a few before committing.

Pousada Arte Urquijo (☎ 3371 1362; www.urquijo.com .br; Rua Dona Geralda 79; d from US$150) This boutique inn wins the style award with charming colonial rooms beautifully decorated with art (some rooms have balconies and sea views), and there's a cozy lounge and swimming pool.

Entertainment

Teatro Espaço (☎ 3371 1575; Rua Dona Geralda 327; ☻ 9pm Wed & Sat) For years the Teatro Espaço has been garnering praise for its famous puppet theater. Even if you can't speak Portuguese, the lifelike puppets and beautifully executed works make for a fine show.

DETOUR

Paraty's resplendent natural setting makes for some fine exploring. Gorgeous beaches lie within a 30-minute drive and a one-hour boat ride, and most are surrounded by green mountains with deep blue seas lapping at the shore. Two of the best beaches are **Praia de Paraty-Mirim**, 27km east of Paraty, where there are a few *barracas* (food stalls) on the beach, and **Praia de Trindade**, with calm seas that reflect the lush vegetation surrounding it. If you'd prefer to hike into the forest, visit a waterfall and take a dip in a natural swimming hole, there's the nearby **Parque Nacional da Serra da Bocaina**. This national park has rich plant and animal life but, sadly, with the park's limited infrastructure it's hard to see much of this. For a short visit, head west out of Paraty about 15 km along the Paraty-Cunha road (Estrada Paraty Cunha), which winds its way uphill. Stop at the Cachoeira (waterfall) do Tobogã (look for signs: it's a brief hike off the Paraty–Cunha road) where you can go for a swim.

On your way back to Paraty, at the 7km marker on the road, stop at the lovely **Vila Verde** (☎ 3371 7808; Paraty-Cunha road; mains US$8-15; ☻ 11am-6pm Tue-Sun low season, 11am until last customer daily high season), which serves homemade pastas, risottos and smoked salmon as well as good desserts and coffee. The restaurant is beautifully landscaped – a small brook trickles through the property, surrounded by lots of greenery.

ILHA GRANDE

☎ 24

Ilha Grande (Big Island) has always dazzled. On the southern coast of Rio, Brazil's third-largest island offers tropical scenery and gorgeous beaches among sheltered bays, brooks and waterfalls. Lush hillsides are remnants of the rapidly disappearing Mata Atlântica.

Before the Portuguese arrival, the island was home to the Tupinambá Indians whose trails around the island are still in use. Once Europeans reached Brazil, Ilha Grande became a shelter for pirates and smugglers from the 16th to the 18th centuries. The island was also the site of a prison (Lazareto), first built at Abraão Bay and later moved to Dois Rios, a tiny settlement on the south side. The latter was demolished in 1994 (you can still see some of the ruins), and since then tourism has fast become the island's chief source of income.

Vila do Abraão is the principal village, and the launchpad for many adventures. From here, you can take schooner tours to gorgeous beaches such as **Praia Lopes Mendes** (which often tops charts listing the world's most beautiful beaches), **Saco do Céu**, **Lagoa Azul** or **Lagoa Verde**. The schooner companies organize regular trips to points around the island, with daily departures to Lopes Mendes. You can also reach the beach via a forest trail by heading east of Vila do Abraão.

There are numerous hikes you can do from Vila do Abraão. One excellent day hike (13km or about three hours each way) takes you over the top of the island to a gorgeous beach framed by two rivers (Dois Rios). This is also the site of the prison ruins and a ghostlike town. You'll find several simple eateries here that serve inexpensive lunches. A shorter walk north from Abraão leads to Praia Preta, where you can see the ruins of **Lazareto**, the island's first prison.

The hike to **Pico do Papagaio** (982m) gives you the chance to see the island's rich flora (and perhaps some wildlife) and, from its summit, take in the splendid views. For this trip, a guide is essential as it's easy to get lost.

There's also excellent diving around the island. **Elite Dive Center** (p196) has a wide range of courses and offers two-tank dives in some fantastic spots.

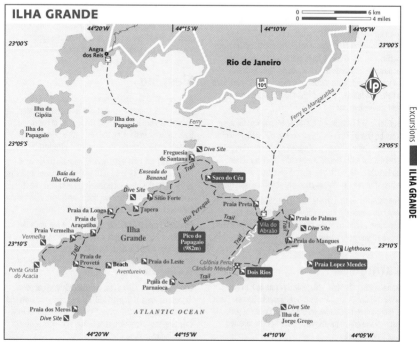

TRANSPORT

Distance from Rio 150km
Direction West
Travel Time Two hours to Mangaratiba or 2½ hours to Angra dos Reis, and then a 90-minute ferry ride.
Car From the Zona Sul, head north on Av D Infante Henrique, which follows the curve of the bay as it goes north to Centro and eventually links up with Av Presidente Kubitschek. Look for signs to merge onto Av Brasil. This turns into BR 101, which leads all the way out to Mangaratiba or Angra. Both places offer long-term parking near the dock for around US$7 per day.
Ferry Once you reach either Mangaratiba or Angra, you'll need to catch the ferry to Vila do Abraão. Boats from Mangaratiba depart at 8am and return at 5:30pm daily. From Angra, boats depart at 3:30pm Monday to Friday and 1:30pm Saturdays, Sundays and bank holidays; they return to Angra at 10am daily. A one-way ferry ride costs US$2.50 Monday to Friday and US$6 Saturday and Sunday. Ferry schedules fluctuate, so it's wise to confirm the times when making a reservation at your hotel.
Bus Costa Verde buses depart every 45 minutes between 5am and 9pm from the main Novo Rio bus station to either Mangaratiba (US$7.50) or Angra (US$10). Make sure you verify ferry connections to avoid getting stuck overnight in Angra or Mangaratiba.

On summer weekends and on holidays the island can get crowded, though during the week (and any time in winter) Ilha Grande nearly always remains quite peaceful.

No cars are allowed on Ilha Grande. Maps of the island and of Vila do Abraão are available at the ferry dock. Be sure to change money before coming to Ilha Grande.

Sights & Information

Elite Dive Center (☎ 9999 9789; www.elitedivecenter .com.br; Travessa Buganville) Offers a wide range of diving courses around the island.

Phoenix Turismo (☎ 3361 5822; www.phoenixturismo .com.br; Rua da Praia 703; excursions US$10-22) A few doors down from O Pescador hotel, Phoenix is one of many outfits offering schooner tours of the island. The most popular destinations are to Praia Lopes Mendes beach, Lagoa Azul and Lagoa Verde. Boat trips last anywhere from a half- to a full day; you can order lunch on the boat and rent snorkeling gear.

Sudoeste SW Turismo (☎ 3361 5516; www.sudoestesw .com.br; Rua da Praia 647) Next door to O Pescador hotel, Sudoeste has excellent Portuguese/English-speaking guides available for hikes around the island – from day climbs up Pico do Papagaio to five-day camping treks around the island. You can also rent kayaks or book private boat tours.

Tourist Information Office (☎ 3361 5508; Rua da Praia) Right alongside the Abraão pier, this small booth has brochures and maps of the island; staff can also call around for you if you need a room.

Eating

Banana Blu (☎ 3361 5160; Rua da Praia 661; mains US$8-14) One of the island's top restaurants, Banana Blu is a charming restaurant facing the ocean. Excellent seafood, risottos and grilled meats are prepared by the talented multilingual chef.

Corsário Negro (☎ 3361 5321; Rua Alice Kury 90; mains for 2 US$20-30) This friendly indoor-outdoor restaurant serves tasty plates of fresh seafood, including paella and the gargantuan *tesouro de tortuga* (mixed seafood platter for two).

Tropicana (☎ 3361 5911; Rua da Praia) Just west of the dock, Tropicana has a lovely garden setting for its tasty seafood. Favorites are pasta with shrimp and the fresh salad Tropicana (salmon, sun-dried tomatoes and veggies).

Sleeping

Aselem (☎ 3361 5602; www.asalem.com.br; d from US$96) A 25-minute walk east of Abraão, this beautiful *pousada* is surrounded by lush scenery. All of the rooms have terraces overlooking the sea, with a sleeping loft upstairs and a lounge with hammock on the first level.

Naturalia (☎ 3361 9583; www.pousadanaturalia.com; Praia do Abraão 149; d from US$82) A 10-minute walk east of the dock, this pleasant *pousada* (guest house) has handsome rooms, each with wood floors, lovely sea views and a hammock in which to while away the afternoon.

Pousada Praia D'Azul (☎ 3361 5091; www.praiadazul .com.br in Portuguese; Rua da Igreja; d from US$48) Straight up from the dock, this newly renovated hotel has small but comfortable rooms that overlook a refreshing swimming pool.

O Pescador (☎ 3361 5114; opescadordailha@uol.com .br; Rua da Praia; d from US$50) Cozily furnished rooms and an excellent restaurant make a great combination at this charming spot overlooking the beach. The friendly owners speak English.

Excursions

ILHA GRANDE

BÚZIOS

📞 22

Armação de Búzios, known simply as Búzios, is a lovely beach resort on a peninsula jutting into the Atlantic, fringed with about 20 beaches. It was a simple fishing village until the early 1960s, when it was 'discovered' by Brigitte Bardot and her Brazilian boyfriend. Today, Búzios offers much more than just its spectacular natural setting. The village has boutiques, elegant restaurants, open-air bars and lavishly decorated B&Bs. Many foreign-owned (especially Argentinean) *pousadas* and restaurants have sprouted along the peninsula's shores, and a mix of international travelers adds to the jumble of languages you'll hear on the streets.

The village itself has two main streets running through it. The posh **Rua das Pedras** hugs the shoreline, with waterfront *pousadas*, bars and restaurants lining the stone-paved street. Rua das Pedras turns into Orla Bardot as it heads north. **Rua Turibe Farias**, just behind Rua das Pedras, has a number of good boutiques, ice-cream parlors and a pleasant square (**Praça Santos Dumont**) that becomes a sceney gathering spot at night.

Pristine white-sand beaches are the daytime attraction in Búzios, and there are over 20 within a short drive from the center. To get a taste of the offerings, take a schooner tour or rent a buggy and explore the area on your own. In general, the southern beaches are trickier

www.lonelyplanet.com

TRANSPORT

Distance from Rio 176km
Direction East
Travel Time 2½ hours

Car From the Zona Sul, head north to the Rio–Niterói bridge (toll US$1.50). After passing the toll, take RJ 101 in the direction of Rio Bonito. After reaching Rio Bonito, take BR 124 (Via Lagos Hwy; toll US$4) west. Stay on this highway until it ends, then continue east another 7km until you reach an Ipiranga gas station at the entrance of São Pedro da Aldeia. Take a left at the gas station and then a right onto BR 106 in the direction of Macaé/Búzios. After another 14km you will reach the Atéque Enfim gas station. Turn right and stay on this road until reaching Búzios. For those who'd rather take the slower, scenic route, a coastal road runs from Itacoatiara out to Cabo Frio then north.
Bus From Novo Rio bus station, **Viação 1001** (📞 2516 1001; per person US$10) buses depart seven times daily. The trip takes 3½ hours. Alternatively, take an hourly bus to Cabo Frio and transfer to Búzios.

to get to, but they're prettier and have better surf. The northern beaches are closer to the towns and more sheltered.

With its long stretch of sand and good surf, **Geribá** remains one of the most popular beaches. Lively restaurants and bars lie scattered along the shore and sunseekers pack the sands. A bit calmer and less developed is the small **Ferradurinha** (Little Horseshoe), just east of Geribá. Continuing counterclockwise you'll find **Ferradura**, another horseshoe-shaped beach that's popular with windsurfers. Next are **Lagoinha**, a rocky beach with rough water, and **Praia da Foca** and **Praia do Forno**, both of which have colder water than the other beaches. **Praia Olho de Boi** (Bull's Eye) has the unique distinction of being named after Brazil's first postage stamp. It's a pocket-sized beach reached by a little trail from the long, clean beach of **Praia Brava**, which lies to the west.

João Fernandinho and **João Fernandes** are good locations for snorkeling, as are the topless beaches of **Azedinha** and **Azeda**. **Praia dos Ossos**, **Praia da Armação**, **Praia do Caboclo** and **Praia dos Amores** are pretty to look at, but not ideal for lounging around on, as they can be crowded

Paradise under the palm fronds in Búzios

197

with boats just offshore, which won't leave you much privacy. **Praia da Tartaruga** is quiet and pretty. **Praia do Gaucho** and **Manguinhos** are town beaches further along the coastal strip.

Although most travelers prefer to base themselves in Buzios, there are two other settlements on the peninsula – **Ossos** and **Manguinhos** – and one a little further north, called **Rasa**. Ossos, at the northernmost tip of the peninsula, is the oldest and most attractive, with a harbor and yacht club, hotels and bars, and a tourist stand. Manguinhos, at the isthmus, is the most commercial; it even has a 24-hour medical clinic. Rasa and the island of Rasa, northwest along the coast, are where Brazil's political dignitaries and CEOs come to relax. Owing to its charm and popularity with Cariocas, prices in Búzios rise substantially on holidays (especially New Year's Eve and Carnaval).

Sights & Information

From any newsstand pick up a copy of *Guia Verão Búzios* (US$5), which has information in English and Portuguese, including a list of places to stay (but no prices). For detailed online information, check www.buziosonline.com.br.

Búzios Trolley (☎ 2623 2763; www.buziostrolley.com.br; Orla Bardot 550; tours US$20) This outfit runs a variety of excursions, including a daily two-hour open-sided bus tour that visits 12 of the peninsula's beaches. You can also book rafting tours and trips by glass-bottomed catamaran.

GusCar (☎ 2623 8225; www.guscar.com.br in Portuguese; Estrada da Usina 444) GusCar offers tours to nearby beaches. It also rents buggies and cars for around US$50 per day.

Queen Lory (☎ 2623 1179; www.queenlory.com.br; Orla Bardot 710; tours from US$20) This outfit offers daily 2½- and five-hour schooner tours to Ilha Feia, Tartaruga and João Fernandinho. Both are good value, with soft drinks, fruit salad and snorkeling gear included in the price. Tours depart from the Pier do Centro in Búzios.

Secretaria de Turismo (☎ 2623 2099; Praça Santos Dumont, Búzios; ☾ 9am-9pm) Pick up a map of the beaches in the area at this tourist-information office, which is one block from Rua das Pedras. Another **branch** (☎ toll-free 0800 249 999; ☾ 24hr) is at the entrance to Búzios.

Eating & Drinking

Bar do Zé (☎ 2623 4986; Orla Bardot 382; ☾ 6pm-midnight; mains US$20-25) This charming restaurant on the

---

DETOUR

Along the way from Rio to Búzios there are a number of scenic beaches, surfing spots and fishing villages.

Follow the directions (p197) for getting to Búzios (ie take the Rio–Niterói bridge, and turn off at Rio Bonito). Turn onto RJ 124 at Rio Bonito (the Via Lagos Hwy), and continue for 23km until you reach the turnoff for **Saquarema**. This small community lies about 100km east of Rio de Janeiro, and enjoys long stretches of open beach, bordered by lagoons and mountains. The town still has a somnolent air to it, though on weekends it attracts a large surfer crowd thanks to waves of up to 3m. A number of beaches lie near the town, including the popular **Barra Nova** and **Praia da Vila**. About 3km north of Saquarema is **Praia Itaúna**, a good spot that hosts an annual surfing contest during the first two weeks of October.

From Saquarema continue east along the coastal road for another 60km and you'll reach **Arraial do Cabo**, a moderate-sized village with beaches that compare to the finest in Búzios. Unlike Búzios, however, Arraial is a sleepy, somewhat blue-collar town. Discovered a few centuries ago by Amerigo Vespucci, Praia dos Anjos has beautiful turquoise water, but a little too much boat traffic for safe swimming. It also has a **Museum of Oceanography** (Praia dos Anjos; ☾ 9am-noon & 1-4:30pm Tue-Sun). Aside from Praia dos Anjos, the most popular beaches in Arraial do Cabo are **Praia do Forno**, **Praia Brava** and **Praia Grande**.

The **Gruta Azul** (Blue Cavern), on the southwestern side of Ilha de Cabo Frio, is another beautiful spot. Be alert to the tides: the entrance to the underwater cavern isn't always open. There are lots of dive operators who run tours here, including **Arraial Sub** (☎ 2622 1945) and **PL Divers** (☎ 2622 2633).

Ten kilometers north of Arraial do Cabo lies **Cabo Frio**, which sits between the Canal do Itajuru on one side and the ocean on the other. It's a bit overdeveloped by tourism, but there is some lovely landscape nearby. East of town, along a scenic road, is the Praia do Forte with bleached white sand and a backdrop of low scrub, cacti and grasses. At the northern end of Praia do Forte is a stone fortress, **Forte São Mateus** (☾ 10am-4pm Tue-Sun), which was built in 1616 and served as a stronghold against pirates.

The **sand dunes** around Cabo Frio are one of the region's most interesting features. The dunes facing the excellent surfing spot of **Praia do Peró** lie 6km north of town in the direction of Búzios. Praia do Pero is near Ogivas and after **Praia Brava** and **Praia das Conchas**. The **Pontal dunes** of Praia do Forte stretch from the Forte São Mateus to Morro de Miranda (Miranda Hill), while the **Dama Branca** (White Lady) sand dunes are on the road to Arraial do Cabo. The dunes can be dangerous due to robberies, so talk to locals before heading out.

main street serves excellent seafood with a fusion twist. Start with the mouth-watering seviche before moving on to the grilled-fish dishes.

Cigalon (☎ 2623 0932; Rua das Pedras 199; mains around US$22) You'll find decadent French cuisine and lovely views at this romantic beachside spot in the center of town.

Sawasdee (☎ 2623 4644; Orla Bardot 422; mains from US$20) Dazzling Thai cuisine made with the region's fresh seafood makes for a winning combination at this highly praised spot. Start the proceedings off with a *kaipilychia* (lychee caipirinha).

Guapo Loco (☎ 2623 2657; Rua das Pedras 233; ⏱ 6pm-4am; mains from US$8) This colorful Mexican eatery draws a young, eager crowd downing burritos and margaritas as DJs spin an eclectic mix overhead. The indoor/outdoor space gets packed on weekends.

Chez Michou Crêperie (☎ 2623 2169; Rua das Pedras 90; crepes US$3-5) This lively outdoor spot serves tasty dinners and savory and sweet crepes. Delicious piña coladas are also served.

Pátio Havana (☎ 2623 2169; Rua das Pedras 101; mains US$8-12) A combination of jazz bar, restaurant, tobacco shop and wine cellar, the Pátio Havana makes a good place to hang out in the evening. Live music shows – *Música Popular Brasileira* (MPB), DJs and jazz – happen in summer.

Sleeping

Brigitta's Guesthouse (☎ 2623 6157; www.buziosonline .com.br/brigitta/pousada.htm in Portuguese; Rua das Pedras 131; s/d US$50/70) Overlooking the water, this charming guest house is one of at least a dozen *pousadas* along this strip. Brigitta's has just four cozy rooms, lending it the feel of a B&B. There's an excellent restaurant attached.

Casas Brancas (☎ 2623 1458; www.casasbrancas.com .br; Morro do Humaitá 10; d from US$250) Set on a hill the Mediterranean-style Casas Brancas has bay views, spacious rooms (some with balconies and living rooms), a swimming pool and a lovely patio. Full spa services.

Hibiscus Beach (☎ 2623 6221; www.hibiscusbeach .com; Rua Primeiro 22, Praia de João Fernandes; bungalows from US$75) On the hillside overlooking João Fernandes beach, Hibiscus Beach offers accommodation in cheerful Polynesian-style bungalows. The lush landscaping, pool and proximity to the beach add to the allure.

PETRÓPOLIS

☎ 24

Just 68km north of Rio, Petrópolis has the air of a European mountain retreat. Horse-drawn carriages still clatter through the streets, and the city's small bridges and canals, manicured parks and old-fashioned lampposts add to its charm. The city makes a fine place for strolls, visiting the museums and taking in the lovely surrounds.

Emperor Dom Pedro I first came across the lovely setting on a journey from Rio to Minas Gerais. It was little more than farmland in the 1830s, but Dom Pedro liked the scenery so much that he decided to buy some land. Although he abdicated the throne and returned to Portugal, the land passed to his son, Dom Pedro II, who built a summer retreat here. By the 1840s, the whole court had jumped on the bandwagon, and a palace rose against the mountains. With mansions and a looming cathedral, Petrópolis earned the nickname 'Imperial City.'

Downtown Petrópolis is a living museum, with that provides a window into the past. One of the city's gems is the neoclassical **Museu Imperial** (p200), which served as the home away from home for Dom Pedro II and his wife, Dona Teresa, when the humidity (and mosquitoes) in Rio became unbearable. The lavish, faithfully preserved building features exhibits from the royal collection, including a 1.7kg crown covered with 639 diamonds and 77 pearls.

North of the palace-museum the **Catedral São Pedro de Alcântara** (p200), houses the tombs

TRANSPORT

Distance from Rio 68km
Direction North
Travel Time 1½ hours
Car Take the Linha Vermelha Hwy from Rio. After passing signs for the international airport, be on the lookout for BR 040; you'll merge onto this highway (also called Rodovia Washington Luís) and follow the signs to Petrópolis.
Bus Every 20 minutes between 5:15am and 7pm. A Viação 1001 (☎ 2516 1001; per person US$6) bus departs from Novo Rio bus station. For the best views be sure to leave well before sundown. Buses arrive at Leonel Brizola station in Bingen, some 10km from downtown, where you'll have to change to a city bus (100 and 10) or taxi to reach the Centro Histórico.

of Dom Pedro II, Dona Teresa and their daughter Princesa Isabel. From the steps of the cathedral you'll have fine views of most of the region, with the spires of the town set against the mountains.

Another eye-catching sight in Petrópolis is the **Palácio de Cristal** (below), which was built for Princesa Isabel in France and brought to the country in 1884. It houses a greenhouse, just as it did back then, and features fountains and lush greenery in front.

Following the imperial era, in the late 19th century Petrópolis became a center for intellectuals and artists, nurturing the talents of Austrian writer Stefan Zweig, composer Rui Barbosa and Santos Dumont, the inventor, architect and writer often dubbed the 'father of Brazilian aviation' for his early flights. You can learn more about the man by touring the small, fascinating home that he designed himself (he also invented the wristwatch) at the **Museu Casa de Santos Dumont** (below).

Some uncommonly charming château-like restaurants lie near Petrópolis, but you'll need a car to visit them as the best places are outside of the city center. If you're just around for the day, you can easily explore the historic center on foot, though with its crisp, calm nights and surplus of cozy cottages and B&Bs, Petrópolis makes a great overnight trip. If you visit, keep in mind that most museums close on Monday.

Sights & Information

Catedral São Pedro de Alcântara (☎ 2242 4300; Rua São Pedro de Alcântara 60; admission free; ☽ 8am-noon & 2-6pm Tue-Sun)

HSBC (Rua do Imperador 884; ☽ 10am-5pm Mon-Fri) It has an ATM.

Museu Casa de Santos Dumont (☎ 2247 3158; Rua do Encanto 22; admission US$2; ☽ 9:30am-5pm Tue-Sun)

Museu Imperial (☎ 2237 8000; Rua da Imperatriz 220; admission US$4; ☽ 11am-5:30pm Tue-Sun)

Palácio de Cristal (☎ 2247 3721; Rua Alfredo Pachá; admission free; ☽ 9am-5:30pm Tue-Sun)

Rios Brasileiros Rafting (☎ 2243 4372; www.rbrafting .com.br; Room 104, Rua Silva Jardim 514) Rios organizes rafting, rappelling and hiking adventures around the area. Portuguese- and English-speaking guides are available.

Tourist Information Office (☎ 2246 9377; Praça dos Expedicionários; ☽ 9am-5pm) Stocks brochures and maps, and can recommend hotels in the area. There's also a good information office at the obelisk on the way into town from Rio.

DETOUR

The lush greenery of the mountains makes a lovely setting for a scenic drive, but if you'd like to see the greenery from the inside, head to **Parque Nacional Da Serra Dos Órgãos** (admission US$3; ☽ 8am-5pm main entrance). The national park has extensive trails through Mata Atlântica rainforest and has a variety of rich plant and animal life). **Dedo de Deus** (God's Finger), **Cabeça de Peixe** (Fish Head) and **Verruga do Frade** (Friar's Wart) are among the more imaginative names. Unfortunately, most of the trails are unmarked and off the extents of available maps. Those interested in hiking, or climbing one of the peaks, should inquire at **Rios Brasileiros Rafting** (above) in Petrópolis.

Those wanting a short hike (and a picnic) can take the 3.5km walking trail, visiting the waterfalls, natural swimming pools, tended lawns and gardens. There are **campsites** (per person US$6) and a **lodge** (per person US$25). There are two entrances to the park, both on BR 116. The one closer to Teresópolis offers more facilities.

Another village in the mountains is **Nova Friburgo**, which has good hotels and restaurants, as well as many lovely natural attractions: woods, waterfalls, trails, sunny mountain mornings and cool evenings. Do be aware that it gets chilly and rainy during the winter months, from June to August.

The area around Nova Friburgo was first settled by families from the Swiss canton of Friburg. During the Napoleonic wars, Dom João encouraged immigration to Brazil. At the time, people were starving in Switzerland, so in 1818 around 300 families packed up and headed for Brazil. The passage overseas was grueling and many families died en route. Those who survived settled in the mountains and established the small village of Nova Friburgo in the New World.

A **tourist information office** (☎ 2523 8000; Praça Dr Demervel B Moreira; ☽ 8am-8pm) is in the center of town. Scout out the surrounding area from **Morro da Cruz** (1800m), which is accessible by **chairlift** (☽ 9am-6pm Sat, Sun & holidays); the chairlift station is in the center at Praça Teleférico. Alternatively, there's **Pico da Caledônia** (2310m), offering fantastic views and launching sites for hang gliders. It's a 6km uphill hike, but the view is worth it.

From Nova Friburgo you can hike to **Pedra do Cão Sentado**, explore the **Furnas do Catete** or visit the mountain towns of **Bom Jardim** (23km northeast on BR 116) or **Lumiar** (25km east of the turnoff at Muri, which is 9km south of Nova Friburgo). In Lumiar, hippies, cheap pensions, waterfalls, walking trails and white-water canoe trips abound.

Trekking Petrópolis (☎ 2235 7607; www.rioserra.com
.br/trekking) Organizes hikes, mountain-biking, rafting and
bird-watching trips through nearby Mata Atlântica rainforest. You can also book through **Pousada 14 Bis** (right).

Eating

Bistrô Petit Palais (☎ 2237 8000; Av Imperatriz 220; mains
from US$8; ☽ noon-7pm Tue-Sun) Within the Museu
Imperial complex, this charming bistro and teahouse serves
tasty croissants, pastries and tortes as well as hot dishes.

Chocolates Katz (☎ 2237 0447; Rua do Imperador 912)
This lovely coffee shop and patisserie makes a fine stop for
a cappuccino and chocolate torte.

Luigi (☎ 2246 0279; Praça da Liberdade 185; mains
US$8-15; ☽ closed Sun) A charming Italian restaurant
set in an old house with high ceilings, creaky floors and
candlelit ambience. It packs in the crowds on Friday and
Saturday nights with its live music.

Majórica Churrascaria (☎ 2242 2498; Rua do Imperador
754; mains US$12-22; ☽ noon-10pm Tue-Sun) This *chur-
rascaria* (barbecue restaurant), a short distance from the
Museu Imperial, has excellent cuts of meat, served à la carte.

Locanda della Mimosa (☎ 2233 5405; Alameda das
Mimosas 30, Vale Florida; 3-course dinner US$60; ☽ 12:30-
3:30pm Sat & Sun, 8-11:30pm Fri & Sat) The work of master
chef Danio Braga dazzles visitors with an ever-changing
menu of exotic bites. Reservations are essential.

TRAVEL TIP

If you have a car, check out the restaurants along the
'culinary highway,' Estrada União Indústria, which is on
the way to Itaipava. About 20km from Petrópolis there
are dozens of excellent spots in lush natural settings.

Sleeping

Pousada 14 Bis (☎ 2231 0946; www.pousada14bis
.com.br; Rua Buenos Aires 192; d from US$35) One of
Petrópolis' most charming hotels, the Pousada 14 Bis has
handsome rooms with wooden floors and large windows
overlooking the street, or views of the pleasant garden
out the back. It's on a quiet street a few blocks from the
bus station.

Casablanca Imperial (☎ 2242 6662; www.casablanca
hotel.com.br in Portuguese; Rua do Imperatriz 286; d from
US$80) Housed in an old mansion near the Museu Imperial,
the Casablanca has a range of rooms: the best feature
high ceilings, old shutters, long bathrooms with tubs, and
antique furnishings.

Hotel Colonial Inn (☎ 2243 1590; www.colonialinn
.com.br in Portuguese; Rua Monsenhor Bacelar 125; d
from US$70) Rooms here feature a mix of antique and
art-nouveau furnishings, and there's a friendly, homelike
feel. It's located just down the street from the Museu Casa
de Santos Dumont.

VISCONDE DE MAUÁ
☎ 24

Set in the Itatiaia, a region of charming country towns, wandering steams and lush forests, Visconde de Mauá is actually made up of three small villages (Mauá, Maringá and
Maromba) scattered a few kilometers apart along the Rio Preto. The chief reason for coming is to soak up the lovely peaceful setting, best enjoyed from one of the cozy chalets in
the region. It's a perfect spot to unwind.
Picturesque walks along quiet lanes lie just
outside your door.

Although the scenery is undoubtedly
new-world tropics, there's an element of
the Old World in Itatiaia. It was first settled by Swiss and German immigrants in
the early 20th century. (Nearby Penedo,
with its saunas, was settled by the Finns.)
Visconde de Mauá lies roughly halfway between Rio and São Paulo, in the alpine Serra
da Mantiqueira.

Hikes in the area include walks to several
waterfalls. The **Santa Clara Cachoeira** is the nicest
in the area. It's a 6km walk north of Maringá on the Ribeirão Santa Clara. Trails on
either side of the falls pass through a series
of bamboo groves.

TRANSPORT

Distance from Rio 152km
Direction Northwest
Travel Time 3½ hours
Car Take Av Brasil north to BR 116. Then, take BR 116
west to Resende, where you'll see signs pointing north
to Visconde de Mauá. The last 10km is unpaved.
Bus From Novo Rio bus station, **Cidade do Aço**
(☎ 2253 8471; www.cidadedoaco.com.br in Portuguese; per person US$12) buses (4½ hours) depart
on Friday at 2:05pm and 7:35pm and on Saturday at
7:05am. They return on Sunday at 5pm and Monday
at 9:30am. Buses stop first in Visconde de Mauá before continuing on to Maringá and Maromba.

For some slippery action, you'll find a **natural pool** in the Rio Preto between Visconde de Mauá and Maringá. You'll reach it by turning left just before the bridge.

Beyond Maromba, you can take a 2.5km walk out of town (follow the signs) to **Cachoeira e Escorrega**, a tiny farm with a naturally formed water slide and a chilly swimming pool at the bottom. If you continue along the same road and take the first left at the fork you'll reach **Cachoeira Veu de Noiva**, another beautiful waterfall.

Sights & Information

Tourist Information Hut (☎ 3387 1283; ☷ 9am-noon & 1-8pm Tue-Sun) At the entrance to the village of Mauá, this small booth can provide information in Portuguese about the region. Several good websites (in Portuguese) are www.viscondedemaua.com.br and www.guiamaua .com.br.

Sleeping

Hotel Casa Alpina (☎ 3387 1390; www.visconde-de -maua.com; d with meals from US$75) This pleasant, German-style chalet has beautiful views and abundant greenery surrounding it. The rooms have handsome wood details, and guests can refresh themselves in the swimming pool or sauna. It's located in Maringá on the Minas Gerais side of the river.

Pousada Terra da Luz (☎ 3387 1306; www.fazenda domel.com.br; Estrada Maringá-Minas; d from US$150) Located north of Maringá, this lovely chalet has gorgeously landscaped grounds and spacious, inviting rooms, perfect for a bit of pampering. There's a good restaurant on-site where you can hear live music most Saturday nights; the *pousada* also has a pool and sauna.

Eating

Gosto com Gosto (☎ 3387 1382; Rua Wenceslau Brás 148, Visconde de Mauá; ☷ noon-6pm) A charming restaurant serving excellent Minas Gerais cuisine. In addition to fresh trout, stuffed sausages and hearty stews, you'll find tasty desserts made from *jaca* (jackfruit) and other luscious fruits.

Casebre Pub (☎ 3387 1605; Rua dos Cavalos, Maringá; ☷ noon-midnight Tue-Sun) This wooden roadhouse-style pizzeria serves a pretty mean trout pizza, as well as fondues.

DETOUR

One of Brazil's loveliest national parks is a short drive from Visconde de Mauá. The **Parque Nacional de Itatiaia** contains virgin rainforest, breathtaking mountain trails and plenty of idyllic rivers, lakes and waterfalls in which to splash about. It's also packed with wildlife, including some 400 bird species as well as monkeys, sloths and many other rainforest creatures. There are numerous trails in the park ranging from hour-long hikes to multiday treks. A recommended day hike (six hours) is the Tres Picos hike, an uphill route that leads past the refreshing **Rio Bonito** before continuing on to a fantastic lookout point. At the park entrance, 7km north of the BR 116, you can pick up trail maps at the **Visitors Centre** (park entrance US$2; ☷ 10am-4pm). To get there from Visconde de Mauá head back to BR 116, take a right and look for the signed turnoff to the right another 6km further on.

Transportation 204

Air 204
Bicycle 204
Boat 205
Bus 205
Car 206
Metro 207
Minivan 207
Taxi 207
Train 207
Tram 207

Practicalities 208

Accommodations 208
Business 208
Children 209
Climate 209
Courses 209
Customs 209
Disabled Travelers 209
Electricity 210
Embassies 210
Emergency 210
Gay & Lesbian Travelers 210
Holidays 211
Internet Access 211
Legal Matters 211
Maps 212
Medical Services 212
Money 212
Newspapers & Magazines 213
Pharmacies 214
Post 214
Radio 214
Safety 214
Telephone 215
Television 216
Time 216
Tipping 216
Tourist information 216
Travel Agencies 217
Visas 217
Women Travelers 217
Work 218

Directory

Directory

TRANSPORTATION

AIR

Many international flights pass through São Paolo before arriving in Rio at the Aeroporto Internacional Antonio Carlos Jobim (commonly called Galeão) on Ilha do Governador (Governor's Island). **Varig** (www .varig.com) is Brazil's biggest international carrier, with flights to many destinations.

Airlines

Most of the major airlines have main offices in Centro. You can also visit their ticket counters in the Aeroporto Santos Dumont.

American Airlines (Map pp244–5; ☎ 0300 789 7778; www.aa.com; Av Atlântica 1702, Copacabana)

British Airways/Qantas (☎ 0300 789 6140; www.ba.com, www.qantas.com.au; Terminal 1, Galeão international airport)

Continental (Map pp238–9; ☎ 2531 1850; www .continental.com; No 3711, Rua da Assembléia 10, Centro)

Gol (☎ 0800 701 2131; www.voegol.com.br; Galeão international airport; Aeroporto Santos Dumont)

United Airlines (☎ 0800 162 323 toll-free; www.ual.com) Centro (5th fl, Av Presidente Antônio Carlos 51, Centro); Copacabana (Map pp244–5; ☎ 2545 6575; Hotel Mariott, Av Atlântica 2600)

Varig (☎ 2510 6650; www.varig.com) Centro (Map pp238–9; Av Rio Branco 277, Centro); Copacabana (Map pp244–5; ☎ 2541 6343; Rua Rodolfo Dantas 16A); Ipanema (Map pp246–7; ☎ 2523 0040; Rua Visconde de Pirajá 351)

Airport

Rio's **Galeão international airport** (Map pp236–7) is 15km north of the city center on Ilha do Governador. **Aeroporto Santos Dumont** (Map pp238–9), used by some domestic flights, is by the bay, in the city center, 1km east of Cinelândia metro station.

DEPARTURE TAX

The international departure tax from Brazil is US$36. This has probably been included in the price of your ticket, but if it's not, you have to pay it in cash (either in US dollars or *reais*) at the airport before departure.

BICYCLE

Although traffic can be intimidating on Rio's roads, the city has many miles of bike paths along the beach, around Lagoa and along Parque do Flamengo. You can rent bikes from a stand along the west side of Lagoa Rodrigo de Freitas for US$8 per hour. Other places to rent bikes include the following:

Ciclovia (Map pp244–5; ☎ 2275 5299; Av Prado Júnior 330, Copacabana; per day US$15) A small selection, but good prices.

GETTING INTO TOWN

The most economical way of reaching the international airport is to take the **Real Auto Bus** (☎ 0800 240 850 toll-free), known locally as the *frescão*. These relatively safe air-conditioned buses go from the international airport (outside the arrivals floor of terminal one or the ground floor of terminal two) to **Novo Rio bus station** (Av Rio Branco, Centro), Aeroporto Santos Dumont, southward through Glória, Flamengo and Botafogo and along the beaches of Copacabana, Ipanema and Leblon to Barra da Tijuca (and vice versa). The buses run every 20 to 30 minutes, 5:20am to 12:10am, and will stop wherever you ask. Fares are around US$3. You can transfer to the metro at Carioca station.

Heading to the airports, you can catch the Real Auto Bus in front of the major hotels along the main beaches, but you have to look alive and flag it down.

Comun (standard) taxis from the international airport are generally safe, though there are occasional robberies reported. Radio taxis are safer, but more expensive. You pay a set fare for them at the airport. A yellow-and-blue *comun* taxi should cost around US$30 to Ipanema if the meter is working. A radio taxi costs about US$40.

Many hotels and hostels also arrange transport to and from the airport. Some do this for free, while others charge between US$40 and US$60.

Consuelo (Map pp244–5; ☎ 2513 0159, 8811 5552; Av Atlântica near Posto 4, Copacabana) In addition to having a pick-up service on Copacabana beach, this place also delivers to all hotels in the Zona Sul.

Special Bike (Map pp246–7; ☎ 2521 2686; Rua Visconde de Pirajá 135B, Ipanema; per hr/day US$7/22; ☾ 9am-7pm Mon-Fri, to 2pm Sat)

BOAT
Ferries
Rio has several islands in the bay that you can visit by ferry; another way to see the city is by taking the commuter ferry to Niterói. See p91 for more information on the following trips.

ILHA DE PAQUETÁ
☎ 2533 6661 (ferries), 2533 7524 (hydrofoils)
The regular ferry takes an hour and costs US$0.50. The more comfortable hydrofoil takes only 25 minutes and costs US$7. The ferry service operates from 5:30am to 11pm, leaving every two to three hours. The hydrofoil leaves daily at 10am, noon, 2pm and 4pm and returns at 7:40am, 11:40am, 12:30pm, 2:30pm and 4:30pm.

ILHA FISCAL Map pp238-9
☎ 3870 6992; per person US$3; ☾ departs 1pm, 2:30pm & 4pm Thu-Sun except on the 2nd weekend of each month
Boats depart from the Espaço Cultural da Marinha (Map pp238–9) three times a day from Thursday to Sunday and include a guided tour of the Palácio da Ilha Fiscal (p91). It's a short ride (15 minutes).

NITERÓI Map pp236-7
Niterói's main attraction is the Museu do Arte Contemporânea (p91), but many visitors board the ferry just for the fine views of downtown and the surrounding landscape. The ferry costs US$1 and leaves every 20 minutes from Praça Quinze de Novembro in Centro (Map pp238–9). Faster, more comfortable catamarans run every 15 minutes from 7am to 4pm and cost US$3.

BUS
City Bus
By far the most widespread form of transport is the city bus. You'll see them traveling at breakneck speeds around hairpin curves or clogged in stifling traffic jams at rush hour. There are hundreds of lines crisscrossing the city, with the most useful for visitors coursing along the corridors between Leblon and Copacabana. Every bus has its destination written on the front and on the side, and if you see the bus for you, hail it by sticking your arm straight out (drivers don't stop unless someone's flagging them down).

Board the bus from the front, and pay the collector sitting toward the front. Conveniently enough, the collector can usually make change. After paying, go through the turnstile and take your seat. You'll exit through the rear. Most buses cost around US$0.75.

Rio buses have a bad reputation in the international media as the setting for robberies, bombings or indiscriminate violence (the 2002 documentary film Bus 174 didn't help matters much). In truth such acts are rare and usually limited to outer-suburban areas where tourists aren't likely to travel. Do keep an eye on your belongings while riding, and don't travel by bus at night; taxis are generally a safer option.

Long-Distance Bus
Buses connect Rio with cities and towns all over the country. Most arrive and depart from the loud Novo Rio Rodoviária (Novo Rio bus station; Map pp236–7; ☎ 2291 5151; www .novorio.com.br in Portuguese; Av Francisco Bicalho 1, São Cristóvão), which lies about five minutes by bus north of the city center. The people at the Riotur desk on the bus station's ground floor can provide information on transportation and lodging.

The other Rio bus station is the Menezes Cortes Rodoviária (Menezes Cortes bus terminal; Map pp238–9; ☎ 2224 7577; Rua São José 35, Centro), which handles services to the Zona Sul and some destinations in Rio de Janeiro state, such as Petrópolis and Teresópolis. You can catch buses to these two destinations from Novo Rio as well.

If you arrive in Rio by bus, it's a good idea to take a taxi to your hotel, or at least to the general area where you want to stay. Traveling on local buses with all your belongings is a little risky. A small booth near the Riotur desk at Novo Rio bus station organizes the yellow cabs out front. Excellent buses leave every 15 minutes or so for São Paulo (six hours). Most major destinations

METRÔ-ÔNIBUS

The safest and often the fastest way to reach the metro is via Metrô-Ônibus (metro buses), which are modern silver buses that make limited stops as they shuttle passengers to and from metro stations. A one-way *Integração* ticket costs as much as a metro ride (US$1.25) but includes both the bus ride and the metro ride (hold onto your ticket). Although there are growing numbers of these buses on Rio's streets, the most useful one for travelers staying in Leblon, Ipanema and southern Copacabana is the metro bus marked 'Gávea' (*not* 'Ipanema,' which goes only as far as Praça General Osório). This will take you to and from the Copacabana metro station Siqueira Campos.

Catch the 'Gávea' metro bus on the following streets:

To Metro	From Metro
Rua Padre Leonel França (Gávea)	Metro station Siqueira Campos
Praça Antero de Quental (Leblon)	Praça General Osório (Ipanema)
Av Ataúlfo de Paiva 19 (Leblon)	Rua Prudente de Moraes 814 (Ipanema)
Rua Visconde de Pirajá 259 (Ipanema)	Rua Prudente de Moraes 1800 (Ipanema)
Praça General Osório (Ipanema)	Praça Antero de Quental (Leblon)
Metro station Siqueira Campos	Rua Marquês de São Vicente 22 (Gávea)
	Rua Padre Leonel França (Gávea)

are serviced by very comfortable *leito* (executive) buses leaving late at night.

It's a good idea to buy a ticket a couple of days in advance if you can, especially if you want to travel on a weekend or during a Brazilian holiday period. Many travel agents in the city sell bus tickets. If you're in Centro, try **Dantur Passagens** (Map pp238–9; downstairs store 134, Av Rio Branco 156, Centro; ⏰ 10am-5pm Mon-Fri).

You can find out all the latest information about bus travel from Rio at www.novorio .com.br. Even though it's in Portuguese, it's pretty easy to navigate. Just click on the *Horários e Preços* (hours and prices) button and plug in your destination city.

CAR

Driving & Parking

In the city itself, driving can be a frustrating experience even if you know your way around. Traffic snarls and parking problems do not make for an enjoyable holiday. If the bus and metro aren't your style, there are plenty of taxis. However, if you do drive in the city, it's good to know a couple of things: Cariocas don't always stop at red lights at night, because of the small risk of robberies at deserted intersections. Late at night, cars slow at red lights and then proceed if no one is around. Another thing to know is that if you park the car on the street, it's common to pay the *flanelinha* (parking

attendant) a few *reais* to look after it. Some of the *flanelinhas* work for the city, others are 'freelance,' but regardless, it's a common practice throughout Brazil.

Rental

Renting a car is relatively cheap, but gasoline is expensive. If you can share the expense with friends, it's a great way to explore some of the remote beaches, mountain towns and national parks near Rio. Getting a car is fairly simple as long as you have a driver's license, a credit card and a passport. To rent a car you must be at least 25 years old. Ideally, you should have an international driver's permit, which you'll need to pick up from your home country. In reality, rental-car companies accept any driver's license – it's the cops who will want to see an international driver's permit.

Prices vary between US$50 and US$90 a day, but they go down a bit in the low season. There is a bit of competition between the major agencies, so it's worth shopping around. If you are quoted prices on the phone, make sure they include insurance, which is compulsory.

Car-rental agencies can be found at either airport or scattered along Av Princesa Isabel in Copacabana. At the international airport, **Hertz** (☎ 3398 4377), **Localiza** (☎ 3398 5445) and **Unidas** (☎ 3398 3452) provide rentals. In Copacabana, among the many are **Hertz** (Map pp244–5; ☎ 2275 7440; Av Princesa Isabel

500) and **Localiza** (Map pp244–5; ☎ 2275 3340; Av Princesa Isabel 150).

METRO

Rio's subway system (Map p250) is an excellent, cheap way to get around. It's open from 5am to midnight Monday through Saturday and 7am to 11pm on Sundays and holidays. During Carnaval the metro operates nonstop from Friday morning until Tuesday at midnight. Both lines are air-conditioned, clean, fast and safe. The main line from Siqueira Campos in Copacabana to Saens Peña has 17 stops. The first 14 – from Copacabana to Estácio – are common to both lines. The lines split at Estácio: the main line continues west toward the neighborhood of Andarai, making stops at Alfonso Pena, São Francisco Xavier and Saens Peña, while the secondary line goes northwest to São Cristóvão, Maracanã and beyond. The main stops in Centro are Cinelândia and Carioca. More stations are planned in the coming years, and the city hopes to integrate Ipanema into the transport system by 2009 with a stop at Praça General Osorio.

You can buy a selection of one-way, round-trip or 10-ride tickets. A basic single costs around US$1, and there's no discount for round-trip or multiple-ride tickets. Free subway maps are available from most ticket booths.

MINIVAN

In the last decade, minivans (Cariocas call them *vans)* have become an alternative form of transportation in Rio. Technically they are illegal but no one seems to mind. They're much quicker than buses and run along Av Rio Branco to the Zona Sul as far as Barra da Tijuca. On the return trip, they run along the coast almost all the way into the center. They run frequently, and the flat fee is US$2. They are probably not a good idea if you have luggage.

TAXI

Rio's yellow-and-blue taxis are prevalent throughout the city. They're fairly inexpensive and provide a good way to zip around. Unfortunately, they aren't completely safe

and hassle-free. A few rare cases have been reported of people being assaulted and robbed by taxi drivers. A much more common problem is fare inflation. Many of the taxi drivers who hang around the hotels are sharks, so it's worth walking a block or so to avoid them.

Make sure the meter works. If it doesn't, ask to be let out of the cab. Meters have a flag that switches the tariff; this should be in the number-one position (80% fare), except on Sunday, holidays, between 9pm and 6am, when driving outside the Zona Sul and during December.

The flat rate is US$2, plus around US$1 per km. **Radio taxis** (☎ 2560 2022) are 30% more expensive than regular taxis, but safer.

Most people don't tip taxi drivers, but it's common to round up the fare.

A few radio-taxi companies include **Centraltáxi** (☎ 2593 2598), **Coopatáxi** (☎ 3899 4343), **JB** (☎ 2501 3026) and **Transcoopass** (☎ 2560 4888).

TRAIN

The suburban train station, **Estação Dom Pedro II** (Central do Brasil; Map pp236–7; ☎ 2296 1244; Praça Cristiano Ottoni, Av Presidente Vargas, Centro) is one of Brazil's busiest commuter stations. To get there, take the metro to Central station and head upstairs. This is the train station which featured in the Academy Award–nominated film *Central do Brasil* (Central Station).

TRAM

Rio was once serviced by a multitude of trams with routes throughout the city. The only one still running is the Santa Teresa tram, known locally as the *bondinho*. It's still the best way to get to this neighborhood from downtown.

The **bonde station** (Map pp238–9; Rua Lélio Gama 65) in Centro is best reached by traveling via Rua Senador Dantas and taking a turn west into Rua Lélio Gama. At the top of the small hill, you'll find the station. *Bondes* (trams) depart every 30 minutes. The two routes currently open have been in operation since the 19th century. Both travel over the **Arcos da Lapa** (p88) and along Rua Joaquim Murtinho before reaching **Largo do Guimarães** (Map p241; Rua Almirante Alexandrino) in the heart of boho Santa Teresa. From there, one line (Paula Matos) takes a northwestern route, terminating at Largo das Neves (Map p241). The longer route (Dois Irmãos) continues from Largo do Guimarães uphill and southwest before terminating near the water reservoir at Dois Irmãos.

Although a policeman often accompanies the tram as a potential deterent, the favelas down the hillsides still make this a high-crime area. Go, by all means, but don't take any valuables with you. See p86 for more details.

PRACTICALITIES

ACCOMMODATIONS

Accommodations listings in the Sleeping chapter (p174) are organized by neighborhood, and arranged alphabetically within each neighborhood section. In Rio, the average double room with bathroom costs about US$100, with seasonal variations (highest in summer, from December to February). Over New Year's Eve and during Carnaval, most hotels charge about double what they normally do, and most will only book a minimum stay of four days. Generally, we've quoted standard rates, which are usually higher than the specials and discounted rates many hotels will give. Booking online can save you quite a bit. See our price guide on p174 for an indication of the standard price range for top-end, midrange and budget accommodations. Two good websites that allow you to peruse listings and make reservations online are www.ipanema.com and Lonely Planet's comprehensive accommodations rundown at www.lonelyplanet.com.

BUSINESS

Be prepared for business negotiations to take longer than you may be accustomed to at home. Cariocas will want to get to know you before getting down to serious business. Meetings can go on for a long time.

Red tape is notorious in Brazil and can be very frustrating. All you can do is find out the regulations and comply with them, no matter how long it takes. If it gets to be too much, you may be tempted to hire a *despachante* to help. *Despachantes* are people who are hired for the express purpose of cutting through red tape and they

are expert at it. They can do in a couple of days what would take you a couple of weeks. It's probably not appropriate here to provide a list of *despachantes,* but your business contacts should be able to put you in touch with one through their network of functional friends.

It pays to make appointments well in advance and confirm them at least once by phone. While Cariocas are known for their tardiness on social occasions, they may not like being kept waiting by a foreigner. Make sure you allow for traffic delays when going to appointments, especially if it's raining.

Business cards are used extensively. It's a good idea to have the information in Portuguese on one side and English on the other.

Hours

Office hours in Rio are from 9am to 6pm, Monday to Friday. Most shops and government services (such as the post offices) are open from 9am to 6pm Monday to Friday, and from 9am to 1pm on Saturday.

Because many Cariocas have little free time during the week, Saturday mornings are often spent shopping. Shops are usually open weekdays from 9am to 7pm and on Saturday from 9am to 1pm. Stores in the large shopping malls are open from 10am to 10pm Monday through Saturday and on Sundays from 3pm to 10pm.

Banks, always in their own little world, generally open from 9am or 10am to 3pm or 4pm Monday to Friday. Currency-exchange places often open an hour after that, when the daily dollar rates become available.

Centers

Before you arrive in Brazil, check out the web pages of Brazilian-American Chamber of Commerce (www.brazilcham.com) and American Chamber of Commerce in Brazil (www.amcham .com.br in Portuguese). Both provide comprehensive information about the various industry sectors and have good links to other business-related sites. Once in Rio, business travelers will find the Rio Convention & Visitors Bureau (p216) most helpful.

The larger hotels have business centers for all your networking needs. For mobile phone rental, see p215. To rent temporary office space in Rio de Janeiro, try one of the following:

Business & Legal Center (☎ 3804 7600; www.blcrio.com .br; 5th fl, Av Presidente Wilson 231, Centro)

Business Quality (☎ 3231 9000; www.bq.com.br in Portuguese; 4th fl, Rua São José 40, Centro)

Tempos Modernos (☎ 2508 8389; www.tmoffice.com .br in Portuguese; sobreloja (1st floor), Travessa do Ouvidor 50, Centro)

CHILDREN

Brazilians are very family oriented, and many hotels let children stay free, although the age limit varies. Baby-sitters are readily available and most restaurants have high chairs.

Don't forget Lonely Planet's *Travel with Children*, by Cathy Lanigan, gives a lot of good tips and advice on traveling with kids in the tropics.

See p88 for more details on sights and activities for children.

CLIMATE

Rio lies only a few dozen kilometers north of the Tropic of Capricorn, so it has a classic tropical climate. In summer (December to February), Rio is hot and humid; temperatures in the high 30°Cs (100°F) are common, and days sometimes reach the low 40°Cs (107°F). Frequent, short rains cool things off a bit, but the summer humidity makes things uncomfortable for people from cooler climates. The rest of the year, it's cooler, with temperatures generally in the mid 20°Cs (77°F), sometimes rising to the low 30°Cs (88°F).

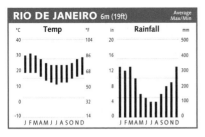

RIO DE JANEIRO 6m (19ft)

COURSES

Rio makes a fine setting for soaking up an exhilarating dose of the tropics, but if action is what you're after, there's a wealth of opportunities for visitors, from diving to surfing to honing one's volleyball game on the sands. See the Activities chapter (p150) for more information on diving, surfing, hang gliding, volleyball and dance classes.

Language Courses

FEEDBACK Map pp246-7
☎ 2522 0598; www.cursofeedback.com.br in Portuguese; Rua Farme de Amoedo 35, Ipanema
Feedback offers group and private courses at its schools throughout the city (there are also locations in Copacabana, Botafogo and Centro). Private classes run to US$25 per hour. Classes for two cost US$15 an hour per person.

INSTITUTO BRASIL-ESTADOS UNIDOS Map pp244-5
IBEU ☎ 2548 8430; www.ibeu.org.br; 5th fl, Av Nossa Senhora (NS) de Copacabana 690, Copacabana
IBEU is one of the older, more respected language institutions in the city. It has four different levels of classes from beginner through to advanced. Classes typically meet two hours a day, three days a week. The cost for a four-week course is about US$440. For information, stop by or visit the website. IBEU also has a decent English library.

CUSTOMS

Travelers entering Brazil can bring in 2L of alcohol, 400 cigarettes, one radio, tape player, typewriter, personal computer, video and still camera. Newly purchased goods worth up to US$500 are permitted duty-free. Meat and cheese products are not allowed.

At Galeão international airport, customs use the random–check system. After collecting your luggage, you pass a post with two buttons; you push the appropriate button depending on whether you have anything to declare. A green light allows you to proceed straight through; a red light means you've been selected for a baggage search. They are usually fairly lenient with foreigners.

DISABLED TRAVELERS

Rio is probably the most accessible city in Brazil for disabled travelers to get around, but that doesn't mean it's always easy. It's convenient to hire cars with driver-guides, but for only one person the expense is quite high compared to the cost of the average bus tour. If there are several people to share the cost, it's definitely worth it.

The metro system has electronic wheelchair lifts, but it's difficult to know whether they're actually functional.

The streets and sidewalks along the main beaches have curb cuts and are wheelchair accessible but most other areas do not have cuts. Many restaurants have entrance steps.

Most of the newer hotels have accessible rooms. Some cable TV is close-captioned.

Organizations

The **Centro de Vida Independente** (Map pp246–7; ☎ 2512 1088; fax 2239 6547; www.cvi-rio .org.br in Portuguese; Rua Marquês de São Vicente 225, Gávea) can provide advice for the disabled about travel in Brazil.

Those in the USA might like to contact the **Society for Accessible Travel & Hospitality** (SATH; ☎ 212-447 7284; www.sath.org). SATH's website is a good resource for disabled travelers. Another excellent website to check is www.access-able.com.

ELECTRICITY

The current is almost exclusively 110V or 120V, 60 Hz, AC. Many hotels also have 220-volt current. The most common power points have two sockets, and most will take both round and flat prongs. If you're packing a laptop – or any electronic device – be sure to take along a surge protector.

Electrical current is not standardized in Brazil, so if you're traveling around the country it's a good idea to carry an adapter. Check the voltage before you plug in. For more information on electricity, plugs and other curious tidbits, visit www.kropla.com.

EMBASSIES

Many foreign countries have consulates or embassies in Rio. If they're not listed here, you'll find consulates listed in the back of Riotur's bimonthly *Rio Guide*.

Argentina (Map pp242–3; ☎ 2553 1646; consar.rio@ openlink.com.br; sobreloja (1st floor) 201, Praia de Botafogo 228, Botafogo)

Australia (Map pp238–9; ☎ 3824 4624; honconau@ terra.com.br; 23rd fl, Av Presidente Wilson 231, Centro)

Canada (Map pp244–5; ☎ 2543 3004; rio@international .gc.ca; 5th fl, Av Atlântica 1130, Copacabana)

France (Map pp238–9; ☎ 2210 1272; consulat.rj@ openlink.com.br; 6th fl, Av Presidente Antônio Carlos 58, Centro)

UK (Map pp242–3; ☎ 2555 9600; www.reinounido.org.br; 2nd fl, Praia do Flamengo 284, Flamengo)

USA (Map pp238–9; ☎ 3823 2000; www.embaixada americana.org.br; Av Presidente Wilson 147, Centro)

EMERGENCY

If you have the misfortune of being robbed, you should report it to the **Tourist Police** (Map pp246–7; ☎ 3399 7170; Rua Afrânio de Melo Franco 159, Leblon; ◷ 24hr). No big investigation is going to occur, but you will get a police form to give to your insurance company.

To call emergency telephone numbers in Rio you don't need a phone card. Useful numbers include the following:

Ambulance ☎ 192

Fire ☎ 193

Police ☎ 190

GAY & LESBIAN TRAVELERS

Rio is the gay capital of Latin America. There is no law against homosexuality in Brazil. During Carnaval, thousands of expatriate Brazilian and gringo gays fly in for the festivities. Transvestites steal the show at all Carnaval balls, especially the gay ones. Outside Carnaval, the gay scene is active, but less visible than in cities like San Francisco and Sydney.

You may hear or read the abbreviation GLS, particularly in the Entertainment section of newspapers and magazines. It stands for Gays, Lesbians and Sympathizers, and when used in connection with venues or events basically indicates that anyone with an open mind is welcome. In general, the scene is much more integrated than elsewhere; and the majority of parties involve a pretty mixed crowd.

The **Rio gay guide** (www.riogayguide.com) is an excellent website full of information for gay and lesbian tourists in Rio, including sections entitled 'Bars & Cafés,' 'Carnival in Rio' and 'Rio for Beginners.' It's available in German, English and Portuguese versions.

Gay travelers interested in meeting others should consider booking an excursion with Rio's best (and only) gay travel agency, **G Brazil** (☎ 2247 4431; www.gbrazil.com; Suite

303, Rua Farme de Amoedo 76, Ipanema). Check the website for a whole range of information on gay activities in the city.

For more details on gay life in Rio de Janeiro see p144.

HOLIDAYS

On public holidays banks, offices, post-offices and most stores close. Public holidays include the following:

New Year's Day January 1

Epiphany January 6

St Sebastian Day January 20

Carnaval February or March

Easter March or April

Tiradentes Day April 21

St George Day April 23

Labor Day May 1

Corpus Christi May or June

Independence Day September 7

Our Lady of Aparecida Day October 12

All Souls' Day November 2

Proclamation Day November 15

Black Consciousness Day November 20

Christmas Day December 25

School break coincides with Rio's summer, running from mid-December to mid-February. It's when the city gets overrun with both Brazilian vacationers and travelers from abroad. Another break occurs in July, when the city will again be crowded.

INTERNET ACCESS

Most top-end hotels and a few midrange ones have the technology to allow you to plug in your laptop and access the Internet from your room. Download the details of your ISP's access numbers before you leave home. The major Internet service providers in Brazil are **Universo Online** (www.uol.com .br in Portuguese) and **Brazil Online** (www.bol .com.br in Portuguese).

Internet cafés are prevalent throughout Rio, with Copacabana having the highest concentration of them. Most places charge between US$2 and US$4 an hour.

Central Fone Centro (Map pp238–9; basement level, Av Rio Branco 156; 9am-9pm Mon-Fri, 10am-4pm Sat);

Ipanema (Map pp246–7; loja (level) B, Rua Vinícius de Moraes 129; 9:30am-8pm Mon-Fri, 11am-6pm Sat & Sun)

Cyber Café (Map pp238–9; Av Rio Branco 43, Centro; 9am-7pm Mon-Fri)

Cyber Café Fundição Progresso (Map pp238–9; Rua dos Arcos 24, Lapa)

El Turf Cyber Bar (Map pp242–3; Shop D91, Rio Sul Shopping Mall, Botafogo; 10am-10pm Mon-Sat)

Fone Rio (Map pp244–5; Rua Constante Ramos 22, Copacabana; 9am-midnight)

Letras e Expressões (Map pp246–7; Rua Visconde de Pirajá 276, Ipanema; 8am-midnight)

Letras e Expressões (Map pp246–7; Av Ataúlfo de Paiva 1292, Leblon; 24hr)

Locutório (Map pp244–5; Av NS Copacabana 1171, Copacabana; 8am-2am)

Museu da República (Map pp242–3; Rua do Catete 153, Catete; 9am-10pm Mon-Fri, to 9pm Sat & Sun) The entrance is in back of the museum through the Parque do Catete.

Telerede (Map pp244–5; Av NS de Copacabana 209A, Copacabana; 8am-2am)

LEGAL MATTERS

In Brazil, 18 is the legal drinking age; it's also the legal age of consent and the minimum driving age.

You are required by law to carry some form of identification. For travelers, this generally means a passport, but a certified copy of the relevant ID page will usually be acceptable.

The police in Rio are very poorly paid, with the honest ones needing two or three other jobs to make ends meet. Corruption and bribery are not uncommon.

Marijuana and cocaine are plentiful in Rio, and both are very illegal. The former military regime had a distinct aversion to drugs and enacted stiff penalties that are still enforced. Nevertheless, marijuana and cocaine are widely used and, as with many things in Brazil, everyone except the authorities has a tolerant attitude toward them.

Be very careful with drugs. If you're coming from one of the Andean countries and have been chewing coca leaves, be especially careful to clean out your pack before arriving in Rio – Brazil is a staging post for a large amount of cocaine smuggled out of Bolivia and Peru.

An allegation of drug trafficking or possession provides the police with the perfect excuse to extract a not-insignificant amount of money from you – and Brazilian prisons are brutal places.

MAPS

The maps used by most Brazilian and foreign travelers are produced by Quatro Rodas, which also publishes the essential *Guia Brasil*, a travel guide in Portuguese that is updated annually. The Rio city maps provided in *Guia Brasil* help with orientation. The guides are generally available at newsstands.

Riotur (p216) also provides a useful map of Rio de Janeiro which has a detailed street layout. It's available free from their information booths.

For topographic maps visit **Editora Geográfica J Paulini** (Map pp238–9; ☎ 2220 0181; shops J & K, Rua Senador Dantas 75, Centro).

MEDICAL SERVICES

Some private medical facilities in Rio de Janeiro are on a par with US hospitals. The UK and US consulates (p210) have lists of English-speaking physicians.

Brazilian blood banks don't always screen carefully. Hepatitis B is rampant. If you require a blood transfusion, do as the Brazilians do: have your friends blood-typed and choose your blood donor in advance. If you need an injection, ask to have the syringe unwrapped in front of you, or use your own.

Pharmacies stock all kinds of drugs and sell them much more cheaply than in the West. However, when buying drugs anywhere in South America, be sure to check the expiration dates and specific storage conditions. Some drugs which are available in Brazil may no longer be recommended, or may even be banned, in other countries. Common names of prescription medicines in South America are likely to be different from the ones you're used to, so ask a pharmacist before taking anything you're not sure about.

Some pharmacists – such as ones in the Drogaleve pharmacy chain – will give injections (with or without prescriptions). If you're concerned about hygiene, always purchase fresh needles.

Hospitals

Hospital Ipanema (Map pp246–7; ☎ 3111 2300; Rua Antônio Parreiras 67, Ipanema)

Miguel Couto (Map pp246–7; ☎ 2274 2121; Av Bartolomeu Mitre 1108, Gávea)

MONEY

Since 1994 the monetary unit of Brazil has been the *real* (R$, pronounced hay-*ow*); the plural is *reais* (pronounced hay-*ice*). The *real* is made up of 100 *centavos*.

Now comes the fun part. There are two types of one-, five-, 10-, 25- and 50-centavo coins in circulation – the old aluminum ones and newer ones that differ from one another in size and color. There's a one-*real* note, as well as both old and new one-*real* coins.

Bank notes are are printed in different colors, so there's no mistaking one denomination for another. In addition to the green one-*real* note, there's a bluish-purple five, a red 10 (and a new plastic 10), a brown 50 and a blue 100.

All prices in this guide are quoted in US dollars.

ATMs

ATMs for most card networks can be found throughout the city, with more and more springing up all the time. Banco do Brasil, Bradesco, Citibank and HSBC are the best banks to try when using a debit or credit card. Look for the sticker of your card's network (Visa, MasterCard, Cirrus or Plus) on the ATM, as usually there's only one ATM in a branch that accepts international cards. Even though many ATMs advertise 24-hour service, these 24 hours usually fall between 6am and 10pm. On holidays, ATM access ends at 3pm.

You can find ATMs in the following locations:

Banco do Brasil Copacabana (Map pp244–5; Av NS de Copacabana 1292); Galeão airport (3rd fl, Terminal 1); Centro (Map pp238–9; Rua Senador Dantas 105)

Banco 24 Horas (Map pp238–9; Centro) Outside Carioca metro stop, near Av Rio Branco.

Citibank Centro (Map pp238–9; Rua da Assembléia 100); Ipanema (Map pp246–7; Rua Visconde de Pirajá 459A); Leblon (Map pp246–7; Av Ataúlfo de Paiva 1260)

HSBC (Map pp238–9; Av Rio Branco 108, Centro)

Changing Money

Good places to exchange money include the following:

Banco do Brasil Centro (Map pp238–9; 2nd fl, Rua Senador Dantas 105); Copacabana (Map pp244–5; Av NS de Copacabana 594); Galeão airport (3rd fl, Terminal 1)

Citibank Centro (Map pp238–9; Rua da Assembléia 100); Ipanema (Map pp246–7; Rua Visconde de Pirajá 459A)

Easier than dealing with banks is going to *casas de câmbio* (money exchanges, usually shortened to *câmbios)*. Recommended *câmbios* include **Casa Aliança** (Map pp238–9; Rua Miguel Couto 35C, Centro; ⏲ 9am-5:30pm) and **Casa Universal** (Map pp244–5; Av NS de Copacabana 371, Copacabana). A number of other *câmbios* can be found in the following areas: in the center of the city on either side of Av Rio Branco and a couple of blocks north of the intersection with Av Presidente Vargas (Map pp238–9). Be very cautious carrying money around town and don't take much to the beach with you.

In Copacabana (Map pp244–5), there is a cluster of money-exchange places behind the Copacabana Palace hotel, near the intersection of Av NS de Copacabana and Rua Fernando Mendes. Ipanema (Map pp246–7) has several money exchanges scattered along Rua Visconde de Pirajá just west of Praça NS de Paz.

US dollars are the preferred foreign currency, and the dollar has gradually been gaining strength against the *real*. It's hard to see this trend changing in the short term, especially as the government has now stopped interfering with the exchange rate.

Anyone can buy or sell US dollars at Rio's *câmbios,* though they take their percentage of course. As a rule, US dollars are easier to exchange and are worth a bit more than other currencies. Have some US dollars in cash to use when the banks are closed.

It's also a good idea to have an emergency stash of US dollars stored separately from your other money, in case your traveler's checks or credit cards are stolen.

There are currently three types of exchange rate operating in Brazil: *comercial, turismo* and *paralelo.*

The commercial and tourist rates are normally a bit lower than the parallel rate. Full parallel rates are available only at borders and at official money exchanges in Rio and São Paulo. If you are changing money

at hotels or travel agencies, you'll have to settle for exchanging cash at a rate a couple of points lower than the full parallel rate quoted for that day.

Exchange rates are written up every day on the front page and in the business section of the major daily papers – *O Globo, Jornal do Brasil* and the *Folha de São Paulo* – and are announced on the evening TV news.

Credit Cards

Visa is the most widely accepted credit card in Rio; MasterCard, American Express and Diners Club are also accepted by many hotels, restaurants and shops.

Credit-card fraud is rife in Rio, so be very careful. When making purchases keep your credit card in sight at all times.

To report lost or stolen credit cards, ring the following emergency numbers:

American Express ☎ 0800 785 050

Diners Club ☎ 0800 784 444

MasterCard/Credicard ☎ 0800 784 411

Visa ☎ 0800 784 556

NEWSPAPERS & MAGAZINES

Ownership of Brazil's media industry is concentrated in the hands of a few organizations. O Globo, based in Rio, controls one of the nation's leading newspapers and TV networks.

Portuguese-Language Press

The *Jornal do Brasil* and *O Globo* are Rio's main daily papers. Both have entertainment listings. *O Povo* is a popular daily with lots of gory photographs.

The country's best-selling weekly magazine is *Veja*. In Rio, it comes with the *Veja Rio* insert, which details the weekly entertainment options (the insert comes out on Sunday). It's a colorful, well-produced magazine, and it's not difficult reading if you're learning Portuguese. *Isto É* has the best political and economic analysis, and reproduces international articles from the British *Economist,* but it's not light reading. It also provides good coverage of current events. *Balcão* is a weekly paper with Rio's only classified advertisements and a good resource for buying anything. *O Nacional* is a weekly paper that has some excellent critical columnists.

Environmental issues (both national and international) are covered in the glossy monthly magazine *Terra*. It seems genuine about environmental concerns, and runs some great photos. *Placar* is the weekly soccer magazine and a must for fans.

The gay and lesbian press is represented in Rio and, more broadly, Brazil by *O Grito* and by the glossy *G Magazine* – both available from most newsstands.

Foreign-Language Press

In Rio you will find three daily newspapers in English: the *Miami Herald, USA Today* and the *International Herald Tribune*. They are usually on the newsstands by noon.

Time and *Newsweek* magazines are available in Brazil. Their coverage is weakest where the *Miami Herald* is strongest: Latin America and sports. The *Economist* is sold in Rio and São Paulo and costs about US$6.

Imported newspapers and magazines are available, but are quite expensive. Newsstands on Av Rio Branco in Centro have the best selection. In Copacabana the newsstand close to Le Meridien has a wide selection of English, French and German newspapers and magazines. The newsstand in Ipanema in front of the Praça NS de Paz has French and English newspapers and magazines. Several bookstores in Ipanema and Leblon offer foreign-language publications. See Shopping (p158) for details.

PHARMACIES

There are scores of pharmacies in town, a number of which stay open 24 hours. In Copacabana try **Drogaria Pacheco** (Map pp244–5; Av NS de Copacabana 115 & 534; 24hr). In Ipanema, visit **Drogaria Pacheco** (Map pp246–7; 2239 5397; Av Visconde de Pirajá 592).

POST

Postal services are decent in Brazil, and most mail seems to get through. Airmail letters to the USA and Europe usually arrive in a week or two. For Australia and Asia, allow three weeks.

There are yellow mailboxes on the street, but it's safer to go to a *corréio* (post office). Most *corréios* are open 8am to 6pm Monday to Friday, and until noon on Saturday. The international airport is open 24 hours.

Other branches include Praia de Botafogo 324 in Botafogo (Map pp242–3), Rua Prudente de Morais 147 in Ipanema (Map pp246–7) and Av NS de Copacabana 540 in Copacabana (Map pp244–5).

Any mail addressed to Poste Restante, Rio de Janeiro, Brazil, ends up at the post office at Rua Primeiro de Março 64, in Centro (Map pp238–9). The post office will hold mail for 30 days and is reasonably efficient. A reliable alternative for American Express customers is to have mail sent to the **American Express office** (Map pp244–5; 2548 7056; loja (level) 1, Av Atlântica 1702, Copacabana).

RADIO

By law at least a third of the music FM radio stations play must be Brazilian. For the latest Brazilian and foreign hits, try tuning into Jovem Pan (94.9FM), 98 (98.1FM), RPC (100.5FM), Transamérica (101.3FM) and Cidade (102.9FM). For jazz, tune into Globo (92.5FM) or MEC (98.9FM).

For authentic Brazilian *pagode* (a relaxed and rhythmic form of samba, first popularized in Rio in the 1970s) and pop, switch to Roquette (94.1FM), O Dia (90.3FM), JB (99.7FM), Tropical (104.5FM) or Universidade (107.9FM).

SAFETY

Rio gets a lot of bad international press about violence, the high crime rate and *balas perdidas* (stray bullets) – but don't let this stop you from coming. Travelers to Rio have as much chance of getting mugged as in any other big city, so the same precautions apply here. If you travel sensibly when visiting the city, you will probably suffer nothing worse than a few bad hangovers. All the same, theft is not uncommon, and you should do what you can to minimize the risks of getting robbed.

Buses are well-known targets for thieves. Avoid taking them after dark, and keep an eye out while you're on them. Take taxis at night to avoid walking along empty streets and beaches. That holds especially true for Centro, which becomes deserted in the evening and on weekends, and is better explored during the week.

Copacabana and Ipanema beaches are safer than others, owing to a police presence there, but don't get complacent. Don't take anything of value to the beach, and always stay alert – especially during holidays when the sands get fearfully crowded. Late at night, don't walk on the beach – stay on the sidewalk – and if you're in Copacabana, it's better to keep to the hotel side of Av Atlântica rather than the beach side.

Get in the habit of carrying only the money you'll need for the day, so you don't have to flash a wad of *reais* or US dollars when you pay for things. Cameras and backpacks attract a lot of attention. Consider using disposable cameras while you're in town; plastic shopping bags also nicely disguise whatever you're carrying. Maracanã football stadium is worth a visit, but take only your spending money for the day and avoid the crowded sections. Don't wander into the favelas at any time, unless you have a knowledgeable guide.

Beaches are the most common places for robbery. A common beach scam is for a thief to approach you from one side and ask you for a light or the time. While you're distracted, the thief's partner grabs your gear from the other side.

If you have the misfortune of being robbed, hand over the goods. Thieves in the city are only too willing to use their weapons if given provocation.

TELEPHONE

Rio is not known for its efficient telephone service, which hasn't improved much after privatization. Lines cross and fail frequently. The only solution is to keep trying.

Public phones are nicknamed *orelhôes,* which means 'floppy ears.' They take *cartão telefônico* (phone cards), which are available from newsstands and street vendors. The cheapest cards are US$2 for 20 units. Prices go up to US$6 for 90-unit cards. All calls in Brazil, including local ones, are timed. Generally, one unit is enough for a brief local call. The phone will display how many units your card has left. Unless you're very lucky, you will have to try at least two or three phones before you find one that works.

Wait for a dial tone and then insert your phone card and dial your number. For information, call ☎ 102. The Portuguese-speaking operator can usually transfer you to an English-speaking operator.

To phone Rio from outside Brazil, dial your international access code, then 55 (Brazil's country code), 21 (Rio's area code) and the number.

Cell Phones

Cell phones are very common in Rio. Locals call them *celular,* which is also the nickname given to hip flasks of liquor.

Cell phones have eight-digit numbers, which usually begin with '9.' You can rent a phone from the following places for around US$5 a day plus call charges:

CONNECTCOM
☎ 2275 8461; www.connectcomrj.com.br
Offers drop-off and pick-up service at your hotel.

FAST CELL Map pp244-5
☎ 2548 1008; www.fastcell.com.br; no 919, Rua Santa Clara 50, Copacabana
Provides excellent service whereby English-speaking staff will deliver to and pick up from your hotel. You can also email before your trip to request that they set you up with a number before you arrive.

HERTZ
☎ 0800 701 7300; www.hertz.com.br
In addition to automobiles, Hertz also rents cell phones. Call or go online to make a reservation (drop-off service available).

Long-Distance & International Calls

International calls aren't cheap in Brazil. You'll pay less if you have an international calling card. Embratel phone cards are available from newsstands (sold in denominations of US$10, $15, and $35). These have a bar on the back that you scratch off to reveal a code to enter along with the number you are calling. (Instructions are printed on the cards in English and Portuguese.) You can make calls through pay phones. Rates generally run at about US$0.50 a minute for calls to the US, US$0.75 a minute to Europe and about twice that to Asia and Australia.

Another way of making long-distance calls is through phone offices. Many Internet cafés in Copacabana also have private phone booths for making calls. Rates, which fluctuate quite a bit, generally run at US$1 per minute to the US, US$1.25 a minute to Europe and much more to Australia and Asia. In Copacabana, try **Telenet**

(Map pp244–5; Rua Domingos Ferreira 59, Copacabana; ☺9am-10pm Mon-Sat, 11am-9pm Sun), **Telerede** (Map pp244–5; Av NS de Copacabana 209, Copacabana; ☺8am-2am) or **Locutório** (Map pp244–5; Av NS Copacabana 1171, Copacabana; ☺8am-2am). In the center of town there is **Central Fone** (basement level, Av Rio Branco 156, Centro; ☺9am-9pm Mon-Fri, 10am-4pm Sat). In Ipanema, **Central Fone** (Map pp246–7; loja (level) B, Rua Vinícius de Moraes 129, Ipanema; ☺9:30am-8pm Mon-Fri, 11am-6pm Sat & Sun) also offers international phone calls.

To make a call to other parts of Brazil, you need to select the telephone company you want to use. To do this, you must insert a two-digit number between the 0 and the area code of the place you're calling. For example, to call Búzios from Rio, you need to dial ☎0 + xx + 22 (0 + phone company code + Búzios city code) + the seven- or eight-digit number. Embratel (code 21) and Intelig (code 23) are Brazil's biggest carriers – and the only ones that permit you to call abroad from Brazil.

Unfortunately, you cannot make collect calls from telephone offices. Public phones and those in hotels are your best bet. For calling collect within Brazil, dial ☎90 + phone company code + area code + phone number. A recorded message (in Portuguese) will ask you to say your name and where you're calling from after the beep.

TELEVISION

The most popular local programs are the *novelas* (soap operas), which are followed religiously by many Brazilians. The *novelas* are on at various times between 7pm and 9pm, and watching them is a good way to practice your Portuguese.

O Globo and Manchete are the two principal national TV networks and both have national news shows. Cable TV is now common in most hotels midrange and up. ESPN, CNN, RAI (Radio Televisione Italia) and MTV are all available. Brazilian MTV is worth tuning into, as it has plenty of local content.

TIME

Brazil has four official time zones. Rio, in the southeastern region, is three hours behind Greenwich Mean Time (GMT). When it's noon in Rio, it's 11am in New York, 8am in Los Angeles, 3pm in London and 1am the next day in Sydney. Daylight saving time runs from February to October.

TIPPING

Most service workers get tipped 10%, and as the people in these services make the minimum wage – which is not nearly enough to live on – you can be sure they need the money. In restaurants the service charge is usually included in the bill and is mandatory; when it is not included in the bill, it's customary to leave a 10% tip. If a waiter is friendly and helpful, you can give more.

There are many other places where tipping is not customary but is a welcome gesture. The workers at local juice stands, bars and coffee corners, and street and beach vendors, are all tipped on occasion. Parking assistants receive no wages and are dependent on tips, usually the equivalent of US$1. Gas-station attendants, shoe shiners and barbers are also frequently tipped. Taxi drivers are not usually tipped, but it is common to round up the fare.

TOURIST INFORMATION

Riotur is the very useful Rio city tourism agency. It operates a tourist information hot line called **Alô Rio** (☎0800 707 1808, 2542 8080) from 9am to 6pm. The receptionists speak English and are very helpful. Riotur's useful multilingual website, at www.rio.rj.gov.br/riotur, is also a good source of information.

All of the Riotur offices distribute maps and the excellent (and regularly updated) bimonthly *Rio Guide,* which lists the major events of the season. The **Centro branch** (Map pp238–9; 9th fl, Rua Assembléia 10; ☺9am-6pm Mon-Fri) is the best. English-speaking staff are always on hand, and they'll call around to find you a hotel if you show up without a reservation.

There is another branch in **Copacabana** (Map pp244–5; ☎2541 7522; Av Princesa Isabel 183; ☺9am-6pm Mon-Fri). Riotur also has information booths with brochures and maps at the **Novo Rio bus station** (Map pp236–7; Av Francisco Bicalho 1, São Cristóvão; ☺8am-8pm), **Maracanã Football Stadium** (Map pp236–7; Rua Professor Eurico Rabelo, São Cristóvão; ☺9am-6pm) and **Galeão airport** (☺6am-11pm).

Another good source of information is the **Rio Convention & Visitors Bureau** (☎ 2259 6165; www.rioconventionbureau.com.br; Suite 610, Rua Visconde de Pirajá 547, Ipanema).

Many hotels have free copies of *Rio this Month,* a publication that provides a useful guide in Portuguese and English to Rio's main attractions.

TRAVEL AGENCIES
AMERICAN EXPRESS Map pp244-5
☎ 2548 2148; Av Atlântica 1702, Copacabana; ☽ 9am-5:30pm Mon-Fri
This agency does a pretty good job of receiving and holding mail and can also book flights for you.

ANDES SOL Map pp244-5
☎ 2275 4370; Av NS de Copacabana 209, Copacabana
A good multilingual agency, offering city and regional tours. Staff can also find discounted lodging in Rio for you.

CASA ALIANÇA Map pp238-9
☎ 2224 4617; casaalianca@casaalianca.com.br; Rua Miguel Couto 35C, Centro; ☽ 9am-5:30pm
Runs a fine outfit and an exchange office, with information on local and regional tours to suit every budget.

LE BON VOYAGE Map pp246-7
☎ 2287 4403; lebonvoyage@hotmail.com; Rua Visconde de Pirajá 82, Ipanema
Particularly noted for its affordable excursions to Búzios and the Costa Verde, this travel agency also offers the convenience of an on-site exchange office.

VISAS
Brazil has a reciprocal visa system, so if your home country requires Brazilian nationals to secure a visa, then you will need one to enter Brazil. US, Canadian, Australian and New Zealand citizens need visas, but UK and French citizens do not. You can check your status with the Brazilian embassy or consulate in your home country.

Tourist visas are issued by Brazilian diplomatic offices. They are valid for arrival in Brazil for a 90-day stay. They are renewable in Brazil for an additional 90 days. In most

Brazilian embassies and consulates, visas can be processed within 24 hours. You will need to present one passport photograph, a round-trip or onward ticket (or a photocopy of it), and a valid passport. If you decide to return to Brazil, your visa is valid for five years.

The fee for visas is also reciprocal. It's usually between US$40 and US$60, though for US citizens visas cost US$100.

Applicants under 18 years of age wanting to travel to Brazil must also submit a notarized letter of authorization from a parent or legal guardian.

Business travelers may need a business visa. These are also valid for 90 days and have the same requirements as a tourist visa. You'll need a letter on your company letterhead addressed to the Brazilian embassy or consulate, stating your business in Brazil, your arrival and departure dates and your contacts. The letter from your employer must also assume full financial and moral (!) responsibility for you during your stay.

For up-to-the-minute advice on visa requirements for Brazil, consult the Lonely Planet website at www.lonelyplanet.com.

Tourist Card
When you enter Brazil, you will be asked to fill out a tourist card, which has two parts. Immigration officials will keep one part, and the other part will be attached to your passport. When you leave the country, this will be detached from your passport by immigration officials.

Make sure you don't lose your part of the tourist card, or your departure could be delayed until officials have checked your story.

For added security, make a photocopy of your section of the tourist card and keep this in a safe place, separate from your passport.

WOMEN TRAVELERS
In Rio, foreign women traveling alone will scarcely be given a sideways glance. Although machismo is an undeniable element in the Brazilian social structure, it is less overt here than in Spanish-speaking Latin America. Flirtation – often exaggerated – is a prominent element in Brazilian male-female relations. It goes both ways

and is nearly always regarded as amusingly innocent banter. You should be able to stop unwelcome attention merely by expressing displeasure.

WORK

Brazil has high unemployment, and visitors who enter the country as tourists are not legally allowed to take jobs. It's not unusual for foreigners to find work teaching English in language schools. The pay isn't great (if you hustle you can make around US$800 a month), but you can still live on it. For this kind of work it's always helpful to speak some Portuguese, although some schools insist that only English be spoken in class. Private language tutoring may pay a little more, but you'll have to do some legwork to find students.

To get this type of work, log on to a Brazilian web server like **terra** (www.terra.com.br in Portuguese) or **uol** (www.uol.com.br in Portuguese) and search for English academies. You should also ask around at the English-language schools.

Language

Pronunciation 220
Social 220
Practical 220
Food 222
Emergencies 222
Health 222

Language

It's true – anyone can speak another language. Don't worry if you haven't studied languages before or that you studied a language at school for years and can't remember any of it. It doesn't even matter if you failed English grammar. After all, that's never affected your ability to speak English! And this is the key to picking up a language in another country. You just need to start speaking.

Learn a few key phrases before you go. Write them on pieces of paper and stick them on the fridge, by the bed or even on the computer – anywhere that you'll see them often.

Locals appreciate travellers trying their language no matter how muddled you may think you sound. So don't just stand there, say something! If you want to learn more of the lingo than we've included here, pick up a copy of Lonely Planet's comprehensive but user-friendly *Brazilian Portuguese Phrasebook*.

PRONUNCIATION

A characteristic of Brazilian Portuguese is the use of nasal vowels. Nasalization is represented by **n** or **m** after a vowel, or by a tilde over it (eg **ã**). The nasal **i** exists only approximately in English, such as the 'ing' in 'sing'. Nasal vowels are pronounced as if you're trying to force the sound out your nose rather than your mouth, creating a similar sound to when you hold your nose.

SOCIAL
Meeting People

Hello.
Olá.
Hi.
Oi.
Goodbye.
Tchau.
Please.
Por favor.
Thank you (very much).
(Muito) obrigado/obrigada.
Yes/No.
Sim/Não.
How's everything?
Tudo bem?
Do you speak (English)?
Você fala (inglês)?
Do you understand?
Você entende?
I (don't) understand.
Eu (não) entendo.

Could you please ...?
Você poderia por favor ...?
  repeat that   repetir istos
  speak more slowly falar mais devagar
  write it down   escrever num papel

Going Out

What's on ...?
O que está acontecendo ...?
  locally   aqui perto
  this weekend   neste final de semana
  today   hoje
  tonight   á noite

Where can I find ...?
Onde posso encontrar ...?
  clubs   um lugar para dançar
  gay venues   lugares gays
  places to eat   lugares para comer
  pubs   um bar

Is there a local entertainment guide?
Existe algum guia de entretenimento dessa área?

PRACTICAL
Question Words

Who?   Quem?
What?   (o) que?
When?   Quando?
Where?   Onde?
How?   Como é que?
Why?   Por que?
Which?   Qual/Quais? (sg/pl)

Numbers & Amounts

0	zero
1	um
2	dois
3	três
4	quatro
5	cinco
6	seis
7	sete
8	oito
9	nove
10	dez
11	onze
12	doze
13	treze
14	quatorze
15	quinze
16	dezesseis
17	dezesete
18	dezoito
19	dezenove
20	vinte
21	vinte e um
22	vinte e dois
30	trinta
40	quarenta
50	cinquenta
60	sessenta
70	setenta
80	oitenta
90	noventa
100	cem
200	duzentos
1000	mil

Days

Monday	segunda-feira
Tuesday	terça-feira
Wednesday	quarta-feira
Thursday	quinta-feira
Friday	sexta-feira
Saturday	sábado
Sunday	domingo

Banking

Where's ...?
Onde tem ...?

an automated teller machine	um caixa automático
a foreign exchange office	uma loja de câmbio

Where can I ...?
Onde posso ...?

I'd like to ...
Gostaria de ...

cash a check	descontar um cheque
change money	trocar dinheiro
change travelers checks	trocar traveller cheques

Post

Where is the post office?
Onde fica o correio?

I want to send a ...
Quero enviar ...

fax	um fax
letter	uma carta
parcel	uma encomenda
postcard	um cartão-postal

I want to buy ...
Quero comprar ...

an aerogram	um aerograma
an envelope	um envelope
stamps	selos

Phones & Cell/Mobiles

I want to make ...
Quero ...

a call (to ...)	telefonar (para ...)
a reverse-charge/ collect call	fazer uma chamada a cobrar

I'd like a/an ...
Eu gostaria de ...

adaptor plug	comprar um adaptador
battery for my phone	comprar uma bateria para o meu telephone
cell/mobile phone for hire	alugar um cellular
phone card	comprar um cartão telefônico
prepaid cell/ mobile phone	comprar um cellular pré-pago
SIM card for your network	comprar um cartão SIM para sua rede

Internet

Where's the local Internet café?
Onde tem um internet café na redondeza?

I'd like to ...
Gostaria de ...

check my email	checar meu e-mail
get online	ter acesso à internet

Transport

When's the ... (bus)?
Quando sai o ... (ônibus)?
  first   primeiro
  last   último
  next   próximo

What time does it leave?
Que horas sai?
What time does it get to (Parati)?
Que horas chega em (Parati)?

Which ... goes to (Niterói)?
Qual o ... que vai para (Niterói)?
  boat   barco
  bus   ônibus
  plane   avião
  train   trem

Is this taxi free?
Este táxi está livre?
Please put the meter on.
Por favor ligue o taxímetro.
How much is it to ...?
Quanto custa até ...?
Please take me to (this address).
Me leve para (este endereço) por favor.

FOOD

breakfast   café da manhã
lunch   almoço
dinner   jantar
snack   lanche

Can you recommend a ...
Você pode recomendar um ...?
  bar/pub   bar
  café   café
  restaurant   restaurante

Is service/cover charge included in the bill?
O serviço está incluído na conta?

For more detailed information on food and dining out, see p103

EMERGENCIES

Help!
Socorro!
It's an emergency.
É uma emergência.
Could you please help?
Você pode ajudar, por favor?
Call a doctor/an ambulance!
Chame um médico/uma ambulância!
Call the police!
Chame a polícia!
Where's the police station?
Onde é a delegacia de polícia?

HEALTH

Where's the nearest ...?
Onde fica ... mais perto?
  (night) chemist   a farmácia (noturna)
  dentist   o dentista
  doctor   o médico
  hospital   o hospital
  medical centre   a clínica médica

I'm ill.
Estou doente.
I need a doctor (who speaks English).
Eu preciso de um médico (que fale inglês).

Symptoms

I have (a) ...
Tenho ...
  diarrhoea   diarréia
  fever   febre
  nausea   náusea
  pain   dor
  sore throat   dor de garganta

GLOSSARY

See p29 for more Carnaval terms.

açaí – juice made from an Amazonian berry
agouti – small rodent; looks like a large guinea pig
a quilo – per kilo
baía – bay
baile – dance, ball
bairro – neighborhood
baixo – popular area with lots of restaurants and bars

banda – a procession of drummers and singers during Carnaval, followed by anyone who wants to dance through the streets
barraca – food stall
batida – mixes of *cachaça*, sugar and assorted fruit juices
beija-flor – hummingbird
berimbau – stringed instrument used to accompany *capoeira*
biblioteca – library
bloco – see *banda*
bonde – tram

bondinho – little tram
boteco – small neighborhood bar
botequim – bar with table service

caboclo – person of mixed European and Brazilian-Indian descent
cachaça – potent cane spirit
cadeira – undercover stadium seats
caipirinha – *cachaça* cocktail
câmbios – money exchange
Candomblé – religion of African origin
capoeira – Afro-Brazilian martial art
capela – chapel
cara – guy, dude (used in slang to denote male or female)
Carioca – native of Rio
carro – car
cartão telefônico – phone card
celular – cellular (mobile) phone
cerveja – beer
cervejaria – pub
chocante – cool, excellent
chope – draft beer
chorinho or **choro** – romantic, intimate samba
churrascaria – traditional barbecue restaurant
cidade maravilhosa – marvelous city (nickname for Rio de Janeiro)
convento – convent
corréio – post office

emergentes – the nouveaux riches; Brazilian yuppies
escola de samba – samba school
estação do metro – metro (subway) station
estrada – road

falou – OK, agreed
farmácia – pharmacy (chemist)
favela – shanty town
fazenda – ranch, plantation, large farm
feira – open-air market
festa – party
fio dental – literally 'dental floss'; a tiny bikini
forró – traditional fast-paced music from the northeast of Brazil
frescão – air-conditioned bus
frescobol – game played on the beach with two wooden racquets and a rubber ball
futebol – football (soccer)

gafieira – dance club/dance hall
gata – attractive young woman

gato – cat (literally); also an attractive young man
gente – people or we

igreja – church
ilha – island

jardim – garden

lagoa – lake
largo – plaza
legal – cool, excellent
livraria – bookshop
loja – level

malandros – con men
mar – sea
Mata Atlântica – Atlantic rainforest
mirante – lookout
morro – mountain
mulatto – person of mixed black and white ancestry
museu – museum

novela – TV soap opera

onibus – bus
orelhões – public telephones
orixá – spirit or deity of the Candomblé religion

pagode – relaxed and rhythmic form of samba; first popularized in Rio in the 1970s
parque – park
ponte – bridge
posto – lifeguard station
pousada – guest house
praça – square
praia – beach
prato feito – fixed plate of the day; often abbreviated to pf

queda – a fall

reais – plural of *real*
real – Brazil's unit of currency since 1994
refrigerante – soft drink
rio – river
rodoviária – bus terminal
rua – street

sobreloja – above the store; first floor up
suco – juice bar
sunga – Speedo-type swimsuit used by Carioca men
supermercado – supermarket

trem – train

Zona Norte – Northern Zone
Zona Sul – Southern Zone

Behind the Scenes

THE LONELY PLANET STORY

The story begins with a classic travel adventure: Tony and Maureen Wheeler's 1972 journey across Europe and Asia to Australia. There was no useful information about the overland trail then, so Tony and Maureen published the first Lonely Planet guidebook to meet a growing need.

From a kitchen table, Lonely Planet has grown to become the largest independent travel publisher in the world, with offices in Melbourne (Australia), Oakland (USA) and London (UK). Today Lonely Planet guidebooks cover the globe. There is an ever-growing list of books and information in a variety of media. Some things haven't changed. The main aim is still to make it possible for adventurous travelers to get out there – to explore and better understand the world.

At Lonely Planet we believe travelers can make a positive contribution to the countries they visit – if they respect their host communities and spend their money wisely. Every year 5% of company profit is donated to charities around the world.

THIS BOOK

This 5th edition of *Rio de Janeiro* was written by Regis St. Louis, with contributions from Paula Gobbi, Thomas Kohnstamm, Dan Littauer, Cassandra Loomis, Carmen Michael, Tom Phillips and Marcos Silviano do Prado. Regis also wrote the 4th edition, while Andrew Draffen wrote editions one to three, with contributions from Heather Schlegel on the 3rd edition. This guidebook was commissioned in Lonely Planet's Oakland office, and produced by:

Commissioning Editor Kathleen Munnelly

Coordinating Editor Louisa Syme

Coordinating Cartographer Andrew Smith

Coordinating Layout Designer Steven Cann

Managing Editor Imogen Bannister

Managing Cartographer Alison Lyall

Assisting Editors Jackey Coyle, Barbara Delissen, Andrea Dobbin and Margedd Heliosz

Assisting Cartographers Chris Crook

Assisting Layout Designers Wibowo Rusli

Cover Designer Yukiyoshi Kamimura

Project Manager Glenn van der Knijff

Language Content Coordinator Quentin Frayne

Thanks to Jessa Boanas-Dewes, David Burnett, Sally Darmody, Bruce Evans, Jennifer Garrett, Mark Germanchis, Martin Heng, Laura Jane, Stephanie Pearson, Christine Weiser and Ceila Wood

Cover photographs Cristo Redentor statue, Ricardo Gomes/ Lonely Planet Images (top); People playing volleyball on Ipanema Beach at sunset, Ricardo Gomes/Lonely Planet Images (bottom); At Ipanema Beach the boy's back tattoo reads 'surf all life long', John Maier Jr/Lonely Planet Images (back).

Internal photographs by Lonely Planet Images, Ricardo Gomes and John Maier Jr except for the following: p70 (#3), p73 (#3), Judy Bellah; p71 (#4) Paul Bigland; p2 (#2), p74 (#3) Lou Jones; p74 (#2) Guy Moberly; p2 (#3), p68 (#1), p69 (#1), p70 (#2, #4), p71 (#1), p197 John Pennock. All images are the copyright of the photographers unless otherwise indicated. Many of the images in this guide are available for licensing from Lonely Planet Images: www.lonelyplanetimages.com.

THANKS
REGIS ST. LOUIS

In Rio, many people helped along the way, and I'd like to thank Carina, Carmen, Gustavo, Fabio, Marcio, Aurelio, Marta and John. I'd also like to thank Marcelo Armstrong, Carlos Roquette, Fabio Sombra, Juliana at Tangará tours and Charlotte Smith at Task Brasil. On Ilha Grande, *abraços* to Rodolfo, Claudia, André for their hospitality and Charlotte and Chris for a lovely walk across the island. Special thanks go to Thomas Kohnstamm, Paula Gobbi and Dan Littauer for their fine contributions. At Lonely Planet, I owe a big thank you to Kathleen Munnelly for all her stellar work on this edition. As always, I'd like to thank the travelers who sent in comments and suggestions for this edition. Lastly, *beijos* to Cassandra and my family for a lovely New Year's together

OUR READERS

Many thanks to the travelers who used the last edition and wrote to us with helpful hints, useful advice and interesting anecdotes:

A Philip Aiken, Steven Amrein, Cédric Argolit, Jörg Ausfelt **B** Roman Baedorf, Fernando Zubikoa Bainales, Nicole Beege, David Berglund, Carol Binder, John Bonallack, Michael Brandenburgsky, John Breski, Nick Bye **C** Hugo Cantalice, Adam Canter, Nick Carney, Donald Carroll, Henry Carson, John

Castro, Nicola Cauchy, Claire Clapshaw, Bjorn Clasen, Alice Conibear, Carol Conte, Ron Coolen **D** Ninna Dalgaard, Candida D'Arcy, Carol Conte, Ron Coolen **D** Ninna Dalgaard, Candida D'Arcy, Joseph Deleonardo, Luisa Doplicher, Kristof Downer, Gene Dunaway **E** Paula Elias **F** Fyaz Faisal, Gabrielle Fennessy, Nuno Ferreira, Kennet & Pernille Föh, Janine Fournier, Damian Francabandiera **G** Margaret Gallery, Robert Garrity, Celia Gerry, Manoel Giffoni da Silveira Netto, John Gillis, Paul Gioffi, Peter Goodwin, Rene Gouweleeuw, Asger Grarup, Giorgio Grazzini, Catherine Grice **H** Tim Harcourt, Paul Harker, Paul Harris, Michael Hartmann, Jake Hefner, Twan Hendriks, Jon Hepworth, Alex Hijmans, Nancy Hirschhorn, Debby & Jim Hogan, Per Holmkvist, David Hornsby, Alex Howarth, David Hunt **I** Michael Ingbar, Jeremy Ireland **J** Caitlin Johnson, Sara Jones, Oscar Juarez **K** Yorgos Kechagioglou, Andrea Kinauer, Lucie Kinkorova, Justine Kirby, Paul Kondratko, Jan Kvet **L** Simon Lago, Johannes Lahti, Gregor Laing, Paul Lambert, Arnaud Leboyer, Sherman Lee, Richard Lee-Hart, Adeline Levine, Sam Levitt, Dirk Luebbers **M** Dylan Mader, Rachael Main, Volker Maiworm, Zukiso Makalima, George Malliaros, Fernando Marins, Slobodan Markovic, Georgina Mason, Nara Mattoso, Michael Maus, Kelly McCarthy, Sandra Mccrossan, Helen McKenna, Michel Mekler, Michael Miano, Clare Middleton, Carlos Millan, Drew Miller, Vicki Monti, **N** Colin Nee, Yannick Neron, Manoel Netto, Gitte Nielsen, Wes Nobelius, Ken Noble, Daniel Norton, Pedro Novak **O** Blon Obrien, Jose Olimpio, Aleksandra Oziemska, Aristea Parissi, Terry Parker, Denise Pendexter, Brad Petersen, Yvonne Pines, M A Pitcher, Vas Pivrnec, Martin Platt, Gordon Price, Leacy Pryor **R** María Concepción Ramos Suárez, Branden Rippey, Simon Robinson, Walace Rodrigues, Wally Rogelstad, Dan Ruff, Ben Rule, Lawrence Ryz **S** Christine Sadler, Al Sandine, Peter Sapper, Urmimala Sarkar, Klaus-Dieter Schmatz, Jerad Schomer, Harvey Schwartz, Bill Seidel, Jacob Seligmann, Sharlene Shah, Igor Shen, Pete Siegfried, Michael Simek, Alastair Simpson, Peter Smolka, Tom Sobhani, David Sowell,

J S Spijker, RL Spolton, Andre Starobin, Louis Stone, Faith Symon **T** Roman Tatarsky, Thomas Teltser, Alan Tensuty, Frank Thianer, Niels Thommesen, Richard Tinker, Theo Tjes, Chris Tjon Kong Hong, Debra Townsend **U** Kalle Ulvstig **V** Eric Vanoncini, Johan Veneman, Zeeger Vink, Fernanda Vitalino, Connie Voeten, Thomas Vogt, Frank von Reeken, Panayiotis Vorrias **W** Colin Walker, Heather Wara, Peter Weis, Nicole Wentz, Sam Williams, Damian Williamson, Rachel Worzencraft **Y** Andrew Young **Z** Rotem Ziv, Aritz Zubikoa

SEND US YOUR FEEDBACK

We love to hear from travelers – your comments keep us on our toes and help make our books better. Our well-traveled team reads every word on what you loved or loathed about this book. Although we cannot reply individually to postal submissions, we always guarantee that your feedback goes straight to the appropriate authors, in time for the next edition. Each person who sends us information is thanked in the next edition – and the most useful submissions are rewarded with a free book.

To send us your updates – and find out about Lonely Planet events, newsletters and travel news – visit our award-winning website: www.lonelyplanet.com /feedback.

Note: We may edit, reproduce and incorporate your comments in Lonely Planet products such as guide-books, websites and digital products, so let us know if you don't want your comments reproduced or your name acknowledged. For a copy of our privacy policy visit www.lonelyplanet.com/privacy.

Notes

Index

See also separate subindexes for Drinking (p231), Eating (p232), Shopping (p232) and Sleeping (p233).

A

A Moreninha 40
accommodations 208,
  see also individual
  neighborhoods, Sleeping
  subindex
airport 187
  long-term rentals 185
  online booking 174
activities 150-6
  capoeira 151
  cycling 97-9, 152, 154
  dancing 11, 27, 33, 43-4,
    128, 144-5, 156
  diving 152, 169, 195
  fishing 58, 152-3, 198
  hang gliding 153, 200
  hiking 153-4, 169, 195,
    202
  jogging 154
  painting 58
  rock climbing 151-2
  surfing 155, 165, 191,
    198
  volleyball 154
  walking 96-102, 154
  yoga 156
Afro-Brazilian people 12-13
AfroReggae 35, 58
agoutis 22
air pollution 21
air travel 204
Alencar, José de 40, 44
Allegro Bistrô Musical
  133, 133
Alô Rio 216
Amado, Jorge 39
Amaral, Luiz 59
Amazon 153
ambulance services 210
Andrade, Jorge 44
Andrade, Mario de 40
Andrade, Oswald de 35
animals
  agoutis 22
  dolphins 58
  monkeys 22

000 map pages
000 photographs

turtles 58
whales 58
antiques 160, 164, 170
Antonio Bernardo 158
Antunes, Arnaldo 36
Aqualung 22
architecture 40-2, 49, 41
  urban planning 22
Armação de Búzios,
  see Búzios
Arraial do Cabo 191, 198
Arte Sesc Cultural Center 128
arts 32-44
  exhibitions 129
Assis, Joaquim Maria
  Machado de 40, 44, 75
ATMs 212
Av Atlântica Fair 168
Azevedo, Anna 38
Azevedo, Artur 44

B

Babenco, Hector 38
Babilônia Feira Hype 16, 168
baile 146
ballet 129
Bambina 179
banks 208, 212
Bar Bofetada 144
Barbosa, Rui 200
barflies 53
bargaining 158
Barra da Tijuca
  accommodations 188
  eating 125-6
  shopping 171-2
Barra Nova 198
Barreto, Bruno 38
Barroso, Ary 34
beaches 56-7, see also
  praia, warnings
  Arraial do Cabo 191
  Azeda 197
  Azedinha 197
  Barra Nova 198
  Búzios 191, 197
  Copacabana 57
  Ferradura 197
  Ferradurinha 197
  Geribá 197
  Ipanema 56-7, 62

Lagoa Azul 195
Lagoa Verde 195
Lagoinha 197
Manguinhos 198
Paraty 191
Praia Vermelha 21
Saco do Céu 195
Santa Teresa 46
Saquarema 191
Bellos, Alex 17
Benjor, Jorge 36
bicycle travel 204-5
birds 22
bird-watching 201
blood banks 212
boat travel 58, 205
Bom Jardim 200
bonde 53, 60, 87, 88, 207-8,
  57, 70
Bonfá, Luiz 35
books 39-40, see also
  literature
  architecture 169
  food 15
  history 35, 169
  music 35, 37, 163
  soccer 17
bookstores 158-9, 161,
  162, 166, 169
bossa nova 35
  books 35, 163
Botafogo 242
  accommodations 184
  drinking 134-5
  eating 118-20
  shopping 166
botanical gardens
  Jardim Botânico 22
Brazilian-American Chamber
  of Commerce 208
bribery 211
Brown, Carlinhos 36
Buarque, Chico 35-6, 40, 53
bus travel 205-6
business
  etiquette 208
  hours 104, 158, 208
  organizations 208-9
Búzios 191, 197-9
Búzios Trolley 198

C

Cabaret Casanova 144
Cabo Frio 198
Cachoeira e Escorrega 202
Cachoeira Veu de Noiva 202
caipirinha 14
Camargo, Luciano di 37
Camargo, Zeze di 37
Camucim people 167
Camus, Marcel 38
cannibalism 47
Capela de Nossa Senhora
  das Dores 194
Capeto, Isabela 161
capoeira 151
capuchin monkeys 22
car travel 191, 206-7
  rental 198, 206-7
Carnaval 8, 10, 11, 24-30,
  2, 24
  balls 26-7
  dance rehearsals 11
  dates 30
  parades 27-8, 27
  tickets 28
Cartola 34
Carvalho, Dani 162
Casa da Cultura 192, 194
Casa da Cultural 58
Casa da Lua 145
Casa França-Brasil 41
Castro, Ruy 35
Catedral Metropolitana
  42
Catedral São Pedro de
  Alcântara 199, 200
Catete 242
  accommodations 186-7
  eating 121
cathedrals, see churches &
  cathedrals
Cavaquinho, Nelson 34
Caymmi, Dorival 34
cell phones 215
Central Fone 211
Centro 96, 238, 71
  accommodations 187
  drinking 135-6
  eating 122-4
Centro Cultural Banco do
  Brasil 32, 57

Centro de Informações
Turísticas 194
Centro de Vida
Independente 210
chairlifts 200
chemists 212
children, travel with 209
choro 32
Christina, Teresa 34
churches & cathedrals
Capela de Nossa Senhora
das Dores 193-4
Catedral Metropolitana 97
Catedral São Pedro de
Alcântara 199, 200
Convento de Santo
Antônio 97
Igreja Nossa Senhora do
Rosário 192
Igreja Santa Rita dos
Pardos Libertos 193
Matriz Nossa Senhora
dos Remédios 192
Cibelle 36
Cidade de Deus 37, 46
Cidade de Música 42
Cidade do Samba 30
cigars 160, 167
Cinco Minutos 40
Cine Idea 145
Cinelândia **96, 238, 71**
accommodations 187
drinking 135-6
eating 122-4
cinema 37-8, 147-8
Cinema Novo 38
climate 9, 209
climbing 169
clubs 144-5
Cobal do Humaitá 167
cocaine 211
Coelho, Gonçalo 47
Coelho, Paulo 32, 39
coffee plantations 50-1
Comte, Auguste de 49
consulates 210
Convento de Santo Antônio
40, 97
Coopa Roca 16
Copa 145
Copacabana **244, 69**
accommodations 179-84
drinking 133-4

eating 115-18
shopping 164-6
Copacabana Palace 40-2
corruption 211
Cosme Velho
accommodations 185-6
drinking 135
eating 120-1
shopping 166-7
cosmetics 160
Costa do Sol 191-202
Costa Verde 191-202
Costa, Lúcio 42
costs 6
accommodations 174
bargaining 158
food 104
taxes 158, 204
courses 209
flying 153
language 209
music 167
surfing 155
yoga 156
credit cards 213
crime 13, 46
drug smuggling 211
personal safety 214
Cristo Redentor 79
cruises 58
culture 12
customs regulations
209
cycling 152, *see also*
mountain biking
bicycle hire 154
tours 97-9

D
Dama Branca 198
Dama de Ferro 145
dance 43-4
classes 156
festivals 11
halls 33
nightlife 144-5
rehearsals 11
schools 27, 33
shows 128
Debret, Jean-Baptiste 43
Democráticus 33
departure tax 204
Dia da Fundação da
Cidade 10
Dia de Independência do
Brasil 10
Dia de São Sebastião 10

Dia do Índio 10
Dias, Gonçalves 44
dictatorship 52-3
Diegues, Carlos 38
díria 18
disabled travelers 209-10
dive operators 198
diving 152, 169, 195
dolphins 58
Dom João VI 49-50
Dom Pedro I 50, 199
Dom Pedro II 50
Donga 33, 52
drinking, *see also individual*
neighborhoods, Drinking
subindex
best neighborhood
bars 132
juice bars 15
wine & spirit stores
161
drinks
cocktails 14
draft beer 14
drugs
illegal 211
prescription 212
Ducha 42-3
Duek, Tufi 160
Dumont, Santos 200

E
El Turf Cyber Ba 211
electricity 210
Elite Dive Center 196
embassies 210
emergencies 210, *see also*
inside front cover
Empório Brasil 160
entertainment 128-48
bookings 128
Carnaval tickets 28-9
dance schools 33
media guides 128
nightlife 144-5
venues 143
environmental issues 20,
21, 46
air pollution 21
recycling 21
urban planning 22
wild rubber 171
Espaço Bndes 128
Estádio Sao Januário
150
Estudantina 33
etiquette 6, 16

F
Faria, Miguel Jr 37
Fasano, Rogerio 110
fashion 16, *see also*
Shopping *subindex*
Brazilian designers 16
etiquette 16
Fashion Rio 16
Favela Rising 37
Favela-Bairro project 8, 20,
22, 46
favelas 8, 37, 46, 58
Coopa Roca 16
tours 59
Feedback 209
feijoada 15
Feira de Arte de Ipanema 168
Feira de Música 168
Feira do Rio Antigo 168
Feira Nordestina 168
Ferradura 197
Ferradurinha 197
festivals 9-2, 148, 193,
see also Carnaval,
special events
film 148
music 11, 32, 35-6
religious 10, 11, 193
fire services 210
fishing 152-3
tours 58
villages 198
fitness 156
Flamengo **242**
accommodations 185-6
drinking 135
eating 120-1
shopping 166-7
Fone Rio 211
food, *see also* Eating
subindex
best international
restaurants 117
bookings 105
Brazilian 105
football (soccer) 150
World Cups 17
foreign-language press 214
Formula One motor
racing 16
Forte de Copacabana
66, **99**
Forte Defensor Perpétuo
192, 194
Forte São Mateus 198
Fosfobox 145
Franco-Brazilian history 49

000 map pages
000 photographs

Index

Freyre, Gilberto 52
Furnas do Catete 200
futebol 17

G
G Brazil 210
gafieiras 33, 139
Galeria Café 145
galleries, *see also* museums
    Centro Cultural Banco do
        Brasil 32, 57
    Museu de Arte Moderna
        (MAM) 32, 42, **92**
    The Maze 58
Garcia-Roza, Luis Alfredo 39
Garotinho, Rosinha 20
Gávea **246**
    drinking 131-3
    food 113-15
    shopping 164
gay travelers 144-5, 210-11
Geiger, Anna Bella 43
gems 161
Geribá 197
Gil, Gilberto 35, 36, 58
Gilberto, Bebel 36
Gilberto, João 35
Glória
    accommodations 186-7
    eating 121
gold rush 48
government 19-20
groceries 106, 113
Grupo Semente 34
Gruta Azul 198
Guarnieri, Gianfranco 44
Guerra dos Canudos 58
Guianás Indians 192
GusCar 198
gyms 156

H
hang gliding 153, 200
Havaianas 16
health 156
    environmental 21
    health-food shops 166
    hospitals 212
    medical services 212
Hepatitis B 212
hiking 153-4, 169, 195, 202
hip-hop 8, 37
Hippie Fair 168
history 46-54
holidays 211
horse racing 150
hospitals 212

I
identification 211
Igreja Nossa Senhora do
    Rosário 192, 194
Igreja Santa Rita dos Pardos
    Libertos 193, 194
Ilha do Araújo 193
Ilha Grande 195-6
independence 50
Instituto Nacional de Belas
    Arte 41
Internet access 211
Ipanema 174-9, **246**, **69**, **70**
    drinking 129-31
    food 106-13
    shopping 158-64
islands
    Ilha do Araújo 193
    Ilha Grande 195-6
Isto É 18
itineraries 56-7
    Búzios 197-9
    Historic Centro 96-7
    Ilha Grande 195-6
    Lagoa to Leme 97-9
    Paraty 192-4
    Petrópolis 199-201
    Santa Teresa 100-1
    Urca 101-2
    Visconde de Mauá 201

J
Jardim Botânico 22
    drinking 131-3
    food 113-15
    shopping 164
jazz 11, 165
Jesus, Clementina de 34
jewelry 159, 160, 161, 169
Jobim, Antonio Carlos
    (Tom) 35
jogging 154
Jornal do Brasil 17-18, 128
juice bars 15

K
kayak hire 196
King Momo 24

L
La Cueva 145
La Girl 145
Lagoa
    drinking 131-3
    food 113-15
    shopping 164
Lagoa Azul 195

Lagoa Verde 195
Lagoinha 197
language 18-19, 220-3
Lapa 100-1, **100**, **238**
    accommodations 188
    drinking 136-7
    eating 124-5
    shopping 170-1
Laranjeiras
    accommodations 185-6
    drinking 135
    eating 120-1
    shopping 166-7
Le Boy 145
Le Corbusier 42
Leal, Maria Teresa 16
Leblon 174-9, **246**, **69**, **70**
    drinking 129-31
    food 106-13
    shopping 158-64
legal matters 211-12
Leme **244**
    accommodations 179-84
    drinking 133-4
    eating 115-18
    shopping 164-6
lesbian travelers 144-5,
    210-11
Letras e Expressões 211
Lins, Paolo 37
literature 15, 17, 35, 37,
    39-40
Lobo, Edu 35
Locutório 211
Lopes, Jarbas 43
Los Hermanos 37
love motels 179
Luiz Amaral Tours 59
Luiz Inácio Lula da Silva 20
Lumiar 200

M
Macedo, Joaquim Manoel
    de 40
Macuco Rio 58
Macunaíma 40
Madame Satã 37, 53
magazines 213-14
Maia, Cesar 8, 20, 46
malandros 53
Manguinhos 198
map legend 235
map sales 212
Maracanã Football Stadium
    150
Marcelo D2 37
marijuana 211

Maringá 201
maritime procession 193
markets 16, 167, 168
Marlin Yacht Tours 58
Maromba 201
Márquez, Gabriel García
    39
martial arts 151
Martins, Gilson 160
Mata Atlântica 22, 200
Matriz Nossa Senhora dos
    Remédios 192, 194
Mauá 201
McGowan, Chris 37
media 17-18
medical services 212
Meireles, Cildo 43
Meirelle, Fernando 37
Meirelles, Victor 43
Melo, Maria Jácome 192
Melo, Patrícia de 39
Meneschal, Roberto 35
Metro 46, 207
Miele, Carlos 16
migration 52
Miguel Couto hospital 212
military 52-3
Minas Gerais 192
minivans 207
Miranda, Carmen 10, 34
mobile phones 215
Monasteiro de São Bento
    40
money 196, 212, 213
monkeys 22
Monte, Marisa 36
Montigny, Grandjean de 49
Moraes, Vinícius de 37, 163
Morro da Cruz 200
motor racing
    Formula One 16
mountain-biking 201
museums, *see also* galleries
    Centro Cultural Banco do
        Brasil 32, 57
    H Stern gem museum 161
    Museu Casa de Santos
        Dumont 200
    Museu da República 211
    Museu de Arte Moderna
        (MAM) 32, 42, **92**
    Museu do Arte
        Contemporânea
        (MAC) 42, **70**
    Museu Imperial 199, 200
    Museum of
        Oceanography 198

music 32, 33-7, 52, 58
  festivals 11, 32, 35-6
  funk 35
  hip-hop 8, 37
  jazz 11
  samba da mesa 140
Música Popular Brasileira
  (MPB) 32, 35-6

N
Nadkarni, Bob 58
Nascimento, Milton 35
national parks
  Parque Nacional da Serra
    da Bocaina 194
  Parque Nacional da
    Serra dos Órgãos
    191, 200
  Parque Nacional da Tijuca
    22, 57
  Parque Nacional de
    Itatiaia 191, 202
newspapers 213-14
Niemeyer, Oscar 42
Noites Cariocas 11, 135
Nova Friburgo 200
Novak, Pedro 59
novelas 18, 216

O
O Dia 17-18
O Globo 17-18, 128
Oiticica, Hélio 43
orchids 22
Orfeu 38
Osklen 16
Ossos 198
Oudin, Dominique 117

P
paddle boating 154
Palácio de Cristal 200
Palácio Monroe 41
Pan American Games 8,
  22, 46
Panorama Rio de Dança 11
Pão de Açúcar 57, **2**
Paraty 191, 192-4
  Carnaval 193
  tours 193, 194
  transport 192
Paraty Tours 193, 194
parking 206

000 map pages
000 photographs

parks & gardens, see also
  national parks
  Jardim Botânico 22
  Parque Lage 22
  Parque Nacional da Serra
    da Bocaina 194
  Parque Nacional da Serra
    dos Órgãos 191, 200
  Parque Nacional da Tijuca
    22, 57
  Parque Nacional de Itatiaia
    191, 202
Passos, Pereira 41, 51-2
passports 217
Pedra do Cão Sentad 200
Penedo 201
peoples
  Afro-Brazilian 12-13
  Camucim 167
  Guianás Indians 192
  Tupinambá Indians 195
performing arts 128-9
Pernambuco, Carla 108
Pessanha, Ricardo 37
Peterson, Joan & David 15
Petrópolis 191, 199-201
pharmacies 212, 214
Phoenix Turismo 196
Photography and Image
  Fair 168
Pico da Caledônia 200
Pico do Papagaio 195
Pixinguinha 33, 52
plants, orchids 22
police 46
politics 20
pollution
  air 21
  beach 21-2
Pontal dunes 198
population 6
Portinari, Cândido 43, 136
Porto, Fernanda 36
Portuguese cooking 15
Portuguese settlers 47
Portzparc, Christian de 42
postal services 214
poverty 54
Powell, Baden 35
Powell, Marcel 35
Praça do Lido Market 168
Praça do Mercado Feira de
  Antiguidades 168
Praça Quinze Handicrafts
  Fair 168
Praça Santos Dumont
  Antique Fair 168

Praia Brava 197, 198
Praia da Armação 197
Praia da Foca 197
Praia da Tartaruga 198
Praia da Vila 198
Praia das Conchas 198
Praia de Paraty-Mirim 194
Praia do Caboclo 197
Praia do Forno 197, 198
Praia do Forte 193
Praia do Gaucho 198
Praia do Jabaquara 193
Praia do Peró 198
Praia do Pontal 193
Praia dos Amores 197
Praia dos Ossos 197
Praia Grande 198
Praia Itaún 198
Praia Lopes Mendes 195
Praia Olho de Boi 197
Praia Vermelha 21
Prazeres, Heitor dos 52
prescription medicines 212
protests 53-4

Q
Queen Lory 198

R
racial identity 12
racism 13
radio 214
Rasa 198
Real Auto Bus 204
Real Gabinete Português de
  Leitura 41, 97-8
recycling 21
Regina, Elis 35
religious festivals 10, 11,
  193
Reveillon 12
Rio Convention & Visitors
  Bureau 208
Rio de Janeiro International
  Film Festival 11, 148
Rio Guesthouse 184
Rio Jazz Festival 11
Rio Marathon 10
Rios Brasileiros Rafting 200
Rita, Maria 36
Rocha, Glauber 38
rock climbing 151-2
Rodrigues, Nelson 44
Rosa, Noel 34
Royal jewels 199
Royal Reading Room 41
running, Rio Marathon 10

S
Sá, Anderson 37
Saco do Céu 195
Sala Cecilia Meireles 128
Salgado, Sebastião 43
samba 33-4, 52, 140
  clubs 139-43
  school rehearsals 11
  schools & shows 141
Sambódromo 24-30, 29
Santa Clara Cachoeira 201
Santa Teresa 57, 100-1,
  100, **241**
  accommodations 188
  drinking 136-7
  eating 124-5
  shopping 170-1
Santos, João Francisco dos
  37, 53
Santos, Nelson Pereira
  dos 38
Saquarema 191, 198
Saramago, José 32
Secretaria de Turismo 198
Senhora 40
Senna, Ayrton 17
Sergio Mendes & Brasil '66
  35
Serra da Mantiqueira
  201
Sexta-Feira da Paixão 10
Shalimar 179
shopping 158-72, 208,
  see also individual
  neighborhoods,
  Shopping subindex
  accessories 159, 161,
    162, 163, 164, 171
  alcohol 161, 169
  antiques 160, 164, 170,
    171
  art-naïf 159, 165
  arts & crafts 161, 162
  bookstores 158-9, 161,
    162, 166, 169
  boutiques 162
  business hours 208
  chocolates 159, 161
  cigars 160, 169
  clothing 159, 161, 160,
    162, 163, 164, 168,
    171
  cosmetics 160
  couture 162
  eclectic 169, 171
  fabrics 163
  fashion 16, 163

Index

230

handbags 160
handicrafts 159, 164, 165, 166, 167, 171
handmade fashion 161
health-food 166
home decor 162, 163
jewelry 158-9, 160, 161, 168, 169
markets 16, 111, 168
music 159, 161, 162, 164, 166, 169
photographic works 168
photography 169
shabby chic 163
shoes 162, 164
souvenirs 159
supermarkets 113
thrift shops 165, 170
shopping centers 161
  Barra Shopping 171
  Botafogo Praia Shopping 166
  Forum 160
  Galeria River 165
  Rio Design Center 172
  Rio Off-Price Shopping 166
  Rio Sul Shopping 166
  São Conrado Fashion Mall 172
  Shopping da Gávea 164
  Via Parque Shopping 172
Sinless 179
slavery 12, 47-8, 151, 192
Smith, Paul 16
smuggling 211
snorkeling 197
soap operas 18, 216
soccer 17, 150-1
Society for Accessible Travel & Hospitality 210
souvenirs 159
Space Club 145
special events, see also Carnaval
  festivals, holidays
  concerts 24-30
  Fashion Rio 16
  Música Popular Brasileira (MPB) 32, 35-6
  Noites Cariocas 135
  Reveillon 12
  Rio Antiques Fair 168
  Rio de Janeiro International Film Festival 148
  Rio Marathon 10
  Tim Festival 11

sport
  beach 56-7, 154
  fishing 58
  Pan American Games 8, 22, 46
  soccer 17
  spectator 150-1
  Star Club 145
  Starck, Phillip 42
  Suassuna, Ariano 44
  Sudoeste SW Turismo 196
  surfing 155, 165, 191, 198
  swimming 21

T
takeout 106
Taunay, Nicolas 43
taxes
  consumer 158
  departure 204
taxis 207
Taylor, Ann 16
Teatro Carlos Gomes 128
Teatro Do Centro Cultural Banco Do Brasil 129
Teatro Espaço 194
Teatro Laura Alvim 129
Teatro Municipal 40-2, 41, 129
telephone services 215-16
Telerede 211
theaters 43-4
  'Nos do Morro'58
  Teatro Carlos Gomes 128
  Teatro Do Centro Cultural Banco Do Brasil 129
  Teatro Laura Alvim 129
  Tristan und Isolde 44
  Um Circo de Rins e Fígados 44
Thomas, Gerald 43-4
Tia Ciata 52
Ticketmaster 128
Ticketronics 128
Tim Festival 11
time 6, 216
tipping 105, 216
tombs 199-200
topless beaches 197
tourist cards 217
tourist information 194, 196, 198, 200, 202, 216-17
tours 58-61
  boating 58, 196
  city 59
  climbing 151-2
  diving 152

favela 59
fishing 153
rafting 198
schooner 193, 198
trolley 198
walking 96-102
train travel 207
trams 53, 60, 87, 88, 207-8, **57, 70**
travel agency 217
Trekking Petrópolis 201
Troisgros, Claude 114
Tropicália 35
Tupinambá Indians 195
Turma OK 145
turtles 58
TV 18-19, 216

U
urban planning 22
Urca 101
  accommodations 184
  drinking 134-5
  eating 118-20
  shopping 166
  walking tour 101-2

V
Valle, Marcos 35
Vargas, President 52
Veja 18-19
Veloso, Caetano 35, 37
Vespucci, Amerigo 47
Vila do Abraão 195
Villard, Roland 117
Vinícius 37
visas 217
Visconde de Mauá 191, 201-02
visual arts 42-3
volleyball 154

W
Waddington, Andrucha 37
walking 154
  tours 96-102
Walter Salles 37-8
warnings
  pollution 21-2
  robberies 198
  swimming 21
whales 58
women travelers 217-18
working in Brazil 218

Y
yoga 156

Z
Zweig, Stefan 200

DRINKING
Academia da Cachaça 129
Adega Flor de Coimbra 136
Allegro Bistrô Musical 133
Amarelinho 135
Arco do Teles 135
Armazém São Thiago 136
Ateliê Odeon 135
Aurora 134
Bar 121 129
Bar d'hotel 130
Bar do Belmiro 134
Bar do Mineiro 136
Bar Lagoa 132
Bar Luiz 135
Beco da Sardinha 135
Bip Bip 137, **34, 138**
Botequim 134
Botequim informal 130
Bracarense 130
Café Neves 136
Caipirinha & Filé 132
Caneco 70 130
Caroline Café 132
Cervantes 133
Champanharia Ovelha Negra 134
Chopp da Lapa 135
Cobal 130
Conversa Fiada 130
Copa Café 133
Copacabana Palace Poolside Bar 134
Cosmopolita 136
da Graça 132
Devassa 130
Dito & Feito 136
Drink Café 132
Empório 131
Esch Café 136
Espirito do Chopp 134
Garota da Urca 135
Garota de Ipanema 131
Goia Beira 136
Guapo Loco 131
Hipódromo Up 132
Horse's Neck 134
Jiló 131
Jobi 131
Jota Bar 132
Lord Jim 131
Mike's Haus 137
Saturnino 132

Seu Martin 131
Shenanigan's 131
Simplesmente 137
Sindicato do Chopp 134
Sitio Lounge 133
Sky Lounge 133
Skylab Bar 134
VIA XV Botequim 136

EATING

00 (zero zero) 113
Academia de Cozinha 194
Adega do Valentim 118
Alessandro E Federico 106
Alho e Óleo 120
Amazónia 121
Amir 115
Antiquarius 106
Aprazível 124
Arab da Lagoa 114
Armazém do Café 106
Arte Temperada 122
Ataúlfo 107
Ateliê Culinário 107
Ateliê Odeon 122
Atrium 122
Azul Marinho 107
Azumi 115 JAPAN
B! 107
Bakers 115
Banana Blu 196
Banana Jack 107
Bar Brasil 124
Bar do Ernesto 124
Bar do Mineiro 124
Bar do Zé 198
Bar Luiz 122
Bar Urca 119
Barra Brasa 107
Barreado 125
Barril 1800 107 BEAR
Bazzar 108
Beduíno 122
Belmonte 120, **120**
Bibi Crepes 108
Bibi Sucos 108
Bira 126
Bistrô do Paço 122
Bistrô Jardins 121
Bistrô Petit Palais 201
Boteco 66 114
Braseiro da Gávea 114
Brasserie Rosário 122
café do Rodrigues 123
Café Fleuri 115
Café Paraty 194
Café Severino 108

Cafeína 108
Cais do Oriente 123, **123**
Carême Bistrô 119
Carlota 108
Carpaccio & Cia 108
Carretão 116
Casa Cavé 123
Casa da Feijoada 108
Casa da Suíça 121
Casebre Pub 202
Catete Grill 121
Cedro do Líbano 123
Celeiro 108
Cervante 116
Chaika 109
Chez Michou Crêperie 199
Chez Pierre 109
Chocolates Katz 201
Chocolatras 109
Churrascaria Majórica 120
Cigalon 199
Cipriani 116
Colher de Pau 109
Confeitaria Colombo 116, 123
Copa Café 116
Corsário Negro 196
Da Silva 109
Delírio Tropical 109
Dito & Feito 123
Doce Delícia 109
Dom João 114
Don Camillo 116
Eça 124
Empório Arabe 109
Emporium Pax 119
Encontras Cariocas 125
Espirito Santa 125
Estação República 121
Fellini 110
Fontes 110
Fratelli 110
Galani 110
Galeto do Leblon 110
Garcia & Rodrigues 110
Garota da Urca 119
Gero 110
Gosto com Gosto 202
Guapo Loco 199
Guimas 114
Gula Gula 110
Hortifruti 111
Juice Co 111
Kilograma 111, 116
Kotobuki 119
Kurt 111
L'Assiette 111

La Fiorentina 116
La Trattoria 117
Lamas 120
Le Blé Noir 117
Le Pré Catalan 117
Le Saint Honoré 117
Lidador 124
Livraria Prefácio 119
Locanda della Mimosa 201
Lope's Confeitaria 117
Lucas 117
Luigi 201
Majórica Churrascaria 201
Margarida Café 194
Marius Carnes 117
Marius Crustáceos 117
Marizé Gourmet 125
Mike's Haus 125
Mil Frutas 111, **111**
Miss Tanaka 114
Museu do Açude 126
Mustafá 111
Nam Thai 112
New Natural 112
Nik Sushi 112
Nova Capela 125
Olympe 114
Osteria Dell'angolo 112
Pátio Havana 99
Peixe Vivo 118
Petronius 112
Pizza Park 119
Plataforma 112
Polis Sucos 112
Porção Rio's 120
Porta Quente 125
Quadrifoglio 115
Quadrucci 112
Quitanda Vegetal 112
Rancho Inn 124
Refúgio 194
Restaurante Albamar 124
Sansushi 125
Sawasdee 199
Senac Bistrô 121
Serafina 118
Shirley 118
Siri Mole & Cia 118
Sobrenatural 125
Stravaganze 119
Sushi Leblon 112
Sushinaka Light 115
Taberna da Glória 121
Tacacá do Norte 121
Talho Capixaba 113
Temperarte 118
Tia Palmira 126

Traiteurs de France 118
Tropicana 196
Vegetariano Social Club 113
Via Sete 113
Vila Verde 194
Yonza 118
Yorubá 119
Zazá Bistrô Tropical 113
Zin 120
Zona Sul Supermarket 113
Zuka 113

SHOPPING

Alfonso Nune's Antiquario 170
Amsterdam Sauer 158
Argumento 158
Arquitetura & Decoração 170
Arte Brasilis 164
Artíndia 166
Av Atlântica Fair 168
Barra Shopping 171-2
Boca do Sapo 159
Botafogo Praia Shopping 166
Brasil & Cia 159
Brechó Antigamente 170
Brechó Arte 70 170
Brumada 166
Casa do Brazão 171
Chez Bonbon 159
Clube Chocolate 171
Cobal do Humaitá 167
Contemporâneo 159
Da Conde 159
Daqu 159
De Salto Alto 165
Eliane Carvalho 159
Escada 160
Esch Café 167
Expand Wine Store 169
Feira de Música 164, 168
Feira Nordestina 168
Florestas 160
Forum 160
Forum de Ipanema 162
Galeria Ipanema Secreta 162
Galeria River 165
Gilson Martins 160
H Stern 160, 169
Hippie Fair 168
Interstudio 161
Ipanema 2000 162
Ipanema.com 161
Isabela Capeto 161

Jeito Brasileiro 167
Juliana Faro 161
Kopenhagen 161
La Vareda 171
Letras e Expressões 161
Lidador 161
Livraria da Travessa 162, 169
Livraria Imperial 169
Livraria Prefácio 166
Loja Novo Desenho 169
Luko 162
Maria de Barro 165
MBR 162
Mixed 162
Modern Sound 164, 165
Mundo Verde 166
Musicale 162, 164, 166
No Meio do Caminho 162
Nova Livraria Leonardo da Vinci 169
O Sol 164
Ooz 163
Osklen 162
Pano Nosso 163
Photography and Image Fair 168
Plano B 164
Praça do Lido Market 168
Praça do Mercado Feira de Antiguidades 168
Praça Quinze Handicrafts Fair 168
Praça Santos Dumont Antique Fair 168
Rasgando Pano 171
Rio Design Center 162, 172
Rio Off-Price Shopping 166
Rio Sul Shopping 166
São Conrado Fashion Mall 172
Shopping Cassino Atlântico Antiques Fair 168
Shopping da Gávea 164
Sub & Sub 169
Tabacaria Africana 169

Teargas 163
Toca do Vinícius 163, 164
Trilhos Urbanos 171
Unimagem 169
Urucum Art & Design 163
Vale das Bonecas 164
Via Parque Shopping 172
Vit 164
Wild Rubber 171
Wöllner Outdoor 164
World Map 164

SLEEPING
Acapulco 179
Ambassador Hotel 187
Apa Hotel 180
Arpoador Inn 174
Aselem 196
Atlântico Sul 188
Atlantis Copacabana Hotel 180
Augusto's Copacabana 180
Blame it on Rio 4 Travel 185
Brigitta's Guesthouse 199
Caesar Park 174
Cama e Café 188
Carioca Easy Hostel 184
Casa 6 Ipanema 174
Casa Áurea 188
Casa Del Mar 188
Casablanca Imperial 201
Casas Brancas 199
Center Hotel 187
Che Lagarto 180
Che Lagarto Iipanema 175
Copacabana Holiday 185
Copacabana Hotel Residência 180
Copacabana Palace 180
Copacabana Praia Hostel 181
Copacabana Praia Hotel 181
Design Hotel Portinar 181
Everest Rio 175

Excelsior Copacabana Hotel 181
Fantastic Rio 185
Flamengo Palace 186
Glória 186
Guanabara Palace 187
Hibiscus Beach 199
Hotel Astoria Copacabana 181
Hotel Casa Alpina 202
Hotel Colonial Inn 201
Hotel Coxixo 194
Hotel Debret 181
Hotel Ferreira Viana 185
Hotel Flórida 185
Hotel Monterrey 186
Hotel Novo Mundo 186
Hotel Paysandu 185
Hotel Pousada Galeão 187
Hotel Praia Ipanema 175
Hotel Regina 185
Hotel Riazor 186
Hotel Rio Claro 187
Hotel Rio internaciona 182
Hotel San Marco 175
Hotel Santa Clara 182
Hotel Solar dos Geránios 194
Hotel Toledo 182
Hotel Turístico 187
Hotel Vermont 176
Hotel Vllamar 182
Imperial Hotel 187
Intercontinental 188
Ipanema Beach House 176
Ipanema Flat Hotel Residência 176
Ipanema Hotel Residência 176
Ipanema Inn 176
Ipanema Plaza 176
Ipanema Sweet 176
Ipanema Tower 176
Ipanema Wave Hostel 177
Itajubá Hotel 187
Le Meridien 182

Leblon Ocean Hotel Residência 177
Lighthouse Hostel 177
Luxor Copacabana 182
Mar ipanema 177
Mar Palace 182
Margarida's Pousada 177
Marina All Suites 177
Marina Palace 177
Mengo Palace Hotel 186
Miramar Palace Hotel 182
Monsieur Le Blond 177
Naturalia 196
O Pescador 196
O Veleiro 184
Olinda Othon Classic 182
Orla Copacabana 183
Parthenon Arpoador 183
Parthenon Queen Elizabeth 178
Plaza Copacabana 183
Pousada 14 Bis 201
Pousada Arte Urquijo 194
Pousada Girassol 183
Pousada Praia D'Azul 196
Pousada Terra da Luz 202
Praia Linda 188
Premier Copacabana Hotel 183
Real Palace Hotel 183
Residencial Apartt 183
Rio Apartment Services 185
Rio Apartments 185
Rio Backpackers 184
Rio Hostel 188
Rio Luxor Aeroporto 187
Rio Othon Palace 184
Rio Roiss Hotel 184
Rio Universe 178
Ritz Plaza Hotel 178
Royal Rio Palace 184
Sheraton 178
Sofitel Rio De Janeiro 184
Sol Ipanema 178
Visconti 179
Yvonne Reimann 185

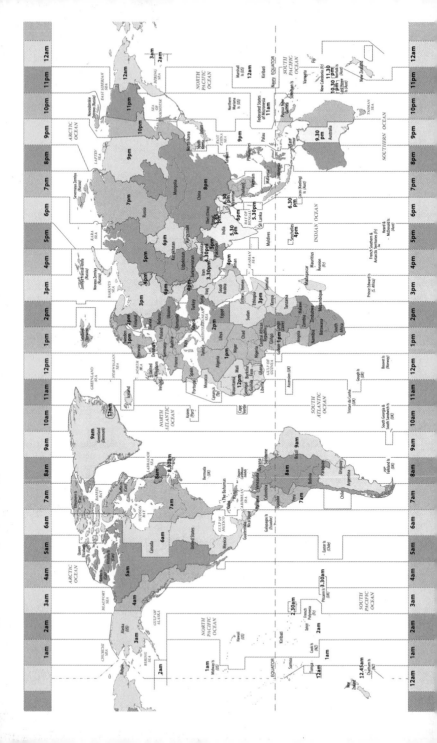

MAP LEGEND

ROUTES

Tollway			One-Way Street
Freeway			Unsealed Road
Primary Road			Mall/Steps
Secondary Road			Tunnel
Tertiary Road			Walking Tour
Lane			Walking Tour Detour
Track			Walking Path

TRANSPORT

Ferry	Rail
Metro	Tram
Bus Route	

HYDROGRAPHY

River, Creek	Mangrove
Intermittent River	Water
Swamp	

BOUNDARIES

State, Provincial	Marine Park

AREA FEATURES

Airport	Cemetery, Christian
Area of Interest	Cemetery, Other
Beach, Desert	Land
Building, Featured	Park
Building, Information	Sports
Building, Other	Urban
Building, Transport	

POPULATION

☯ CAPITAL (NATIONAL)	◉ CAPITAL (STATE)
● Large City	● Medium City
● Small City	● Town, Village

SYMBOLS

Sights/Activities
- Beach
- Monument
- Museum, Gallery
- Picnic Area
- Point of Interest
- Ruin
- Snorkeling
- Zoo, Bird Sanctuary

Eating
- Eating

Drinking
- Drinking
- Café

Entertainment
- Entertainment

Shopping
- Shopping

Sleeping
- Sleeping

Transport
- Airport, Airfield
- Bus Station
- Cycling, Bicycle Path
- General Transport
- Taxi Rank

Information
- Bank, ATM

- Embassy/Consulate
- Hospital, Medical
- Information
- Internet Facilities
- Parking Area
- Petrol Station
- Police Station
- Post Office, GPO
- Telephone
- Toilets

Geographic
- Lookout
- Mountain, Volcano

Rio de Janeiro 236
Centro, Cinelândia & Lapa 238
Santa Teresa 241
Flamengo, Botafogo & Catete 242
Copacabana & Leme 244
Ipanema, Leblon & Gávea 246
Floresta da Tijuca 249
Rio de Janeiro Transport Map 250

Maps

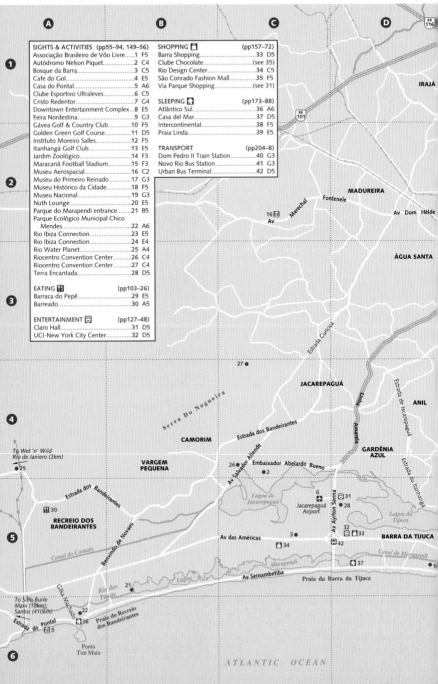

SIGHTS & ACTIVITIES (pp55–94, 149–56)
Associação Brasileiro de Vôo Livre.....1 F5
Autódromo Nelson Piquet.................2 C4
Bosque da Barra.............................3 C5
Cafe do Gol....................................4 E5
Casa do Pontal...............................5 A6
Clube Esportivo Ultraleves...............6 C5
Cristo Redentor..............................7 G4
Downtown Entertainment Complex...8 E5
Feira Nordestina............................9 G3
Gávea Golf & Country Club............10 F5
Golden Green Golf Course.............11 D5
Instituto Moreira Salles..................12 F5
Itanhangá Golf Club......................13 E5
Jardim Zoológico...........................14 F3
Maracanã Football Stadium...........15 F3
Museu Aerospacial........................16 C2
Museu do Primeiro Reinado...........17 G3
Museu Histórico da Cidade............18 F3
Museu Nacional............................19 G3
Nuth Lounge.................................20 E5
Parque do Marapendi entrance......21 B5
Parque Ecológico Municipal Chico
  Mendes....................................22 A6
Rio Ibiza Connection.....................23 E5
Rio Ibiza Connection.....................24 E4
Rio Water Planet...........................25 A4
Riocentro Convention Center.........26 C4
Riocentro Convention Center.........27 C4
Terra Encantada...........................28 D5

EATING (pp103–26)
Barraca do Pepê...........................29 E5
Barreado.....................................30 A5

ENTERTAINMENT (pp127–48)
Claro Hall....................................31 D5
UCI-New York City Center............32 D5

SHOPPING (pp157–72)
Barra Shopping.............................33 D5
Clube Chocolate.......................(see 35)
Rio Design Center.........................34 C5
São Conrado Fashion Mall.............35 F5
Via Parque Shopping..................(see 31)

SLEEPING (pp173–88)
Atlântico Sul................................36 A6
Casa del Mar...............................37 D5
Intercontinental............................38 F5
Praia Linda..................................39 E5

TRANSPORT (pp204–8)
Dom Pedro II Train Station.............40 G3
Novo Rio Bus Station....................41 G3
Urban Bus Terminal......................42 D5

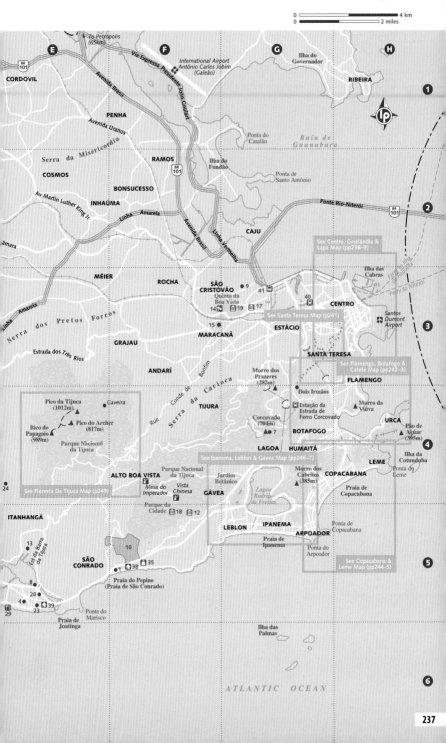

0 ——————— 4 km
0 ——————— 2 miles

E To Petrópolis (65km)
To Petrópolis (65km)
Via Expressa Presidente João Goulart

F International Airport Antônio Carlos Jobim (Galeão)

G Ilha do Governador

H

CORDOVIL

Avenida Brasil
Avenida Uranos

PENHA

Baía de Guanabara

Ponta do Catalão

Serra da Misericórdia

RAMOS

BR 101

Ilha do Fundão

COSMOS

BONSUCESSO

Ponta de Santo Antônio

Av Martin Luther King Jr

INHAÚMA

Linha Amarela

Ponte Rio-Niterói

BR 101

MÉIER

Linha Amarela

ROCHA

SÃO CRISTÓVÃO
Quinta da Boa Vista

9
41
40

See Centro, Cinelândia & Lapa Map (pp238–9)

Ilha das Cabras

Ferry to Ilha de Paquetá

Ferry to Niterói

14
15
19
17

See Santa Teresa Map (p241)

CENTRO

Santos Dumont Airport

Serra dos Pretos Forros

GRAJAÚ

Estrada dos Três Rios

MARACANÃ

ESTÁCIO

SANTA TERESA

See Flamengo, Botafogo & Catete Map (pp242–3)

ANDARÍ

Bonfim

Morro dos Prazeres (282m)

FLAMENGO

Serra da Carioca

TIJUCA

Dois Irmãos

Estação da Estrada de Ferro Corcovado

Morro da Viúva

URCA

Pão de Açúcar (395m)

Pico da Tijuca (1012m)

Caveira

Bico do Papagaio (989m)

Pico do Archer (817m)

Rue Conde de

Corcovado (704m)

7

BOTAFOGO

Parque Nacional da Tijuca

LAGOA

HUMAITÁ

LEME

Ilha da Cotunduba

Ponta do Leme

24

See Floresta Da Tijuca Map (p249)

ALTO BOA VISTA

Mesa do Imperador

Parque Nacional da Tijuca

Vista Chinesa

Jardim Botânico

See Ipanema, Leblon & Gávea Map (pp246–7)

Morro dos Cabritos (385m)

COPACABANA

Praia de Copacabana

GÁVEA

Lagoa Rodrigo de Freitas

Parque da Cidade

18
12

ITANHANGÁ

13

Est do Barra da Tijuca

10

LEBLON

IPANEMA

Praia de Ipanema

ARPOADOR

Ponta do Arpoador

Ponta de Copacabana

See Copacabana & Leme Map (pp244–5)

8

SÃO CONRADO

1
38
35

Praia do Pepino (Praia de São Conrado)

20

4

29
23

39

Ponta do Marisco

Praia de Joatinga

Ilha das Palmas

ATLANTIC OCEAN

1
2
3
4
5
6

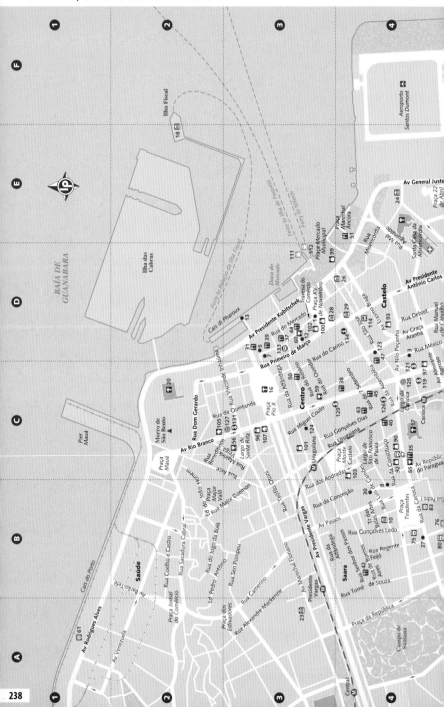

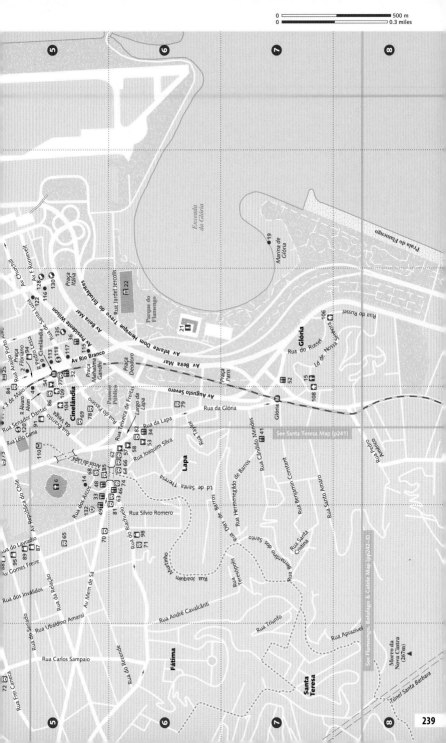

SIGHTS & ACTIVITIES (pp55–94, 149–56)
Arco de Teles..1 D3
Biblioteca Nacional..............................2 D5
Calypso..3 D4
Câmara Municipal.................................4 C5
Casa França-Brasil.................................5 D3
Catedral Metropolitana.......................6 C5
Centro Cultural Banco do Brasil (CCBB)..7 D3
Centro Cultural Carioca.......................8 B4
Centro Cultural Justiça Federal..........9 D5
Centro de Arte Hélio Oiticica..........10 B4
Centro Excursionista Brasileira........11 C5
Claudio Affonso..................................12 D3
Convento de Santo Antônio..........(see 17)
Espaço Cultural da Marinha.............13 D3
Fundição Progresso............................14 C5
Igreja da NS da Glória do Outeiro...15 D7
Igreja de NS de Candelária................16 C3
Igreja São Francisco da Penitência...17 C4
Ilha Fiscal..18 E2
Macuco Rio.......................................(see 19)
Mar do Rio.......................................(see 19)
Marlin Yacht Charters........................19 E7
Monasteiro de São Bento..................20 C2
Monumento Nacional dos Mortos da II Guerra
   Mundial...21 D6
Museu de Arte Moderna....................22 D6
Museu Histórico e Diplomático........23 A3
Museu Histórico Nacional.................24 E4
Museu Nacional de Belas Artes........25 D5
Museu Naval e Oceanográfico..........26 D4
Núcleo de Dança.................................27 B4
Paço Imperial.......................................28 D3
Palácio Tiradentes...............................29 D4
Real Gabinete Português de Leitura..30 D4
Saveiros Tours...................................(see 19)
Universidade da Pesca.....................(see 3)

EATING 🍴 (pp103–26)
Arte Temporada...................................31 D3
Ateliê Odeon..32 D5
Atrium...(see 28)
Bar Brasil..33 C5
Bar do Ernesto....................................34 C6
Bar Luiz...35 C4
Beduíno...36 D5
Bistro do Paço..................................(see 28)
Brasserie Rosário.................................37 D3
Café do Rodrigues..............................38 C4
Cais do Oriente....................................39 D3
Casa Cavé..40 C4
Casa da Suíça.......................................41 C7
Cedro do Líbano..................................42 B4
Confeitaria Colombo...........................43 C4
Dito & Feito..44 D3
Eça..45 C4
Encontras Cariocas.............................46 C6

Lidador..47 D4
Marizè Gourmet...................................48 C5
Nova Capela..49 B5
Rancho Inn..50 C3
Restaurante Albamar...........................51 E4
Taberna da Glória.................................52 D7

DRINKING 🍷 (pp127–48)
Adega Flor de Coimbra........................53 C6
Amarelinho..54 D5
Bar Luiz..55 C4
Beco da Sardinha..................................56 C3
Chopp da Lapa......................................57 C6
Cosmopolita..58 C6
Esch Café...59 C3
VIA XV Botequim.................................60 D3

ENTERTAINMENT 🎭 (pp127–48)
Armazem do Rio...................................61 A1
Asa Branca...62 C6
Carioca da Gema..................................63 C6
Cariolapa...64 C6
Casa de Mãe Joana...............................65 B5
Casarão Cultural dos Arcos.................66 C6
Cine Ideal...67 C4
Circo Voador..68 C5
Club Six..69 C5
Dama da Noite......................................70 B5
Democraticus...71 B6
Elite..72 A5
Espaço BNDES......................................73 C5
Estação Paço.....................................(see 28)
Estrela da Lapa......................................74 C6
Estudantina Café..................................75 B4
Mangue Seco Cachaçaria.....................76 B4
Odeon BR..77 D5
Palácio..78 C5
Point da Lapa..79 C6
Río Scenarium.......................................80 B4
Sacrilégio...81 C6
Sala Cecília Mierelles...........................82 C6
Teatro Carlos Gomes............................83 B4
Teatro do Centro Cultural Banco do
   Brasil..(see 7)
Teatro Municipal...................................84 C5
Teatro Odisséia.....................................85 C5
Teatro Rival Petrobras.........................86 C5

SHOPPING 🛍 (pp157–72)
Alfonso Nune's Antiquario..................87 B5
Arquitetura & Decoração.....................88 B5
Casa do Brazão......................................89 B5
Casa Oliveira...90 C4
Editora Geográfica J Paulini................91 C5
Empório Musicale.................................92 C4
Expand Wine Store...............................93 D4
Feira de Música....................................94 D5

Feira do Rio Antigo..............................95 B5
H Stern...(see 45)
Livraria da Travessa.............................96 C3
Livraria da Travessa.........................(see 38)
Livraria Imperial..............................(see 28)
Loja Novo Desenho..........................(see 22)
Nova Livraria Leonardo da Vinci........97 C4
Plano B...98 B6
Praça do Mercado Feira de
   Antiguidades.....................................99 D3
Praça XV Handicrafts Fair..................100 D3
Sub & Sub..101 C3
Tabacaria Africana.............................102 D3
Unimagem...103 C4

SLEEPING 🛏 (pp173–88)
Ambassador Hotel..............................104 C5
Center Hotel.......................................105 C2
Glória...106 D7
Guanabara Palace..............................107 C3
Hotel Turístico...................................108 C7
Itajubá Hotel......................................109 C5

TRANSPORT (pp204–8)
Bonde to Santa Teresa.......................110 C5
Continental Airlines.......................(see 134)
Ferry to Ilha de Paquetá....................111 D3
Ferry to Niterói...................................112 D3
Mangue Seco Cachaçaria....................113 D5
Menezes Cortes Bus Teminal............114 D4
TAP Portugal Airlines.........................115 D5
United Airlines....................................116 D5
Varig..117 D5

INFORMATION
Australian Consulate......................(see 122)
Avipam Turismo.................................118 D5
Banco 24 Horas..................................119 C4
Banco do Brasil..................................120 C5
Bradesco ATM....................................121 C4
Business & Legal Center.....................122 D5
Business Quality.................................123 D4
Casa Aliança.......................................124 C3
Central Fone.......................................125 C4
Citibank...126 C4
Cyber Café..127 C3
Cyber Café Fundição
   Progresso......................................(see 14)
Dantur Passagens..........................(see 125)
French Consulate...............................128 D5
HSBC..129 C4
Italian Consulate................................130 D5
Navegantes...131 C3
Police Post..132 B5
Post Office...133 D3
Riotur..134 D4
USA Consulate....................................135 D5

SANTA TERESA

0 ———————————————— 500 m
0 ———————————————— 0.3 miles

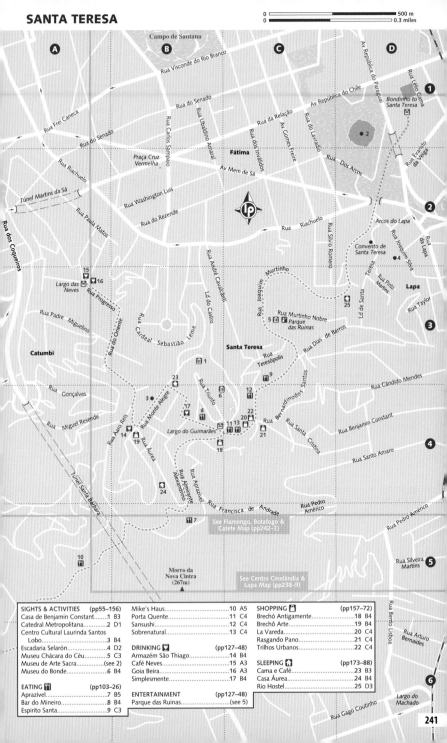

SIGHTS & ACTIVITIES	(pp55–156)
Casa de Benjamin Constant	1 B3
Catedral Metropolitana	2 D1
Centro Cultural Laurinda Santos	
Lobo	3 B4
Escadaria Selarón	4 D2
Museu Chácara do Céu	5 C3
Museu de Arte Sacra	(see 2)
Museu do Bonde	6 B4

EATING	(pp103–26)
Aprazível	7 B5
Bar do Mineiro	8 B4
Espirito Santa	9 C3

Mike's Haus	10 A5
Porta Quente	11 C4
Sansushi	12 C4
Sobrenatural	13 C4

DRINKING	(pp127–48)
Armazém São Thiago	14 B4
Café Neves	15 A3
Goia Beira	16 A3
Simplesmente	17 B4

ENTERTAINMENT	(pp127–48)
Parque das Ruinas	(see 5)

SHOPPING	(pp157–72)
Brechó Antigamente	18 B4
Brechô Arte	19 B4
La Vareda	20 C4
Rasgando Pano	21 C4
Trilhos Urbanos	22 C4

SLEEPING	(pp173–88)
Cama e Café	23 B3
Casa Áurea	24 B4
Rio Hostel	25 D3

See Flamengo, Botafogo &
Catete Map (pp242–3)

See Centro Cinelândia &
Lapa Map (pp238–9)

FLAMENGO, BOTAFOGO & CATETE

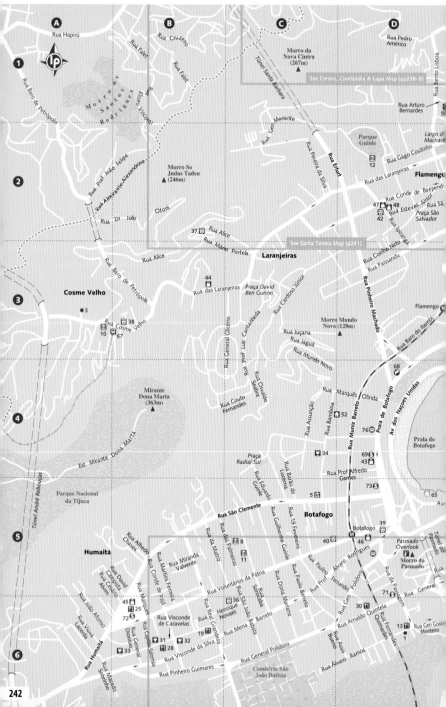

See Centro, Cinelândia & Lapa Map (pp238-9)

See Santa Teresa Map (p241)

Rua Hapirú

Rua Cruzeiro

Rua Falet

Rua Falet

Rua Eliseu Visconti

Rua Gen Mariante

Rua Pereira da Silva

Rua Pedro Américo

Rua Bento Lisboa

Rua Arturo Bernardes

Túnel Santa Bárbara

Morro da Nova Cintra (267m)

Morro de Santos Rodrigues

Rua Baro de Petrópolis

Rua Pref João Felipe

Rua Almirante Alexandrina

Morro So Judas Tadeu (246m)

Parque Guinle

Rua Gago Coutinho

Rua Erfurt

Flamengo

Rua das Laranjeiras

Rua Conde de Baependi

Rua Esteves Júnior

Rua Sá

Praça São Salvador

Rua Ipiranga

Otoni

Rua Dr Julio

Rua Alice

Rua Mário Portela

Laranjeiras

Rua Alice

Rua Baro de Petrópolis

Rua das Laranjeiras

Praça David Ben Gurion

Rua Cardoso Júnior

Rua Coelho Neto

Rua Paissandu

Cosme Velho

Rua Cosme Velho

Morro Mundo Novo (128m)

Rua Pinheiro Machado

Flamengo

Rua General Glicério

Rua Juçana

Rua Jaguá

Rua Mundo Novo

Rua Baro do Itambi

Rua Prof Luís Cantanheda

Rua Osvaldo Seabra

Mirante Dona Marta (363m)

Rua Couto Fernandes

Rua Marquês Olinda

Praia de Botafogo

Rua Assunção

Rua Bambina

Rua Muniz Barreto

Av dos Nações Unidas

Est Mirante Dona Marta

Praia do Botafogo

Túnel André Rebouças

Parque Nacional da Tijuca

Praça Radial Sul

Rua Barão de Lucena

Rua Eduardo Guinle

Rua Prof Alfredo Gomes

Rua São Clemente

Rua Guilherme Guinle

Rua 19 Fevereiro

Botafogo

Botafogo

Pasmado Overlook

Túnel do Pasmado

Humaitá

Rua Alfredo Chaves

Rua das Palmeiras

Rua da Matriz

Morro do Pasmado

Rua David Campista

Rua Campos Alvim

Rua Conde de Iraja

Rua Miranda Valverde

Rua Martins Ferreira

Rua Voluntários da Pátria

Rua Sorocaba

Rua Paulino

Rua Paulo Barreto

Rua Prof Fernandes

Rua Álvaro Rodrigues

Rua da Passagem

Rua General

Rua João Afonso

Rua Viúva Lacerda

Rua Marquês

Rua Henrique Novaes

Rua São Grandra

Rua João Batista

Rua Dona Mariana

Rua Gen Polidoro

Rua Arnaldo Quintela

Rua Fernandes Guimarães

Rua Gen Goiás Monteiro

Rua Humaitá

Rua Macedo Sobrinho

Rua Capela Salomão

Rua Dionísio

Rua Visconde de Caravelas

Rua Mena Barreto

Rua Visconde da Silva

Rua Assis Bueno

Rua Álvaro Ramos

Rua Pinheiro Guimarães

Rua General Polidoro

Cemitério São João Batista

242

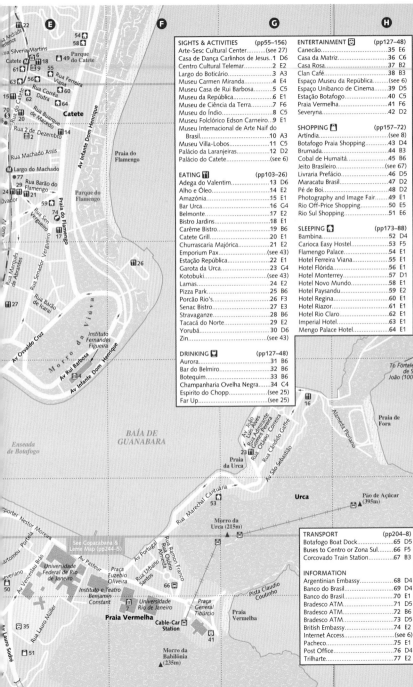

SIGHTS & ACTIVITIES (pp55–156)
Arte-Sesc Cultural Center............(see 27)
Casa de Dança Carlinhos de Jesus..1 D6
Centro Cultural Telemar................2 E2
Largo do Boticário...........................3 A3
Museu Carmen Miranda................4 E4
Museu Casa de Rui Barbosa...........5 C5
Museu da República.......................6 E1
Museu de Ciência da Terra.............7 F6
Museu do Índio..............................8 C5
Museu Folclórico Edson Carneiro...9 E1
Museu Internacional de Arte Naïf do
    Brasil.......................................10 A3
Museu Villa-Lobos.......................11 C5
Palácio da Laranjeiras..................12 D2
Palácio do Catete........................(see 6)

EATING (pp103–26)
Adega do Valentim.....................13 D6
Alho e Óleo.................................14 E2
Amazónia....................................15 E1
Bar Urca.....................................16 G4
Belmonte...................................17 E2
Bistro Jardins.............................18 E1
Carême Bistro............................19 B6
Catete Grill................................20 E1
Churrascaria Majórica.................21 E2
Emporium Pax.........................(see 43)
Estação República......................22 E1
Garota da Urca...........................23 G4
Kotobuki.................................(see 43)
Lamas..24 E2
Pizza Park..................................25 B6
Porção Rio's...............................26 F3
Senac Bistro..............................27 E3
Stravagance...............................28 B6
Tacacá do Norte.........................29 E2
Yorubá.......................................30 D6
Zin..(see 43)

DRINKING (pp127–48)
Aurora.......................................31 B6
Bar do Belmiro..........................32 B6
Botequim...................................33 B6
Champanharia Ovelha Negra.......34 C4
Espirito do Chopp....................(see 25)
Far Up.....................................(see 25)

ENTERTAINMENT (pp127–48)
Canecão.....................................35 E6
Casa da Matriz............................36 C6
Casa Rosa...................................37 B2
Clan Café....................................38 B3
Espaço Museu da República.......(see 6)
Espaço Unibanco de Cinema........39 D5
Estação Botafogo........................40 C5
Praia Vermelha...........................41 F6
Severyna....................................42 D2

SHOPPING (pp157–72)
Artíndia...................................(see 8)
Botafogo Praia Shopping............43 D4
Brumada....................................44 B3
Cobal de Humaitá.......................45 B6
Jeito Brasileiro........................(see 67)
Livraria Prefácio.........................46 D5
Maracatu Brasil...........................47 D2
Pé de Boi....................................48 D2
Photography and Image Fair.........49 E1
Rio Off-Price Shopping................50 E5
Rio Sul Shopping.........................51 E6

SLEEPING (pp173–88)
Bambina.....................................52 D4
Carioca Easy Hostel.....................53 F5
Flamengo Palace.........................54 E1
Hotel Ferreira Viana.....................55 E1
Hotel Flórida...............................56 E1
Hotel Monterrey.........................57 D1
Hotel Novo Mundo......................58 E1
Hotel Paysandu...........................59 E2
Hotel Regina...............................60 E1
Hotel Riazor................................61 E1
Hotel Rio Claro...........................62 E1
Imperial Hotel............................63 E1
Mengo Palace Hotel....................64 E1

TRANSPORT (pp204–8)
Botafogo Boat Dock....................65 D5
Buses to Centro or Zona Sul........66 F5
Corcovado Train Station.............67 B3

INFORMATION
Argentinian Embassy....................68 D4
Banco do Brasil............................69 D4
Banco do Brasil............................70 E1
Bradesco ATM.............................71 D5
Bradesco ATM.............................72 B6
Bradesco ATM.............................73 D5
British Embassy...........................74 E2
Internet Access.........................(see 6)
Pacheco......................................75 D4
Post Office..................................76 D4
Trilharte......................................77 E2

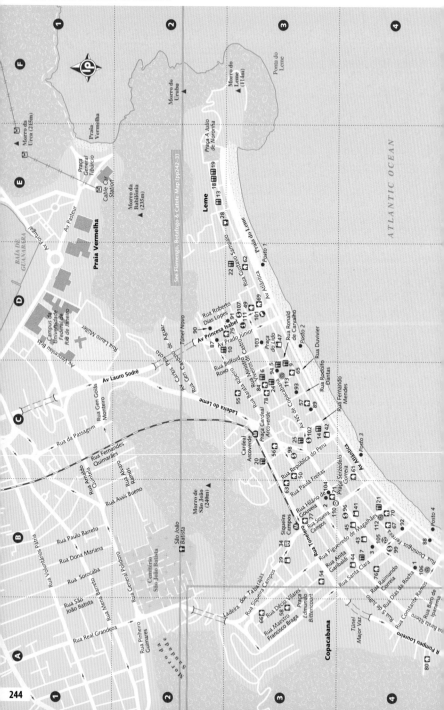

SIGHTS & ACTIVITIES (pp55–94, 149–56)
Antonio Carioca...........................(see 83)
Body Tech (Copacabana)...................1 B4
Clube Excursionista Carioca...............2 B3
Instituto Brasil Estados Unidos............3 B4
Museu Histórico do Exército Forte de
  Copacabana................................4 B6

EATING 🍴   (pp103–26)
Amir...5 C3
Azumi...6 C3
Bakers..7 B4
Bibi Crepes.................................8 A5
Café Fleuri.................................(see 69)
Carretão....................................9 C3
Cervantes..................................10 D2
Cipriani...................................(see 57)
Don Camillo..............................11 B5
Kilograma..................................12 A5
La Fiorentina.............................13 E2
La Trattoria..............................14 A5
Le Blé Noir...............................15 A5
Le Pré Catalan.........................(see 85)
Le Saint Honore.........................(see 69)
Lope's Confeitaria.....................16 A6
Lucas.......................................17 A6
Marius Carnes...........................18 E2
Marius Crustáceos.....................19 E2
Peixe Vivo.................................20 C3
Serafina....................................21 B4
Shirley......................................22 D3
Siri Mole & Cia..........................23 A6
Temperarte...............................24 C3
Traiteurs de France....................25 C3
Yonza..26 B5

DRINKING 🍷   (pp127–48)
Allegro Bistro Musical.................(see 44)
Confeitaria Colombo...................27 B5
Copa Café.................................(see 85)
Horse's Neck.............................28 E2
Sindicato do Chopp....................29 A6
Sindicato do Chopp....................30 B5

ENTERTAINMENT 🎭   (pp127–48)
Bip Bip......................................31 A5
Blue Angel.................................32 A6

                                          33 A6
                                          34 B3
                                        (see 35)
Le Boy......................................35 A6
Roxy...36 B4

SHOPPING 🛍   (pp157–72)
Arte Brasilis..............................37 A6
Av Atlantica Fair.........................38 B5
De Salto Alto.............................39 B3
Galeria River.............................40 A6
Kopenhagen...............................41 B4
Maria de Barro............................42 C3
MBR..43 B4
Modern Sound............................44 B4
Mundo Verde.............................45 B4
Musicale..................................46 A5
Praça do Lido Market...................47 D3
Shopping Cassino Atlantica to
  Antiques Fair...........................48 B6

SLEEPING 🛏   (pp173–88)
Acapulco..................................49 D3
Apa Hotel.................................50 C3
Atlantis Copacabana Hotel............51 A6
Augusto's Copacabana................52 B5
Blame it on Rio 4 Travel..............53 B5
Che Lagarto..............................54 B3
Copacabana Holiday....................55 C3
Copacabana Hotel Residência........56 C3
Copacabana Palace.....................57 C3
Copacabana Praia Hostel.............58 A3
Copacabana Praia Hotel..............59 A6
Design Hotel Portinari.................60 A6
Excelsior Copacabana Hotel..........61 C4
Fantastic Rio.............................62 D3
Hotel Astoria Copacabana............63 B3
Hotel Debret.............................64 A5
Hotel Rio Internacional................65 C3
Hotel Santa Clara.......................66 A3
Hotel Toledo.............................67 B4
Hotel Vilamar............................68 A5
Le Meridien Othon Palace............69 D3
Luxor Copacabana......................70 B4
Mar Palace................................71 B3
Miramar Palace Hotel..................72 A5
Orla Copacabana.......................73 B4

Plaza Copacabana.......................75 D3
Pousada Girassol.......................76 B4
Premier Copacabana Hotel............77 B3
Real Palace Hotel.......................78 C3
Residencial Apartt......................79 A6
Rio Backpackers.........................80 A4
Rio Guesthouse..........................81 A6
Rio Othon Palace.......................82 B5
Rio Roiss Hotel...........................83 B5
Royal Rio Palace........................84 C3
Soffel Rio Palace.......................85 B6
Yvonne Reimann.......................86 B6

TRANSPORT   (pp204–8)
American Airlines......................(see 57)
Ciclovia....................................87 D2
Consuelo..................................88 B4
Continental Airlines....................89 C3
Hertz.......................................90 D2
Localiza...................................91 D3
United Airlines..........................92 B4
Varig..93 C3

INFORMATION
American Express.....................(see 57)
Andes Sol................................94 D2
Banco do Brasil.........................95 A5
Banco do Brasil.........................96 B4
Bradesco..................................97 A5
Bradesco ATM...........................98 C3
Bradesco ATM...........................99 B4
Bradesco ATM.........................100 D3
Canadian Consulate..................101 D3
Casa Universal.........................102 C3
Drogaria Pacheco.....................103 D3
Drogaria Pacheco.....................104 B4
Fast Cell..................................105 B4
Fone Rio.................................106 D3
HSBC.....................................107 D3
HSBC.....................................108 A6
Locutório...............................109 A5
Post Office..............................110 B3
Riotur....................................111 D3
Telenet..................................112 B4
Telerede................................113 C3
Ticketronics..........................(see 44)

SIGHTS & ACTIVITIES (pp55–94, 149–56)
                                        (see 83)
La Girl..1 B4
Le Boy...2 B3
Bunker 94....................................3 B4
Fosfobox

IPANEMA, LEBLON & GÁVEA

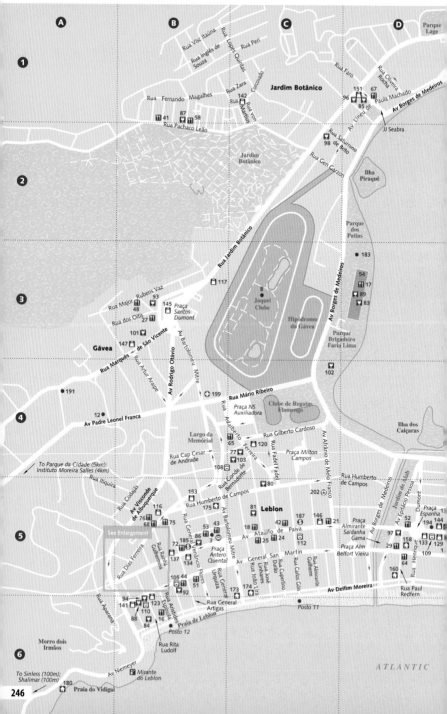

A **B** **C** **D**

1

Parque Lage

Rua Visc Itaúna
Rua Inglês de Souza
Rua Lopes Quintas
Rua Peri
Corcovado

Rua Faro
Rua Oliveira Rocha

Jardim Botânico

Rua Zara
Rua von Martius

151
67
96
85
Paula Machado

Av Borges de Medeiros

Rua Fernando Magalhes
142

Rua Saturnino de Brito
98

Av L Inêu de

JJ Seabra

41
87
58
Rua Pachaco Leão

Rua Gen Garzon

Ilha Piraquê

2

Jardim Botânico

Parque dos Patins

Rua Jardim Botânico

183
54
17
89
83

3

117

Rua Major
Rubens Vaz
93
48
145
Praça Santos Dumont
Rua dos Oitis
27
101
147
Rua Marques de São Vicente

8
Joquei Clube

Hipódromo da Gávea

Parque Brigadeiro Faria Lima

Gávea

Av Rodrigo Otávio
Rua Artur Araipe
Rua Bartolomeu Mitre

102

191

199
Rua Mário Ribeiro
Praça NS Auxiliadora
Clube de Regatas Flamengo

4

12
Av Padre Leonel Franca

Largo da Memórial
65
120
Rua Gilberto Cardoso
Praça Milton Campos

Ilha dos Caiçaras

Rua Cap Cesar de Andrade
77
103
108
Rua Conde de Bernadotte
80
202

Av Afranio de Melo Franco
Rua Humberto de Campos

To Parque da Cidade (5km);
Instituto Moreira Salles (4km)
Rua Itiquira

153
175
Rua Humberto de Campos

81
Leblon
187
146
21

Av Borges de Medeiros
Jardim Epitácio Pessoa
52
194
Praça Espanha
13
144

Rua Codajás
Av Visconde de Albuquerque
116
76
68
75

134
53
43
3
86
18
42
24
25
112
Praça Almirante Saldanha Gama
97
29
158
133
129
109

5

See Enlargement
72
185
137
Praça Antero Quental
Av General San Martim
Rua José Linhares
Rua Cupertino Coêlho
Rua Carlos Góis
Rua Almirante Guilhem
Praça Alm Belfort Vieira
64
160

Rua Dias Ferreira
Rua Rainha Guilherma
105
44
51
92
173
174
Rua General Artigas
Posto 11

Av Delfim Moreira
Rua Paul Redfern

Rua Aperana
94
141
88
110
123
84
16
Praia de Leblon
Posto 12

6

Morro dois Irmãos

Rua Rita Ludolf

To Sinless (100m);
Shalimar (100m)
180
Praia do Vidigal
Av Niemeyer
Mirante do Leblon

ATLANTIC

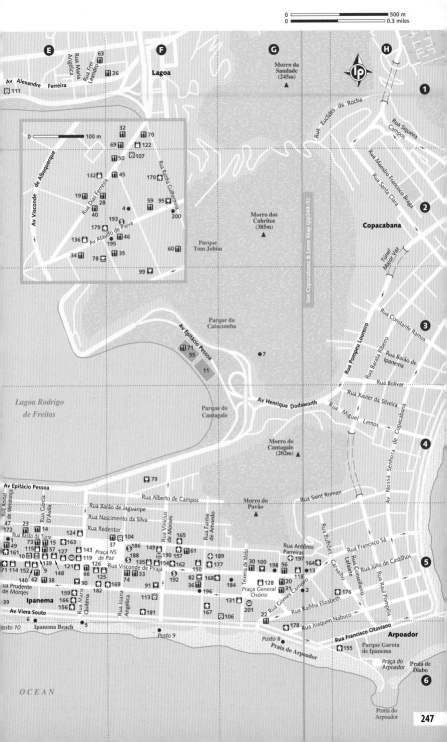

E

Rua Maria
Angélica

63
Rua Frei
Leandro

26

Av Alexandre Ferreira

111

F

Lagoa

G

Morro da
Saudade
(245m)

H

Rua Euclides da Rocha

Rua Siqueira
Campos

1

Rua Maestro Francisco Braga

Rua Santa Clara

2

Copacabana

0   100 m

32

70

69   122

50   107

132   45

170

Av Visconde de Albuquerque

19   28
40

Rua Das Ferreira

4

59 95
200

Rua Rainha Guilhermina

193
179
136   46
195
34 78   35

99

60

Morro dos
Cabritos
(385m)

Túnel
Mão Vaz

Rua Constante Ramos

3

Parque
Tom Jobim

Rua Pompeu Loureno

Rua Barata Ribeiro

Rua Barão de
Ipanema

Parque da
Catacumba

Av Epitácio Pessoa

71
55

11

7

Rua Bolívar

Rua Xavier da Silveira

Av Henrique Dodsworth

Rua Miguel Lemos

Lagoa Rodrigo
de Freitas

Parque do
Cantagalo

Morro do
Cantagalo
(202m)

Av Nossa Senhora de Copacabana

4

79

Av Epitácio Pessoa

Rua Alberto de Campos

Rua Barão de Jaguaripe

Rua Nascimento da Silva

Rua Redentor

Rua Anibal
de Mendonça

Rua Garcia
D'Ávila

47 23
172
14
73 15
115 57
127
126
121
140 62 139 148
71 114 152
90
38

125
169

Rua Maria Quitéria

159
166
156

39   Ipanema

Av Viera Souto

6

osto 10   Ipanema Beach   5

Posto 9

Morro do
Pavão

Rua Saint Roman

Rua Antônio
Parreiras

Rua Vinícius
de Moraes

Rua Farme
de Amoedo

Rua Barão da Torre

49
161
10
117

143
104
186
188
135
74

37

149
33
190
157
162
150
192

165
61

189
177

168
196

91

113
181

Praça NS
de Paz

Rua Visconde de Pirajá

Rua Joana
Angélica

Rua Prudente
de Moraes

167

Teixeira de Melo

Rua Gomes Carneiro

Praça General
Osório

131
201
106

82 30 100
36 31
128
198 56
118
20
164
13
197

22
178

Rua Raínha Elizabeth

Rua Bulhões
Carvalho

Rua Conselheiro
Lafaiete

Rua Francisco Sá

Rua Júlio de Castilhos

Rua Raul Pompéia

176

5

Rua Francisco Otaviano

Arpoador

155

Parque Garota
de Ipanema

Praça do
Arpoador

Praia de
Diabo

Posto 8

Praia do Arpoador

O C E A N

Ponta do
Arpoador

247

SIGHTS & ACTIVITIES (pp55–94, 149-56)
Body Tech (Ipanema)......................................1 E5
Body Tech (Ipanema)......................................2 G5
Body Tech (Leblon)..3 B5
Dive Point...4 F2
Escolinha de Surf Paulo Dolabella............5 E5
Escolinha de Vôlei...6 E5
Fundição Eva Klabin Rapaport...................7 G3
Joquei Clube...8 C3
Museu Amsterdam Sauer..............................9 E5
Museu H Stern..10 F3
Paddle Boats...11 F3
Planetário..12 A4
Yôga Center...13 G5

EATING (pp103–26)
00..(see 12)
Alessandro E Federico................................14 E5
Alessandro E Federico................................15 E5
Antiquarius..16 B6
Arab Da Lagoa..17 D3
Ataúlfo..18 C5
Ateliê Culinário..19 E2
Azul Marinho......................................(see 155)
Banana Jack..20 C5
Barra Brasa..21 C5
Barril 1800...22 G5
Bazzar...23 E5
Bibi Crepes..24 C5
Bibi Sucos...25 C5
Boteco 66...26 F1
Braseiro da Gávea..27 B3
Carlota..28 E2
Carpaccio & Cia...29 D5
Carretão...30 G5
Casa da Feijoada..31 G5
Celeiro..32 F1
Chaika...33 F5
Chez Pierre...(see 167)
Chocolatras...34 E2
Colher de Pau...35 F2
Colher de Pau...36 F5
Da Silva..37 F5
Delírio Tropical...38 E5
Doce Delícia..39 E5
Doce Delícia..40 E2
Dom João...41 B1
Empório Arabe..42 C5
Fellini...43 B5
Fontes..(see 109)
Fratelli..44 B5
Galani..(see 156)
Galeto do Leblon...45 F2
Garcia & Rodrigues......................................46 F2
Gero...47 E5
Guimas..48 B3
Gula Gula...49 E5
HortiFruti..50 F2
Juice Co..51 B5
Kilograma...52 D5
Kurt...53 B5
Lagoa Kiosks..54 D3
Lagoa Kiosks..55 F3
L'Assiette...56 G5
Mil Frutas..57 E5
Miss Tanaka..58 B1
Mustafá..59 F2
Nam Thai..60 F2
New Natural...61 F5
Nik Sushi..62 E5
Olympe...63 E1
Osteria Dell'Angelo.....................................64 D5
Petronius...(see 156)
Plataforma...65 C4
Polis Sucos..66 E5
Quadrifoglio..67 D1
Quadrucci..68 B5
Quitanda Vegetal...69 F1
Sushi Leblon..70 F1
Sushinaka Light...71 F3
Talho Capixaba...72 B5
Via Sete..73 E5
Zazá Bistrô Tropical.....................................74 F5
Zona Sul Supermarket.................................75 B5
Zuka..76 B5

DRINKING (pp127–48)
Academia da Cachaça..................................77 C4
Armazém do Café...78 E2
Bl..(see 138)
Bar 121..(see 121)
Bar D'Hotel...(see 173)
Bar Lagoa...79 F4
Botequim Informal.......................................80 C5
Bracarense..81 C5
Café Severino.....................................(see 116)
Cafeína...82 F5
Caipirinha & Filé...83 D3
Caneco 70..84 B6
Caroline Café..85 D1
Conversa Fiada...86 B5
Da Graça..87 B1
Devassa...88 B6
Drink Café..89 D3
Empório..90 E5
Garota de Ipanema......................................91 F5
Guapo Loco...92 B5
Hipódromo Up...93 B3
Jiló...94 B6
Jobi...95 F2
Jota Bar..96 D1
Lord Jim...97 D5
Saturnino...98 C2
Seu Martin...99 F3
Shenanigan's..100 C5
Sitio Lounge..101 B3
Sky Lounge..102 C4
Vegetariano Social Club............................103 C4

ENTERTAINMENT (pp127–48)
Bar do Tom..(see 65)
Baronneti...104 F5
Bombar...105 B5
Casa da Cultura Laura Alvim....................106 G5
Esch Cafe...107 F2
Espaço Leblon...108 B4
Estação Ipanema...109 D5
Melt..110 B6
Mistura Fina...111 E1
Teatro Laura Alvim...........................(see 106)
Teatro Leblon..112 C5
Vinícius Piano Bar......................................113 F5

SHOPPING (pp157–72)
Amazon Life..114 E5
Amsterdam Sauer...............................(see 9)
Antonio Bernardo.......................................115 E5
Argumento..116 B5
Babilônia Feira Hype...................................117 B3
Boca do Sapo...118 G5
Brasil & Cia...(see 166)
Chez Bonbon...119 E5
Cobal de Leblon..120 C4
Contemporâneo..121 E5
Da Conde..(see 108)
Daqui... (see 4)
Eliane Carvalho...122 F1
Emporio Brasil...................................(see 129)
Escada..123 B6
Florestas...(see 119)
Forum..124 E5
Forum de Ipanema.....................................125 E5
Galeria Ipanema Secreta...........................126 E5
Gilson Martins...127 E5
H Stern...(see 10)
Hippie Fair..128 G5
Interstudio...129 D5
Ipanema 2000...130 D5
Ipanema.com...131 G5
Isabela Capeto...132 E2
Juliana Faro..133 D5
Kopenhagen...134 B5
Letras e Expressões (Ipanema).................135 F5
Letras e Expressões (Leblon).....................136 E2

Lidador..137 B5
Livraria da Travessa....................................138 D5
Luko...(see 130)
MBR...(see 119)
Mixed..139 E5
Musicale...140 E5
No Meio do Caminho..................................141 B6
O Sol...142 C1
Osklen...143 E5
Oz...144 D5
Pano Nosso..(see 129)
Praça Santos Dumont Antique Fair.....145 B3
Rio Design Center.......................................146 C5
Shopping da Gávea.....................................147 B3
Teargas..148 E5
Toca do Vinícius...149 E5
Urucum Art & Design......................(see 109)
Vale das Bonecas...150 F5
VIT...151 D1
Wöllner Outdoor..152 E5
World Map...153 B5
World Map...154 F5

SLEEPING (pp173–88)
Arpoador Inn..155 H6
Caesar Park...156 E5
Casa 6 Ipanema...157 F5
Che Lagarto Ipanema.................................158 D5
Everest Rio..159 E5
Hotel Praia Ipanema..................................160 D5
Hotel San Marco..161 E5
Hotel Vermont...162 F5
Ipanema Beach House................................163 E5
Ipanema Flat Hotel Residência................164 G5
Ipanema Hotel Residência........................165 F5
Ipanema Inn...166 E5
Ipanema Plaza..167 F5
Ipanema Sweet..168 F5
Ipanema Tower..169 F5
Leblon Ocean Hotel Residência..............170 F2
Lighthouse Hostel..............................(see 157)
Mar Ipanema...171 E5
Margarida's Pousada..................................172 E5
Marina All Suites...173 C5
Marina Palace..174 C5
Monsieur Le Blond......................................175 B5
Parthenon Queen Elizabeth......................176 H5
Rio Apartments..177 F5
Rio Universe...178 G6
Ritz Plaza Hotel...179 E2
Sheraton...180 A6
Sol Ipanema..181 F5
Visconti..182 E5
Wave Hostel.......................................(see 157)

TRANSPORT (pp204–8)
Gray Line Tours..................................(see 180)
Heliport...183 D3
Special Bike..184 G5
Varig..(see 125)

INFORMATION
Banco do Brasil..185 B5
Banco do Brasil..186 F5
Banco do Brasil & Bradesco.......................187 F5
BankBoston & Bradesco Info....................188 F5
Cardio Trauma Ipanema............................189 F5
Central Fone...190 F5
Centro de Vida Independente...................191 A4
Citibank...192 F5
Citibank...193 F2
Drogaria Pacheco.......................................194 D5
Farmácia Piaíí...195 F2
Feedback..196 F5
Hospital Ipanema.......................................197 G5
Le Bon Voyage...198 G5
Miguel Couto Hospital...............................199 B4
Pacheco..200 F2
Post Office..201 G5
Rio Convention & Visitors
Bureau...(see 130)
Tourist Police..202 C5